A Documentary History
of the Arab-Israeli Conflict

A Documentary History
of the Arab-Israeli Conflict

Edited with
Historical Introductions
by CHARLES L. GEDDES

PRAEGER

New York
Westport, Connecticut
London

Library of Congress Cataloging-in-Publication Data

A Documentary history of the Arab-Israeli conflict / edited with
historical introductions by Charles L. Geddes.
    p. cm.
  Includes index.
  ISBN 0-275-93858-1 (alk. paper)
    1. Jewish-Arab relations—1917- —Sources. 2. Israel-Arab
conflicts—Sources.   I. Geddes, C. L. (Charles L.), 1928-
DS119.7.D616 1991
956—dc20   90-23949

British Library Cataloguing in Publication Data is available.

Library of Congress Catalog Card Number: 90-23949
ISBN: 0-275-93858-1

First published in 1991

Praeger Publishers, One Madison Avenue, New York, NY 10010
An imprint of Greenwood Publishing Group, Inc.

Printed in the United States of America

The paper used in this book complies with the
Permanent Paper Standard issued by the National
Information Standards Organization (Z39.48-1984).

10 9 8 7 6 5 4 3 2 1

Copyright Acknowledgments

The editor and publisher gratefully acknowledge permission to use extracts from:

Various documents and papers are reproduced with the permission of the
Controller of Her Majesty's Stationery Office.

King-Crane Commission Report, *Editor & Publisher*, vol. 55, no. 27, December
2, 1922 is reproduced with the permission of *Editor & Publisher*.

The Letters of Sidney and Beatrice Webb, ed. Norman Mackenzie, vol. 3 (Cambridge: Cambridge University Press, 1978) is reproduced with permission of Cambridge University Press.

Every reasonable effort has been made to trace the owners of copyright materials
in this book, but in some instances this has proven impossible. The author and
publisher will be glad to receive information leading to more complete acknowl-
edgments in subsequent printings of the book and in the meantime extend their
apologies for any omissions.

Dedicated to the Memory
of my beloved parents
James E. and Dorothy M. Geddes

Contents

Preface

During the nearly quarter of a century that I have been teaching a course on the Arab-Israeli conflict on a regular basis I have had my students read a major portion of the relevant documents so that they might gain a greater understanding of the subject. Although some of these documents have been more or less readily available either in the text or in supplementary readers, others I have had to have duplicated for them. It was as an outgrowth of this practice that I decided to prepare a collection of the most important of these documents, originally for my students and then to meet the request of others who are no longer students. When I decided to publish this collection I was encouraged by some of those previous students to prepare relatively short introductions so as to place each document in its historical context. As with the documents themselves, I decided to return once again to the primary sources in the preparation of these introductions. The result has been that the historical notes are, themselves, based primarily upon other documents, published memoirs of the participants, printed and unprinted letters, international reporting services, and other "raw" materials, and, in one instance, personal correspondence with a onetime congressman. In addition to the introductions many of the documents have been provided with epilogues so as to provide the reader with detailed information regarding the results or reaction to that particular document. So as to ensure total accuracy in the reprinting of each document, I have, insofar as possible, returned to the original sources, as so noted. Also, I have attempted to reproduce the documents in the same format as they appear in the sources, rather than trying to force them into a uniform pattern. In this way, I believe, it will be possible for the reader to obtain a better "feel" for each document. Most of the documents are reproduced in their entirety; except for those that were too lengthy (there are a few which are well over three hundred pages), repeated documents which are included within this collection, or contain information that I do not believe is any longer applicable only the conclusions or recommendations have been fully included. However, I wish to assure the reader that in no instance has any relevant information been omitted, and not one of the documents has been paraphrased or truncated. It has been my aim to produce a scholarly work that might serve as both a supplementary text for college courses on the subject and that could also "stand alone." How well I have succeeded in the latter I shall have to leave to the reader. It must be stressed, however, that it has never been my intention to provide a thorough running history of the subject, thus the stress upon the documents, many of which have not previously been reprinted in any collection.

This work provides the documentary background to political Zionism and the means by which Great Britain attempted, first, to support the establishment of a Jewish homeland in Palestine, and second, to ease the fears of the Arab inhabitants regarding such a refuge. In addition, for the first time in any of the surprisingly few collections of the documents, it brings out the involvement of the United States in the dispute in which she has become a major element, whether for good or for bad.

I wish to thank the Honorable Hamilton Fish, Sr., for responding so thoroughly, frankly, and quickly to my questions regarding the 1922 and 1944 congressional resolutions. I am also indebted to Mr. Peter Drummey, Associate Librarian of the Massachusetts Historical Society, for his invaluable information regarding the papers in the Henry Cabot Lodge collection. There are many others, too numerous to mention by name, in a number of embassies, information offices of foreign states and organizations, Her Majesty's Stationery Office, the U.S. Department of State, the Dag Hammarskjöld Library of the United Nations, University of Cambridge Library, the British Library, the University of Colorado Library, and, of course, the University of Denver Library, who have all rendered yeoman service to me in the preparation of this volume. My sincerest thanks to them all.

Brief Chronology of
the Arab-Israeli Conflict

B.C.

1004 Approximate date of the founding of the ancient state of Israel.

586 Destruction of the first Jewish temple, built by Solomon, by King Nebuchadnezzar of Babylonia and the "Babylonian Captivity" of the Jews.

538 Jews released from captivity by Cyrus the Great of the Achaemenian Empire of Persia. Cyrus assists Jews in reconstruction of the temple.

520-516 Completion of second temple.

168 Temple either completely destroyed or seriously damaged by earthquake.

37-34 Construction of third temple, or reconstruction of second temple, by Herod the Great.

A.D.

71-72 Temple and entire city of Jerusalem destroyed by order of Roman Emperor Titus. Construction of an entirely new city that is forbidden to the Jews. Beginning of the "diaspora."

638 Surrender of Jerusalem to Muslims completes the conquest of Palestine.

683 Construction of the Dome of the Rock on Mount Zion ("Temple Mount") by Umayyad Caliph 'Abd al-Malik.

1071 Saljuk Turks take Jerusalem and Holy Land.

1099　Capture of Jerusalem by the Crusaders and establishment of the "Kingdom of Jerusalem."

1516　Ottoman Turkish conquest of Syria and Palestine by Selim the Grim. Entire Fertile Crescent absorbed into Ottoman Empire. Palestine created as "Sanjak of Jerusalem."

1881　Assassination of Alexander II, "Tsar of all the Russians." Organized riots (*pogroms*) break out against the Jews on behalf of the Russian Orthodox Church. Pogroms spread westward into Central Europe.

1882　Leo Pinsker publishes pamphlet *Auto-emancipation* , calling for the creation of a "Jewish state somewhere on earth."

1896　Publication of *Der Judenstaat* ("The Jewish State") by Theodor Herzl.

1897　First Zionist Congress held in Basel, Switzerland, 29-31 August. Adoption of the "Basel Program." Until his death seven years later Herzl attempts to obtain land in Palestine for Jews from Ottoman Sultan.

1903　Seventh Zionist Congress held in Basel. Great Britain offers huge tract of land in highlands of British East Africa for Jewish national home, which is refused.

1904　Death of Theodor Herzl. Leadership of Zionist Organization passes into hands of David Woffson.

1908　"Committee of Union and Progress" effects revolution against the Ottoman Government. Extreme Turkish nationalism and Ottomanism eliminates any possibility of Zionists obtaining land in Palestine by legal means.

1914　Outbreak of World War I in Europe in August. Ottoman Empire enters conflict on side of Central Powers (Germany and the Austro-Hungarian Empire) in November.

1915　4 July—10 March 1916 exchange of ten letters between Sharif of Two Holy Cities of Mecca and Medina and British Government — "Husayn—McMahon Correspondence." Arabs promise military assistance to Great Britain in return for recognition of their independence.

1916　Exchange of notes between British, French, and Russian Governments leads to "Sykes—Picot Agreement" 9—16 May in which the three states agree to divide Fertile Crescent among themselves. 2 November Sharif Husayn proclaims himself "King of the Arab Countries." Great Britain and France officially recognize him as "King of the Hijaz."

1917   British War Cabinet, in exchange for promise of Jews worldwide to support war effort of allies, issues to Baron Rothschild a letter on 2 November known as the "Balfour Declaration." Previously accepted by Prime Minister Georges Clemenceau of France and President Woodrow Wilson of United States.

1918   President Wilson delivers "Fourteen Points" speech before U.S. Congress on 8 January. States that self-determination of peoples is one of the objectives of the war. Three days previously, 5 January, Prime Minister David Lloyd George of Great Britain makes a similar declaration. On 1 October Arabs under command of Prince Faysal, son of King Husayn, enter Damascus. Proclamation of "Arab Constitutional Government" over Syria and Palestine. Ottoman Turks surrender in the Near East on 30 October. Publication of "Anglo-French Declaration" on 7 November.

1919   King-Crane Commission delivers its final recommendations concerning the Near East to President Wilson on 28 August. Not published until 1922.

1920   San Remo Conference of Entente Powers (Great Britain, France, Italy, and Japan) establishes mandates for Great Britain over Palestine and Iraq, and France over Syria on 25 April.

1922   Issuance of "Churchill White Paper" in June as official British position regarding virtually unlimited Jewish immigration into Palestine. On 24 July Palestine Mandate "officially assigned" to Great Britain by Council of the League of Nations. U.S. Congress endorses "Balfour Declaration" by Public Resolution on 21 September. Beginning of U.S. involvement in coming dispute.

1924   By Anglo-American Convention United States accepts British mandate over Palestine.

1930   Issuance of "Passfield White Paper." Publication of public letter from British Prime Minister Ramsay McDonald to Chaim Weizmann in *The*

Times to elucidate "White Paper" ("McDonald Letter").

1936   General strike by Palestinian Arabs against British mandate and Zionist program from April to October.

1937   22 June publication of Peel Commission Report recommending partitioning of Palestine. Woodhead Commission appointed January 1938 to put partition into effect. Government finds partitioning "impracticable."

1939   London Conference in attempt to find solution fails. Publication of "1939 White Paper" on 17 May recognizing impossibility of partition and placing limit on further Jewish immigration and land purchases and proposing establishment of independent Palestinian state at end of 10 years. Rejected by both Jews and Arabs as not going far enough to meet their respective, and opposing, demands. Outbreak of World War II on 3 September.

1945   Formation of League of Arab States 22 March. Germany and Austria surrender 7 May.

1946   Recommendations of the Anglo-American Commission of Inquiry signed 20 April call for future single state in Palestine. Until hostilities cease territory is to remain under mandate or given over in trusteeship to United Nations. Joint six—member committee formed by United States and Great Britain to examine recommendations of Commission results in "Grady-Morrison Plan," which supports the concept of a single state. Conference on Palestine convened in London 10 September between British, Arab, and Zionist leaders.

1947   London talks recognized as complete failure 14 February. In letter to Secretary-General of United Nations, 2 April, Britain announces decision to surrender mandate over Palestine. 29 November U.N. General Assembly passes Resolution 181 (II) calling for partitioning of Palestine into three states: Jewish, Arab, and an internationalized Jerusalem by a vote of 33 to 13 with 10 abstentions.

1948   Proclamation of state of Israel 14 May, immediately recognized by President Harry Truman. British mandate over Palestine officially ends on

15 May with withdrawal of troops. 15 May outbreak of first Arab-Israeli war lasting until July 1949. Israel occupies new section of Jerusalem. Beginning of Palestine refugee problem with hundreds of thousands fleeing conflict.

1949   Israel admitted into membership of United Nations. General Assembly establishes United Nations Relief and Works Agency to assist destitute Arab Palestinian refugees.

1956   President Jamal 'abd al-Nasir of Egypt nationalizes Suez Canal 26 July. Israel, France, and Great Britain attack Egypt leading to "Suez War."

1964   Palestine Liberation Organization (PLO) founded in Jerusalem 2 June with adoption of Palestinian National Covenant and Constitution.

1967   "Six Day War" of June leads to Israeli capture of old city of Jerusalem and territories in West Bank. U.N. Security Council passes Resolution 242.

1973   "Yom Kippur War," October, leads to Israeli capture of Syrian Golan Heights, West Bank from Jordan and Gaza Strip from Egypt.

1974   PLO granted "Observer Status" in U.N. General Assembly.

1975   Israeli-Egyptian Agreement signed in September for withdrawal of forces from Sinai Peninsula and establishment of American observers along the cease-fire line ("Sinai I" and "Sinai II").

1978   "Camp David Accord" signed 17 September between President Jimmy Carter of the United States, President Anwar al-Sadat of Egypt, and Prime Minister Menachem Begin of Israel.

1979   Peace treaty between Egypt and Israel signed in Washington, D.C., on 26 March. 31 March "Baghdad Resolution" of Islamic Conference leads to isolation of Egypt from most other Arab countries. President al-Sadat. assassinated.

1980   European Community leaders issue "Venice Declaration" as basis for peace.

1981   Crown Prince Fahd of Sa'udi Arabia enunciates "Fahd Peace Plan" on 8 August. Adopted by other Arab states as "Fez Declaration."

1982   Israeli invasion and occupation of southern Lebanon begins 5 June. PLO withdraws from Lebanon under U.S. sponsorship.

1987   Uprising (*intifada*) of Palestinians in West Bank
          and Gaza Strip, which Israeli army attempts to
          suppress with "iron fist" policy, without suc-
          cess.
1988   Palestinian National Council declares independent
          state of Palestine in West Bank and Gaza Strip
          15 November.   In statement issued 14 December
          Yasir Arafat, Chairman of the PLO Executive
          Committee, explicity recognizes Israel's right to
          exist.   By Resolution 43/177, 15 December, U.N.
          General Assembly acknowledges   the procla-
          mation of the state of Palestine.   On 16 Decem-
          ber United States opens talks with PLO at its
          headquarters in Tunis.
1990   President Bush calls off talks with PLO, 20 June. 2
          August   Iraqi   troops   invade   neighboring
          Kuwait.   That evening, in an emergency ses-
          sion, the Security Council passes the first of a
          series of 12 resolutions calling for withdrawal
          of Iraq and establishing an international mili-
          tary force to implement decisions.   PLO leader
          Yasir Arafat and large numbers of Palestinians
          declare support for Saddam Husayn, President
          of Iraq.   8 October, a Jewish fundamentalist
          group, "Faithful of the Temple Mount,"
          marches on al-Aqsa Mosque to symbolically
          place a stone for rebuilding of Jewish Temple,
          although forbidden by Israeli supreme court.
          Muslims gathered to prevent action begin
          throwing stones at marchers.   Israeli police
          shoot at demonstrators with live ammunition,
          killing 17-20, wounding approximately 150.
          Security Council, 12 October, passes resolution
          672 condemning Israel for use of excessive
          force.   Resolution denounced by Israeli Gov-
          ernment.
1991   International force of 28 nations begins action
          against Iraq to force withdrawal from Kuwait,
          16 January.   28 February truce implemented
          when Iraq agrees to comply with all Security
          Council resolutions.   President Bush announces
          time propitious to settle disputes in Near East,
          including Arab-Israeli conflict.   5 March Sec-
          retary of State James Baker begins lengthy
          series of talks with leaders.   During summit
          meeting in Moscow Presidents Bush and Gor-

bachev of U.S.S.R. announce on 31 July to
jointly sponsor Arab-Israeli peace conference
to begin 10 October. Israeli Government and
PLO agree to participate 4 August.

1

Auto-emancipation, 1882

Although Leo Pinsker is not regarded as the
founder of modern political Zionism, he was the
first to expound the idea for the establishment
of a Jewish national state. Both Pinsker's *Auto-
emancipation* ("Self-liberation") and Herzl's
Der Judenstaat ("The Jewish State") have surprisingly similar ideas, but Herzl, following the
publication of his own pamphlet, maintained
that he had no prior knowledge of Pinsker's
work. Without, therefore, the same widespread
impact as *Der Judenstaat,* Pinsker's intellec-
tualized concept of a secularized home-land is
of interest for an understanding of Zionism.

Leo Pinsker, the son of the noted Hebrew
scholar Simchah Pinsker, was born in
Tomashov in the then—Russian province of
Poland in 1821. While Leo was still a child the
family moved to the Black Sea port of Odessa,
where he lived until his death in 1891. Unlike
most boys of his faith and class, Leo received a
secular education in Russian schools and, after
a brief study of the law in his home city,
received a medical degree from the University
of Moscow. He returned to Odessa and

Source: Leo Pinsker, *Road to Freedom: Writings and Addresses*
(New York: Scopus Publishing Co., 1944). *Auto-emancipation* is
included on pp. 74-106 (translated by D.S. Blondheim). Translation
first published by Federation of American Zionists, New York, 1916.

established his practice. In middle life he became an outspoken advocate of Jewish assimilation into Russian life. These ideas came into conflict, however, with the outbreak of anti—Jewish riots (*pogroms*) in the southern Russian provinces following the assassination of the Tsar Alexander II and the accession of his son Alexander III in March of 1881. Although Pinsker and his family were not physically harmed during the lengthy and devastating course of these riots, the violent anti-Semitism had a profound emotional impact upon him, leading to the conviction that state-hood, not assimilation, was the remedy.

Failing to convince Jewish leaders in central and western Europe of the necessity of his ideas, Pinsker returned to Odessa where he published anonymously, and at his own ex-pense, his brief tract in German, only 36 pages in length in the original. The major portion of *Auto-emancipation* is concerned with what in his mind was the cause of anti-Jewish feeling and the nationhood of a people without a na-tion. The last few pages, the portion that fol-lows, contains the argument for a Jewish state somewhere on earth and the means by which it could be established.

The following excerpt begins on page 97 of *Road to Freedom: Writings and Addresses.*

VIII

. . . In the life of peoples, as in the life of individuals, there are important moments which do not often recur, and which, according as they are utilized or not utilized, exercise a decisive influence upon the future of the people as of the individual, whether for weal or for woe. We are now passing through such a moment. The consciousness of the people is awake. The great ideas of the eighteenth century have not passed by our people without leaving a trace. We feel not only as Jews; we feel as men. As men, we, too, would fain live and be a nation like the others. And if we seriously desire that, we must first of all extricate ourselves from the old yoke, and rise manfully to our full height. We must first of all desire to help ourselves.... Only then will the help of others as well be sure to come.

But the time in which we live is adapted for decisive action not merely because of our own inner experience, not merely in consequence of our newly-aroused self-consciousness. The general history of the present day seems called to be our ally. In a few decades we have seen rising into new life nations which at an earlier time would not have dared to dream of a resurrection. The dawn already appears amid the darkness of traditional statesmenship. The governments are already inclining their ears — first, to be sure, in those cases in which they cannot do otherwise — to the louder and louder voices of national self-consciousness. It is true that those happy ones who attained their national independence were not Jews. They lived upon their own soil and spoke one language, and therein they certainly had the advantage of us.

But what if our position is more difficult? That is all the more reason why we should strain every energy to the task of ending our national misery in honorable fashion. We must go to work resolved and ready for sacrifice, and we did not lack resolution to hold our banner fast, even if not to hold it high. But we sailed the surging ocean of universal history without a compass, and such a compass must be invented. Far off, very far off, is the haven for which our soul longs. As yet we do not even know where it is, whether in the East or the West. For the wanderer of a thousand years, however, no way, no matter how distant, may be too long. . . .

IX

But how can we find that haven without sending out an expedition? If we are once so happy as to know what we need, and if only we are resolved, we must go forward with all care and foresight, step by step, without undue haste, and we must struggle with all our strength against being diverted into by-paths. We probably lack a leader of the genius of Moses — history does not grant a people such guides repeatedly. But a clear recognition of what we need most, a recognition of the absolute necessity of a home of our own, would arouse among us a number of energetic, honorable, and distinguished friends of the people, who would take the leadership, and would, perhaps, be no less able than one man to deliver us from disgrace and persecution.

What should we do first of all, how should we make a beginning? We believe that a nucleus for this beginning is already at hand; it consists of societies already in existence. It is encumbent upon them, they are called and in duty bound, to lay the foundation of that lighthouse to which our eyes will turn. If they are to be equal to their new task, these societies must, of course, be completely transformed. They must convoke a national congress, of which they are to form the center. If they decline this function, however, and if they think that they may not overstep the boundaries of their previous activity, they must at least form some of their numbers into a national institute, let us say a directorate, which will have to supply the place of that unity which we lack, without which the success of our endeavors is unthinkable. As a representative of our national interest this institute must comprise the leaders of our people, and it must energetically take in hand the direction of our general, national affairs. Our greatest and best forces — men of finance, of science, and of affairs, statesmen and publicists — must join hands with one accord in steering toward the common destination. This would aim chiefly and especially at creating a secure and inviolable home for the surplus of those Jews who live as proletarians in the different countries and are a burden to the native citizens.

There can, of course, be no question whatever of a united emigration of the entire people. The comparatively small number of Jews in the Occident, who constitute an insignificant percentage of the population, and for this reason, perhaps, are better situated and even to a certain extent naturalized, may in the future remain where they are. The wealthy may also remain even where the Jews are not readily tolerated. But, as we have said before, there is a certain point of saturation, beyond which their numbers may not increase, if the Jews are not to be exposed to the dangers of persecution as in Russia, Roumania, Morocco and elsewhere. It is this surplus which, a burden to itself and to others, conjures up the evil fate of the entire people. It is now high time to create a refuge for this surplus. We must occupy ourselves with the foundation of such a lasting refuge, not with the purposeless collection of donations for pilgrims or fugitives who forsake, in their consternation, a hospitable home, to perish in the abyss of a strange and unknown land.

The first task of this national institute, which we miss so much and must unconditionally call into existence, would have to be the discovery of a territory adapted to our purpose, as far as possible continuous in extent and of uniform character. In this respect there would probably commend themselves most highly those two lands, situated in opposite parts of the world, which have lately vied with each other for first place in creating two opposite currents in the Jewish emigration. This division was the cause of the failure of the entire movement.

Without plan, destination, or unity, as the emigration was, it would really have to be regarded as entirely unsuccessful and as having disappeared without a trace, had it not been so instructive as to what we should do and what we should leave undone in the future. With the total lack of foresight, reasonable consideration, and wise unity, it was impossible to recognize in the chaos of wandering, famishing fugitives a movement with any prospects whatever, directed toward a clearly marked goal. It was no emigration, but a portentous flight. For the poor fugitives the years 1881 and 1882 were a highway covered with wounded and corpses. And even the few who were so happy as to reach the goal of their desires, the longed-for haven, found the latter no whit better than the dangerous road. Wherever they came, people tried to get rid of them. The emigrants were soon confronted by the desperate alternative of either roaming about without shelter, without help, and without a plan in a strange land, or wandering back shamelessly to their no less strange and loveless homecountry. This emigration was for our people nothing but a new date in its martyrology. But this aimless wandering in the labyrinth of exile, to which our people have always been accustomed, does not cause them to advance a step; they rather sink deeper in the sticky morass of their wanderings. In the last emigration no sign of progress toward a better state of things is to be observed. Persecution, flight, dispersion, and a new exile — just as in the good old times. The weariness of the persecutors now allows us a little respite; will we be satisfied with it? Or will we rather use this respite to draw the proper moral from the experience accumulated, in order that we may escape the new blows which are sure to come? ... .

It is to be hoped that we have now passed that stage in which the Jews of the Middle Ages wretchedly vegetated. The sons of modern culture among our people esteem their dignity no less highly than our oppressors do theirs. But we shall not be able successfully to defend this dignity until we stand upon our own feet. As soon as an asylum is found for our poor people, for the fugitives whom our historic and predestined fate will always create for us, we shall simultaneously rise in the opinion of the peoples. We shall forthwith cease to be surprised by such tragic happenings as in the last few years, happenings which promise, alas, to be repeated more than once, not only in Russia, but also in other countries. We must labor actively to complete the great work of self-liberation. We must use all means which human intellect and human experience have devised, in order that the sacred work of national regeneration may not be left to blind chance.

X

The land which we are about to purchase must be productive and well situated and of an area sufficient to allow the settlement of several millions. The land, as national property, must be inalienable. Its selection is, of course, of the first and highest importance, and must not be left to offhand decision or to certain preconceived sympathies or individuals, as has, alas, happened lately. This land must be uniform and continuous in extent, for it lies in the very nature of our problem that we must possess as a counterpoise to our dispersion *one single refuge*, since a *number of refugees* would again present the features of our old dispersion. Therefore, the selection of a national and permanent land, meeting all requirements, must be made with all care, and confided to one single national institute, to a commission of experts selected from our directorate. Only such a supreme tribunal will be able, after thorough and comprehensive investigation, to give an opinion and decide upon which of the two continents and upon *which* territory in them our final choice should fall.

Only then, and not before, should the directorate, together with an associated body of capitalists, as founders of a stock company later to be organized, purchase a piece of land upon which in the course of time several million Jews could settle. This piece of land might form a small territory in North America, or a sovereign Pashalik in Asiatic Turkey recognized by the Porte and the other Powers as neutral. It would certainly be an important duty of the directorate to secure the assent of the Porte, and probably of the other European cabinets to this plan.

The land purchased would have to be divided by surveyors, under the supervision of the directorate, into small parcels, which could be assigned according to the local conditions to agricultural, or building, or manufacturing purposes. Every parcel laid off thus (for agriculture, house and garden, townhall, factory, etc.) would form a lot which would be transferred to the purchaser in accordance with his wishes.

After a complete survey and publication of detailed maps and a comprehensive description of the land, a part of the lots would be sold to Jews for an adequate payment at a price in exactly determined proportion to the cost-price, perhaps somewhat higher than the latter. The proceeds of the sale, together with the profits, would belong in part to the stock company, and be turned in part into a fund to be administered by the directorate, for the maintenance of destitute immigrants. For the establishment of this fund the directorate could also open a subscription. It is definitely to be expected that our brethren everywhere would hail with joy such an appeal for subscriptions, and that the most liberal donations would be made for such a sacred purpose.

In the title-deed given every purchaser, made out in his name, and signed by the directorate and the company, the exact number of the lot upon the general map would be given, so that every one could see clearly the location of the piece of ground —field, or building lot — which he purchases as his individual property.

Assuredly, many a Jew, perhaps momentarily fettered to his old home by an occupation little to be envied, would joyfully grasp the opportunity to throw out an anchor to windward by such a deed, and to escape those sad experiences in which the immediate past is so rich.

That part of the territory which would be assigned to the directorate for free distribution, in return for the national subscription mentioned, and for the financial returns to be expected, would be given to destitute but able-bodied immigrants, recommended for consideration by local committees.

As for the donations to the national subscription, these would have to come in, not at once, but say in annual installments, and the settlement, too, would have to be made gradually and in a fixed order.

If the experts give their opinion in favor of Palestine or Syria, this decision would have to be based on the hypothesis that the country could be transformed in time by labor and industry into a quite productive one. In this case the price of land would rise in the future.

If the decision of those selected should be in favor of North America, however, we must hasten. If one considers that in the last thirty-eight years the population of the United States of America has risen from seventeen millions to fifty millions, and that the increase in population for the next forty years will probably continue in the same proportion, we can well understand that *immediate* action is necessary, if we do not desire to eliminate for all time the possibility of establishing in the New World a secure refuge for our unhappy brethren.

Every one who has the slightest judgment can see at first glance that the purchase of lands in America would, because of the swift rise of that country, not be a risky undertaking, but a lucrative enterprise. Whether this act of national self-help on our part would be a more or less productive enterprise, however, is of little importance in comparison with the great significance which such an undertaking would have for the future of our unsettled people; for our future will remain insecure and precarious so long as a radical change in our position is not made. This change cannot be brought about by the civil emancipation of the Jews in this or that state, but only by the auto-emancipation of the Jewish people as a nation, the foundation of a colonial community belonging to the Jews, which is some day to become our inalienable home, our fatherland.

There will certainly be no lack of objection to our plans. We will be charged with reckoning with our host. What land will grant us permission to constitute a nation within its borders? At first glance, our building would appear from this standpoint to be a house of cards to divert children and wits. We think, however, that only thoughtless childhood could be diverted by the sight of shipwrecked voyagers who desire to build a little boat in order to leave an inhospitable country. We even go as far as to say that we expect, strangely enough, that those inhospitable people will aid us in our departure. Our "friends" will see us leave with the same pleasure with which we turn our back upon them.

Of course, the establishment of a Jewish refuge cannot come about without the support of the governments. In order to attain the latter and to insure the perpetual existence of a refuge, the creators of our national regeneration will have to proceed with patience and care. What we seek is at bottom neither new nor dangerous to anyone. Instead of *many refuges* which we have always been accustomed to seek, we would fain have *one single refuge*, the existence of which, however, would have to be politically assured.

Let "Now or never!" be our watchword. Woe to our descendants, woe to the memory of our Jewish contemporaries, if we let this moment pass by!

SUMMARY

The Jews are not a living nation; they are everywhere aliens; therefore they are despised.

The civil and political emancipation of the Jews is not sufficient to raise them in the estimation of the peoples.

The proper, the only remedy would be the creation of a Jewish nationality, of a people living upon its own soil, the auto-emancipation of the Jews; their emancipation as a nation among nations by the acquisition of a home of their own.

We should not persuade ourselves that humanity and enlightenment will be radical remedies for the malady of our people.

The lack of national self-respect and self-confidence, of political initiative and of unity, are the enemies of our national renaissance.

In order that we may not be constrained to wander from one exile to another, we must have an extensive productive place of refuge, a *rendezvous* which is our own.

The present moment is more favourable than any other for the plan unfolded.

The international Jewish question must receive a national solution. Of course, our national regeneration can only proceed slowly. *We* must take the first step. Our *descendants* must follow us in measured and not over-hasty time.

A way must be opened for the national regeneration of the Jews by a congress of Jewish notables.

No sacrifice would be too great in order to reach the goal which will assure our people's future, everywhere endangered.

The financial accomplishment of the undertaking can in the present state of the case encounter no insuperable difficulties.

Help yourselves, and God will help you!

2

Der Judenstaat, 1896

With the publication of his short book, *Der Judenstaat* ("The Jewish State") on 14 February 1896, Theodor Herzl came to be regarded as the father of modern political Zionism. The ideas expressed by Herzl for the establishment of a Jewish secular state and the methods to be employed in doing so are astonishingly similar to those propounded by Leo Pinsker fifteen years earlier, but in his diary entry of 20 September 1895, Herzl wrote: "In Odessa, for example, there had lived a man named Pinsker who had fought the same cause, namely, the regaining of a Jewish national home. Unfortunately, Pinsker was already dead. His writings are said to be worthwhile. Shall read them as soon as I have time."[1]

The lives of the two men were similar as well. Herzl was born into easy circumstances on 2 May 1860, in Budapest, the second capital of the then Austro-Hungarian Empire. He too received a secular education and in 1878 entered the University of Vienna for the study of

Source: Theodor Herzl. *The Jewish State (Der Judenstaat)* trans. Harry Zohn (New York: Herzl Press, 1970). Courtesy of American Zionist Federation. Translation reproduced covers pages 49-58 and 94-98.

[1]Raphael Patai, ed., and Harry Zohn, trans., *The Complete Diaries of Theodor Herzl*, vol. 1 (New York: Thomas Yoseloff, 1960), 243.

law. He was admitted to the bar in 1884.
Although as a child he was taken to the nearby
liberal-reform temple by his father, by his
early adulthood he seldom visited a synagogue.
He was a Jew not by faith but by birth. After
practicing law in state service for only a year
Herzl resigned his position in favor of earning
his livelihood as a writer. In 1892 he joined the
staff of the noted Viennese newspaper *Neue
Freie Presse*, and shortly afterward became that
paper's Paris correspondent. He retained, however, his interest in drama and print literature.

It was as a student in Vienna that Herzl
began to perceive the Jewish Question: the
rising tide of anti-Jewish sentiment that was
starting to engulf Europe in the last quarter of
the nineteenth century. At first he attempted
to understand it, and then, in the spring of
1895, he sought a solution through the emigration of the Jews. Like Pinsker before him,
Herzl attempted to obtain support for his ideas
from amongst the wealthy and powerful Jews
of Western Europe, with so little success, that
he too turned to the expedient of publishing
them in a short seventy-one page pamphlet
published in Vienna at his own expense. It was
shortly thereafter translated into several languages, not, however, including Russian. Although it received praise from some Jewish authors and highly-placed officials, it made an almost immediate impression upon the masses,
particularly in Russia.

In the introduction he posed the question, "assimilation or emigration?" and came
out wholeheartedly in favor of emigration. His
entire thesis was succinctly made in the first
sentence of the work: "The idea which I have
developed in this pamphlet is a very old one: it
is the restoration of the Jewish state." Following a brief, impassioned description defining
the Jewish Question, Herzl launched into a detailed description of his "Plan."

II. GENERAL PART

THE PLAN

The entire plan is in its essence perfectly simple, as it must be if it is to be come comprehensible to all.

Let sovereignty be granted us over a portion of the earth's surface that is sufficient for our rightful national requirements; we shall take care of everything else ourselves.

The creation of a new sovereign state is neither ludicrous nor impossible. After all, we have seen it happen in our own day — among nations which are not largely middle-class, as we are, but poorer, uneducated, and therefore weaker than ourselves. The governments of the countries scourged by anti-Semitism will be keenly interested in securing a sovereign status for us.

Two great agencies will be created for this task which is simple in design but complicated in execution: The Society of Jews and the Jewish Company.

What the Society of Jews has prepared scientifically and politically, the Jewish Company will put into effect.

The Jewish Company will handle the liquidation of all business interests of departing Jews and will organize trade and commerce in the new country.

As has already been stated, the departure of the Jews must not be imagined as a sudden one. It will be gradual, taking decades. The poorest will go first and make the land arable. In accordance with a predetermined plan, they will build roads, bridges, and railways, set up telegraph installations; regulate rivers and provide themselves with homesteads. Their labor will bring trade, trade will create markets and markets will attract new settlers — for everyone will come voluntarily, at his own expense and his own risk. The labor that we put into the soil will enhance value of the land. The Jews will soon realize that a new and permanent field has opened up for their spirit of enterprise which has heretofore been met with hatred and contempt.

Whoever wants to found a state today must not go about it in the manner that a thousand years ago would have been the only possible one. It is foolish to revert to old levels of civilization, which is what Zionists would like to do. If, for example, we were required to clear a country of wild beasts, we would not tackle it in the fashion of fifth-century Europeans. We would not set out individually with spears and lances to hunt bears; but would organize a large, jolly hunting party, drive the beasts together, and throw a melinite bomb into their midst.

If we wish to erect buildings, we shall not put up ungainly piles at the shore of some lake; we shall build the way it is done now. We shall build more boldly and more magnificently than has ever been done before; for we now have means that are unprecedented in history.

The emigrants standing lowest in the economic scale will be gradually be followed by those of the next grade. Those who are now in desperate straits will go first. They will be led by the average intellects whom we overproduce and who are persecuted everywhere.

This pamphlet is intended to open a general discussion on the question of Jewish migration. This does not mean, however, that it is to be put to a vote, for that would ruin the cause from the outset. Let anyone who does not want to go along stay behind. The opposition of individuals is immaterial.

Let all those who wish to join us line up behind our banner and fight for it with word, pen, and deed.

Those Jews who espouse our idea of a state will rally round the Society of Jews. Thereby they will give it the authority to speak in the name of the Jews and negotiate with governments in their behalf. To put it in the terminology of international law, the Society will be recognized as a state-creating power, and this in itself will mean the formation of the State.

If the Powers show themselves willing to grant the Jewish people sovereignty over a neutral territory, the Society will negotiate for the land to be taken. Two regions are possibilities: Palestine and Argentina. Noteworthy experiments in colonization have been made in both places, although they have been based on the mistaken principle of a gradual infiltration of Jews. Infiltration is always bound to end badly. For there invariably comes a moment when the government, under pressure of the native population — which feels itself threatened — bars any further influx of Jews. Consequently, emigration will be pointless unless it is based upon our guaranteed sovereignty.

The Society of Jews will negotiate with the present authorities of the country — under the protectorate of the European Powers, if the matter makes sense to them. We shall be able to offer the present authorities enormous advantages — assume part of their national debt, build new thoroughfares (which we should require ourselves), and do many other things. But the very creation of the Jewish State will be beneficial to the neighboring countries, because the cultivation of an area enhances the value of its surroundings, on a large as on a small scale.

PALESTINE OR ARGENTINA?

Is Palestine or Argentina preferable? The Society will take whatever is given, whatever is favored by the public opinion of the Jewish people. The Society will determine both points.

Argentine is a country with some of the greatest natural resources in the world; it extends over a vast area, is sparsely populated, and has a temperate climate. It would be very much to the interest of the Republic of Argentina to cede a portion of its territory to us. The present infiltration of Jews, to be sure, has produced some ill feeling there; it would be necessary to enlighten Argentina on the intrinsic difference of the new Jewish immigration.

Palestine is our unforgettable historic homeland. The very name would be a powerfully moving rallying cry for our people. If His Majesty the Sultan were to give us Palestine, we could in return pledge ourselves to regulate the entire finances of Turkey. For Europe we could constitute part of the wall of defense against Asia; we would serve as an outpost of civilization against barbarism. As a neutral state we would remain in contact with all Europe, which would have to guarantee our existence. Some form of extraterritoriality under international law could be found for the Holy Places of Christendom. We would form a guard of honor around the Holy Places, answering for the fulfilment of this duty with our existence. This guard of honor would be the symbol of the solution of the Jewish Question after what were for us eighteen centuries of affliction.

III. THE JEWISH COMPANY

BASIC FEATURES

The Jewish Company is conceived partly along the lines of the great land-acquisition companies. It might be called a Jewish "Chartered Company". However, it is not endowed with sovereign powers and has other than merely colonial tasks.

The Jewish Company will be founded as a joint-stock company incorporated in England, under British English laws and protection. Its headquarters will be in London. I cannot tell at this time how large the share capital should be; our numerous financial experts will work that out. But to avoid vague terminology I shall estimate it at a billion marks; it may have to be either more or less than that. The form of subscription, which will be discussed later, will determine what fraction of that amount must actually be paid in at the start of the Company's operations.

The Jewish Company will be a transitional organization. It is strictly a business operation which must always be carefully distinguished from the Society of Jews.

The first task of the Jewish Company will be to liquidate the immovable property of the emigrating Jews. This will be done in such a way as to prevent crises, safeguard every man's interests, and permit that internal migration of Christian fellow citizens which has already been indicated.

PURCHASE OF LAND

The land that is guaranteed to the Society of Jews under international law must, of course, be purchased under civil law as well.

The arrangements made by individuals for their own settlement do not come within the scope of this discussion. But the Company will require large tracts of land for its own needs and ours, and it must secure the necessary land by centralized purchase. It will mainly be a matter of acquiring state domains now belonging to the present government of the country. The aim will be to acquire land "over there" without driving prices sky-high, just as "over here" sales will be made without causing prices to drop. There is no need to worry about any wild rigging of the market, for the value of the land will be created by the Company, which will direct the settlement of the land in cooperation with the supervising Society of Jews. The latter will see to it that the enterprise becomes a Suez rather than a Panama.[2]

---

[2] The reference is to the Suez Canal, whose construction was successfully completed in 1869, as contrasted with the Panama Canal,

The Company will sell its official building sites at favorable rates to the Company, for it is entitled to an unlimited premium for having borne the risk, like any free entrepreneur. When an undertaking involves risk, the entrepreneur should be encouraged to make a generous profit.

V. SOCIETY OF JEWS AND JEWISH STATE

THE GESTOR OF THE JEWS

This organ of the National Movement, whose nature and functions we are only now discussing, will actually come into being before anything else. Its formation is extremely simple. This "moral person" will arise out of the circle of valiant English Jews whom I informed about my plan in London.[3]

The Society of Jews will be the center of the incipient Jewish movement.

The Society will have scientific and political tasks. The founding of the Jewish State, as I envisage it, presupposes modern, scientific methods. If we journey out of Egypt today, this cannot be done in the simple fashion of ancient times. We shall first obtain an idea of our numbers and our strength in a different way. The Society of Jews is the new Moses of the Jews. The undertaking of that great, old *gestor* of the Jews in primitive times is to ours as some beautiful old *Singspiel* is to modern. We shall play the same melody with many, many more violins, flutes, harps, violincellos, and strong basses; with electric lights, scenery, choruses, magnificent costumes, and star signers.

This pamphlet is intended to initiate a general discussion of the Jewish Question. Friend and foe will take part in

---

whose name became a byword for administrative corruption. As a result of the corrupt practices of many officials of the French Panama Canal Company, Ferdinand de Lesseps resigned and was tried in 1888, and the Company was dissolved in 1889. [Editor's note].

[3] Herzl here refers to his visit to London which took place in the second half of November 1895, during which he was received with sympathy and was promised support by several leading British Jews [members of the Maccabean Club of London, before whom Herzl presented his ideas on 24 November 1895.] Cf. *The Complete Diaries of Theodor Herzl*. New York: 1960, vol. I, 276-84. [Editor's note].

it; but   no longer, I hope, in the form of sentimental defense and vulgar invective.   Let the debate be objective, grand, serious, and political.

The Society of Jews will collect all pronouncements of statesmen, parliaments, Jewish communities, and organizations which are made orally or in writing,   at meetings or in newspapers and books.

Thus the Society learn and determine for the first time whether the time has come when the Jews want to, or have to, migrate to the Promised Land.   From Jewish communities all over the world the Society will receive the materials for a comprehensive collection of Jewish statistics.

Subsequent tasks, such as expert investigation of the new country and its natural resources, the uniform plan for the migration and the settlement, preliminary work on legislation and administration, etc., will be developed logically in line with the objective.

Externally, the Society, as I have already explained in the general section, must attempt to be recognized as a state-forming power. From the free assent of many Jews it can derive the authority required to deal with the governments concerned.

Internally — that is to say, in its relations with the Jewish people — the Society will create the institutions that are indispensable in the early period — the germ cell, to use a scientific term, from which the public institutions of the Jewish State are to develop later.

Our first object is, as has already been stated, sovereignty assured by international law over an area that is adequate for our rightful needs.

What must be done next?

THE OCCUPATION OF THE LAND

When peoples migrated in ancient   times, they let themselves be carried along, tossed about by historical chance.   Like swarms of locusts they alighted wherever their random course took them.   For in ancient times the globe was not known to man.

The new migration of the Jews must proceed in accordance with scientific principles. ... .

And so the new Jewish land must be explored and taken possession of with all modern aids.

As soon as we have secured the land, a ship will sail to take possession of it.

This ship will carry representatives of the Society, the Company, and the Local Groups.

These pioneers will have three tasks: first, the exact scientific investigation of all natural properties of the land; second, the establishment of a tightly centralized administration; third, the distribution of the land. These tasks complement one another and are to be carried out in accordance with the objective which is by now sufficiently familiar.

Only one thing remains to be clarified — namely, how the occupation of the land by Local Groups should proceed.

In America the occupation of a newly opened territory still takes place in a naive manner. The settlers gather at the border, and at the appointed hour make a simultaneous and violent dash for it.

It cannot be done that way in the new land of the Jews. Plots in the provinces and towns will be auctioned off — not for money, but for achievements. It will have been established according to the general plan which roads, bridges, dams, etc., are necessary for traffic. These will be grouped according to provinces. Within each province the sites for towns will be auctioned off in a similar manner. The Local Groups will assume the responsibility of carrying this out in an orderly fashion, and they will defray the costs from local assessments. After all, the Society will be in a position to know in advance whether or not the Local Groups are undertaking too great a sacrifice. The big communities will get a lot of elbow-room for their activities. Greater sacrifices will be rewarded by certain concessions: Universities, technical schools, academies, research institutes, etc., and those government institution which do not have to be located in the capital will be dispersed throughout the country.

The proper execution of what is undertaken will be guaranteed by the personal interest of the buyers, and, if need be, by local assessments. For just as we cannot, and do not wish to, abolish differences among individuals, differences among the Local Groups will continue. Everything will fall into place in a natural way. All acquired rights will be protected, every new development will get sufficient scope.

Our people will be fully informed of all these matters.

Just as we will not take others by surprise or cheat them, we shall not deceive ourselves either.

Everything will be systematically worked out in ad-

vance. In the elaboration of this plan, which I am capable
only of suggesting, our keenest minds will participate.   Every achievement in the fields of social science and technol-
ogy   of our own age and of the even more advanced age
which will dawn over the protracted execution of the plan
must be utilized for the cause.   Every happy invention
which is already available or will become available must be
used.   Thus the land   can be occupied and the state founded
in a manner as yet unknown to history, and with unprecedented chances of success. ... .

The Basel Program, 1897

The publication of *Der Judenstaat* was greeted
with disdain by some and with acclaim by
others, particularly from amongst the Jews of
Russia who had suffered the most from the
pograms of the 1880s. Frustrated by the refusal
of Jewish philanthropists and religious leaders
to support his scheme for the establishment of
a Jewish state Herzl decided to make of it a mass
movement. To this end, on Sunday, 7 March
1897, at his home in Vienna, Herzl, together
with a few fellow Zionists from Germany and
Austria determined to convene a "General
Zionist Congress" to meet the following August
in Munich. Later, however, because of the
objections of the rabbis of that city, the locale
of the Congress was moved to Basel,
Switzerland. The second method employed to
reach the ordinary Jew was the establishment
by Herzl of a Zionist newspaper, *Die Welt* [The
World], first published on 4 June 1897.

Between 29-31 August 1897, 197 specially
invited delegates met in Basel for the momen-
tous first Zionist Congress.. Herzl was proclaimed president by acclamation. The immediate and long-term results of this meeting
were two-fold: firstly, the institutionalization
of the Congress as the supreme organ of

Source: *The Jewish Chronicle*, September 3, 1897, p. 13.

Zionism (the "National Assembly," as Herzl termed it), thus transforming this previously inchoate movement into an international political organization; secondly, the adoption of the "Basel Program," here quoted in its entirety. To provide for continuity, direction, and political action an executive committee was formed with Herzl as its chairman. For the next six years, until his death in July of 1904, Herzl devoted himself to the goal of persuading the Sultan to grant Palestine to the Zionist organization in order to put his plan into effect, but without success.

The aim of Zionism is to create for the Jewish people a home in Palestine secured by public law.
The Congress contemplates the following means to the attainment of this end:

1. The promotion, on suitable lines, of the colonization of Palestine by Jewish agricultural and industrial workers.

2. The organization and binding together of the whole of Jewry by means of appropriate institutions, local and international, in accordance with the laws of each country.

3. The strengthening and fostering of Jewish national sentiment and consciousness.

4. Preparatory steps towards obtaining government consent, where necessary, to the attainment of the aim of Zionism.

Husayn-McMahon Correspondence, 1915–1916

Following the 1908 *coup d'état* that overthrew the autocratic regime of Sultan 'Abd al-Hamid in the Ottoman Empire, the government came into the hands of the Turkish nationalists of the "Committee of Union and Progress," decidedly pro-German. In that year the Sharif Husayn ibn 'Ali, a descendant of the Prophet Muhammad and considered in Istanbul as pro-Turkish, was appointed the Grand Sharif of the Holy Cities of Mecca and Medina by the new administration. The second of his three sons, 'Abd Allah, had been elected to a seat in the new Turkish parliament. Prior to the outbreak of the war 'Abd Allah, enroute to Mecca, stopped in Cairo in February of 1914 to discuss with the then British Consul, Lord Kitchener,

Source: Great Britain. Parliamentary Papers, *Miscellaneous No. 3 (1939). Correspondence Between Sir Henry McMahon, G.C.M.G., G.C.F.O., K.C.I.E., C.S.I., His Majesty's High Commissioner at Cairo and the Sherif Hussein of Mecca July 1915 - March 1916* (London, His Majesty's Stationery Office, 1939) Cmd. 5957. Reprinted here are two of the letters that were exchanged between the Sharif Husayn ibn 'Ali, the guardian of the two Holy Cities of Mecca and Medina and Sir Henry representing the British Government. The first is dated 14 July 1915 and the second (the fourth letter) is dated 24 October 1916. Each represents the respective views of the Arab nationalists and the British cabinet in regards to Syria-Palestine. Reprinted by permission of the Controller of Her Majesty's Stationery Office.

the possibility of British support for an Arab revolt against the Ottoman Government.

With the outbreak of the war in August of that year, Lord Kitchener was recalled to London and appointed Minister of War and was replaced in Cairo by Sir Henry McMahon as High Commissioner, with Egypt having been proclaimed a protectorate of Great Britain. In November the Ottoman Empire entered the war on the side of the Central Powers. Early in 1915 Lord Kitchener, perhaps recalling his earlier conversation with 'Abd Allah, requested that Sir Henry obtain from the Sharif Husayn the Arab requirements for a revolt in order to open a southern front to occupy Turkish troops so that they could not be deployed in Europe. Meanwhile the Sharif had sent his youngest son, Faysal, to Damascus to assure the Ottoman governor of the family's loyalty to Istanbul. There he met the leaders of the al-Fatat society seeking independence of the Arabs who gave to him the so-called "Damascus Protocol" that came to serve as the basis for the Sharif Husayn's first letter to Sir Henry.

In response to an oral message relayed to him in Mecca by a representative of Sir Henry, the Sharif Husayn sent his first letter to the High Commissioner.

Mecca, Ramadan 2, 1333

[July 14, 1915]

Whereas the entire Arab nation without exception is determined to assert its right to live, gain its freedom and administer its own affairs in name and in fact;

And whereas the Arabs believe it to be in Great Britain's interest to lend them assistance and support in the fulfillment of their steadfast and legitimate aims to the exclusion of all other aims;

And whereas it is similarly to the advantage of the Arabs, in view of their geographical position and their economic interests, and in view of the well-known attitude of the Government of Great Britain, to prefer British assistance to any other;

For these reasons, the Arab nation has decided to approach the Government of Great Britain with a request for the approval, through one of their representatives if they think fit, of the following basic provisions which, as time presses, have not been made to include matters of relatively smaller importance, since such matters can wait until the time comes for their consideration:-

1. Great Britain recognises the independence of the Arab countries which are bounded: on the north, by the line Mersin-Adana to parallel 37° N. and thence along the line Birejik-Urfa-Mardin-Midiat Jazirat (ibn 'Umar) - Amadia to the Persian frontier; on the east, by the Indian Ocean (with the exclusion of Aden whose status will remain as at present); on the west, by the Red Sea and the Mediterranean Sea back to Mersin.

2. Great Britain will agree to the proclamation of an Arab Caliphate for Islam.

3. The Sharifian Arab Government undertakes, other things being equal, to grant Great Britain preference in all economic enterprises in the Arab countries.

4. With a view to ensuring the stability of Arab independence and the efficacy of the promised preference in economic enterprises, the two contracting parties undertake, in the event of any foreign state attacking either of them, to come to each other's assistance with all the resources of their military and naval forces; it being understood that peace will be concluded only when both parties concur.

In the event of one of the two parties embarking upon a war of offence, the other party will adopt an attitude of neutrality, but, if invited to join, will agree to confer with the other party as the the conditions of joint action.

5. Great Britain agrees to the abolition of the Capitulations in the Arab countries, and undertakes to assist the Sharifian Government in summoning an international congress to decree their abolition.

6. Clauses 3 and 4 of the present Agreement are to remain in force for a period of fifteen years. Should either party desire an extension, due notice of one year before the expiry of that period will have to be given.

Therefore, since the entire Arab nation is (God be praised!) united in its resolve to pursue its noble aim to the end, at whatever cost, it requests the Government of Great Britain to return an answer, whether negatively or in the affirmative, within thirty days of the receipt of this message, in default of which it reserves its right to complete freedom of action, just as we will consider ourselves absolved from the letter and the spirit of the declaration which we made earlier through 'Ali Efendi.

In his response, dated 30th August, Sir Henry reiterated Great Britain's desire for Arab independence and the establishment of an Arab caliphate. However, he stated that the question regarding the frontiers of the proposed Arab state was premature and "a waste of time." On this Husayn was adamant. Therefore, on 24 October, McMahon wrote:

Cairo, October 24, 1915

I have, with gratification and pleasure, received your note of the 29th Shawwal, 1333 [9 September 1915], and its tokens of sincere friendship have filled me with satisfaction and contentment.

I regret to find that you inferred from my last note that my attitude towards the question of frontiers and boundaries was one of hesitancy and lukewarmth. Such was in no wise the intention of my note. All I meant was that I considered that the time had not yet come in which that question could be discussed in a conclusive manner.

But, having realized from your last note that you considered the question important, vital and urgent, I hastened to communicate to the Government of Great Britain the purport of your note. It gives me the greatest pleasure to convey to you, on their behalf, the following declarations which, I have not doubt, you will receive with satisfaction and acceptance.

The districts of Mersin and Alexandretta, and portions of Syria lying to the west of the districts of Damascus, Homs, Hama and Aleppo, cannot be said to be purely Arab, and must on that account be excepted from the proposed delimitation.

Subject to that modification, and without prejudice to the treaties concluded between us and certain Arab Chiefs, we accept that delimitation.

As for the regions lying within the proposed frontiers, in which Great Britain is free to act without detriment to the interests of her ally France, I am authorised to give you the following pledges on behalf of the Government of Great Britain, and to reply as follows to your note:

(1) That, subject to the modifications stated above, Great Britain is prepared to recognise and uphold the independence of the Arabs in all the regions lying within the frontiers proposed by the Sharif of Mecca;

(2) That Great Britain will guarantee the Holy Places against all external aggression, and will recognise the obligation of preserving them from aggression;

(3) That, when circumstances permit, Great Britain will help the Arabs with her advice and assist them in the establishment of governments to suit those diverse regions;

(4) That it is understood that the Arabs have already decided to seek the counsels and advice of Great Britain exclusively; and that such European advisers and officials as may be needed to establish a sound system of administration shall be British;

(5) That, as regards the two vilayets of Baghdad and Basra, the Arabs recognize that the fact of Great Britain's established position and interests there will call for the setting up of special administrative arrangements to protect those regions from foreign aggression, to promote the welfare of their inhabitants, and to safeguard our mutual economic interests.

I am confident that this declaration will convince you, beyond all doubt, of Great Britain's sympathy with the aspirations of her friends the Arabs; and that it will result in a lasting and solid alliance with them, of which one of the immediate consequences will be the expulsion of the Turks from the Arab countries and the liberation of the Arab peoples from the Turkish yoke which has weighed on them all these long years.

I have confined myself in this note to vital questions of primary importance. If there are any other matters in your notes, which have been overlooked, we can revert to them at some suitable time in the future.

I have heard with great satisfaction and pleasure that the Sacred Kiswa and the charitable gifts which had gone with it, had arrived safely and that, thanks to your wise directions and arrangements, they were landed without trouble or damage in spite of the risks and difficulties created by the present deplorable war. We pray to Almighty God that He may bring a lasting peace and freedom to mankind.

I am sending this note with your faithful messenger, Shaikh Muhammad ibn 'Aref ibn 'Uraifan, who will lay before you certain interesting matters which, as they are of secondary importance, I have abstained from mentioning in this note.

On the basis of Sir Henry's pledge to assist in the establishment of Arab independence following the victory of the allies, Husayn declared war against the Ottomans on 5 June 1916.

Sykes-Picot Agreement, 1916

Although the war had reached such a stalemate that the principal allies, France, Great Britain, and Russia, could not be assured of a victory, early in March of 1915 they had already begun to divide the spoils between themselves, particularly the division of the Ottoman Empire. Britain and France desperately needed to have the eastern front kept alive so that the combined forces of Germany and the Austro-Hungarian Empire could not be concentrated in the West. Tsar Nicholas II demanded a price for continued Russian participation in the war, and that was that Constantinople and the Straits should be added to his empire. In return for her recognition of this claim, France required recognition of her "historical right" to Syria, including Palestine; Great Britain, in turn, desired that Constantinople be declared an open port and the Holy Cities of Mecca and Medina and an undefined Arabia be constituted as an independent Muslim state.

It was in July of that year that the first War Cabinet under Herbert Asquith initiated its secret correspondence with the Sharif Husayn

Source: E. L. Woodward & Rohan Butler, eds., *Documents on British Foreign Policy 1919-1939: First Series, vol. IV: 1919* (London: Her Majesty's Stationery Office, 1952), 245-47. Reprinted by permission of the Controller of Her Majesty's Stationery Office.

to bring the Arabs in on the side of the Entente. However, it was not until 21 October 1915 that the British Foreign Secretary, Sir Edward Gray, informed the French Government, through its ambassador in London, Paul Cambon, of this action and of Husayn's own demands, suggesting that they should meet to discuss their mutual interests in the Middle East. Cambon thereupon requested Charles-George Picot, one of his political advisors, to represent France. Sir Arthur Nicolson, the permanent undersecretary of state for foreign affairs, was selected to negotiate for his government. On 23 November Picot and Nicolson began their discussions, but after only two days the two had reached an impasse. Nicolson was thereupon replaced by Sir Mark Sykes, Middle East advisor in the War Office and regarded as a friend of the Arabs. The two initialed a basic agreement on 3 January 1916. Following the approval of the draft by both the French and British Governments in early February, Sykes and Picot traveled to Moscow to present it to the Tsarist government for approval. The Russian foreign minister agreed to the division of the Fertile Crescent in return for support of Russian annexation of the northern Turkish regions of Erzeroum, Trebizond, Van, Bitlis, and Kurdistan. The resultant agreement was established in a series of letters exchanged between the three parties between 26 April and 23 October 1916. The terms of the arrangement for the division of the Arab lands between Britain and France are contained in a letter from Sir Edward Gray to Ambassaor Cambon dated 16 May 1916, and for the proposed cessation of Turkish territories to Russia in a letter from Sir Edward to Count Benckendorff, the Russian ambassador to the Court of St. James, dated 23 May. Both Italy and Japan were informed of these agreements, but, of course, not the Arabs. Writing later, David Lloyd George, the leader of the second War Cabinet, wrote, "It was a foolish document." and quoted Lord Curzon as stating,"'When the Sykes-Picot Agreement was drawn up it was, no

doubt, intended by its authors ... as a sort of
fancy sketch to suit a situation that had not
then arisen, and which it was thought extremely unlikely would ever arise; that, I suppose must be the principal explanation of the
gross ignorance with which the boundary
lines in that agreement were drawn.'"[1]

      It is accordingly understood between the
French and the British Governments—
      1. That France and Great Britain are prepared to
recognise and protect an independent Arab State or a Confederation of Arab States in the areas (A) and (B) marked on
the annexed map, under the suzerainty of an Arab chief.
That in area (A) France, and in area (B) Great Britain, shall
have priority of right of enterprise and local loans.   That in
area (A) France, and in area (B) Great Britain, shall alone
supply advisers or foreign functionaries at the request of
the Arab State or Confederation of Arab States.
      2. That in the blue area France, and in the red area
Great Britain, shall be allowed to establish such direct or
indirect administration or control as they desire and as they
may think fit to arrange with the Arab State or Confederation of Arab States.
      3. That in the brown area [Palestine] there shall be
established an international administration, the form of
which is to be decided upon after consultation with Russia,
and subsequently in consultation with the other Allies, and
the representatives of the Shereef of Mecca.
      4. That Great Britain be accorded (1) the ports of Haifa
and Acre, (2) guarantee of a given supply of water from the
Tigris and Euphrates in area (A) for area (B).   His Majesty's
Government, on their part, undertake that they will at no
time enter into negotiations for the cession of Cyprus to any
third Power without the previous consent of the French
Government.
      5. That Alexandretta shall be a free port as regards the
trade of the British Empire, and there shall be no discrimination in port charges or facilities as regards British ship-

---

[1]David Lloyd George, *Memoirs of the Peace Conference,* vol. 2 (New
Haven: Yale University Press, 1939), 664-65.

ping and   goods; that there shall be freedom of transit for British goods through Alexandretta and by railway through the blue area, whether those goods are intended for or originate in the red area, or (B), or area (A); and there shall be no discrimination, direct or indirect, against   British goods on any railway or against British goods or ships at any port serving the areas mentioned.

That Haifa shall be a free port as regards the trade of France, her dominions and protectorates, and there shall be no discrimination in port charges or facilities as regards French shipping and French goods.   There shall be freedom of transit for French goods through Haifa and by the British railway through the brown area, whether those goods are intended for or originate in the blue area, area (A) and area (B), and there shall be no discrimination, direct or indirect, against French goods on any railway, or against French goods or ships at any port serving the areas mentioned.

6. That in area (A) the Baghdad Railway shall not be extended southwards beyond Mosul, and in area (B), northwards beyond Samarra, until a railway connecting Baghdad with Aleppo via the Euphrates Valley has been completed, and then only with the concurrence of the two Governments.

7. That Great Britain has the right to build, administer, and be sole owner of a railway connecting Haifa with area (B). and shall have a perpetual right to transport troops along such a line at all times.

It is to be understood by both Governments that this railway is to facilitate the connexion of Baghdad with Haifa by rail, and it is further understood that, if the engineering difficulties and expense entailed by keeping this connecting line in the brown area only make the project unfeasible, that the French Government shall be prepared to consider that the line in question may also   traverse the polygon Banias-Keis Marib-Salkhad Tell Otsda-Mesmie before reaching area (B).

8. For a period of twenty years the existing Turkish customs tariff shall remain in force throughout the whole of the blue and red areas, as well as in areas (A) and (B), and no increase in the rates of duties or conversion from *ad valorem* to specific rates shall be made except by agreement between the two powers.

There shall be no interior customs barriers between any of the above mentioned areas. The customs duties leviable on goods destined for the interior shall be collected at

the port of entry and handed over to the administration of
the area of destination.

9. It shall be agreed that the French Government will
at no time enter into any negotiations for the cession of
their rights and will not cede such   rights in the blue area to
any third Power, except   the Arab State or Confederation of
Arab States, without the previous agreement of His Majesty's
Government, who, on their part, will give a similar undertaking to the French Government regarding the red area.

10. The British and French Governments, as the pro-
tectors of the Arab State, shall agree that they themselves
acquire and will not   consent to a third Power acquiring
territorial possessions in the Arabian peninsula, nor   consent to   a third Power installing   a naval base either on the
east coast, or on the islands, of the Red Sea.   This, however,
shall not prevent such adjustment of the Aden frontier as
may be necessary in consequence of the recent Turkish aggression.

11. The negotiations with the Arabs as to the boundaries of the Arab State or Confederation of Arab States shall
be continued through the same channel as heretofore on
behalf of the two Powers.[2]

12. It is agreed that measures to control the importa-
tion of arms into the Arab territories will be considered by
the two Governments.

I have the honour to state that, in order to make the
agreement complete, His Majesty's Government are proposing to the Russian Government to exchange notes analogous
to those exchanged by the latter and your Excellency's Government on the 26th April last.   Copies of these notes will be
communicated to your Excellency as soon as exchanged...

Shortly after the successful revolution
in November of 1917 the new Bolshevik government of Russia published all of the secret
agreements and treaties discovered in the
archives of the former Imperial Foreign Min-
istry, including the "Sykes-Picot Agreement."
This was almost at once brought to the attention
of the Sharif Husayn and other leaders of the
Arab national movement, who, to say the least,
were quite angry at the duplicity of Great Britain.   It would have appeared that the Agree-

----

[2] *I.e.,* continuation of the Husayn-McMahon Correspondence.

ment was no longer valid since the Bolshevik government renounced it;the French, however, considered the Agreement still valid for it was the basis for France's claim to Syrian territory. Even prior to this action the British Cabinet in the Spring of 1917 had begun to reconsider portions of the Agreement, particularly regarding Palestine. In April the "Sub-committee on Territorial Desiderata", led by Lord Curzon, in its recommendations to the Cabinet stated: "It is of great importance that both Palestine and Mesopotamia should be under British control. To ensure this it is desirable that His Majesty's Government should secure such modification of the Agreement with France of May 1916 as would give Great Britain definite and exclusive control over Palestine."[3] This, and the question of Mosul, became the bases for Britain's willingness to keep the Agreement alive. In December 1918 Georges Clemenceau, the French premier, arrived in London for conversations with Prime Minister Lloyd George. In his memoirs Lloyd George provides an account of the verbal agreement reached by the two leaders:

When Clemenceau came to London after the War I drove with him to the French Embassy through cheering crowds who acclaimed him with enthusiasm. After we reached the Embassy he asked me what it was I specially wanted from the French. I instantly replied that I wanted Mosul attached to Iraq, and Palestine from Dan to Beersheba under British control. Without any hesitation he agreed. Although that agreement was not reduced to writing, he adhered to it honourably in subsequent negotiations.[4]

---

[3] Quoted in Jon Kimche, *The Second Arab Awakening* (London: Thames and Hudson, 1970), 55.

[4] David Lloyd George *Memoirs of the Peace Converence*, vol. 2, 673.

6

Balfour Declaration, 1917

This vague and apparently innocuous statement of policy issued by the British Cabinet and
sent by the Foreign Secretary to a private citizen, Baron Lionel Rothschild, came to be one of
the most important and far-reaching documents in the entire history of the Arab-Israeli
conflict. It served as both the basis for large-
scale Jewish immigration into Palestine under
the auspices of Great Britain, leading in 1948 to
the foundation of the State of Israel, and as the
pretext by which Britain could obtain control
over this strategic area, because the text of the
letter was included within the League of
Nations Mandate for Palestine.

The immediate background to the issuance of the Declaration is very complex so
that all that can be included here is a brief
summary of its history.

One of the leading personna behind the
Declaration was Dr. Chaim Weizmann, a bril-
liant Russian Jewish chemist and an outspoken
advocate of Zionism, later to become the first
President of the State of Israel. He emigrated
first from his homeland to Switzerland, and
from there to England in 1904, where he settled
in Manchester, then the center of his particu-

Source: Harold W. V. Temperley, ed. *A History of the Peace Conference of Paris,* vol. 6 (London: Henry Frowde and Hodder & Stoughton, 1924) 170.

lar specialization. As he later wrote in his autobiography, his move to England was predi-
cated upon the belief that there he would find
the greatest sympathy for Zionism. As with
Herzl, Weizmann was a firm advocate in the necessity for the Zionists to gain Palestine by legal means rather than through infiltration as
proposed by many other Russian Zionists. This
necessitated obtaining the support of the leading British politicians, whose cooperation was
achieved because of their own devout Christian
upbringings and imperialist ideals. In 1906 he
gained his first convert, Arthur James Balfour,
a former Unionist Prime Minister and later
Foreign Secretary in the Second War Cabinet,
Eight years later he was introduced to the
Minister of Munitions, and soon to be Prime
Minister, David Lloyd George. These two were
not alone in their support of the Zionist dream,
but they were shortly to be of inestimable
value. A third supporter of great influence was
Sir Mark Sykes, one of the authors of the
"Sykes-Picot Agreement," who, when they met
in 1916, was Principal Secretary of the War
[inner] Cabinet. Sir Mark was especially es-
teemed by the others because of his supposed
"special knowledge" of the Middle East gained
from a year's travel there prior to the war.

Between the outbreak of the war in 1914
and the end of 1916, Weizmann and his allies
prepared public opinion for the acceptance of
Zionism through the newspapers, particularly
the highly respected Manchester *Guardian* and
The Times, and pamphlets. Finally, in January
1917, Weizmann, now President of the English
Zionist Federation, and others of the executive
committee, gave Sir Mark a document titled
"Outline of Program for the Jewish
Resettlement of Palestine in Accordance with
the Aspirations of the Zionist Movement,"
which Sir Mark, in turn, could submit to the
new cabinet under the premiership of Lloyd
George. The time was most propitious.

By 1917 the allies were in desperate
condition in their conflict with the Central

Powers: the loss of men at the fronts had been horrendous; the financial conditions of Britain and France were precarious, requiring new influx of capital from the United States; vast amounts of food and war materials were being lost to German U-boats; Russian losses had been so great that there was fear that she might come to separate terms, thereby freeing German troops to be moved to the western front and also depriving the allies of foodstuffs from the Ukraine. The cabinet believed that if the government came out in official support of Zionist immigration and settlement in Palestine, the Jews of the world, and particularly those in the United States and Russia, would, in return, place political pressure upon their respective governments for even greater support of the war effort. Later, in his memoirs, Lloyd George wrote: "The Zionist leaders gave us a definite promise that, if the Allies committed themselves to giving facilities for the establishment of a National Home for the Jews in Palestine, they would do their best to rally to the Allied cause Jewish sentiment and support throughout the world. They kept their word in the letter and the spirit,... ."[1] There was, furthermore, a fear that Germany might come out in support of the Zionists to increase Jewish support for the Central Powers.

Although most of the members of the cabinet were in favor of such a declaration there was opposition, led by the Jewish Secretary of State for India, Edwin Montagu. Throughout most of the year the three interest groups, the Zionists, the Jewish anti-Zionists, and the government agonized over the precise wording of the statement through six successive drafts. Finally, following approval by the leaders of the American and French governments, on 31 October, the cabinet approved the final text.

---

[1] *Memoires of the Peace Conference*, II, 737.

Foreign Office,
November 2nd, 1917

Dear Lord Rothschild,

I have much pleasure in conveying to you, on behalf of His Majesty's Government, the following declaration of sympathy with Jewish Zionist aspirations which has been submitted to, and approved by, the Cabinet.

"His Majesty's Government view with favour the establishment in Palestine of a national home for the Jewish people, and will use their best endeavours to facilitate the achievement of this object, it being clearly understood that nothing shall be done which may prejudice the civil and religious rights of existing non-Jewish communities in Palestine, or the rights and political status enjoyed by Jews in any other country."

I should be grateful if you would bring this declaration to the knowledge of the Zionist Federation.

[Signed]

Arthur James Balfour

7

The Hogarth Message, 1918

Shortly after the issuance of the Balfour Declaration it was widely disseminated to the Jewish communities throughout Europe and the United States through newspapers and pamphlets dropped from the air to those behind enemy lines so that its hoped-for effect could be made as soon as possible. Presumably, however, a similar effort was not made for its publication or release within the Middle East. However, news of the Declaration did reach the Arab populations in Egypt and the Arabian Peninsula. The Arab leaders, including the Sharif, now King, Husayn, believed that the promise thus made to the Zionists was not in accord with the earlier assurances given by the British Government in 1916 for the establishment of an Arab state or states within the same area. The king, understandably, requested clarification of these conflicting promises.

The Director of the Arab Bureau in Cairo, Commander D. G. Hogarth, the noted British

Source: Great Britain. Parliamentary Papers. *Miscellaneous No. 4 (1939). Statements made on behalf of His Majesty's Government during the year 1918 in regard to the Future Status of certain parts of the Ottoman Empire.* (London: His Majesty's Stationery Office, 1939), Cmd. 5964. 7 pp. Reprinted by permission of the Controller of Her Majesty's Stationery Office.

archaeologist, was directed to deliver the response, formulated in London, personally to the king. It appears that when the two met in Jiddah on 4 January 1918, Hogarth read each section of the message separately to allow for explanation on his part and notetaking and oral response by the king, for Hogarth's notes of the conversation are appended to the official statement as published by HMSO. This brief transcript is reprinted here as well. Upon his return to Cairo, Hogarth reported to the High Commissioner, where he again took notes. In the latter notes he wrote: "*International control of the Palestine Holy Places* [original italics]. — The King left me little doubt that he secretly regards this as a point to be reconsidered after the Peace, in spite of my assurances that it was to be a definite arrangement. . . , but I have no doubt that in his own mind he abates none of his original demands on behalf of the Arabs, or in the fullness of time, of himself." Then, in regards to the settlement of Jews in Palestine, he wrote: "The King would not accept an independent Jew State in Palestine, nor was I instructed to warn him that such a State was contemplated by Great Britain"

The first public notice of this message was made by George Antonious in his *The Arab Awakening* (page 268), first published in 1938. Because Antonious did not have the official English text available for the writing of his book he relied upon the Arabic notes made by King Husayn during the course of the conversation. Without printing the full text, Antonious quotes one sentence he translated from the Arabic, which should be compared with the English text reprinted below in paragraph (3) as well as with the text of the Balfour Declaration: "Jewish settlement in Palestine would only be allowed in so far as would be consistent with the political and economic freedom of the Arab population." It is to be noted that the full text was not made

public by Great Britain until 1939, the year
following the publication of Antonious' book.

No. 1

THE HOGARTH MESSAGE

(a)

The following is the text of a message which
Commander D. G. Hogarth, C.M.G., R.N.V.R., of the Arab
Bureau in Cairo, was instructed on the 4th January, 1918, to
deliver to King Hussein of the Hejaz at Jedda:-
"(1)   The Entente Powers are determined that the Arab
race shall be given full opportunity of once again forming a
nation in the world.   This can only be achieved by the Arabs
themselves uniting, and Great Britain and her Allies will
pursue a policy with this ultimate unity in view.

"(2) So far as Palestine is concerned, we are determined that no people shall be subject to another, but-
(a)   In view of the fact that there are in Palestine
shrines, Wakfs and Holy places, sacred in some cases to
Moslems alone, to Jews alone, to Christians alone, and in
others to two or all three, and inasmuch as these places are
of interest to vast masses of people outside Palestine and
Arabia, there must be a special regime to deal with these
places approved of by the world.
(b)   As regards the Mosque of Omar, it shall be considered as a Moslem concern alone, and shall not be subjected
directly or indirectly to any non-Moslem authority.

"(3)   Since the Jewish opinion of the world is in
favour of a return of Jews to Palestine, and inasmuch as this
opinion must remain a constant factor, and, further, as His
Majesty's Government view with favour the realisation of
this aspiration, His Majesty's Government are determined
that in so far as is compatible with the freedom of the existing population, both economic and political, no obstacle
should be put in the way of the realisation of this ideal.

"In this connexion the friendship of world Jewry to the Arab cause is equivalent to support in all States where Jews have a political influence. The leaders of the movement are determined to bring about the success of Zionism by friendship and co-operation with the Arabs, and such an offer is not one to be lightly thrown aside."

(b)

The following is the record of the conversation which Commander Hogarth had with King Hussein about the message which he had delivered:-

"I read Foreign Office Formula No. 1 (Arab Nation and need of Unity). King assented cordially saying it expressed the basis of all our Agreement. I said that owing to long lapse of time Allies thought it well to repeat it now.

"King then said that if any minor modifications of our Agreement with him were imposed on us by war necessities he would frankly recognise such necessity, but asked he should be frankly informed of modification and necessity.

"I then introduced Formula No. 2 (International Administration in Palestine) by reminding King of proviso in original Agreements safeguarding special interests of our Allies and especially France. He interpolated humorous reference to Fashoda, implying doubt of real and permanent community of interest between France and us. I let this pass with gesture of dissent and said France had come to see eye to eye with us in Arab matters, favoured as much as we Feisal's plans, took the view so strongly held in America that people should have the government they desire, and wished only to protect and assist in the development of independent Government in Syria.

"I then read No. 2. King assented, saying that brain which could formulate this could devise form of administration to safeguard all interests. He lauded Great Britain's action in case Omar Mosque, comparing Caliph Omar's abstention from Christian shrines in Jerusalem. If we could draw up statement similar to No. 2 with omission of reference to political administrative control, he would publish it to all Islam.

"I passed to Formula No. 3 (Jewish Settlement in Palestine) prefacing it by statement of growth of Zionism during war and great value of Jew interests and alliance. King seemed quite prepared for formula and agreed enthusiastically, saying he welcomed Jews to all Arab lands. I explained that His Majesty's Government's resolve safeguarded existing local population."

8

Fourteen Point Speech, 1918

On 8 January 1918, President Woodrow Wilson delivered the annual address to a joint session of Congress. Because it was presented during the war, rather than this speech being on the "State of the Union" and his program of action, it was devoted exclusively to the fourteen points that he had previously expressed for the achievement of peace. For the subject peoples of the world this speech held out a promise for their own independence and self-government. It is not because his idealism was achieved, but rather because it was a ray of hope, that it was so frequently cited by the leaders of those peoples. It is for this reason that the speech has been included within this collection of documents.

GENTLEMEN OF THE CONGRESS: Once more, as repeatedly before, the spokesmen of the Central Empires have indicated their desire to discuss the objects of the war and the possible bases of a general peace. Parleys have been in progress at Brest-Litovsk between Russian representatives and representatives of the Central Powers to which the attention of all the belligerents has been invited for the purpose of ascer-

---

Source: United States. Department of State. *Papers Relating to the Foreign Relations of the United States. 1918. Supplement I: The World War* , vol. I (Washington D.C.: United States Government Printing Office, 1933) 12-17.

taining whether it may be possible to extend these parleys into a general conference with regard to terms of peace and settlement.   The Russian representatives presented not only a perfectly definite statement of the principles upon which they would be willing to conclude peace but also an equally definite programme of the concrete application of those principles.   The representatives of the Central Powers, on their part, presented an outline of settlement which, if much less definite, seemed susceptible of liberal interpretation until their specific programme of practical terms was added.   That programme proposed no concessions at all either to the sovereignty of Russia or to the preferences of the populations with whose fortunes it dealt, but meant, in a word, that the Central Empires were to keep every foot of territory their armed forces had occupied,— every province, every city, every point of advantage,— as a permanent addition to their territories and their power.   It is a reasonable conjecture that the general principles of settlement which they at first suggested originated with the more liberal statesmen of Germany and Austria, the men who have begun to feel the force of their own peoples' thought and purpose, while the concrete terms of actual settlement came from the military leaders who have no thought but to keep what they have got.   The negotiations have broken off.   The Russian representatives were sincere and in earnest.   They can not entertain such proposals of conquest and domination.

The whole incident is full of significance.   It is also full of perplexity.   With whom are the Russian representatives dealing?   For whom are the representatives of the Central Empires speaking?   Are they speaking for the majority of their respective parliaments or for the minority parties, that military and imperialistic minority which has so far dominated their whole policy and controlled the affairs of Turkey and of the Balkan states which have felt obliged to become their associates in this war?   The Russian representatives have insisted, very justly, very wisely, and in the true spirit of modern democracy, that the conferences they have been holding with the Teutonic and Turkish statesmen should be held within open, not closed, doors, and all the world has been audience, as was desired.   To whom have we been listening, then?   To those who speak the spirit and intention of the resolutions of the German Reichstag of the 9th [19th] July last, the spirit and intention of the liberal leaders and parties of Germany, or to those who resist and defy that spirit and intention and insist upon conquest and subjugation?   Or are we listening, in fact, to both, unreconciled and in open and hopeless contradiction?   These are very serious and pregnant questions.   Upon the answer to them depends the peace of the world.

But whatever the results of the parleys at Brest-Litovsk, whatever the confusions of counsel and of purpose in the utterances of the spokesmen of the Central Empires, they have again attempted to acquaint the world with their objects in the war and have again challenged their adversaries to say what their objects are and what sort of settlement they would deem just and satisfactory.   There is no good reason why that challenge should not be responded to, and responded to with the utmost candor.   We did not wait for it. Not once, but again and again, we have laid our whole thought and purpose before the world, not in general terms only, but each time with sufficient definition to make it clear what sort of definitive terms of settlement must necessarily spring out of them.   Within the last week Mr. Lloyd George has spoken with admirable candor and in admirable spirit for the people and Government of Great Britain.   There is no confusion of counsel among the adversaries of the Central Powers, no uncertainty of principle, no vagueness of detail.   The only secrecy of counsel, the only lack of fearless frankness, the only failure to make definite statement of the objects of the war lies with Germany and her allies.   The issues of life and death hang upon these definitions.   No statesman who has the least conception of his responsibility ought for a moment to permit himself to continue this tragical and appalling outpouring of blood and treasure unless he is sure beyond a peradventure that the objects of the vital sacrifice are part and parcel of the very life of society and that the people for whom he speaks think them right and imperative as he does.

There is, moreover, a voice calling for these definitions of principle and of purpose which is, it seems to me, more thrilling and more compelling than any of the many moving voices with which the troubled air of the world is filled.   It is the voice of the Russian people.   They are prostrate and all but helpless, it would seem, before the grim power of Germany, which has hitherto known no relenting and no pity.   Their power, apparently is shattered.   And yet their soul is not subservient.   They will not yield either in principle or in action.   Their conception of what is right, and of what it is humane and honorable for them to accept,

has been stated with a frankness, a largeness of view, a generosity of spirit, and a universal human sympathy which
must challenge the admiration of every friend of mankind;
and they have refused to compound their ideals or desert
others that they themselves may be safe.   They call to us to
say what it is we desire, in what, if in anything, our purpose
and our spirit differ from theirs; and I believe that the people of the United States would wish me to respond, with utter
simplicity and frankness.   Whether their present leaders
believe it or not, it is our heartfelt desire and hope that some
way may be opened whereby we may be privileged to assist
the people of Russia to attain their utmost hope of liberty
and ordered peace.

It will be our wish and purpose that the processes of
peace, when they are begun, shall be absolutely open and
that they shall involve and permit henceforth no secret understandings of any kind.   The day of conquest and aggran-
dizement is gone by; so is also the day of secret covenants
entered into in the interest of particular governments and
likely at some unlooked-for moment to upset the peace of the
world.   It is this happy fact, now clear to the view of every
public man whose thoughts do not still linger in an age that
is dead and gone, which makes it possible for every nation
whose purposes are consistent with justice and the peace of
the world to avow now or at any other time the objects it has
in view.

We entered this war because violations of right had
occurred which touched us to the quick and made the life of
our own people impossible unless they were corrected and
the world secured once for all against their recurrence.
What we demand in this war, therefore, is nothing in particular to ourselves.   It is that the world be made fit and safe
to live in; and particularly that it be made safe for every
peace-loving nation which, like our own, wishes to live its
own life, determine its own institutions, be assured of justice
and fair dealing by the other peoples of the world as against
force and selfish aggression.   All the peoples of the world
are in effect partners in this interest, and for our own part
we see very clearly that unless justice be done to others it
will not be done to us.   The programme of the world's peace,
therefore, is our programme; and that programme, the only
possible programme, as we see it, is this:

I.   Open covenants of peace, openly arrived at,
after which there shall be no private understandings of any
kind but diplomacy shall proceed always frankly and in the

public view.

II.   Absolute freedom of navigation upon the seas, outside territorial waters, alike in peace and in war, except as the seas may be closed in whole or in part by international action for the enforcement of international covenants.

III.   The removal, so far as possible, of all economic barriers and the establishment of an equality of trade conditions among all the nations consenting to the peace and associating themselves for its maintenance.

IV.   Adequate guarantees given and taken that national armaments will be reduced to the lowest point consistent with domestic safety.

V.   A free, open-minded and absolutely impartial adjustment of all colonial claims, based upon a strict observance of the principle that in determining all such questions of sovereignty the interests of the populations concerned must have equal weight with the equitable claims of the government whose title is to be determined.

VI.   The evacuation of all Russian territory and such a settlement of all questions affecting Russia as will secure the best and freest cooperation of the other nations of the world in obtaining for her an unhampered and unembarrassed opportunity for the independent determination of her own political development and national policy and assure her of a sincere welcome into the society of free nations under institutions of her own choosing; and, more than a welcome, assistance also of every kind that she may need and may herself desire.   The treatment accorded Russia by her sister nations in the months to come will be the acid test of their good will, of their comprehension of her needs as distinguished from their own interests, and of their intelligent and unselfish sympathy.

VII.   Belgium, the whole world will agree, must be evacuated and restored, without any attempt to limit the sovereignty which she enjoys in common with all other free nations.   No other single act will serve to restore confidence among the nations in the laws which they have themselves set and determined for the government of their relations with one another.   Without this healing act the whole structure and validity of international law is forever impaired.

VIII. All French territory should be freed and the invaded portions restored, and the wrong done to France by

Prussia in 1871 in the matter of Alsace-Lorraine, which has unsettled the peace of the world for nearly fifty years, should be righted, in order that peace may once more be made secure in the interest of all.

IX.   A readjustment of the frontiers of Italy should be effected along clearly recognizable lines of nationality.

X.   The peoples of Austria-Hungary, whose place among the nations we wish to see safeguarded and assured, should be accorded the freest opportunity of autonomous development.

XI.   Rumania, Serbia, and Montenegro should be evacuated; occupied territories restored; Serbia accorded free and secure access to the sea; and the relations of the several Balkan states to one another determined by friendly counsel along historically established lines of allegiance and nationality; and international guarantees of the political and economic independence and territorial integrity of the several Balkan states should be entered into.

XII.   The Turkish portions of the present Ottoman Empire should be assured a secure sovereignty, but the other nationalities which are now under Turkish rule should be assured an undoubted security of life and an absolutely unmolested opportunity of autonomous development, and the Dardenelles should be permanently opened as a free passage to the ships and commerce of all nations under international guarantees.

XIII.   An independent Polish state should be erected which should include the territories inhabited by indisputably Polish populations, which should be assured a free and secure access to the sea, and whose political and economic independence and territorial integrity should be guaranteed by international covenant.

XIV.   A general association of nations must be formed under specific covenants for the purpose of affording mutual guarantees of political independence and territorial integrity to great and small states alike.

In regard to these essential rectifications of wrong and assertions of right we feel ourselves to be intimate partners of all the governments and peoples associated together against the Imperialists. We cannot be separated in interest or divided in purpose. We stand together until the end.

For such arrangements and covenants we are willing to fight and to continue to fight until they are achieved; but only because we wish the right to prevail and desire a just and stable peace such as can be secured only by removing the chief provocations to war, which this programme does remove. We have no jealousy of German greatness, and there is nothing in this programme that impairs it. We grudge her no achievement or distinction of learning or pacific enterprise such as have made her record very bright and very enviable. We do not wish to injure her or to block in any way her legitimate influence or power. We do not wish to fight her either with arms or with hostile arrangements of trade if she is willing to associate herself with us and the other peace-loving nations of the world in covenants of justice and law and fair dealing. We wish her only to accept a place of equality among the peoples of the world, — the new world in which we now live, — instead of a place of mastery.

Neither do we presume to suggest to her any alteration or modification of her institutions. But it is necessary, we must frankly say, and necessary as a preliminary to any intelligent dealings with her on our part, that we should know whom her spokesmen speak for when they speak to us, whether for the Reichstag Majority or for the military party and the men whose creed is imperial domination.

We have spoken now, surely, in terms too concrete to admit of any further doubt or question. An evident principle runs through the whole programme I have outlined. It is the principle of justice to all peoples and nationalities, and their right to live on equal terms of liberty and safety with one another, whether they be strong or weak. Unless this principle be made its foundation no part of the structure of international justice can stand. The people of the United States could act upon no other principle; and to the vindication of this principle they are ready to devote their lives, their honor, and everything that they possess. The moral climax of this the culminating and final war for human liberty has come, and they are ready to put their own strength, their own highest purpose, their own integrity and devotion to the test.

This statement of the war aims of the United States and their allies was quickly transmitted to the Near East where points IV and XII were particularly welcomed as a means by which those peoples who had lived for four centuries under Ottoman domination could achieve their independence.

On 5 January, three days previous to President Wilson's Congressional address, as Prime Minister Lloyd George of Great Britain delivered a speech before the Trade Unions meeting in London in which he set forth his Government's war aims. In this he stated: *"Therefore is that we feel that government with the consent of the governed must be the basis of any territorial settlement in this war* [his italics]."[1]   A few minutes further in this speech he reiterated this sentiment in speaking of the Near East:

Outside Europe we believe that the same principles should be applied. While we do not challenge the maintenance of the Turkish Empire in the homelands of the Turkish race with its capital at Constantinople — the passage between the Mediterranean and the Black Sea being internationalised and neutralised — Arabia, Armenia, Mesopotamia, Syria and Palestine are in our judgment entitled to a recognition of their separate national conditions.[2]

The text of this speech was widely publicized as well, also reaching the Near East.

---

[1] Reprinted in: David Lloyd George, *War Memoirs of David Lloyd George*, vol. 5 (Boston: Little, Brown, and Company, 1936) 67.

[2] Ibid., 70.

9

Declaration to the Seven, 1918

The conflicting agreements and statements made by the British Government during the two years 1916-1918, i.e., Sir Henry McMahon's last letter to Sharif Husayn, the Sykes-Picot Agreement, the Balfour Declaration, and now both Lloyd George's and Wilson's public pronouncements of policy, were, understandably, confusing to the Arab nationalist leaders. Seven of these leaders therefore, probably about the beginning of June of 1918, requested clarification from His Majesty's Government. The resultant reply has come to be known as "The Declaration to the Seven," first brought to public attention by George Antonius in *The Arab Awakening* (Appendix D). As with The Hogarth Message this Declaration was not made public until after the publication of Antonius's book.

NO. 2

THE DECLARATION TO THE SEVEN

The following is the text of a message which His Majesty's High Commissioner in Cairo was instructed to con-

Source: Great Britain. Parliamentary Papers. *Miscellaneous No. 4 (1939). Statements made on behalf of His Majesty's Government during the year 1918 in regard to the Future Status of certain parts of the Ottoman Empire* (London: His Majesty's Stationery Office, 1939), 5-6. Reprinted by permission of the Controller of Her Majesty's Stationery Office.

vey to seven Arab leaders resident in Cairo who had presented a memorial to His Majesty's Government. The message was delivered to representatives of the seven memorialists on about the 16th June, 1918, by Commander D. G. Hogarth, C.M.G., R. N.V.R., and Mr. O. Walrond, C.M.G.:-

"His Majesty's Government have considered the memorial of the seven with the greatest care. His Majesty's Government fully appreciate the reasons why the memorialists desire to retain their anonymity, and the fact that the memorial is anonymous has not in any way detracted from the importance which His Majesty's Government attribute to the document.
"The areas mentioned in the memorandum fall into four categories:-
"1. Areas in Arabia which were free and independent before the out-break of war;
"2. Areas emancipated from Turkish control by the action of the Arabs themselves during the present war;
"3. Areas formerly under Ottoman dominion, occupied by the Allied forces during the present war;
"4. Areas still under Turkish control.

"In regard to the first two categories, His Majesty's Government recognise the complete and sovereign independence of the Arab inhabiting these areas and support them in their struggle for freedom.
"In regard to the areas occupied by Allied forces, His Majesty's Government draw the attention of the memorialists to the texts of the proclamations issued respectively by the General Officers Commanding-in-Chief on the taking of Bagdad and Jerusalem. These proclamations embody the policy of His Majesty's Government towards the inhabitants of those regions. It is the wish and desire of His Majesty's Government that the future government of these regions should be based upon the principle of the consent of the governed, and this policy has and will continue to have the support of His Majesty's Government.[1]

---

[1] All of Palestine, the former Ottoman Sanjak of Jerusalem, would have been included, therefore, under this third area that had been entirely liberated by December of 1917 by a mixed Arab and British army under the command of General Sir Edmund Allenby. Lloyd George, in his *Memoires of the Peace Conference* (II, 667), wrote: "In the military operations on the Palestine front, the Arab cavalry and

"In regard to the areas mentioned in the fourth category, it is the wish and desire of His Majesty's Government that the oppressed peoples of these areas should obtain their freedom and independence, and towards the achievement of this object His Majesty's Government continue to labour.

"His Majesty's Government are fully aware of, and take into consideration, the difficulties and dangers which beset those who work for the regeneration of the populations of the areas specified.

"In spite, however, of these obstacles His Majesty's Government trust and believe that they can and will be overcome, and wish to give all support to those who desire to overcome them. They are prepared to consider any scheme of co-operation which is compatible with existing military operations and consistent with the political principles of His Majesty's Government and the Allies."

---

camelry rendered invaluable service. They took part in no great battles, but they harrassed the Turks, constantly cut their lines of communication, and absorbed a considerable number of enemy troops in protecting these lines. ... The Arabs were entitled to claim that they rendered undoubted aid to the British armies that defeated the Turks and finally drove them out of the Arab regions of the Turkish Empire." [Editor's note].

10

Anglo-French Declaration, 1918

On 30 October 1918 the Ottoman Government signed an armistice with the Allies on the Island of Mudros to take effect the following day, under the conditions of the armistice, the Ottoman Government abandoned all claims to Arab lands. Precisely one week previously, the Allied commander of the forces operating in the Fertile Crescent, General Sir Edmund Allenby, issued instructions for the military administration of those areas already liberated and those that likely would be shortly occupied. By these orders the whole of the Fertile Crescent was placed under "Occupied Enemy Territory Administration" (O.E.T.A.). Whereas Iraq was treated as a single administrative unit, the Syrian region was subdivided into three, along the lines of the Sykes—Picot Agreement: O.E.T.A. East, the interior of Syria from Aqaba to Aleppo, was placed under the authority of General Ali Pasha al-Rikabi with Arab occupation troops; O.E.T.A. West, the Lebanese and Syrian coast from Tyre to Cilicia, was to be occupied by French troops; O.E.T.A. South, Palestine, was placed under British administration.

In view of their contributions to the war

Source: David Lloyd George, *Memoirs of the Peace Conference*, vol. 2 (New Haven: Yale University Press, 1939), 672.

effort in the Near East on behalf of the Allies,
to many Arabs the institution of military administration, and particularly, the breakup of
Greater Syria into three zones, appeared to be
the replacement of one hated foreign domination by two others. To allay these fears and
suspicions the British and French Governments
agreed upon a joint declaration on 7 November
that was telegraphed that same day, in French,
to Sir Reginald Wingate, High Commissioner in
Egypt, for immediate publication in the Arab
newspapers in Egypt and Syria. The text reproduced here is the official Foreign Office translation.

The goal aimed at by France and Great Britain in their
conduct in the East of a war unchained by German ambition
is the complete and definite freedom of the peoples so long
oppressed by the Turks, and the establishment of national
governments and administrations deriving their authority
from the initiative and free choice of the native population.
In order to fulfill these intentions, France and Great
Britain are agreed in the desire to encourage and assist in
the establishment of native governments and administrations in Syria and Mesopotamia, at this moment freed by the
Allies, and in the territories of which they are attempting
the liberation, and on the recognition of these as soon as
they are effectively established. Far from wishing to impose
on the populations of these regions such or such institutions, they have no other care than to assure by their support and practical aid the normal working of the governments and institutions which these populations have freely
set up. To ensure equal and impartial justice for all, to aid
the economic development of the country by inspiring and
encouraging local initiative, to facilitate the spread of education, to put an end to the divisions too long exploited by
Turkish policy — such is the role which the two
Governments proclaim in the liberated territories.

11

Covenant of the League of Nations (The Mandate Article), 1919

During the course of the war the allied leaders of Great Britain and the United States repeatedly stated that the annexation of territory was not one of their aims. The question therefore arose regarding the disposition of the conquered German colonies in East Africa and the South Pacific. However, in regards to the Turkish-held regions in the Near East there was the unfortunate Sykes-Picot Agreement that had come to be an embarrassment to the British. Unwilling to return the conquered territories to their former masters, and also not desirous of flaunting world opinion with expanding already extensive empires, and with internationalization having been unsuccessful in the past, a form of trusteeship appeared to be the only answer. In November of 1918, General Jan C. Smuts, the official representative of the Union of South Africa on the Imperial War Cabinet, presented a written proposal for the concept of mandates whereby these regions would be handed over to the developing idea of a League of Nations which would, in turn, assign them as mandataries to the more "civilized" countries, specifically the victors.

Source: Pitman B. Potter, *The Covenant of the League of Nations: text, index, interpretation* (New York: Carnegie Endowment for International Peace, Division of Intercourse and Education, 1927) 26-30.

The idea that France would be responsible for her mandates to the League was not at all appealing to Georges Clemenceau, the French premier. When it was pointed out to him by Lloyd George during the Peace Conference in February 1919 that the authority of the League was more conceptual than real, and that, at any rate, France was automatically a member of the Supreme Council of the League, he acquiesced in the principle. It was only then that the "Mandate Article" (XXII) could be incorporated within the Covenant of the League of Nations, that itself was brought into being under Article I of the Treaty of Versailles, signed on 28 June 1919.

Although the Supreme Council of the four principal powers — France, Great Britain, Italy, and the United States — at its meeting in Paris on 7 May 1919 divided the class "B" and "C" mandated territories among France, Great Britain, Australia, New Zealand, and the Union of South Africa, the assignment of the class "A" mandates was postponed until a later meeting at San Remo in 1920, at which the United States was not a participant.

ARTICLE XX

The Members of the League severally agree that this Covenant is accepted as abrogating all obligations or understandings *inter se* which are inconsistent with the terms thereof, and solemnly undertake that they will not hereafter enter into any engagements inconsistent with the terms thereof.

ARTICLE XXII

To those colonies and territories which as a consequence of the late war have ceased to be under the sovereignty of the States which formerly governed them and which are inhabited by peoples not yet able to stand by themselves under the strenuous conditions of the modern world, there should be applied the principle that the wellbeing and development of such peoples form a sacred trust of civilization, and that securities for the performance of this trust should be embodied in this Covenant.

The best method of giving practical effect to this principle is that the tutelage of such peoples should be entrusted to advanced nations who by reason of their resources, their experience or their geographical position, can best undertake this responsibility, and who are willing to accept it, and that this tutelage should be exercised by them as Mandataries on behalf of the League.

The character of the mandate must differ according to the stage of the development of the people, the geographical situation of the territory, its economic conditions and other similar circumstances.

[A] Certain communities formerly belonging to the Turkish Empire have reached a stage of development where their existence as independent nations can be provisionally recognized subject to the rendering of administrative advice and assistance by a Mandatary until such time as they are able to stand alone.   The wishes of these communities must be a principal consideration in the selection of the Mandatary.

[B] Other peoples, especially those of Central Africa, are at such a stage that the Mandatary must be responsible for the administration of the territory under conditions which will guarantee freedom of conscience or religion, subject only to the maintenance of public order and morals, the prohibition of abuses such as the slave trade, the arms traffic and the liquor traffic, and the prevention of the establishment of fortifications or military and naval bases and of military training of the natives for other than police purposes and the defence of the territory, and will also secure equal opportunities for the trade and commerce of other Members of the League.

[C] There are territories, such as Southwest Africa and certain of the South Pacific Islands, which, owing to the sparseness of their population, or their small size, or their remoteness from the centers of civilization, or their geographical contiguity to the territory of the Mandatary, and other circumstances, can be best administered under the laws of the Mandatary as integral portions of its territory, subject to the safeguards above-mentioned in the interests of the indigenous population.

In every case of mandate, the Mandatary shall render to the Council an annual report in reference to the territory committed to its charge.

The degree of authority, control, or administration to

be exercised by the Mandatary shall if not previously agreed upon by the Members of the League be explicitly defined in each case by the Council.

A permanent Commission shall be constituted to receive and examine the annual reports of the Mandataries and to advise the Council on all matters relating to the observance of the mandates.

King-Crane Commission Report, 1919

In February of 1919 the Supreme Council of the Peace Conference, France, Great Britain, Italy, and the United States, meeting in Paris at the Quay d'Orsay, began their discussions regarding the future of the former Near Eastern territories of the Ottoman Empire. On the 6th the Amir Faysal, son of King Husayn of the Hijaz, accompanied by Colonel T. E. Lawrence, was permitted to address the Conference to present the Arab case for independence. During the course of his speech Faysal suggested that an international enquiry be made to determine the wishes of the peoples of the Fertile Crescent regarding immediate independence or that state which they wished as the mandatary power to assist in their economic advancement. Following the conclusion of his appeal Dr. Howard Bliss, an American missionary and Principal of the American University of Beirut, addressed the Council in which he also urged the appointment of such a commission because of the fear within Syria that France would be appointed the mandatary authority.

Because of his firm belief in the concept

Source: Editor & Publisher, vol. 55, no. 27, December 2, 1922, 2d section, pp. IV-XXVI. Reprinted by permission of *Editor and Publisher*.

of self-determination this idea held great at-
traction for President Wilson.   On 20 March,
during the course of the debate Wilson
... suggested that the fittest men that could be obtained should be selected to form an Inter-Allied
Commission to go to Syria, extending their inquiries,
if they led them beyond the confines of Syria. Their
object should be to elucidate the state of opinion and
the soil to be worked on   by   any mandatory.   They
should be asked to come back and tell the Conference
what they found with regard to these matters.   He made
this suggestion, not because he lacked confidence in
the experts whose views he had heard, such as Dr.
Howard Bliss and General Allenby.   These, however,
had been   involved in some way with the population,
with special objects either educational or military. If
we were to send a Commission of men with no
previous contact with Syria, it would, at any rate,
convince the world that the Conference had tried to do
all it could to find the most scientific basis possible
for a settlement.   The Commission should be composed
of an equal number of French, British, Italian and
American representatives.   He would send it with
carte blanche to tell the facts as they found them.[1]

To this suggestion Clemenceau agreed
"in principle" with the reservation that the investigation should   not   be limited strictly to
Syria, but should also include Palestine and
Mesopotamia.   Lloyd George stated that he had
"no objection."   At a subsequent meeting of the
Council on the 25th the proposal for the establishment of the "Inter-Allied Commission on
Mandates in Turkey" was formally adopted and
signed. The American, British, and Italian
members were appointed, but France continued
to delay to designate its members and finally
refused to participate in the Commission despite
her original agreement.   With the withdrawal
of the French, Lloyd George decided that Great
Britain could not participate.   The Italian
Government, without any definite reason, also

---

[1]   From the official transcript of the Peace Conference, as quoted in
Lloyd George, *Memoirs of the Peace Conference*, vol. 2, 693.

withdrew.   Nevertheless, Wilson was determined that the investigation should be undertaken, with the result that his appointees, Dr.
Henry C. King, President of Oberlin College, and
Mr. Charles R. Crane, an industrialist, with
their staff, began their interviews in Jaffa on
11 June 1919.   After visiting thirty-six of the
more important towns and hearing numerous
delegations from throughout Syria and
Palestine they completed their task on 21st
July, after the Peace Treaty had been signed.
Although their final report was submitted to
the president it was not formally presented to
the Peace Conference because it was so hostile
to the French claims in Syria, although copies
were given to both the British and French governments.   In fact, the report was never officially published, although it was finally
printed in 1922 in *Editor & Publisher*, a weekly
magazine for the newspaper field.   It is from
this that the following extract has been taken.

RECOMMENDATIONS

Syria-Palestine

A.   We recommend, as most important of all, and in
strict harmony with our Instructions, that whatever foreign
administration (whether of one or more Powers) is brought
into Syria, should come in, not at all as a colonising Power in
the old sense of that term, but as a Mandatory under the
League of Nations with the clear consciousness that 'the
well-being and development', of the Syrian people form for
it a 'sacred trust'.
   (1)   To this end the Mandate should have a limited
term, the time of expiration to be determined by the League
of Nations, in the light of all the facts as brought out from
year to year, in the annual reports of the Mandatory to the
League or in other ways.
   (2)   The mandatory Administration should have, however, a period and power sufficient to ensure the success of
the new state; and especially to make possible carrying
through important educational and economic undertakings,
essential to secure founding of the State.

(3)   The mandatory Administration should be characterised from the beginning by a strong and vital educational emphasis in clear recognition of the imperative necessity of education for the citizens of a democratic state, and for the development of a sound national spirit. This systematic cultivation of national spirit is particularly required in a country like Syria, which has only recently come to self-consciousness.

(4)   The Mandatory should definitely seek, from the beginning of its trusteeship, to train the Syrian people to independent self-government as rapidly as conditions allow, by setting up all the institutions of a democratic state, and by sharing with them increasingly the work of administration, and so forming gradually an intelligent citizenship, interested unselfishly in the progress of the country, and forming at the same time a large group of disciplined civil servants.

(5)   The period of 'tutelage' should not be unduly prolonged, but independent self-government should be granted as soon as it can safely be done; remembering that the primary business of governments is not the accomplishment of certain things, but the development of citizens.

(6)   It is peculiarly the duty of the Mandatory in a country like Syria, and in this modern age, to see that complete religious liberty is ensured, both in the constitution and in the practice of the state, and that a jealous care is exercised for the rights of all minorities. Nothing is more vital than this for the enduring success of the new Arab State.

(7)   In the economic development of Syria, a dangerous amount of indebtedness on the part of the new state should be avoided, as well as any entanglements financially with the affairs of the mandatory Power. On the other hand, the legitimate established privileges of foreigners, such as rights to maintain schools, commercial concessions, etc., should be preserved, but subject to review and modification under the authority of the League of Nations in the interest of Syria. The mandatory Power should not take advantage of its position to force a monopolistic control at any point to the detriment either of Syria or of other nations; but it should seek to bring the new State as rapidly as possible to economic independence as well as to political independence.

Whatever is done concerning the further recommendations of the Commission, the fulfillment of at least the conditions now named should be assured, if the Peace Conference and the League of Nations are true to the policy of the mandatories already embodied in the Covenant of the League of Nations. This should effectively guard the most essential interests of Syria, however the machinery of administration is finally organised. The Damascus Congress betrayed in many ways their intense fear that their country would become, though under some other name, simply a colonial possession of some other Power. That fear must be completely allayed.

B. We recommend, in the second place, that the unity of Syria be preserved, in accordance with the earnest petition of the great majority of the people of Syria.

(1) The territory concerned is too limited, the population too small, and the economic, geographic, racial and language unity too manifest, to make the setting up of independent States with its boundaries desirable, if such division can possible be avoided. The country is very largely Arab in language, culture, traditions, and customs.

(2) This recommendation is in line with important 'general considerations' already urged, and with the principles of the League of Nations, as well as in answer to the desires of the majority of the population concerned.

(3) The precise boundaries of Syria should be determined by a special commission on boundaries, after the Syrian territory has been in general allotted. The Commissioners believe, however, that the claim of the Damascus Conference to include Cilicia in Syria is not justified, either historically or by commercial or language relations. The line between the Arabic-speaking and the Turkish-speaking populations would quite certainly class Cilicia with Asia Minor, rather than with Syria. Syria, too, has no such need of further seacoast as the large interior sections of Asia Minor.

(4) In standing thus for the recognition of the unity of Syria, the natural desires of regions like the Lebanon, which have already had a measure of independence, should not be forgotten. It will make for a real unity, undoubtedly, to give a large measure of local autonomy, and especially in the case of strongly unified groups. Even the 'Damascus Programme' which presses so earnestly the unity of Syria, itself urges a government 'on broad decentralisation principles'.

Lebanon has achieved a considerable amount of prosperity and autonomy within the Turkish Empire. She certainly should not find her legitimate aspirations less possible within a Syrian national State. On the contrary, it may be confidently expected that both her economic and political relations with the rest of Syria would be better if she were a constituent member of the State rather than entirely independent of it.

As a predominantly Christian country, too, Lebanon naturally fears a Moslem domination in a unified Syria. But against such domination she would have a four-fold safeguard: her own large autonomy; the presence of a strong mandatory for the considerable period in which the constitution and practice of the new State would be forming; the oversight of the League of Nations, with its insistence upon religious liberty and the rights of minorities; and the certainty that the Arab Government would feel the necessity of such a State, if it were to commend itself to the League of Nations. Moreover, there would be less danger of a reactionary Moslem attitude, if Christians were present in the State in considerable numbers, rather than largely segregated outside the State, as experience of the relations of different religious faiths in India suggest.

As a predominantly Christian country, it is also to be noted that Lebanon would be in a position to exert a stronger and more helpful influence if she were within the Syrian State, feeling its problems and needs, and sharing all its life, instead of outside it, absorbed simply in her own narrow concerns. For the sake of the larger interests, both of Lebanon and Syria, then, the unity of Syria is to be urged. It is certain that many of the more thoughtful Lebanese themselves hold this view. A similar statement might be made for Palestine; though, as the Holy Land for Jews and Christians and Moslems alike, its situation is unique, and might more readily justify unique treatment, if such treatment were justified anywhere. This will be discussed more particularly in connexion with the recommendation concerning Zionism.

C. We recommend, in the third place, that Syria be placed under one mandatory Power, as the natural way to secure real and efficient unity.

(1) To divide the administration of the provinces of Syria among several mandatories, even if existing national unity were recognised; or to attempt a joint mandatory of the whole on the commission plan: — neither of these courses would be naturally suggested as the best way to secure and promote the unity of the new State, or even the general unity of the whole people. It is conceivable that circum-

stances might drive the Peace Conference to some such form of divided Mandate; it is not a solution to be voluntarily chosen, from the point of view of the larger interests of the people, as considerations already urged indicate.

(2) It is not to be forgotten, either, that, however they are handled politically, the people of Syria are there, forced to get on together in some fashion. They are obliged to live with one another — the Arabs of the East and the people of the coast, the Moslems and the Christians. Will they be helped or hindered, in establishing tolerable and finally cordial relations, by a single mandatory? No doubt the quick mechanical solution of the problem of difficult relations is to split the people up into little independent fragments. And sometimes, undoubtedly, as in the case of the Turks and Armenians, the relations are so intolerable as to make some division imperative and inevitable. But in general, to attempt complete separation only accentuates the differences and increases the antagonism. The whole lesson of the modern social consciousness points to the necessity of understanding 'the other half', as it can be understood only by close and living re-lations. Granting reasonable local autonomy to reduce friction among groups, a single mandatory ought to form a constant and increasingly effective help to unity of feeling throughout the State, and ought to steadily improve group relations.

The people of Syria, in our hearings, have themselves often insisted that, so far as unpleasant relations have hitherto prevailed among various groups, it has been very largely due to the direct instigation of the Turkish Government. When justice is done impartially to all; when it becomes plain that the aim of the common government is the service of all classes alike, not their exploitation, then can decent human relations be secured — a foundation which could not be obtained by dividing men off from one another in antagonistic groups.

The Commissioners urge, therefore, for the largest future good of all groups and regions alike, the placing of the whole of Syria under a single Mandate.

D. We recommend, in the fourth place, that Amir Faisal be made head of the new united Syrian State.

(1) This is expressly and unanimously asked for by the representative Damascus Congress in the name of the Syrian people, and there seems to be no reason to doubt that the great majority of the population of Syria sincerely desire to have Amir Faisal as ruler.

(2)   A constitutional monarchy along democratic
lines, seems naturally adapted to the Arabs, with their long
training under tribal conditions, and with their traditional
respect for their Chiefs.   They seem to need, more than most
people, a king as the personal symbol of the powers of the
State.

(3)   Amir Faisal has come, too, naturally into his present place of power, and there is no one else who could well
replace him.   He has the great advantage of being the son of
the Sharif of Mecca, and as such honoured throughout the
Moslem world.   He was one of the prominent Arab leaders
who assumed responsibility for the Arab uprising against
the Turks, and so shared in the complete deliverance of the
Arabic-speaking portions of the Turkish Empire.   He was
consequently hailed by the Damascus Congress as having
merited their full confidence and entire reliance.   He was
taken up and supported by the British as the most promising
candidate for the head-ship of the new Arab State — an Arab
of the Arabs, but with a position of wide appeal through his
Sharifian connection, and through his broad sympathies
with the best in the Occident.   His relations with the Arabs to
the east of Syria are friendly, and his kingdom would not be
threatened from that side.   He undoubtedly does not make so
strong an appeal to the Christians of the West Coast, as the
the Arabs of the East; but no man can be named who would
have a stronger general appeal.   He is tolerant and wise,
skilfull in dealing with men, winning in manner, a man of
sincerity, insight and power.   Whether he has the full
strength needed for his difficult task it is too early to say;
but certainly no other Arab leader combines so many elements of power as he, and he will have invaluable help
throughout the mandatory period.

The Peace Conference may take genuine satisfaction
in the fact that an Arab of such qualities is available for the
headship of this new state in the Near East.

E. We recommend, in the fifth place, serious modification of the extreme Zionist programme for Palestine of
unlimited immigration of Jews, looking finally to making
Palestine distinctly a Jewish State.

(1)   The Commissioners began their study of Zionism
with minds predisposed in its favour, but the actual facts in
Palestine, coupled with the force of the general principles
proclaimed by the Allies and accepted by the Syrians have
driven them to the recommendation here made.

(2)   The Commission was abundantly supplied with lit-

erature on the Zionist programme by the Zionist Commission to Palestine; heard in conferences much concerning the Zionist colonies and their claims; and personally saw something of what had been accomplished. They found much to approve in the aspirations and plans of the Zionists, and had warm appreciation for the devotion of many of the colonists, and for their success, by modern methods, in overcoming great natural obstacles.

(3) The Commission recognised also that definite encouragement had been given to the Zionists by the Allies in Mr. Balfour's often-quoted statement, in its approval by other representatives of the Allies. If, however, the strict terms of the Balfour Statement are adhered to — favouring 'the establishment in Palestine of a national home for the Jewish people', 'it being clearly understood that nothing shall be done which may prejudice the civil and religious rights of existing non-Jewish communities in Palestine' — it can hardly be doubted that the extreme Zionist programme must be greatly modified.

For a national home for the Jewish people is not equivalent to making Palestine into a Jewish State; nor can the erection of such a Jewish State be accomplished without the gravest trespass upon the civil and religious rights of existing non-Jewish communities in Palestine. The fact came out repeatedly in the Commission's conferences with Jewish representatives, that the Zionists looked forward to a practically complete dispossession of the present non-Jewish inhabitants of Palestine, by various forms of purchase.

In his address of July 4, 1918, President Wilson laid down the following principle as one of the four great 'ends for which the associated peoples of the world were fighting': 'The settlement of every question, whether of territory, of sovereignty, of economic arrangement, or of political relationship upon the basis of the free acceptance of that settlement by the people immediately concerned, and not upon the basis of the material interest or advantage of any other nation or people which may desire a different settlement for the sake of its own exterior influence or mastery.' If that principle is to rule, and so the wishes of Palestine's population are to be decisive as to what is to be done with Palestine, then it is to be remembered that the non-Jewish population of Palestine - nearly nine-tenths of the whole — are emphatically against the entire Zionist programme. The tables show that there was no one thing upon which the population of Palestine were more agreed than upon this. To subject a people so minded to unlimited Jewish immigration, and to steady financial and social pressure to surrender the land, would be a gross violation of the principle just quoted, and of the people's rights, though it kept within the forms of law.

It is to be noted also that the feeling against the Zionist programme is not confined to Palestine, but shared very generally by the people throughout Syria, as our conferences clearly showed. More than seventy-two per cent — 1,350 in all — of all the petitions in the whole of Syria were directed against the Zionist programme. Only two requests — those for a united Syria and for independence — had a larger support. This general feeling was duly voiced by the General Syrian Congress in the seventh, eighth and tenth resolutions of the statement.

The Peace Conference should not shut its eyes to the fact that the anti-Zionist feeling in Palestine and Syria is intense and not lightly to be flouted. No British officer, consulted by the Commissioners, believed that the Zionist programme could be carried out except by force of arms. The officers generally thought that a force of not less than 50,000 soldiers would be required even to initiate the programme. That of itself is evidence of a strong sense of the injustice of the Zionist programme, on the part of the non-Jewish populations of Palestine and Syria. Decisions requiring armies to carry out are sometimes necessary, but they are surely not gratuitously to be taken in the interests of serious injustice. For the initial claim, often submitted by Zionist representatives that they have a 'right' to Palestine, based on an occupation of 2,000 years ago, can hardly be seriously considered.

There is a further consideration that cannot justly be ignored, if the world is to look forward to Palestine becoming a definitely Jewish State, however gradually that may take place. That consideration grows out of the fact that Palestine is the Holy Land for Jews, Christians, and Moslems alike. Millions of Christians and Moslems all over the world are quite as much concerned as the Jews with conditions in Palestine, especially with those conditions which touch upon religious feeling and rights. The relations in these matters in Palestine are most delicate and difficult. With the best possible intentions, it may be doubted whether the Jews could possibly seem to either Christians or Moslems proper guardians of the holy places, or custodians of the Holy Land as a whole.

The reason is this: The places which are most sacred to Christians — those having to do with Jesus — and which are also sacred to Moslems, are not only not sacred to Jews, but abhorrent to them. It is simply impossible, under those circumstances, for Moslems and Christians to feel satisfied to have these places in Jewish hands, or under the custody of the Jews. There are still other places about which Moslems must have the same feeling. In fact, from this point of view, the Moslems, just because the sacred places of all three religions are sacred to them, have made very naturally much more satisfactory custodians of the holy places than the Jews could be. It must be believed that the precise meaning in this respect of the complete Jewish occupation of Palestine has not been fully sensed by those who urge the extreme Zionist programme. For it would intensify, with a certainty like fate, the anti-Jewish feeling both in Palestine and in all other portions of the world which look to Palestine as the Holy Land.

In view of all these considerations, and with a deep sense of sympathy for the Jewish cause, the Commissioners feel bound to recommend that only a greatly reduced Zionist programme be attempted by the Peace Conference, and even that, only very gradually initiated. This would have to mean that Jewish immigration should be definitely limited, and that the project for making Palestine distinctly a Jewish commonwealth should be given up.

There would then be no reason why Palestine could not be included in a united Syrian State, just as other portions of the country, the holy places being cared for by an international and inter-religious commission, somewhat as at present, under the oversight and approval of the Mandatory and of the League of Nations. The Jews, of course, would have representation upon this commission.

The recommendations now made lead naturally to the necessity of recommending what power should undertake the single Mandate for Syria.

(1) The considerations already dealt with suggest the qualifications ideally to be desired in the mandatory Power: First of all, it should be freely desired by the people. It should be willing to enter heartily into the spirit of the mandatory system, and its possible gift to the world, and so be willing to withdraw after a reasonable period, and not seek selfishly to exploit the country. It should have a passion for democracy, for the education of the common people and for the development of the national spirit. It needs un-

limited sympathy and patience in what is practically certain to be a thankless task; for no Power can go in honestly to face actual conditions (like land-ownership, for example) and seek to correct these conditions, without making many enemies. It should have experience in dealing with less developed peoples, and abundant resources in men and money.

(2) Probably no Power combines all these qualifications, certainly not in equal degree. But there is hardly one of these qualifications that has not been more or less definitely indicated in our conference with the Syrian people and they certainly suggest a new stage in the development of the self-sacrificing spirit in the relations of peoples to one another. The Power that undertakes the single Mandate for all Syria, in the spirit of these qualifications, will have the possibility of greatly serving not only Syria but the whole world, and of exalting at the same time its own national life. For it would be working in direct line with the high aims of the Allies in the War, and give proof that those high aims had not been abandoned. And that would mean very much just now, in enabling the nations to keep their faith in one another and in their own highest ideals.

(3) The Resolutions of the Peace Conference of January 30, 1919, quoted in our instructions, expressly state for regions to be 'completely severed from the Turkish Empire', that 'the wishes of these communities must be a principal consideration in the selection of the mandatory Power'. Our survey left no room for doubt of the choice of the majority of the Syrian people. Although it was not known whether America would take a Mandate at all; and although the Commission could not only give no assurances upon that point, but had rather to discourage expectations; nevertheless, upon the face of the returns, America was the first choice of 1,152 of the petitions presented — more than sixty per cent — while no other Power had as much as fifteen per cent for first choice.

And the conferences showed that the people knew the grounds upon which they registered their choice for America. They declared that their choice was due to knowledge of America's record; the unselfish aims with which she had come into the War; the faith in her felt by multitudes of Syrians who had been in America; the spirit revealed in American educational institutions in Syria, especially the College in Bairut, with its well-known and constant encouragement of Syrian national sentiment; their belief that America had no territorial or colonial ambitions, and would

willingly withdraw when the Syrian State was well established as her treatment of Cuba and the Philippines seemed
to them to illustrate; her genuinely democratic spirit; and
her ample resources.

From the point of view of the desires of the 'people
concerned', the Mandate should clearly go to America.

(4)   From the point of view of qualifications, too, already stated as needed in the Mandatory for Syria, America,
as first choice of the people, probably need not fear careful
testing, point by point, by the standard involved in our discussion of qualifications; though she has much less experience in such work than Great Britain, and is likely to show
less patience; and though her definite connexions with
Syria have been less numerous and close than those of
France.   She would have at least the great qualification of
fervent belief in the new mandatory system of the League of
Nations, as indicating the proper relations which a strong
nation should take toward a weaker one.   And, though she
would undertake the Mandate with reluctance she could
probably be brought to see how logically the taking of such
responsibility follows from the purposes with which she
entered the War, and from her advocacy of the League of
Nations.

(5)   There is the further consideration that America
could probably come into the Syrian situation, in the beginning at least, with less friction than any other Power.
The great majority of Syrian people, as has been seen,
favour her coming, rather than that of any other Power.
Both the British and the French would find it easier to yield
their respective claims to America than to each other.   She
would have no rival imperial interests to press.   She would
have abundant resources for the development of the sound
prosperity of Syria; and this would inevitably benefit in a
secondary way the nations which have had closest connexion with Syria, and so help to keep relations among the
Allies cordial.   No other Power probably would be more welcome as a neighbour to the British with their large interests
in Egypt, Arabia and Iraq; or to the Arabs and Syrians in
these regions; or to the French with their long-established
and many-sided interests in Bairut and the Lebanon.

(6)   The objections to recommending at once a single
American Mandate for all Syria are: First of all, that it is not
certain that the American people would be willing to take
the Mandate; that it is not certain that the British or French
would be willing to withdraw, and would cordially welcome

America's coming, a situation which might prove steadily harassing to an American administration; that the vague but large encouragement given to the Zionist aims might prove particularly embarrassing to America, on account of her large influential Jewish population; and that, if America were to take any mandate at all, and were to take but one mandate, it is probable that an Asia Minor Mandate would be more natural and important. For there is a task there of such peculiar and world-wide significance as to appeal to the best in America, and demand the utmost from her, and as certainly to justify her in breaking with her established policy concerning mixing in the affairs of the eastern hemisphere. The Commissioners believe, moreover, that no other Power could come into Asia Minor, with hands so free to give impartial justice to all the peoples concerned.

To these objections, as a whole, it is to be said that they are all of such a kind that they may resolve themselves; and that they only form the sort of obstacles that must be expected in so large and significant undertaking. In any case they do not relieve the Commissioners from the duty of recommending the course which, in their honest judgment, is the best course, and the one for which the whole situation calls.

The Commissioners, therefore, recommend, as involved in the logic of the facts, that the United States of America be asked to undertake the single Mandate for all Syria.

If for any reason the mandate for Syria is not given to America, then the Commissioners recommend, in harmony with the express request of the majority of the Syrian people, that the mandate be given to Great Britain. The tables show that there were 1,073 petitions in all Syria for Great Britain as mandatory, if America did not take the Mandate. This is very greatly in excess of any similar expression for the French.

On the contrary — for whatever reason — more than sixty per cent of all the petitions presented to the Commission directly and strongly protested against any French mandate. Without going into discussion of the reasons for this situation, the Commissioners are reluctantly compelled to believe that this situation itself makes it impossible to recommend a single French Mandate for all Syria.

The feeling of the Arabs of the East is particularly strong against the French. And there is grave reason to believe that the attempt to enforce a French Mandate would precipitate war between the Arabs and the French, and force upon Great Britain a dangerous alternative. The Commissioners may perhaps be allowed to say that this conclusion is contrary to their own earlier hope, that — because of France's long and intimate relations with Syria, because of her unprecedented sacrifices in the War, and because the British Empire seemed certain to receive far greater accessions of territory from the War — it might seem possible to recommend that France be given the entire Mandate for Syria. But the longer the Commission remained in Syria, the more clear it became that that course could not be taken.

The Commissioners recommend, therefore, if America cannot take the mandate for all Syria, that it be given to Great Britain; because of the choice of the people concerned; because she is already on the ground and with much of the necessary work in hand; because of her trained administrators; because of her long and generally successful experience in dealing with less developed peoples; and because she has so many of the qualifications needed in a mandatory Power, as we have already considered them.

We should hardly be doing justice, however, to our sense of responsibility to the Syrian people, if we did not frankly add some at least of the reasons and misgivings, variously expressed and implied in our conferences, which led to the preference for an American Mandate over a British Mandate. The people repeatedly showed honest fear that in British hands the mandatory power would become simply a colonising power of the old kind; that Great Britain would find it difficult to give up the colonial theory, especially in case of a people thought inferior; that she would favour a civil service and pension budget too expensive for a poor people; that the interests of Syria would be subordinated to the supposed needs of the Empire; that there would be, after all, too much exploitation of the country for Britain's benefit; that she would never be ready to withdraw and give the country real independence; that she did not really believe in universal education, and would not provide adequately for it; and that she already had more territory in her possession — in spite of her fine colonial record — than was good for herself or for the world.

These misgivings of the Syrian people unquestionably largely explain their demand for 'absolute independence', for a period of 'assistance' of only twenty years, their protest against Article XXII of the Covenant of the League of

Nations, etc.   They all mean that whatever Power the Peace Conference shall send into Syria, should go in as a true mandatory under the League of Nations, and for a limited term.   Anything else would be a betrayal of the Syrian people.

It needs to be emphasised, too, that under a true mandatory for Syria, all the legitimate interests of all the nations in Syria would be safeguarded.   In particular, there is no reason why any tie that France has had with Syria in the past should be severed or even weakened under the control of another mandatory Power, or in an independent Syria.

13

San Remo Agreement, 1920

Although the peace treaty and the disposition of the former Ottoman domains in the Near East had been discussed by the Peace Conference in Paris in May and June 1919, political and philosophical differences precluded the completion of the remaining problems. Accordingly, following a conference held in London in February 1920, among the leaders of France, Great Britain, and Italy, the Supreme Council convened again at the Villa Devachan in San Remo, Italy, 18-26 April 1920, to settle the assignment of the mandates and the final terms of the Turkish treaty. Finally, on 25 April, the four Powers, with the Japanese representative present, formally reached the following agreement by which France and Great Britain assigned to themselves the mandates in the Fertile Crescent with the agreement to be later ratified by the Council of the League of Nations.

It was agreed—

(*a*) To accept the terms of the mandates article as given be-

Source: Rohan Butler and J. P. T. Bury, eds., *Documents on British Foreign Policy 1919-1939: First Series, Vol. VIII: 1920* (London: Her Majesty's Stationery Office, 1958) 176-77. Reprinted by permission of the Controller of Her Majesty's Stationery Office.

low with reference to Palestine, on the understanding that there was inserted in the *procès-verbal* an undertaking by the mandatory Power that this would not involve the surrender of the rights hitherto enjoyed by the non-Jewish communities in Palestine; this undertaking not to refer to the question of the religious protectorate of France, which had been settled earlier in the previous afternoon by the undertaking given by the French Government that they recognised this protectorate as being at an end.

(*b*) That the terms of the mandates article should be as follows:—

The high contracting parties agree that Syria and Mesopotamia shall, in accordance with the fourth paragraph of article 22, Part I (Covenant of the League of Nations), be provisionally recognised as independent States, subject to the rendering of administrative advice and assistance by a mandatory until such time as they are able to stand alone. The boundaries of said States will be determined, and the selection of the mandatories made, by the Principal Allied Powers.

The high contracting parties agree to entrust, by application of the provisions of article 22, the administration of Palestine, within such boundaries as may be determined by the Principal Allied Powers,[1] to a mandatory, to be selected by the said Powers. The mandatory will be responsible for putting into effect the declaration originally made on the 8th [2nd] November, 1917, by the British Government, and adopted by the other Allied Powers, in favour of establishment in Palestine of a national home for the Jewish people, it being clearly understood that nothing shall be

---

[1] These were agreed upon between France and Great Britain in two separate conventions based, primarily, on the wishes of Lloyd George, upon the boundaries of ancient Israel as established by George Adam Smith in his *Atlas of the Historical Geography of the Holy Land*, first published in 1908. Great Britain. Parliamentary Papers. *Franco-British Convention of 23rd December, 1920, on Certain Points Connected with the Mandates for Syria and the Lebanon, Palestine and Mesopotamia* (London: His Majesty's Stationery Office, 1921), Cmd. 1195, and, Great Britain. Parliamentary Papers. *Agreement Between the British and the French Governments Respecting the Boundary Line Between Syria and Palestine from the Mediterranean to El Hammé* (London: His Majesty's Stationery Office, 1923), Cmd. 1910. [Editor's note.]

done which may prejudice the civil and religious rights of the existing non-Jewish communities in Palestine, or the rights and political status enjoyed by Jews in any other country:--

'La Puissance mandataire s'engage à nommer dans le plus bref délai une commission spéciale pour étudier toute question et toute réclamation concernant les différentes communautés religieuses et en établir le réglement. Il sera tenu compte dans la composition de cette commission des intérêts religieux en jeu. Le président de la commission nommé par le Conseil de la Société des Nations.'

[The mandatory power is engaged to name with the least delay a special commission to study all questions and claims concerning the different religious communities and to establish the regulations. It will take into account in the composition of this commission the religious interests in play. The president of the commission will be named by the Council of the League of Nations.]

The terms of the mandates in respect of the above territories will be formulated by the Principal Allied Powers and submitted to the Council of the League of Nations for approval.

Turkey hereby undertakes, in accordance with the provisions of article [blank], to accept any decisions which may be taken in this connection.

(c) 'Les mandataires choisis par les principales Puissances alliées sont: la France pour la Syrie, et la Grande-Bretagne pour la Mésopotamie et la Palestine.'

[The mandatories chosen by the Principal Allied Powers are: France for Syria and Great Britain for Mesopotamia and Palestine.] 2

---

2 This agreement was basically repeated in the Treaty of Sèvres with Turkey, signed on 20 August 1920, in Section VII, Articles 94-96. Article 95, which pertains to Palestine, again includes the "Balfour Declaration" in its entirety. Article 97 states: "Turkey hereby undertakes, in accordance with the provisions of Article 132, to accept any decisions which may be taken in relation to the questions dealt with in this Section." Carnegie Endowment for International Peace, *The Treaties of Peace 1919-1923* , vol. 1 (New York: Carnegie Endowment for International Peace, 1924) 817. [Editor's note and translations].

14

Resolutions of the Council of the League of Nations, 1920

The Mandates Article (no. XXII) of the Covenant of the League of Nations was the subject of intense controversy within the so-called Council of Ten (comprised of two representatives each from France, Great Britain, Italy, Japan, and the United States), not surprisingly, considering that most of its member states were desirous of obtaining additional territory as a result of the war. It was this Council which, therefore, drafted a carefully written compromise which was then presented to the Commission on the League of Nations responsible for preparing the Covenant, and left untouched by it. Although under this article the mandates were made the responsibility of the League neither the League Council nor the Assembly was given the authority to appoint the mandataries. This was left to the Supreme Allied Council which, as we saw above, determined the fate of the "liberated" peoples, who, it must be pointed out, were given no choice in the selection.

In the following resolutions, adopted by the Council of the League on 26 October 1920, it will be noted that the League abdicated its responsibilities in bowing to the decisions of the,

Source: Reprinted in: Harold W. V. Temperley, ed., *A History of the Peace Conference of Paris*, vol. 6 (London: Henry Frowde and Hodder & Stoughton, 1924), 505-6.

by now, three Principal Powers (France, Great Britain, and Italy) regarding which should obtain what mandate, what the boundaries were to be, and even their conditions, as determined in the case of the Fertile Crescent, at the San Remo Conference.

I. The Council decides to request the principal Powers to be so good as: (*a*) to name the Powers to whom they have decided to allocate the Mandates provided for in Article XXII; (*b*) to inform it as to the frontiers of the territories to be administered under these Mandates; (*c*) to communicate to it the terms and the conditions of the Mandates that they propose should be adopted by the Council in accordance with the prescriptions of Article XXII.

II. The Council will take cognizance of the Mandatory Power appointed and will examine the draft Mandates communicated to it, in order to ascertain that they conform to the prescriptions of Article XXII of the Covenant.

III. The Council will notify to each Power appointed that it is invested with the Mandate, and will, at the same time, communicate to it the terms and conditions thereof.

IV. The Council instructs the Secretary-General to prepare in accordance with the recommendations set forth in this report, a draft scheme for the organization of the Mandates Commission provided for by Article XXII, Paragraph 9.

15

Churchill White Paper, 1922

By 1922, in addition to the objections voiced by the Christian and Muslim Arab communities in Palestine, serious reservations regarding British policy, and particularly the Mandate, had begun to be made in both Houses of Parliament. In the debates beginning in 1920 following the San Remo Conference the main objections made by the opposition were that the inhabitants of Palestine had not been consulted officially, aside from the findings of the King-Crane Commission, respecting the appointment of the Mandatary, contrary to the Mandate Article (XXII) of the Covenant of the League of Nations: "The wishes of these communities must be a principal consideration in the selection of the Mandatary." The second major objection was the inclusion of the Balfour Declaration as a principal doctrine in the terms of the proposed Mandate, contrary to the wishes of the Palestinians who comprised over 90 percent of the population.

On the 21st of June, 1922, Lord Islington, one of the leading opponents of the Mandate

Source: Great Britain. Parliamentary Papers. *Palestine. Correspondence with the Palestine Arab Delegation and the Zionist Organisation* (London: His Majesty's Stationery Office, 1922), Cmd. 1700. Reprinted by permission of the Controller of Her Majesty's Stationery Office.

document still under consideration by the government, presented to the House of Lords a motion to modify its terms:

That the Mandate for Palestine in its present form is inacceptable to this House, because it directly violates the pledges made by His Majesty's Government to the people of Palestine in the Declaration of October 1915 [the letter of 24 October from Sir Henry McMahon to the Sharif Husayn], and again in the Declaration of November, 1918 [the Anglo-French Joint Communiquè, 7 November], and is, as at present formed, opposed to the sentiments and wishes of the great majority of the people of Palestine; that, therefore, its acceptance by the Council of the League of Nations should be postponed until such modifications have therein been effected as will comply with pledges given by His Majesty's Government.[1]

In his speech in support of the motion Lord Islington stated that the second paragraph of the Preamble (which repeated verbatum the Balfour Declaration) and Articles 4, 6, and 11 were inconsistent with the pledges made to the Arab inhabitants of Palestine. Despite the opposition of Arthur Balfour, who had been elevated to the peerage as the Earl of Balfour, the motion was agreed to by a vote of 60 to 29. A similar motion presented to the House of Commons was defeated, largely through the efforts of Winston Churchill, Secretary of State for the Colonies, and Major W. G. A. Ormsby-Gore. Responsibility for Palestine in Whitehall was transferred from the Foreign Office to the Colonial Office at the beginning of 1921, thus coming under the authority of Churchill, who had long been an advocate of Zionism.

With this widespread and extensive opposition to the Mandate policy directed to the establishment of a Jewish national home in

---

[1] Great Britain. *Parliamentary Debates (Official Record). House of Lords. 5th Session - 31st Parliament 1922*, vol. 50 (London: His Majesty's Stationery Office, 1922) 994. Reprinted by permission of the Controller of Her Majesty's Stationery Office.

Palestine the Government took the unusual step of issuing a statement of policy in June of that year, prior to the acceptance of the document by the Council of the League. It was believed at the time that this statement had been drafted by Sir Herbert Samuel, the Zionist High Commissioner for Palestine, who had been appointed to the position at the request of the Zionist Executive. Despite its total support for the Zionist program in Palestine, Chaim Weizmann and his colleagues considered the statement ". . . a serious whittling down of the Balfour Declaration"[2] because it separated the area of the trans-Jordan from Palestine and proposed a legislative council.

The Secretary of State for the Colonies has given renewed consideration to the existing political situation in Palestine, with a very earnest desire to arrive at a settlement of the outstanding questions which have given rise to uncertainty and unrest among certain sections of the population. After consultation with the High Commissioner for Palestine the following statement has been drawn up. It summarises the essential parts of the correspondence that has already taken place between the Secretary of State and a Delegation from the Moslem—Christian Society of Palestine, which has been for some time in England, and it states the further conclusions which have since been reached.

The tension which has prevailed from time to time in Palestine is mainly due to apprehensions, which are entertained both by sections of the Arab and by sections of the Jewish population. These apprehensions, so far as the Arab are concerned, are partly based upon exaggerated interpretations of the meaning of the Declaration made on behalf of His Majesty's Government on 2nd November, 1917. Unauthorised statements have been made to the effect that the purpose in view is to create a wholly Jewish Palestine. Phrases have been used such as that Palestine is to become "as Jewish as England is English." His Majesty's Government regard any such expectation as impracticable and have no such aim in view. Nor have they at any time contemplated,

---

[2] Chaim Weizmann. *Trial and Error: the Autobiography of Chaim Weizmann*, vol. 2 (Philadelphia: The Jewish Publication Society of America, 5709-1949) 290.

as appears to be feared by the Arab Delegation, the disappearance or the subordination of the Arabic population, language or culture in Palestine. They would draw attention to the fact that the terms of the Declaration referred to do not contemplate that Palestine as a whole should be converted into a Jewish National Home, but that such a home should be founded in Palestine. In this connection it has been observed with satisfaction that at the meeting of the Zionist Congress, the supreme governing body of the Zionist Organisation, held at Carlsbad in September, 1921, a resolution was passed expressing as the official statement of Zionist aims "the determination of the Jewish people to live with the Arab people on terms of unity and mutual respect, and together with them to make the common home into a flourishing community, the upbuilding of which may assure to each of its peoples an undisturbed national development."

It is also necessary to point out that the Zionist Commission in Palestine, now termed the Palestine Zionist Executive, has not desired to possess, and does not possess, any share in the general administration of the country. Nor does the special position assigned to the Zionist Organisation in Article IV of the Draft Mandate for Palestine imply any such functions. That special position relates to the measures to be taken in Palestine affecting the Jewish population, and contemplates that the Organisation may assist in the general development of the country, but does not entitle it to share in any degree in its Government.

Further, it is contemplated that the status of all citizens of Palestine in the eyes of the law shall be Palestinian, and it has never been intended that they, or any section of them, should possess any other juridicial status.

So far as the Jewish population of Palestine are concerned, it appears that some among them are apprehensive that His Majesty's Government may depart from the policy embodied in the Declaration of 1917. It is necessary, therefore, once more to affirm that these fears are unfounded, and that that Declaration, re-affirmed by the Conference of the Principal Allied Powers at San Remo and again in the Treaty of Sèvres, is not susceptible of change.

During the last two or three generations the Jews have recreated in Palestine a community, now numbering 80,000, of whom about one-fourth are farmers or workers upon the land. This community has its own political organs; an elected assembly for the direction of its domestic concerns; elected councils in the towns; and an organisation for

the control of its schools. It has its elected Chief Rabbinate
and Rabbinical Council for the direction of its religious affairs. Its business is conducted in Hebrew as a vernacular
language, and a Hebrew press serves its needs. It has its distinctive intellectual life and displays considerable economic
activity. This community, then, with its town and country
population, its political, religious and social organisations,
its own language, its own customs, its own life, has in fact
"national" characteristics. When it is asked what is meant
by the development of the Jewish National Home in
Palestine, it may be answered that it is not the imposition of
a Jewish nationality upon the inhabitants of Palestine as a
whole, but the further development of the existing Jewish
community, with the assistance of Jews in other parts of the
world, in order that it may become a centre in which the
Jewish people as a whole may take, on grounds of religion
and race, an interest and a pride. But in order that this
community should have the best prospect of free development and provide a full opportunity for the Jewish people to
display its capacities, it is essential that it should know that it
is in Palestine as of right and not on sufferance. That is the
reason why it is necessary that the existence of a Jewish
National Home in Palestine should be internationally guaranteed, and that it should be formally recognised to rest
upon ancient historic connection.

       This, then, is the interpretation which His Majesty's
Government place upon the Declaration of 1917, and, so understood, the Secretary of State is of opinion that it does not
contain or imply anything which need cause either alarm to
the Arab population of Palestine or disappointment to the
Jews.

       For the fulfillment of this policy it is necessary that
the Jewish community in Palestine should be able to increase its numbers by immigration. This immigration cannot be so great in volume as to exceed whatever may be the
economic capacity of the country at the time to absorb new
arrivals. It is essential to ensure that the immigrants should
not be a burden upon the people of Palestine as a whole, and
that they should not deprive any section of the present
population of their employment. Hitherto the immigration
has fulfilled these conditions. The number of immigrants
since the British occupation has been about 25,000.

       It is necessary also to ensure that persons who are
politically undesirable are excluded from Palestine, and ev-

ery precaution has been and will be taken by the Administration to that end.

It is intended that a special committee should be established in Palestine, consisting entirely of members of the new Legislative Council elected by the people, to confer with the Administration upon matters relating to the regulation of immigration. Should any difference of opinion arise between this committee and the Administration, the matter will be referred to His Majesty's Government, who will give it special consideration. In addition, under Article 81 of the draft Palestine Order in Council, any religious community or considerable section of the population of Palestine will have a general right to appeal, through the High Commissioner and the Secretary of State, to the League of Nations on any matter on which they may consider that the terms of the Mandate are not being fulfilled by the Government of Palestine.

With reference to the Constitution which it is now intended to establish in Palestine, the draft of which has already been published, it is desirable to make certain points clear. In the first place, it is not the case, as has been represented by the Arab delegation, that during the war His Majesty's Government gave an undertaking that an independent national government should be at once established in Palestine. This representation mainly rests upon a letter dated the 24th October, 1915, from Sir Henry McMahon, then His Majesty's High Commissioner in Egypt, to the Sherif of Mecca, now King Hussein of the Kingdom of the Hejaz. That letter is quoted as conveying the promise to the Sherif of Mecca to recognise and support the independence of the Arabs within the territories proposed by him   But this promise was given subject to a reservation made in the same letter, which excluded from its scope, among other territories, the portions of Syria lying to the west of the district of Damascus. This reservation has always been regarded by His Majesty's Government as covering the vilayet of Beirut and the independent Sanjak of Jerusalem. The whole of Palestine west of the Jordan was thus excluded from Sir H. McMahon's pledge.

Nevertheless, it is the intention of His Majesty's Government to foster the establishment of a full measure of self-government in Palestine. But they are of opinion that, in the special circumstances of that country, this should be accomplished by gradual stages and not suddenly. The first step was taken when, on the institution of a civil

Administration, the nominated Advisory Council, which now exists, was established. It was stated at the time by the High Commissioner that this was the first step in the development of self-governing institutions, and it is now proposed to take a second step by the establishment of a Legislative Council containing a large proportion of members elected on a wide franchise. It was proposed in the published draft that three of the members of this Council should be non-official persons nominated by the High Commissioner, but representations having been made in opposition to this provision, based on cogent considerations, the Secretary of State is prepared to omit it. The Legislative Council would then consist of the High Commissioner as President and twelve elected and ten official members. The Secretary of State is of opinion that before a further measure of self-government is extended to Palestine and the Assembly placed in control over the Executive, it would be wise to allow some time to elapse. During this period the institutions of the country will have become well established; its financial credit will be based on firm foundations, and the Palestinian officials will have been enabled to gain experience of sound methods of government. After a few years the situation will be again reviewed, and if the experience of the working of the constitution now to be established so warranted, a larger share of authority would then be extended to the elected representatives of the people.

The Secretary of State would point out that already the present Administration has transferred to a Supreme Court elected by the Moslem community of Palestine the entire control of Moslem religious endowments (Wakfs), and of the Moslem religious Courts. To this Council the Administration has also voluntarily restored considerable revenues derived from ancient endowments which had been sequestrated by the Turkish Government. The Education Department is also advised by a committee respresentative of all sections of the population, and the Department of Commerce and Industry has the benefit of the cooperation of the Chambers of Commerce which have been established in the principal centres. It is the intention of the Administration to associate in an increased degree similar representative committees with the various Departments of the Government.

The Secretary of State believes that a policy upon these lines, coupled with the maintenance of the fullest religious liberty in Palestine and with scrupulous regard for the rights of each community with reference to its Holy

Places cannot but commend itself to the various sections of the population, and that upon this basis may be built up that spirit of co-operation upon which the future progress and prosperity of the Holy Land must largely depend.

16

Mandate for Palestine, 1922

The drafting of the mandate, like the Balfour Declaration earlier, became the responsibility of the Foreign Office, now under Lord Curzon. His private secretary, Eric Forbes-Adam, an avowed Zionist sympathizer, was given responsibility to work over the several drafts, together with an American member of the Zionist Executive, Ben V. Cohen, beginning in March of 1920 and extending through the summer.

Despite the intensive opposition within the government, Parliament, and the press to the mandate document in the manner in which it was worded (as well as to Britain assuming responsibility for the mandate over Palestine at all), the mandate was placed on the agenda of the Council of the League of Nations at its last meeting in London on Saturday, 24 July 1922. Ratification of the mandate, by constitution, had to be unanimous by the eight members of the Council. Fearful that a few of the member

Source: Great Britain. Parliamentary Papers. *League of Nations. Mandate for Palestine, Together with a Note by the Secretary-General Relating to Its Application to the Territory Known as Trans-Jordan* (London: His Majesty's Stationery Office, 1922), Cmd. 1785. Reprinted by permission of the Controller of Her Majesty's Stationery Office.

states of the Council that had small Jewish populations might not be favorably disposed to the document as submitted, Chaim Weizmann and his colleagues began an intensive lobbying effort, particularly towards the representatives from Italy, Spain, and Brazil. These were won over to the Zionist position, with the result that the mandate was accepted without difficulty.[1]

The Council of the League of Nations:

Whereas the Principal Allied Powers have agreed, for the purpose of giving effect to the provisions of Article 22 of the Covenant of the League of Nations, to entrust to a Mandatory selected by the said Powers the administration of the territory of Palestine, which formerly belonged to the Turkish Empire, within such boundaries as may be fixed by them; and

Whereas the Principal Allied Powers have also agreed that the Mandatory should be responsible for putting into effect the declaration originally made on November 2nd, 1917, by the Government of His Britannic Majesty, and adopted by the said Powers, in favour of the establishment in Palestine of a national home for the Jewish people, it being clearly understood that nothing should be done which might prejudice the civil and religious rights of existing non-Jewish communities in Palestine, or the rights and political status enjoyed by Jews in any other country; and

Whereas recognition has thereby been given to the historical connection of the Jewish people with Palestine and the grounds for reconstituting their national home in that country; and

Whereas the Principal Allied Powers have selected His Britannic Majesty as the Mandatory for Palestine; and

Whereas the mandate in respect of Palestine has been formulated in the following terms and submitted to the Council of the League for approval; and

Whereas His Britannic Majesty has accepted the mandate in respect of Palestine and undertaken to exercise it

---

[1] Chaim Weizmann, *Trial and Error: the Autobiography of Chaim Weizmann*, vol. 2 (Philadelphia: The Jewish Publication Society of America, 5709-1949) 292-93.

on behalf of the League of Nations in conformity with the following provisions, and

Whereas by the afore-mentioned Article 22 (paragraph 8), it is provided that the degree of authority, control or administration to be exercised by the Mandatory, not having been previously agreed upon by the Members of the League, shall be explicitly defined by the Council of the League of Nations;

Confirming the said mandate, defines its terms as follows:

Art. 1.   The Mandatory shall have full powers of legislation and of administration, save as they may be limited by the terms of this mandate.

Art. 2.   The Mandatory shall be responsible for placing the country under such political, administrative and economic conditions as will secure the establishment of the Jewish national home, as laid down in the preamble, and the development of self-governing institutions, and also for safeguarding the civil and religious rights of all the inhabitants of Palestine, irrespective of race and religion.

Art. 3.   The Mandatory shall, so far as circumstances permit, encourage local autonomy.

Art. 4.   An appropriate Jewish agency shall be recognised as a public body for the purpose of advising and co-operating with the Administration of Palestine in such economic, social and other matters as may affect the establishment of the Jewish national home and the interests of the Jewish population in Palestine, and, subject always to the control of the Administration, to assist and take part in the development of the country.

The Zionist organisation, so long as its organisation and constitution are in the opinion of the Mandatory appropriate, shall be recognised as such agency.   It shall take steps in consultation with His Britannic Majesty's Government to secure the co-operation of all Jews who are willing to assist in the establishment of the Jewish national home.

Art. 5.   The Mandatory shall be responsible for seeing that no Palestine territory shall be ceded or leased to, or in any way placed under the control of, the Government of any Foreign Power.

Art. 6.   The Administration of Palestine, while ensuring that the rights and position of other sections of the population are not prejudiced, shall facilitate Jewish immigration under suitable conditions and shall encourage, in co-operation with the Jewish agency referred to in Article 4, close settlement by Jews on the land, including State lands and waste lands not required for public purposes.

Art. 7. The Administration of Palestine shall be responsible for enacting a nationality law. There shall be included in this law provisions framed so as to facilitate the acquisition of Palestinian citizenship by Jews who take up their permanent residence in Palestine.

Art. 8. The privileges and immunities of foreigners, including the benefits of consular jurisdiction and protection as formerly enjoyed by Capitulation or usage in the Ottoman Empire, shall not be applicable in Palestine.

Unless the Powers whose nationals enjoyed the aforementioned privileges and immunities on August 1st, 1914, shall have previously renounced the right to their reestablishment, or shall have agreed to their non-application for a specified period, these privileges, and immunities shall, at the expiration of the mandate, be immediately re-established in their entirety or with such modifications as may have been agreed upon between the Powers concerned.

Art. 9. The Mandatory shall be responsible for seeing that the judicial system established in Palestine shall assure to foreigners, as well as to natives, a complete guarantee of their rights.

Respect for the personal status of the various peoples and communities and for their religious interests shall be fully guaranteed. In particular, the control and administration of Wakfs shall be exercised in accordance with religious law and the dispositions of the founders.

Art. 10. Pending the making of special extradition agreements relating to Palestine, the extradition treaties in force between the Mandatory and other foreign Powers shall apply to Palestine.

Art. 11. The Administration of Palestine shall take all necessary measures to safeguard the interests of the community in connection with the development of the country, and, subject to any international obligations accepted by the Mandatory, shall have full power to provide for public ownership or control of any of the natural resources of the country or of the public works, services and utilities established or to be established therein. It shall introduce a land system appropriate to the needs of the country, having regard, among other things, to the desirability of promoting the close settlement and intensive cultivation of the land.

The Administration may arrange with the Jewish agency mentioned in Article 4 to construct or operate, upon fair and equitable terms, any public works, services and utilities, and to develop any of the natural resources of the country, in so far as these matters are not directly undertaken by the Administration. Any such arrangements, shall provide that no profits distributed by such agency, directly or indirectly, shall exceed a reasonable rate of interest on the capital, and any further profits shall be utilised by it for the benefit of the country in a manner approved by the Administration.

Art. 12. The Mandatory shall be entrusted with the control of the foreign relations of Palestine and the right to issue exequaturs to consuls appointed by foreign Powers. He shall also be entitled to afford diplomatic and consular protection to citizens of Palestine when outside its territorial limits.

Art. 13. All responsibility in connection with the Holy Places and religious buildings or sites in Palestine, including that of preserving existing rights and of securing free access to the Holy Places, religious buildings and sites and the free exercise of worship, while ensuring the requirements of public order and decorum, is assumed by the Mandatory, who shall be responsible solely to the League of Nations in all matters connected herewith, provided that nothing in this article shall prevent the Mandatory from entering into such arrangements as he may deem reasonable with the Administration for the purpose of carrying the provisions of this article into effect; and provided also that nothing in this mandate shall be construed as conferring upon the Mandatory authority to interfere with the fabric or the management of purely Moslem sacred shrines, the immunities of which are guaranteed.

Art. 14. A special Commission shall be appointed by the Mandatory to study, define and determine the rights and claims in connection with the Holy Places and the rights and claims relating to the different religious communities in Palestine. The method of nomination, the composition and the functions of this Commission shall be submitted to the Council of the League for its approval, and the Commission shall not be appointed or enter upon its functions without the approval of the Council.

Art. 15. The Mandatory shall see that complete freedom of conscience and the free exercise of all forms of worship, subject only to the maintenance of public order and morals, are ensured to all. No discrimination of any kind shall be made between the inhabitants of Palestine on the ground of race, religion or language. No person shall be excluded from Palestine on the sole ground of his religious belief.

The right of each community to maintain its own schools for the education of its own members in its own language, while conforming to such educational requirements of a general nature as the Administration may impose, shall not be denied or impaired.

Art. 16. The Mandatory shall be responsible for exercising such supervision over religious or eleemosynary bodies of all faiths in Palestine as may be required for the maintenance of public order and good government. Subject to such supervision, no measures shall be taken in Palestine to obstruct or interfere with the enterprise of such bodies or to discriminate against any representative or member of them on the ground of his religion or nationality.

Art 17. The Administration of Palestine may organise on a voluntary basis the forces necessary for the preservation of peace and order, and also the defence of the country, subject, however, to the supervision of the Mandatory, but shall not use them for purposes other than those specified save with the consent of the Mandatory. Except for such purposes, no military, naval or air forces shall be raised or maintained by the Administration of Palestine.

Nothing in this article shall preclude the Administration of Palestine from contributing to the cost of the maintenance of the forces of the Mandatory in Palestine.

The Mandatory shall be entitled at all times to use the roads, railways and ports of Palestine for the movement of armed forces and the carriage of fuel and supplies.

Art. 18. The Mandatory shall see that there is no discrimination in Palestine against the nationals of any State Member of the League of Nations (including companies incorporated under its laws) as compared with those of the Mandatory or of any foreign State in matters concerning taxation, commerce, or navigation, the exercise of industries or professions, or in the treatment of merchant vessels or civil aircraft. Similarly, there shall be no discrimination in Palestine against goods originating in or destined for any of the said States, and there shall be freedom of transit under equitable conditions across the mandated area.

Subject as aforesaid and to the other provisions of this mandate, the Administration of Palestine may, on the advice of the Mandatory, impose such taxes and customs duties as it may consider necessary, and take such steps as it may think best to promote the development of the natural resources of the country and to safeguard the interests of the population. It may also, on the advice of the Mandatory, conclude a special customs agreement with any State the territory of which in 1914 was wholly included in Asiatic Turkey or Arabia.

Art. 19. The Mandatory shall adhere on behalf of the Administration of Palestine to any general international conventions already existing, or which may be concluded hereafter with the approval of the League of Nations, respecting the slave traffic, the traffic in arms and ammunition, or the traffic in drugs, or relating to commercial equality, freedom of transit and navigation, aerial navigation and postal, telegraphic and wireless communication or literary, artistic or industrial property.

Art. 20. The Mandatory shall co-operate on behalf of the Administration of Palestine, so far as religious, social and other conditions may permit, in the execution of any common policy adopted by the League of Nations for preventing and combating disease, including diseases of plants and animals.

Art. 21. The Mandatory shall secure the enactment within twelve months from this date, and shall ensure the execution of a Law of Antiquities based on the following rules. This law shall ensure equality of treatment in the matter of excavations and archaeological research to the nations of all States Members of the League of Nations.

(1) "Antiquity" means any construction or any product of human activity earlier than the year A.D. 1700.

(2) The law for the protection of antiquities shall proceed by encouragement rather than by threat.

(3) No antiquity may be disposed of except to the competent Department, unless this Department renounces the acquisition of any such antiquity.

No antiquity may leave the country without an export licence from the said Department.

(4) Any person who maliciously or negligently destroys or damages an antiquity shall be liable to a penalty to be fixed.

(5)   No clearing of ground or digging with the object of finding antiquities shall be permitted, under penalty of fine, except to persons authorised by competent Department.

(6)   Equitable terms shall be fixed for expropriation, temporary or permanent, of lands which might be of historical or archæological interest.

(7)   Authorisation to excavate shall only be granted to persons who show sufficient guarantees of archaeological experience.   The Administration of Palestine shall not, in granting these authorities, act in such a way as to exclude scholars of any nation without good grounds.

(8)   The proceeds of excavations may be divided between the excavator and the competent Department in a proportion fixed by that Department. If division seems impossible for scientific reasons, the excavator shall receive a fair indemnity in lieu of a part of the find.

Art. 22.   English, Arabic and Hebrew shall be the official languages of Palestine. Any statement or inscription in Arabic on stamps or money in Palestine shall be repeated in Hebrew; any statement or inscription in Hebrew shall be repeated in Arabic.

Art. 23.   The Administration of Palestine shall recognise the holy days of the respective communities in Palestine as legal days of rest for the members of such communities.

Art 24.   The Mandatory shall make to the Council of the League of Nations an annual report to the satisfaction of the Council as to the measures taken during the year to carry out the provisions of the mandate.   Copies of all laws and regulations promulgated or issued during the year shall be communicated with the report.

Art. 25.   In the territories lying between the Jordan and the eastern boundary of Palestine as ultimately determined, the Mandatory shall be entitled, with the consent of the Council of the League of Nations, to postpone or withhold application of such provisions of this mandate as he may consider inapplicable to the existing local conditions, and to make such provision for the administration of the territories as he may consider suitable to those conditions, provided that no action shall be taken which is inconsistent with the provisions of Articles 15, 16 and 18.

Art. 26   The Mandatory agrees that, if any dispute whatever should arise between the Mandatory and another

Member of the League of Nations relating to the interpretation or the application of the provisions of the mandate, such dispute, if it cannot be settled by negotiation, shall be submitted to the Permanent Court of International Justice provided for by Article 14 of the Covenant of the League of Nations.

Art. 27. The consent of the Council of the League of Nations is required for any modification of the terms of the mandate.

Art. 28. In the event of the termination of the mandate hereby conferred upon the Mandatory, the Council of the League of Nations shall make such arrangements as may be deemed necessary for safeguarding in perpetuity, under guarantee of the League, the rights secured by Articles 13 and 14, and shall use its influence for securing, under the guarantee of the League, that the Government of Palestine will fully honour the financial obligations legitimately incurred by the Administration of Palestine during the period of the mandate, including the rights of public servants to pensions or gratuities.

17

Joint Resolution of Congress, 1922

At the time of considerable debate in Great Britain regarding the government's policy in Palestine, and even before the final wording of the mandate itself had been finalized, the Congress of the United States gratuitously involved itself in the controversy by unanimously passing a Joint Resolution favoring the establishment of a Jewish National Home in Palestine.

Although the United States had not joined the League of Nations and therefore had no voice in the acceptance of the Mandate over Palestine by the League when it should be brought before it, the Zionist leaders in the United States were, understandably, desirous of exerting whatever influence they could in the acceptance of the Balfour Declaration by both the British Government and the League. On 26 March 1922 an American Zionist conference held in Philadelphia passed a resolution "... urging support of the British mandate and ap-

Source: United States of America. *The Statutes at Large of the United States of America from April 1921 to March 1923. Concurrent Resolutions of the Two Houses of Congress and Recent Treaties, Conventions, and Executive Proclamations* [H.J. Res. 322; Pub. Res., No. 731, vol. 42 (Washington D.C.: Government Printing Office, 1923) 1012.

pealing to the United States Government to give
public expression' to its sympathy with the
cause [of the Jewish national home]."[1] Three
days later, on the 29th, Coleman Silbert,   an
American Zionist member of the Massachusetts
legislature from Boston, introduced   the following resolution into that body:

Order relative to recognizing Palestine as the homeland of the Jewish people.
     Whereas the supreme council of the Allied
Peace Conference meeting at San Remo recognized the
right of the Jewish nation to a national existence in
Palestine and conferred upon Great Britain a mandate
over Palestine; and
     Whereas the various great nations of the world
have approved the establishment of the national
homeland for the Jews in Palestine; and
     Whereas the the people of the United States,
individually and through their spokesmen in Congress
and by leading men in all walks of life, have expressed
their gratification at the realization of the national
hopes of the Jews; and
     Whereas the General Court of Massachusetts
views with pleasure the progress of the Jewish people
in Palestine, in developing the economic resources of
the country, in founding institutions of learning, and
in creating a spiritual center, so that it may the better
serve mankind: Therefore be it
     Ordered. That the General Court of Mas-
sachusetts urges the Government of the United States
of America formally to recognize the present status of
the Jewish people in Palestine and thus to approve the
fulfillment of its yearning desire for a national home
in the land of its forefathers; and be it further
     Ordered. That copies of this order be sent by
the secretary of the Commonwealth to the President of
the United States, to the presiding officers of both
branches of Congress, to each of the Senators and

---

[1] *The New York Times,* 27 March 1922, p. 17, quoting from the resolution.

Representatives in Congress from Massachusetts, and to the Zionist organization of America.[2]

The resolution was passed in both houses of the state's legislature on that same date. The following morning a delegation of Jewish voters from Massachusetts met with Senator Henry Cabot Lodge in his office in Washington, D.C., where they presented him with a copy of the resolution. Shortly after noon that day Lodge had read into the record of the Senate the same resolution and demanded that as many senators as needed be called into the chamber to constitute a quorum, although no vote was required. (The following 17 May Senator Colt of Rhode Island had read into the record a resolution passed by the legislature of that state on 28 April with the exact same wording!). On 11 April another Jewish group had a conference with Senator Lodge at which it was requested that he introduce a resolution favoring the establishment in Palestine of the Jewish national home into the Senate Committee on Foreign Relations, of which he was Chairman. The very next day such a resolution was brought to the Committee for vote. On the 3rd of May, Lodge reported to the Senate the version of the resolution passed upon by the Committee (S.J. Res. 191) and demanded that it be voted upon immediately without debate, which was accomplished.

Three factors were at work to account for the speedy adoption of a resolution not immediately involving the United States: 1) Senator Lodge and Arthur Balfour (of the Balfour Declaration) had become close friends following their first meeting in 1894 in London. At the Washington Conference on the Limitation of Armaments of 1921, Lodge was a member of the U.S. delegation and Balfour was the head of the British delegation. On at least one occasion Lodge entertained Balfour at a time when seri-

---

[2] United States of America. Congress of the United States. *Congressional Record - Senate* 30 March 1922, p. 4757.

ous debate about the Declaration was proceeding in England. 2) It is known that Lodge was favorable toward the establishment of the British Mandate over Palestine and the Jewish national home in that country as early as 1919, for he had written a letter to the Zionist Organization of America in that year expressing his interest. 3) Perhaps more importantly, 1922 was an election year and Senator Lodge was up for re-election; however, as early as March, it was realized that it would be a very closely contested election and his letters indicate his concern. In a later letter to an American acquaintance residing in Paris, dated 21 October 1922, Lodge wrote, "My reporting of the Palestine Resolution will give me a very much stronger vote among the Jews than you suggest. That is a matter on which they have a great deal of sentiment. I do not expect for that reason support from Mr. [Supreme Court Justice] Brandeis or Mr. Filene, but of the mass of them I think there can be no doubt."[3]

In the meanwhile, Mr. Hamilton Fish, the freshman Representative from upper New York state, an area with a large Jewish population, was approached on 4 April by a number of American Zionist leaders, including Judge Julian W. Mack. Despite his exalted position as a member of the federal judiciary, Mack had recently served as President of the Zionist Organization of America. These Zionist leaders wanted Fish to introduce a resolution into the House of Representatives favoring the Jewish national home in Palestine. Fish was a junior member of the House Committee on Foreign Affairs, and a long-term Zionist sympathizer. Fish does not recall who wrote the resolution that he brought before his Committee, but it was reported out on 23 May after public hearings with the demand that it be voted upon without debate. The following reprint of the

---

[3] Lodge to William Astor Chanler, 21 October 1922. Reprinted by permission of the Director of the Massachusetts Historical Society, in which the Lodge papers are housed.

joint Resolution, finally passed by Congress on 30 June, was an amalgam of the Senate and House resolutions were very similar in wording.[4]

In two editorials published in *The New York Times* (7 and 28 May 1922) these congressional representatives were accused of "pandering to the Jewish vote," thus dividing the Jewish population of the country between those who supported the Zionist cause and those who did not care; contravening the Constitutional separation of religion and state; and interfering in a political matter that was of no concern to the United States.

Despite these and other objections to the Joint Resolution, it was signed by President Warren Harding on 21 September 1922, thus bringing the United States into what was to become the Arab—Israeli conflict.

Resolve by the Senate and House of Representatives of the United States of America in Congress assembled, That the United States of America favors the establishment in Palestine of the national home for the Jewish people, it being clearly understood that nothing shall be done which may prejudice the civil and religious rights Christian and all other non-Jewish communities in Palestine, and that the holy places and religious buildings and sites in Palestine shall be adequately protected.

Approved, September 21, 1922.

---

[4] In private communication with the editor of this collection Mr. Fish stated that he does not recall that he and Senator Lodge had conferred about their respective resolutions prior to this time.

18

Anglo-American Convention, 1924

By Article 8 of the Mandate, as approved by the Council of the League of Nations, the Capitulatory Treaties that those nations, including the United States, had had with the former Ottoman Empire were unilaterally abolished in Palestine by Great Britain. Furthermore, with the refusal of Congress to ratify the Treaty of Versailles (containing the Covenant of the League of Nations as Article I) the United States and its citizens were deprived of any regularized position within the country. It was therefore necessary for Britain and the United States to sign this convention to place the United States upon an equal footing with other nations in Palestine.

During the course of the negotiations the United States Government expressed its desire that the Anglo-American Convention should be worded as nearly alike the Franco-American Convention in recognition of the mandate over Syria/Lebanon as possible. The British Government, in turn, wished to have the convention regarding Palestine be also operable in regards to her mandate over Trans-

Source: United States. Department of State. *Papers Relating to the Foreign Relations of the United States 1924*, vol. 2 (Washington, D.C.: Government Printing Office, 1939) 212-22.

Jordan, and insisted that the Mandate document be included within the Convention, thereby obtaining U.S. acceptance of the Mandate as worded.

Whereas by the Treaty of Peace concluded with the Allied Powers, Turkey renounces all her rights and title over Palestine; and

Whereas article 22 of the Covenant of the League of Nations in the Treaty of Versailles provides that in the case of certain territories which, as a consequence of the late war, ceased to be under the sovereignty of the States which formerly governed them, mandates should be issued, and that the terms of the mandate should be explicitly defined in each case by the Council of the League; and

Whereas the Principal Allied Powers have agreed to entrust the mandate for Palestine to His Britannic Majesty; and

Whereas the terms of the said mandate have been defined by the Council of the League of Nations, as follows:-

[Here follows a reprinting of the Mandate, eliminated in this present reproduction of the Convention]   and

Whereas the mandate in the above terms came into force on the 29th September, 1923; and

Whereas the United States of America, by participating in the war against Germany, contributed to her defeat and the defeat of her Allies in the territory transferred by them but has not ratified the Covenant of the League of Nations embodied in the Treaty of Versailles; and

Whereas the Government of the United States and the Government of His Britannic Majesty desire to reach a definite understanding with respect to the rights of the two Governments and their respective nationals in Palestine;

The President of the United States of America and His Britannic Majesty have decided to conclude a convention to this effect, and have named as their plenipotentiaries:-

The President of the United States of America:

His Excellency the Honourable Frank B. Kellogg, Ambassador Extraordinary and Plenipotentiary of the United States at London:

His Majesty of the King of the United Kingdom of Great Britain and Ireland and of the British Dominions beyond the Seas, Emperor of India:

The Right Honourable Joseph Austen Chamberlain, M.P., His Majesty's Principal Secretary of State for Foreign Affairs:
who, after having communicated to each other their respective full powers, found in good and due form, have agreed as follows:-

ARTICLE 1

Subject to the provisions of the present convention the United States consents to the administration of Palestine by His Britannic Majesty, pursuant to the mandate recited above.

ARTICLE 2

The United States and its nationals shall have and enjoy all the rights and benefits secured under the terms of the mandate to members of the League of Nations and their nationals, notwithstanding the fact that the United States is not a member of the League of Nations.

ARTICLE 3

Vested American property rights in the mandated territory shall be respected and in no way impaired.

ARTICLE 4

A duplicate of the annual report to be made by the Mandatory under article 24 of the mandate shall be furnished to the United States.

ARTICLE 5

Subject to the provisions of any local laws for the maintenance of public order and public morals, the nationals of the United States will be permitted freely to establish and maintain educational, philanthropic and religious institutions in the mandated territory, to receive voluntary applicants and to teach in the English language.

ARTICLE 6

The extradition treaties and conventions which are, or may be, in force between the United States and Great Britain, and the provisions of any treaties which are, or may be, in force between the two countries which relate to extradition or consular rights shall apply to the mandated territory.

ARTICLE 7

Nothing contained in the present convention shall be affected by any modification which may be made in the terms of the mandate as recited above, unless such modifications shall have been assented to by the United States.

ARTICLE 8

The present convention shall be ratified in accordance with the respective constitutional methods of the High Contracting Parties. The ratifications shall be exchanged in London as soon as practicable. The present convention shall take effect on the date of the exchange of ratifications.

In witness whereof, the undersigned have signed the present convention, and have thereunto affixed their seals.

Done in duplicate at London, this 3rd day of December, 1924.

[SEAL]   Frank B. Kellogg

[SEAL] Austen Chamberlain

Ratifications exchanged at London, December 3, 1925.

19

Passfield White Paper, 1930

In August of 1929, after nearly eight years of relative calm, conflict between the Arab and Jewish communities broke out all over Palestine, but with particular ferocity in Hebron, Jaffa, Haifa, and Safed, resulting in the deaths of over two hundred people on both sides. Although a dispute over the Wailing Wall was partially to blame, the primary cause was the economic distress of a large number of Arab cultivators, together with general fears on the part of the non-Jewish communities about being overrun by foreign immigrants. In the decade between 1920 and 1929 the *legal* immigration of Jews from Europe amounted to 99,806. Because the original concept of Zionism was a return to agriculture by the "returning" Jews, the Jewish National Fund, in order to provide for the immigrants, undertook large-scale purchases of land, largely from absentee landowners. This was in addition to "waste" lands and "state" lands made available to the

Source: Great Britain. Parliamentary Papers. *Palestine. Statement of Policy by His Majesty's Government in the United Kingdom. Presented by the Secretary of State for the Colonies to Parliament by Command of His Majesty, October 1930* (London: His Majesty's Stationery Office, 1930), Cmd. 3692. Reprinted by permission of the Controller of Her Majesty's Stationery Office.

Jews by the Palestine Administration under the terms of the mandate. The land thus obtained was declared "national land" and therefore neither cultivable by nor transferable to non-Jews. The Arab peasants, whose forefathers had cultivated the same soil for generations, were now evicted from their homes. With other land unavailable to them, or too expensive for them to purchase in competition with the Jewish National Fund, the dispossessed farmers flocked to the cities to find alternative employment, but, without adequate education or other skills, little was available. Furthermore, under the terms of the mandate, the Palestine Administration encouraged the development of the infrastructure and small-scale industries by the Jewish Agency, so that immigrant Jews from throughout the world — generally with better education, greater managerial skills, and greater capital, provided by Jewish communities — undertook this important task. Even here the better paying jobs were reserved for the Jews. It was inevitable that conflict should occur.

Surprised by the outbreak of violence on such a wide scale, the Colonial Office, on 14 September, announced the appointment of a Commission of Inquiry under the chairmanship of a former colonial chief justice, Sir Walter Shaw. Following a tour of investigation throughout Palestine, the commissioners published their report on 12 March 1930. In this they stated that the fundamental cause for the disturbances seemed to be Arab fears of loss of livelihood and eventual Jewish domination through change in landownership and continued large-scale immigration.[1] Their primary recommendations were: (a) a restatement of policy regarding the safeguarding of the rights of the non-Jewish communities, (b) a

---

[1] Great Britain. Parliamentary Papers. *Report of the Commission on the Palestine Disturbances of August 1929* (London: His Majesty's Stationery Office, 1930), Cmd. 3530. This Commission of Inquiry is generally known as the "Shaw Commission".

clearer statement about and closer supervision over immigration, (c) greater protection for the Arab peasantry through a more explicit policy on land tenure, and, (d) a re-emphasis of the earlier declaration that the Zionist Organization was not entitled to share in the Government of Palestine.

The findings and recommendations of the "Shaw Commission" were at such variance with the general understanding of the Palestine situation in London and were met with so much hostility on the part of the Zionist leaders that the Government decided to send Sir John Hope Simpson to Jerusalem in order to undertake an even more thorough investigation. His report (Cmd. 3686) served as the basis for the following "Statement of Policy", although Dr. Weizmann considered Simpson's commission "... either a superfluity or a propaganda instrument for the Government's predetermined policy."[2] He, nevertheless, had been provided with an advance copy of the report prior to its publication.

Sidney Webb was both an early member of the Fabian Society and of the Labour Party, which he had represented in Parliament for a number of years. Upon the formation of the Labour Government in 1929 Webb was elevated to the peerage as Lord Passfield and appointed to the position of Secretary of State for the Colonies in the Cabinet. At the time of the issuance of the "White Paper" that bears his name, Beatrice Webb wrote in her diary on 30 October, "Sidney started with a great admiration for the Jew and a contempt for the Arab — but he reports that all the officials, at home and in Palestine, find the Jews, even many accomplished and cultivated Jews, intolerable as negotiators and colleagues."[3]

[2] Chaim Weizmann. *Trial and Error: the Autobiography of Chaim Weizmann*, vol. 2 (Philadelphia: The Jewish Publication Society of America, 5709-1949) 332.

[3] Quoted in *The Letters of Sidney and Beatrice Webb*, ed. Norman MacKenzie, vol. 3 (Cambridge: Cambridge University Press, 1978)

1. The Report of the Special Commission, under the Chairmanship of Sir Walter Shaw, which was published in April [1930], gave rise to acute controversy, in the course of which it became evident that there is considerable misunderstanding about the past actions and future intentions of His Majesty's Government in the United Kingdom in regard to the administration of Palestine. It was realised that the publication of a clear and full statement of policy, designed to remove such misunderstanding and the resultant uncertainty and apprehension, was a matter of urgent importance. The preparation of such a statement, however, necessitated certain essential preliminary steps which have inevitably delayed its completion.

The Report of the Shaw Commission drew attention to certain features of the problem, which, in the opinion of His Majesty's Government, called for prompt and full investigation, in view of their important bearing upon future policy. It was therefore decided to send to Palestine a highly qualified investigator (Sir John Hope Simpson) to confer with the High Commissioner and to report to His Majesty's Government on land settlement, immigration and development. Owing to the dominating importance of these subjects, and their close inter-connection, His Majesty's Government recognised that no statement of policy could be formulated without first taking into account a full and detailed exposition of the situation in Palestine under these three important heads, such as Sir John Hope Simpson was eminently qualified to furnish. Considerable pressure has been brought to bear upon His Majesty's Government to anticipate the receipt of Sir John Hope Simpson's Report by a declaration of policy, but, while appreciating the urgent need for as early a declaration as possible, His Majesty's Government felt bound to adhere to their decision to await the receipt of Sir John Hope Simpson's Report, especially having regard to the evidence which was accumulating as to the extreme difficulty and complexity of the problem and the need for the fullest investigation of the facts before arriving at any definite conclusions.

Sir John Hope Simpson's Report has now been received, and the present statement of policy has been framed after very careful consideration of its contents and of other information bearing upon the Palestine situation which has recently become available.

---

335. Reprinted by permission of Cambridge University Press.

2.   In a country such as Palestine, where the interests and aims of two sections of the community are at present diverse and in some respects conflicting, it is too much to expect that any declaration of policy will fully satisfy the aspirations of either party.   His Majesty's Government have, however, permitted themselves to hope that the removal of existing misunderstandings and the more precise definition of their intentions may go far to allay uneasiness and to restore confidence on both sides.   It will be the endeavour of His Majesty's Government, not only by the present statement of policy but by the administrative actions which will result from it, to convince both Arabs and Jews of their firm intention to promote the essential interests of both races to the utmost of their power, and to work consistently for the development, in Palestine, of a prosperous community, living in peace under an impartial and progressive Administration. It is necessary, however, to emphasise one important point, viz., that in the peculiar circumstances of Palestine no policy, however enlightened or however vigorously prosecuted, can hope for success, unless it is supported not merely by the acceptance, but by the willing co-operation of the communities for whose benefit it is designed.

It is unnecessary here to dwell upon the unhappy events of the past year and the deplorable conditions which have resulted from them.   His Majesty's Government feel bound, however, to remark that they have received little assistance from either side in healing the breach between them during the months of tension and unrest which have followed on the disturbances of August 1929, and that to the difficulties created by the mutual suspicions and hostilities of the two races has been added a further grave obstacle, namely, an attitude of mistrust towards His Majesty's Government fostered by a press campaign in which the true facts of the situation have become obscured and distorted.   It cannot be too strongly emphasised that on the establishment of better relations between Arabs and Jews depend the future peace and prosperity of the country which is dear to both races.   This is the object which His Majesty's Government have constantly in view, and they feel that it is more likely to be attained if both sides will willingly co-operate with the Government and with the Palestine Administration, and endeavour to realise that, in the discharge of their mandatory obligations and indeed in all their relations with Palestine, His Majesty's Government may be trusted to safeguard and promote the interests of both races.

3.   Many of the misunderstandings which have un-
happily arisen on both sides appear to be the result of a failure to appreciate the nature of the duty imposed upon His
Majesty's Government by the terms of the Mandate.   The next
point, therefore, which His Majesty's Government feel it
necessary to emphasise, in the strongest manner possible, is
that in the words of the Prime Minister's statement in the
House of Commons on the 3rd April last, "a double undertaking is involved, to the Jewish people on the one hand and to
the non-Jewish population of Palestine on the other."
    Much of the agitation which has taken place during
the past year seems to have arisen from a failure to realise
the full import of this fundamental fact.   Both Arabs and
Jews have assailed the Government with demands and re-
proaches based upon the false assumption that it was the
duty of His Majesty's Government to execute policies from
which they are, in fact, debarred by the explicit terms of the
Mandate.
    The Prime Minister, in the statement above referred
to, announced, in   words which could not have been made
more plain, that it is the intention of His Majesty's
Government to continue to administer Palestine in accordance with the terms of the Mandate, as approved by the
Council of the League of Nations.   "That" said Mr. Ramsay
MacDonald, "is an international obligation from which there
can be no question of receding."   In spite of so unequivocal a
statement, the hope seems to have been entertained that, by
some means or other, an escape could be found from the
limitations plainly imposed by the terms of the Mandate.   It
must be realised, once and for all, that it is useless for Jewish
leaders on the one hand to press His Majesty's Government to
conform their policy in regard, for example, to immigration
and land, to the aspirations of the more uncompromising
sections of Zionist opinion.   That would be to ignore the
equally important duty of the Mandatory Power towards the
non-Jewish inhabitants of Palestine.   On the other hand, it is
equally useless for Arab leaders to maintain their demands
for a form of Constitution, which would render it impossible
for His Majesty's Government to carry out, in the fullest
sense, the double undertaking already referred to.   His
Majesty's Government have reason to think that one of the
reasons for the sustained tension and agitation on both sides
has been the creation by misguided advisers of the false
hope that efforts to intimidate and to bring pressure to bear
upon His Majesty's Government would eventually result in
forcing them into a policy which weighted the balances in

favour of one or the other party.

It becomes, therefore, essential that at the outset His Majesty's Government should make it clear that they will not be moved, by any pressure or threats, from the path laid down in the Mandate, and from the pursuit of a policy which aims at promoting the interests of the inhabitants of Palestine, both Arabs and Jews, in a manner which shall be consistent with the obligations which the Mandate imposes.

4.   This is not the first time that His Majesty's Government have endeavoured to make clear the nature of their policy in Palestine. In 1922 a full statement was published and was communicated both to the Palestine Arab Delegation, then in London, and to the Zionist Organisation. This statement met with no acceptance on the part of the Arab Delegation, but the Executive of the Zionist Organisation passed a Resolution assuring His Majesty's Government that the activities of the Organisation would be conducted in conformity with the policy therein set forth. Moreover, in the letter conveying the text of this Resolution to His Majesty's Government, Dr. Weizmann wrote:-

> "The Zionist Organisation has, at all times, been sincerely desirous of proceeding in harmonious co-operation with all sections of the people of Palestine. It has repeatedly made it clear, both in word and deed, that nothing is further from its purpose than to prejudice in the smallest degree the civil or religious rights, or the material interests of the non-Jewish population."

The experience of the intervening years has inevitably brought to light certain administrative defects and special economic problems, which have to be taken into account in considering the welfare of all sections of the community. Nevertheless, the statement of policy, issued after prolonged and careful consideration in 1922, provides the foundations upon which future British policy in Palestine must be built up.

5.   Apart from proposals for the establishment of a Constitution in Palestine which will be dealt with in later paragraphs, there are three important points dealt with in this statement which must now be recalled:-

(a) *The meaning attached by His Majesty's Government of*

the expression "the Jewish National Home" which is contained in the Mandate.

On this point, the following passage may be quoted from the 1922 Statement:-

"During the last two or three generations the Jews have recreated in Palestine a community, now numbering 80,000, of whom about one-fourth are farmers or workers upon the land. This community has its own political organs; an elected assembly for the direction of its domestic concerns; elected councils in the towns; and an organisation for the control of its schools. It has its elected Chief Rabbinate and Rabbinical Council for the direction of its religious affairs. Its business is conducted in Hebrew as a vernacular language and a Hebrew press serves its needs. It has its distinctive intellectual life and displays considerable economic activity. This community then, with its town and country population, its political, religious and social organisation, its own language, its own customs, its own life, has in fact "national" characteristics. When it is asked what is meant by the development of the Jewish National Home in Palestine, it may be answered that it is not the imposition of a Jewish nationality upon the inhabitants of Palestine as a whole, but the further development of the existing Jewish community, with the assistance of Jews in other parts of the world, in order that it may become a centre in which the Jewish people as a whole may take, on grounds of religion and race, an interest and a pride. But in order that this community should have the best prospect of free development and provide a full opportunity for the Jewish people to display its capacities, it is essential that it should know that it is in Palestine as of right and not on sufferance. That is the reason why it is necessary that the existence of a Jewish National Home in Palestine should be internationally guaranteed, and that it should be formally recognised to rest upon ancient historic connection.

"This, then, is the interpretation which His Majesty's Government place upon the Declaration of 1917, and, so understood, the Secretary of State is of opinion that it does not contain or imply anything which need cause either alarm to the Arab population or disappointment to the Jews."

(b) *The principles which should govern immigration.*
   On this point the statement of policy continues as follows:-

> "For the fulfilment of this policy it is necessary that the Jewish community in Palestine should be able to increase its numbers by immigration. This immigration cannot be so great in volume as to exceed whatever may be the economic capacity of the country at the time to absorb new arrivals. It is essential to ensure that the immigrants should not be a burden upon the people of Palestine as a whole, and that they should not deprive any section of the present population of their employment. Hitherto the immigration has fulfilled these conditions. The number of immigrants since the British occupation has been about 25,000.
>
> "It is necessary also to ensure that persons who are politically undesirable are excluded from Palestine and every precaution has been and will be taken by the Administration to that end."

It will be observed that the principles enunciated above render it essential that in estimating the absorptive capacity of Palestine at any time account should be taken of Arab as well as Jewish unemployment in determining the rate at which immigration should be permitted. It is the intention of His Majesty's Government to take steps to ensure a more exact application of these principles in the future.

(c) *The position of the Jewish Agency.*
   In the passage quoted below, an attempt was made to indicate the limitations, implicit in the Mandate, necessarily imposed upon the scope of the Jewish Agency provided for in Article 4 of the Mandate:-

> "It is also necessary to point out that the Zionist Commission in Palestine, now termed the Palestine Zionist Executive, has not desired to possess, and does not possess, any share in the general administration of the country. Nor does the special position assigned to the Zionist Organisation in Article IV of the draft Mandate for Palestine imply any such functions. That special position relates to the measures affecting the Jewish population, and contemplates that the Organisation may assist in the general development of the country, but does not enti-

tle it to share in any degree in its Government."

6.   His Majesty's Government desire to reaffirm generally the policy outlined in the 1922 Statement, and, in particular, the three passages quoted above.   On these three important points it is not thought that anything but barren controversy would result from an attempt further to elaborate their conceptions.   It is recognised, however, in the light of past experience that much remains to be done to improve the practical application of the principles enunciated in the foregoing passages, and it is the intention of the Government,   in   consultation   with   the   Palestine Administration, to take active steps to provide improved machinery for meeting the requirements of both Arabs and Jews, under these three heads.   In particular, it is recognised as of the greatest importance that the efforts of the High Commissioner towards some closer and more harmonious form of co-operation and means of consultation between the Palestine Administration and the Jewish Agency should be further developed, always consistently, however, with the principle which must be regarded as basic, that the special position of the Agency, in affording advice and co-operation, does not entitle the Agency, as such, to share in the government of the country.   Similarly, machinery must be provided to ensure that the essential interests of the non-Jewish sections of the Community should at the same time be fully safeguarded, and that adequate opportunity should be afforded for consultation with the Palestine Administration on matters affecting those interests.

7.   At this point it becomes desirable to remove any ground of misunderstanding that may exist as to the passages in the Mandate bearing upon the safeguarding of the rights of the non-Jewish community in Palestine.   The passages in the Mandate specially bearing on this point will be found in-

Article 2.   "The Mandatory shall be responsible for placing the country under such political administrative and economic conditions as will secure the establishment of the Jewish National Home, as laid down in the preamble, and the development of self-governing institutions, and also for safeguarding the civil and religious rights of all the inhabitants of Palestine, irrespective of race and religion."

Article 6.   "The Administration of Palestine, while ensuring that the rights and position of other sections of the population are not prejudiced, shall facilitate Jewish immigration under suitable conditions, and shall encourage, in co-operation with the Jewish agency referred to in Article 4, close settlement by Jews on the land, including State lands and waste lands not required for public purposes."

Article 9.   "The Mandatory shall be responsible for seeing that the judicial system established in Palestine shall assure to foreigners, as well as to natives, a complete guarantee of their rights.

Respect for personal status of the various peoples and communities and for their religious interests shall be fully guaranteed.   In particular, the control and administration of Wakfs shall be exercised in accordance with religious law and the dispositions of the founders."

Article 13.   "All responsibility in connection with the Holy Places and religious buildings or sites in Palestine, including that of preserving existing rights and of securing free access to the Holy Places, religious buildings and sites, and the free exercise of worship, while ensuring the requirements of public order and decorum, is assumed by the Mandatory, who shall be responsible solely to the League of Nations in all matters connected herewith, provided that nothing in this article shall prevent the Mandatory from entering into such arrangements as he may deem reasonable with the Administration for the purpose of carrying the provisions of this article into effect, and provided also that nothing in this Mandate shall be construed as conferring upon the Mandatory authority to interfere with the fabric or the management of purely Moslem sacred shrines, the immunities of which are guaranteed."

Article 15.   "The Mandatory shall see that complete freedom of conscience and the free exercise of all forms of worship, subject only to the maintenance of public order and morals, are ensured to all.   No discrimination of any kind shall be made between the inhabitants of Palestine on the ground of race, religion or language.   No person shall be excluded from Palestine on the sole ground of his religious belief.

The right of each community to maintain its own schools for the education of its own members in its own language, while conforming to such educational requirements of a general nature as the Administration may impose, shall not be denied or impaired."

On the other hand, special reference to the Jewish National Home and to Jewish interests are contained in *Article 4*:-

Article 4. "An appropriate Jewish agency shall be recognised as a public body for the purpose of advising and co-operating with the Administration of Palestine in such economic, social and other matters as may affect the establishment of the Jewish National Home and the interests of the Jewish population in Palestine, and, subject always to the control of the Administration, to assist and take part in the development of the country.

The Zionist organisation, so long as its organisation and constitution are in the opinion of the Mandatory appropriate, shall be recognised as such agency. It shall take steps in consultation with His Britannic Majesty's Government to secure the co-operation of all Jews who are willing to assist in the establishment of the Jewish National Home."

Article 6. (Already quoted above.)

Article 11. "The Administration of Palestine shall take all necessary measures to safeguard the interests of the community in connection with the development of the country, and, subject to any international obligations accepted by the mandatory, shall have full power to provide for public ownership or control of any of the natural resources of the country or of the public works, services and utilities established or to be established therein. It shall introduce a land system appropriate to the needs of the country, having regard, among other things, to the desirability of promoting the close settlement and intensive cultivation of the land.

The Administration may arrange with the Jewish Agency mentioned in Article 4 to construct or operate, upon fair and equitable terms, any public works, services and utilities, and to develop any of the natural resources of the country, in so far as these matters are not directly undertaken by the Administration. Any such arrangements shall provide that no profits distributed by such agency directly or indirectly, shall exceed a reasonable rate of interest on the capital, and any further profits shall be utilised by it for the benefit of the country in a manner approved by the Administration."

8. In the first place, it will be observed that Article 2 makes the Mandatory responsible for safeguarding the civil and religious rights of all the inhabitants of Palestine, irrespective of race or religion; and secondly, that the obligation contained in Article 6 to facilitate Jewish immigration and to encourage close settlement by Jews on the land, is qualified by the requirement to ensure that the rights and position of other sections of the population are not prejudiced. Moreover, by Article 11 "the Administration of Palestine is required to take all necessary measures to safeguard the interests of the community in connection with the development of the country." It is clear from the wording of this Article that the population of Palestine as a whole, and not any sectional interest, is to be the object of the Government's care, and it may be noted that the provision for arranging with the Jewish Agency for the construction or operation of public works, services and utilities, is only permissive and not obligatory, and could not be allowed to conflict with the general interests of the community. These points are emphasised because claims have been made on behalf of the Jewish Agency to a position in regard to the general administration of the country, which His Majesty's Government cannot but regard as going far beyond the clear intention of the Mandate. Moreover, attempts have been made to argue, in support of Zionist claims, that the principal feature of the Mandate is the passages regarding the Jewish National Home, and that the passages designed to safeguard the rights of the non-Jewish community are merely secondary considerations qualifying, to some extent, what is claimed to be the primary object for which the Mandate has been framed.

This is a conception which His Majesty's Government have always regarded as totally erroneous. However difficult the task may be it would, in their view, be impossible, consistently with the plain intention of the Mandate, to attempt to solve the problem by subordinating one of these obligations to the other. The British Accredited Representative, when appearing before the Permanent Mandates Commission on the 9th of June last, endeavoured to make clear the attitude of His Majesty's Government towards the difficulties inherent in the Mandate. In commenting on his statements in their report to the Council, the Permanent Mandates Commission made the following important pronouncement:-

"From all these statements two assertions emerge, which should be emphasised:-
(1) that the obligations laid down by the Mandate in regard to the two sections of the population are of equal weight;
(2) that the two obligations imposed on the Mandatory are in no sense irreconcilable."

"The Mandates Commission has no objection to raise to these two assertions, which, in its view, accurately express what it conceives to be the essence of the Mandate for Palestine and ensure its future."

His Majesty's Government are fully in accord with the sense of this pronouncement and it is a source of satisfaction to them that it has been rendered authoritative by the approval of the Council of the League of Nations.

It is the difficult and delicate task of His Majesty's Government to devise means whereby, in the execution of its policy in Palestine, equal weight shall at all times be given to the obligations laid down with regard to the two sections of the population and to reconcile those two obligations where, inevitably, conflicting interests are involved.

It is hoped that the foregoing explanation of the nature of the task imposed by the Mandate upon His Majesty's Government will make clear the necessity, already emphasised, for willing co-operation with the Palestine Administration and with His Majesty's Government on the part of both Arab and Jewish leaders.

9. The preceding paragraphs contain an exposition of the general principles which have to be taken into account as governing policy in Palestine and the limiting conditions under which it must be carried out. The practical problems with which His Majesty's Government are faced in Palestine must now be considered in detail.

These may be regarded as falling roughly under three heads:-
(1) Security,
(2) Constitutional development,
(3) Economic and Social development.
They will be dealt with in that order.

(1) *Security*

10. It it *[sic]*   a primary duty of the Administration to ensure peace, order and good government in Palestine.   In an earlier paragraph His Majesty's Government have intimated that they will not be moved from their duty by any pressure or threats.

Outbreaks of disorder in the past have been promptly repressed and special measures have been taken to deal with any future emergencies.   It must be clearly understood that incitements to disorder or disaffection, in whatever quarter they may originate, will be severely punished and the powers of the Administration will, so far as may be necessary, be enlarged to enable it to deal the more effectively with any such dangerous and unwarrantable attempts.

His Majesty's Government have decided to retain in Palestine, for the present, two battalions of infantry; in addition to these, two squadrons of air craft and four sections of armoured cars will be available in Palestine and Trans-Jordan.   It will be recalled that Mr. Dowbiggin, Inspector-General of Police, Ceylon, was sent to Palestine to enquire into the organisation of the Palestine Police Force.   His elaborate and valuable report has been received and is under detailed consideration.   Certain of his recommendations have already been carried out, including those involving an increase in the strength of the British and Palestinian sections of the Force and those providing for a scheme of defence for Jewish Colonies, to which reference was made in paragraph 9 of the statement with regard to British Policy in Palestine, published as Command Paper 3582.   The remainder of the many recommendations in Mr. Dowbiggin's report are under consideration in consultation with the High Commissioner for Palestine, and further changes will be made when decisions are taken on these recommendations.   His Majesty's Government avail themselves of this opportunity to reiterate their determination to take all possible steps to suppress crime and maintain order in Palestine.   They desire to emphasise, in this connexion, that in determining the nature and composition of the security forces necessary for this purpose they must be guided by their expert advisers, and must aim at ensuring that the forces employed are suitable for the duties which they have to carry out, without regard to any political considerations.

(2) *Constitutional Development.*

11.   Reference has already been made to the demands of Arab leaders for a form of constitution which would be

incompatible with the mandatory obligations of His Majesty's Government. It is, however, the considered opinion of His Majesty's Government that the time has now come when the important question of the establishment of a measure of self-government in Palestine must, in the interests of the community as a whole, be taken in hand without further delay.

It may be convenient, in the first instance, to give a brief résumé of the history of this question since the establishment of the civil administration.

In October 1920 there was set up in Palestine an Advisory Council composed in equal parts of official and nominated unofficial members. Of the ten unofficial members, four were Moslems, three were Christians and three were Jews.

On the 1st September, 1922, the Palestine Order in Council was issued, setting up a Government in Palestine under the Foreign Jurisdiction Act. Part 3 of the Order in Council directed the establishment of a Legislative Council to be composed of the High Commissioner as President, with ten other official members, and 12 elected non-official members. The procedure for the selection of the non-official members was laid down in the Legislative Council, Order in Council, 1922, and in February and March 1923 an attempt was made to hold elections in accordance with that procedure.

The attempt failed owing to the refusal of the Arab population as a whole to co-operate (a detailed report of these elections is contained in the papers relating to the elections for the Palestine Legislative Council, 1923, published as Command Paper 1889).

The High Commissioner thereupon suspended the establishment of the proposed Legislative Council, and continued to act in consultation with an Advisory Council as before.

Two further opportunities were given to representative Arab leaders in Palestine to co-operate with the Administration in the government of the country, first, by the reconstitution of a nominated Advisory Council, but with membership conforming to that proposed for the Legislative Council, and, secondly, by a proposal for the formation of an Arab agency. It was intended that this Agency should have functions analogous to those entrusted to the Jewish Agency by Article 4 of the Palestine Mandate.

Neither of these opportunities was accepted and, accordingly, in December 1923, an Advisory Council was set up consisting only of official members. This position still continues; the only change being that the Advisory Council has been enlarged by the addition of more official members as the Administration developed.

It will be recalled that, under the terms of Article 2 of the Mandate, His Majesty's Government are responsible for placing the country under such political, administrative and economic conditions as will secure the establishment of the Jewish National Home and the development of self-governing institutions, and for safeguarding the civil and religious rights of the inhabitants. The action taken with regard to constitutional development in the early years of the Civil Administration is briefly described above.

With the object of enabling the people of Palestine to obtain practical experience of administrative methods and the business of government and to learn discrimination in the selection of their representatives, Lord Plumer, who was High Commissioner for Palestine from 1925 to 1928, introduced a wider measure of local self-government than had previously obtained under the British régime.

Sir John Chancellor considered the question of constitutional development on his assumption of the office of High Commissioner in December 1928. He consulted representatives of various local interests and, after a careful examination of the position, put forward certain proposals in June 1929. Discussion of the question was, however, suspended in consequence of the disturbances in August 1929.

12. His Majesty's Government have now carefully considered this question in the light of the present stage of progress and development and with special regard to their obligation to place the country under such political, administrative and economic conditions as will secure the development of self-governing institutions. They have decided that the time has arrived for a further step in the direction of the grant to the people of Palestine, of a measure of self-government compatible with the terms of the Mandate.

His Majesty's Government accordingly intend to set up a Legislative Council generally on the lines indicated in the statement of British policy in Palestine issued by Mr. Churchill in June 1922, which is reproduced as Appendix 5 to the Report of the Commission on the Palestine disturbances of August 1929.

His Majesty's Government trust that on this occasion they will secure the co-operation of all sections of the population of Palestine. His Majesty's Government desire to make it quite clear that while they would deeply regret an attempt on the part of any section of the population to prevent them from giving effect to their decision, all possible steps will be taken to circumvent such an attempt, if made, since they consider it in the interests of the population of the country as a whole that the further step now proposed should no long be deferred.

His Majesty's Government would point out that had this Legislature been set up at the time when it was first contemplated the people of Palestine would by now have gained more experience of the working of constitutional machinery. Such experience is indispensable for any progress in constitutional development. The sooner all sections of the population show a desire to co-operate with His Majesty's Government in this respect, the sooner will it be possible for such constitutional development to take place as His Majesty's Government hope to see in Palestine.

There are obvious advantages to be gained by all sections of the population from the establishment of such a Council. It should be of special benefit to the Arab section of the population, who do not at present possess any constitutional means for putting their views on social and economic matters before the Government. Their representatives on the Council which is to be set up will, of course, be in the position, not only to present the views of the Arab section of the population on these and other matters, but also to participate in discussions thereon. A further advantage may accrue to the country as a whole from the establishment of the Legislative Council, viz., that the participation of representatives of both sections of the community as members of the Legislative Council, will tend to improve the relations between the Jews and the Arabs.

13.   As stated above, the new Legislative Council will be on the lines indicated in the statement of policy issued in 1922. It will consist of the High Commissioner and 22 members, of whom ten will be official members and 12 unofficial members. Unofficial members of the Council will normally be elected by primary and secondary elections. It is, however, in the view of His Majesty's Government, so important to avoid the repetition of the deadlock which occurred in 1923 that steps will be devised to ensure the appointment of the requisite number of unofficial members to the Council in the event of one or more members failing to be elected on account of the non-co-operation of any section of the population, or for any other reason. The High Commissioner will

continue to have the necessary power to ensure that the Mandatory shall be enabled to carry out its obligations to the League of Nations, including any legislation urgently required, as well as the maintenance of order.

When difference arises as to the fulfilment by the Government of Palestine of the terms of the Mandate, a petition to the League of Nations is admissible under Article 85 of the Order in Council of 1922.

(3) *Economic and Social Development.*

14.   Under this head the practical problems to be considered are mainly concerned with questions relating to land, immigration and unemployment.   These three questions are intimately interrelated, with political as well as economic aspects, and upon their solution must depend any advance that can be hoped for towards settled conditions of peace and prosperity in Palestine.

Since attention was drawn to these matters in the Report of the Shaw Commission, they have formed the subject of detailed investigations on the spot by a Committee appointed by the High Commissioner in April, to examine into the economic condition of agriculturists and the fiscal measures of Government in relation thereto, and also by Sir John Hope Simpson who, on instructions from the Secretary of State for the Colonies, proceeded to Palestine in May in order to examine the questions of immigration, land settlement and development.

15.   As a result of these extensive and elaborate investigations, certain conclusions have emerged and certain facts have been established which will now be set out briefly:-

(1) *Land.*

It can now be definitely stated that at the present time and with the present methods of Arab cultivation there remains no margin of land available for agricultural settlement by new immigrants, with the exception of such undeveloped land as the various Jewish agencies hold in reserve.

There has been much criticism in the past in regard to the relatively small extent of State land which has been made available for Jewish settlement.   It is, however, an error to imagine that the Palestine Government is in possession of large areas of vacant land which could be made available for Jewish settlement. The extent of unoccupied areas of Government land is negligible. The Government claims considerable areas which are, in fact, occupied and cultivated by Arabs. Even were the title of the Government to these areas admitted, and it is in many cases disputed, it would not be possible to make these areas available for Jewish settlement, in view of their actual occupation by Arab cultivators and of the importance of making available additional land on which to place the Arab cultivators who are now landless.

The Provision of a margin available for settlement depends upon the progress made in increasing the productivity of the land already occupied.

16.   It now appears, in the light of the best available estimates, that the area of cultivable land in Palestine (excluding the Beer-Sheba region) is 6,544,00 dunams. This area is considerably less than had hitherto been estimated, previous official estimates being in the neighbourhood of 10 to 11 million dunams.

It also appears that while an area of at least 130 dunams is required to maintain a fellah family in a decent standard of life in the unirrigated tracts, the whole of the cultivable land in the country, excluding the area already in the hands of the Jews, would, were it divided among the existing Arab cultivators, provide an average holding of not more than 90 dunams. In order to provide an average holding of 130 dunams for all Arab cultivators, about 8 million dunams of cultivable land would be required.

It also appears that of the 86,980 rural Arab families in the villages, 29.4 per cent. are landless. It is not known how many of these are families who previously cultivated and have since lost their land. This is one point, among others, upon which, at present, it is not possible to speak with greater precision, but which will, it is hoped, be ascertained in the course of the Census which is to be taken next year.

17.   The condition of the Arab fellah leaves much to be desired, and a policy of land development is called for if an improvement in his conditions of life is to be effected.

The sole agencies which have pursued a consistent policy of land development have been the Jewish Colonisation organisations, public and private.

The Jewish settlers have had every advantage that

capital, science and organisation could give them. To these and to the energy of the settlers themselves their remarkable progress is due. On the other hand, the Arab population, while lacking the advantages enjoyed by the Jewish settlers, has, by the excess of births over deaths, increased with great rapidity, while the land available for its sustenance has decreased by about a million dunams. This area has passed into Jewish hands.

18.   Reference has been made to the energy evinced and the remarkable progress made in Jewish land settlement. It would be unjust to accept the contention, which has been advanced in the course of the controversy regarding relations between Jews and Arabs in Palestine, that the effect of Jewish settlement upon the Arab population has in all cases been detrimental to the interests of the Arabs. This is by no means wholly true, but it is necessary in considering this aspect of the problem to differentiate between colonisation by such bodies as the Palestine Jewish Colonisation Association (commonly known as the P.I.C.A.) and colonisation under Zionist auspices.

In so far as the past policy of the P.I.C.A. is concerned, there can be no doubt that the Arab has profited largely by the installation of the Colonies, and relations between the colonists and their Arab neighbours have in the past been excellent. The cases which are now quoted by the Jewish authorities in support of the contention that the effect of Jewish colonisation on the Arabs in the neighbourhood has been advantageous, are cases relating to Colonies established by the P.I.C.A. before colonisation financed from the Palestine Foundation Fund, which is the main financial instrument of the Jewish Agency, came into existence.

Some of the attempts which have been made to prove that Zionist colonisation has not had the effect of causing the previous tenants of land acquired to join the landless class have on examination proved to be unconvincing, if not fallacious.

19.   Moreover, the effect of Jewish colonisation on the existing population is very intimately affected by the conditions on which the various Jewish bodies hold, utilise and lease their land. It is provided by the Constitution of the Enlarged Jewish Agency, signed at Zürich on the 14th August, 1929 (Article 3 (d) and (e)), that the land acquired shall be held as the "inalienable property of the Jewish people," and that in "all the works or undertakings carried out

or furthered by the Agency, it shall be deemed to be a matter of principle that Jewish labour shall be employed." Moreover, by Article 23 of the draft lease, which it is proposed to execute in respect of all holdings granted by the Jewish National Fund, the lessee undertakes to execute all works connected with the cultivation of the holdings only with Jewish labour.   Stringent conditions are imposed to ensure the observance of this undertaking.

An undertaking binding settlers in the Colonies of the Maritime Plain to hire Jewish workmen only, whenever they may be obliged to hire help, is inserted in the Agreement for the repayment of advances made by the Palestine Foundation Fund.   Similar provision is contained in the Agreement for the Emek Colonies.

These stringent provisions are difficult to reconcile with the declaration at the Zionist Congress of 1921 of "the desire of the Jewish people to live with the Arab people in relations of friendship and mutual respect, and, together, with the Arab people, to develop the homeland common to both into a prosperous community which would ensure the growth of the peoples."

20.   The Jewish leaders have been perfectly frank in their justification of this policy.   The Executive of the General Federation of Jewish Labour, which exercises a very important influence on the direction of Zionist policy, has contended that such restrictions are necessary to secure the largest possible amount of Jewish immigration and to safeguard the standard of life of the Jewish labourer from the danger of falling to the lower standard of the Arab.

However logical such arguments may be from the point of view of a purely national movement, it must, nevertheless, be pointed out that they take no account of the provisions of Article 6 of the Mandate, which expressly requires that, in facilitating Jewish immigration and close settlement by Jews on the land, the Administration of Palestine must ensure that "the rights and position of other sections of the population are not prejudiced."

(2) Agricultural Development.

21.   As indicated in the immediately preceding paragraph, it is the duty of the Administration under the Mandate to ensure that the position of the "other sections of the population" is not prejudiced by Jewish immigration. Also, it is its duty under the Mandate to encourage close set-

tlement of the Jews on the land, subject always to the former condition.

22.   As a result of recent investigations, His Majesty's Government are satisfied that, in order to attain these objects, a more methodical agricultural development is called for with the object of ensuring a better use of the land.

23.   Only by the adoption of such a policy will additional Jewish agricultural settlement be possible consistently with the conditions laid down in Article 6 of the Mandate.   The result desired will not be obtained except by years of work.   It is for this reason fortunate that the Jewish organisations are in possession of a large reserve of land not yet settled or developed.   Their operations can continue without break, while more general steps of development, in the benefits of which Jews and Arabs can both share, are being worked out.   During this period, however, the control of all disposition of land must of necessity rest with the authority in charge of the development.   Transfers of land will be permitted only in so far as they do not interfere with the plans of that authority.   Having regard to the responsibilities of the Mandatory Power, it is clear that this authority must be the Palestine Administration.

24.   Among the problems which will have to be considered are those of irrigation, the co-ordination of development with the activities of the Department of Agriculture and other Government Departments, and the determination of their respective spheres of action so as to avoid friction and overlapping, and to obtain the greatest efficiency in co-ordinated effort.

Consideration must also be given to the protection of tenants by some form of occupancy right, or by other means, to secure them against ejectment or the imposition of excessive rental.

Closely associated with any development must be the acceleration of the work of settlement by the ascertainment of title and the registration of tenancies.   In this connection an important problem is presented by the large proportion of Arab village land which is held under the tenure-in-common known as mesha'a.   Nearly half of the Arab villages are held on mesha'a tenure and there is a consensus of opinion that this system is a great obstacle to the agricultural development of the Country.

The constitution of co-operative societies among the

fellahin appears to be an important preliminary to their advancement. The whole question has recently been under examination on behalf of the Palestine Government by an expert with great experience.

25.   The finances of Palestine have been severely strained by the necessity of providing for large increases in its security forces.   These increases have been deemed essential in the light of the events of the autumn of 1929, and it is not possible to forecast the time that must elapse before it will be thought safe to reduce expenditure on this account.   That must largely depend on the success of the policy now envisaged, and on the extent of the improvement in mutual relations between Arabs and Jews which His Majesty's Government hope will be one of its results.
    It is part of the general policy of His Majesty's Government that Palestine should be self-supporting.   The improvement of agricultural conditions contemplated will not only take time, but will involve considerable expenditure, though it is to be hoped that part of the outlay will prove to be recoverable.   His Majesty's Government are giving earnest consideration to the financial position which arises out of this situation, and steps are being taken to concert the necessary measures to give effect to their policy.

(3) *Immigration*.

26.   The whole system under which immigration into Palestine is controlled by the Administration has recently been most carefully examined, and in the month of May it was considered necessary by His Majesty's Government, whilst leaving undisturbed Jewish immigration in its various forms, to suspend the further issue of certificates for the admission of immigrants under the Labour Schedule — i.e., as employed persons (over and above the 950 already sanctioned) for the half year ending the 30th September, 1930, pending the result of this examination and the determination of future policy.   This examination has revealed certain weaknesses in the existing system.   It has been shown that under it there have been many cases of persons being admitted, who, if all the facts had been known, should not have received visas.   No effective Government control exists in regard to the selection of immigrants from abroad, with the result that there are no adequate safeguards against irregularities in connection with the issue of immigration certificates, and also against the immigration of undesirables.   A

further unsatisfactory feature is that a large number of
travellers, who enter Palestine with permission to remain
for a limited time, stay on without sanction. It is calculated
that the number of such cases during the last three years
amounted to 7,800. Another serious feature is the number of
persons who evade the frontier control.

In any attempt to devise adequate Government machinery for the control of immigration, account must be
taken of the important part at present played in connection
with Jewish immigration by the General Federation of
Jewish Labour. The influence of the General Federation is
far-reaching and its activities are manifold. It constitutes
an important factor within the World Zionist movement, and
at the last Zionist Congress more than a quarter of the total
number of delegates represented such Zionist circles, both
in Palestine and abroad, as are identified with the
Federation. The influence which the Federation is able to
exert upon immigrants is shown by the fact that its members
are not permitted to have recourse to the Courts of the
country in cases of dispute with another member. It has its
own Courts of First and Second Instance and its Labour High
Court, to which appeals from the subordinate Tribunals lie.
The Federation has adopted a policy which implies the introduction in Palestine of a new social order based on commu-
nal settlements and the principle of "self-labour" (i.e., that
each man should work for himself and avoid the employment of hired labourers). Where self-labour is impossible it
insists on the employment of Jewish labour exclusively by
all Jewish employers.

In view of its responsibilities under the Mandate, it is
essential that the Palestine Government, as the agent of the
Mandatory Power, should be the deciding authority in all
matters of policy relating to immigration, especially having
regard to its close relation to unemployment and land development policy. No adequate improvement in existing machinery can be devised unless a *modus vivendi* is established
between the Government on the one hand and the Jewish
Agency on the other, in regard to their respective functions, and full account must be taken of the influence exerted in the policy of the Agency by the General Federation
of Jewish labour.

27. As regards the relation of immigration to unemployment, great difficulties at present exist owing to the absence of efficient machinery for estimating the degree of
unemployment existing at any time. This is especially true

as regards the Arab section of the community. While no reliable statistics are available, sufficient evidence has been adduced to lead to the conclusion that there is at present a serious degree of Arab unemployment, and that Jewish unemployment likewise exists to an extent which constitutes a definitely unsatisfactory feature. It may be regarded as clearly established that the preparation of the Labour Schedule must depend upon the ascertainment of the total of unemployed in Palestine. It follows that the extent of that unemployment must be accurately determined, and His Majesty's Government will give serious consideration to devising machinery for this purpose. The economic capacity of the country to absorb new immigrants must therefore be judged with reference to the position of Palestine as a whole in regard to unemployment, and care must also be exercised in ascertaining that economic capacity, to make allowances for any demand for labour, which, owing to increased circulation of money connected with expenditure on development or for other causes, may be regarded as of a temporary character.

28.   Article 6 of the Mandate directs that the rights and position of the other sections of the population shall not be prejudiced by Jewish immigration. Clearly, if immigration of Jews results in preventing the Arab population from obtaining the work necessary for its maintenance, or if Jewish unemployment unfavourably affects the general labour position, it is the duty of the Mandatory Power under the Mandate to reduce, or, if necessary, to suspend, such immigration until the unemployed portion of the "other sections" is in a position to obtain work. It may here be remarked that in the light of the examination to which immigration and unemployment problems have been subjected, His Majesty's Government regard their action in the suspension of immigration under the Labour Schedule last May as fully justified.
It has been argued that the High Commissioner's approval of the issue of Immigration Certificates under the Labour Schedule implied that there was room for the admission of immigrants of the working class, and that, in consequence, His Majesty's Government, in suspending the issue of those certificates, must have been influenced by political considerations. This is not the case. In arriving at their decision to suspend the issue of the certificates, His Majesty's Government had in mind the opinions expressed in the Report of the Shaw Commission that there was a shortage of

land and that immigration should be more closely controlled. It was realised that these issues called for expert examination, but His Majesty's Government felt that, until they had been so examined, no steps should be taken which might aggravate an economic situation which in the opinion of the majority of the Shaw Commission, was already such as to afford ground for anxiety.

Any hasty decision in regard to more unrestricted Jewish immigration is to be strongly deprecated, not only from the point of view of the interests of the Palestine population as a whole, but even from the special point of view of the Jewish community. So long as widespread suspicion exists, and it does exist, amongst the Arab population, that the economic depression, under which they undoubtedly suffer at present, is largely due to excessive Jewish immigration, and so long as some grounds exist upon which this suspicion may be plausibly represented to be well founded, there can be little hope of any improvement in the mutual relations of the two races. But it is upon such improvement that the future peace and prosperity of Palestine must largely depend.

It is hoped that changes may be devised in the method of the preparation of the Labour Schedule which will tend to promote amicable relations between the Jewish authorities in Palestine and the Immigration Department. It is clearly desirable to establish closer co-operation and consultation between the Jewish authorities and the Government, and the closer and more cordial co-operation becomes, the easier it should be to arrive at an agreed Schedule based upon a thorough understanding, on both sides, of the economic needs of the country.

29. As has been shown in the foregoing paragraphs, the three problems of development, immigration and unemployment are closely inter-related, and upon the evolution of a policy which will take full account of these three factors must depend the future of Palestine. It is only in a peaceful and prosperous Palestine that the ideals of the Jewish National Home can in any sense be realised, and it is only by cordial co-operation between the Jews and the Arabs and the Government that prosperity can be secured.

The situation revealed by exhaustive examination of the various economic, political and social factors involved, makes it clear that Palestine has reached a critical moment in its development. In the past it may be said that the Government has left economic and social forces to operate with the minimum of interference or control, but it has become increasingly clear that such a policy can no longer continue. It is only the closest co-operation between the Government and the leaders of the Arab and Jewish communities that can prevent Palestine from drifting into a situation which would imperil, on the one hand, the devoted work of those who have sought to build up the Jewish National Home, and, on the other, the interests of the majority of the population who at present possess few resources of their own with which to sustain the struggle for existence. What is required is that both races should consent to live together and to respect each other's needs and claims. To the Arabs His Majesty's Government would appeal for a recognition of the facts of the situation, and for a sustained effort at co-operation in obtaining that prosperity for the country as a whole by which all will benefit. From the Jewish leaders, His Majesty's Government ask a recognition of the necessity for making some concessions on their side in regard to the independent and separatist ideals which have been developed in some quarters in connection with the Jewish National Home, and for accepting it as an active factor in the orientation of their policy that the general development of the country shall be carried out in such a way that the interests of the Arabs and Jews may each receive adequate consideration, with the object of developing prosperity throughout the country under conditions which will give no grounds for charges of partiality upon the one side or upon the other, but will permit of the Arab and Jewish communities developing in harmony and contentment.

The MacDonald Letter, 1931

The White Paper, and Lord Passfield himself, was virulently attacked by the Zionists, with Dr. Chaim Weizmann in the forefront. To show his opposition to the policy set forth within the "Statement of Policy" Weizmann resigned as president of the Jewish Agency. In a special cabinet committee meeting held a few days before the issuance of the White Paper Dr. Weizmann succinctly stated the Zionists' opposition:

If the obligation of the Mandatory is reduced to an obligation toward one hundred and seventy thousand people as against seven hundred thousand people, a small minority juxtaposed to a great majority, then of course everything else can perhaps be explained. *But the obligation of the Mandatory Power is toward the Jewish people* of which the one hundred and seventy thousand are merely the vanguard. I must take issue, as energetically as I can, with the formulation of the obligation of the Mandatory Power as an obligation toward *both* sections of the Palestine population.[1]

Source: *The Times*, Saturday, 14 February 1931.

[1] Chaim Weizmann. *Trial and Error: the Autobiography of Chaim Weizmann* , vol. 2 (Philadelphia: The Jewish Publication Society of America, 5709-1949) 334 (italics added).

In a letter to his wife of 22nd October Passfield wrote:

3) The Jewish hurricane continues. I see Felix Warburg (in U.S.) has resigned his Zionist posts. They seem to go wild with excitement and rage, on mere partisan telegraphic summaries and interpretations of a lengthy document. We are (i) putting *n o* limitations on continued colonisation, (ii) making no change as regards the previous limit on non-rural immigration and (iii) expressly and defiantly declaring we will carry out the Mandate, whatever the Arabs say or do. The Jews have therefore no *ground* of complaint against us. But we *do* negative the idea of a Jewish State, which the British Government has consistently done - and this (rather than a National Home *in* Palestine) is what so many of them want.[2]

As a result of the political furor Prime Minister MacDonald agreed to issue a public letter addressed to Weizmann explaining the White Paper. The wording of this letter was undertaken by a special cabinet committee in association with the Zionist leaders. Three days before its publication Passfield wrote in a private letter to a friend:

The Jews quibbled and fought over every sentence. [Arthur] Henderson (as Chairman of the Cabinet Committee) did his job about as well as it could have been done; but the position was very ticklish politically, and he *had* to get a statement which the Jews would accept, whilst not ignoring the High Commissioner with whom we were in telegraphic communication — and ˙not doing anything to incense the Arabs. ...

It has been a bad three months; and all the more vexatious because there was really nothing in the White Paper of October (which the Cabinet itself passed), to which the Jews can honestly object. The present letter to Dr Weizmann really takes nothing back, and contradicts nothing in the White Paper. But

---

[2] *The Letters of Sidney and Beatrice Webb*, ed. Norman MacKenzie, vol. 3 (Cambridge, Cambridge University Press, 1978) 335. Reprinted by permission of Cambridge University Press. (original emphasis).

Dr Weizmann saw fit in October to use it as a means of stirring the emotions of World Jewry, in order to revive the flow of donations — he has to raise £400,000 a year to keep the work in Palestine going — and the flow had very seriously fallen off owing to the American slump. Well, his scheme has had a partial and temporary success. He has got some money; how much we don't know, but certainly not enough to relieve him from anxiety.[3]

Dear Dr. Weizmann,

In order to remove certain misconceptions and misunderstandings which have arisen as to the policy of his Majesty's Government with respect to Palestine, as set forth in the White Paper of October, 1930, and which were the subject of a debate in the House of Commons on November 17, and also to meet certain criticisms put forward by the Jewish Agency, I have pleasure in forwarding you the following statement of our position, which will fall to be read as the authoritive interpretation of the White Paper on the matters with which this letter deals.

2. It has been said that the policy of his Majesty's Government involves a serious departure from the obligations of the Mandate as hitherto understood, that it misconceives the Mandatory obligations, and it foreshadows a policy which is inconsistent with the obligations of the Mandatory to the Jewish people.

UNDERTAKING OF THE MANDATE

3. His Majesty's Government did not regard it as necessary to quote *in extensio* the declarations of policy which have been previously made, but attention is drawn to the fact that, not only does the White Paper of 1930 refer to, and endorse, the White Paper of 1922, which has been accepted by the Jewish Agency, but it recognizes that the undertaking of the Mandate is an undertaking to the Jewish people, and not only to the Jewish population of Palestine. The White Paper placed in the foreground of its statement my speech in the House of Commons on April 3, 1930, in which I announced, in words which could not have been made more plain, that it was the intention of his Majesty's

---

[3] Ibid., vol. 2, 345-46.

Government to continue to administer Palestine in accordance with the terms of the Mandate as approved by the Council of the League of Nations. That position has been reaffirmed and again made plain by my speech in the House of Commons on November 17. In my speech on April 3 I used the following language:-

His Majesty's Government will continue to administer Palestine in accordance with the terms of the Mandate as approved by the Council of the League of Nations. This is an international obligation from which there can be no question of receding.

Under the terms of the Mandate his Majesty's Government are responsible for promoting the establishment in Palestine of a National Home for the Jewish people, it being clearly understood "that nothing shall be done which might prejudice the civil and religious rights of existing non-Jewish communities in Palestine or the rights and political status enjoyed by Jews in any other country."

A double undertaking is involved, to the Jewish people, on the one hand, and to the non-Jewish population of Palestine, on the other; and it is the firm resolve of his Majesty's Government to give effect, in equal measure, to both parts of the Declaration, and to do equal justice to all sections of the population of Palestine. That is a duty from which they will not shrink, and to the discharge of which they will apply all the resources at their command.

That declaration is in conformity not only with the articles, but also with the preamble of the Mandate, which is hereby explicitly reaffirmed.

4.   In carrying out the policy of the Mandate the Mandatory cannot ignore the existence of differing interests and viewpoints. These, indeed, are not in themselves irreconcilable, but they can only be reconciled if there is a proper realization that the full solution of the problem depends on an understanding between the Jews and the Arabs. Until that is reached consideration of balance must inevitably enter into the definition of policy.

5.   A good deal of criticism has been directed to the White Paper upon the assertion that it contains injurious allegations against the Jewish people and Jewish Labour organization. Any such intention on the part of his Majesty's Government is expressly disavowed. It is recognized that the

Jewish Agency have all along given willing cooperation in carrying out the policy of the Mandate, and that the constructive work done by the Jewish people in Palestine has had beneficial effects on the country as a whole. His Majesty's Government also recognize the value of the services of labour and trade union organization in Palestine, to which they desire to give every encouragement.

"CIVIL AND RELIGIOUS RIGHTS"

6.   A question has arisen as to the the meaning to be attached to the words "safeguarding the civil and religious rights of all inhabitants of Palestine, irrespective of race and religion," occurring in Article 2, and the words "ensuring that the rights and position of other sections of the population are not prejudiced," occurring in Article 6 of the Mandate. The words "safeguarding the civil and religious rights," occurring in Article 2, cannot be read as meaning that the civil and religious rights of individual citizens are to be unalterable. In the case of Suleiman Murra, to which reference has been made, the Privy Council, in construing these words of Article 2, said: "It does not mean ... that all the civil rights of every inhabitant of Palestine which existed at the date of the Mandate are to remain unaltered throughout its duration; for if this were to be a condition of the Mandatory jurisdiction, no effective legislation would be possible," The words, accordingly must be read in another sense, and the key to the true purpose and meaning of the sentence is to be found in the concluding words of the article: "irrespective of race and religion." These words indicate that, in respect of civil and religious rights, the Mandatory is not to discriminate between persons on the ground of religion or race, and this protective provision applies equally to Jews, Arabs, and all sections of the population.

7.   The words "rights and position of other sections of the population." occurring in Article 6, plainly refer to the non-Jewish community. These rights and position are not be be prejudiced, that is, are not to be impaired or made worse. The effect of the policy of immigration and settlement on the economic position of the non-Jewish community cannot be excluded from consideration. But the words are not be be read as implying that existing economic conditions in Palestine should be crystallized. On the contrary, the obligation to facilitate Jewish immigration and to en-

courage close settlement by Jews on the land remains a positive obligation of the Mandate, and it can be fulfilled without prejudice to the rights and position of other sections of the population of Palestine.

JEWISH SETTLEMENT

8.   We may proceed to the contention that the Mandate has been reinterpreted in a manner highly prejudicial to Jewish interests in the vital matters of land settlement and immigration.   It has been said that the policy of the White Paper would place an embargo upon immigration and would suspend, if not, indeed, terminate, the close settlement of the Jews on the land, which is a primary purpose of the Mandate.   In support of this contention particular stress has been laid upon the passage referring to State lands in the White Paper, which says that "it would not be possible to make these areas available for Jewish settlement in view of their actual occupation by Arab cultivators, and of the importance of making available additional land on which to place the Arab cultivators who are now landless."

9.   The language of this passage needs to be read in the light of the policy as a whole.   It is desirable to make it clear that the landless Arabs to whom it was intended to refer in the passage quoted were such Arabs as can be shown to have been displaced from the lands which they occupied in consequence of the lands passing into Jewish hands, and who have not obtained other holdings on which they can establish themselves, or other equally satisfactory occupation.   The number of such displaced Arabs must be a matter for careful inquiry.   It is to landless Arabs within this category that his Majesty's Government feel themselves under an obligation to facilitate their settlement upon the land. The recognition of this obligation in no way detracts from the larger purposes of development, which his Majesty's Government regards as the most effectual means of furthering the establishment of a national home for the Jews.

10.   In framing a policy of land settlement, it is essential that his Majesty's Government should take into consideration every circumstance that is relevant to the main purposes of the Mandate.   The area of cultivable land, the possibilities of irrigation, the absorptive capacity of the country in relation to immigration are all elements perti-

nent to the issues to be elucidated, and the neglect of any one of them would be prejudicial to the formulation of a just and stable policy.

A NEW INQUIRY

It is the intention of his Majesty's Government to institute an inquiry as soon as possible to ascertain, *inter alia*, what State and other lands are, or properly can be made, available for close settlement by Jews under reference to the obligation imposed upon the Mandatory by Article 6 of the Mandate. This inquiry will be comprehensive in its scope, and will include the whole land resources of Palestine. In the conduct of the inquiry provision will be made for all interests, whether Jewish or Arab, making such representations as it may be desired to put forward.

11. The question of the congestion among the fellaheen in the hill districts of Palestine is receiving the careful consideration of his Majesty's Government. It is contemplated that measures will be devised for the improvement and intensive development of the land, and for bringing into cultivation areas which hitherto may have remained uncultivated, and thereby securing to the fellaheen a better standard of living without, save in exceptional cases, having recourse to transfer.

12. In giving effect to the policy of land settlement, as contemplated in Article 11 of the Mandate, it is necessary, if disorganization is to be avoided and if the policy is to have a chance to succeed, that there should exist some centralized control of transactions relating to the acquisition and transfer of land during such interim period as may reasonably be necessary to place the development scheme upon a sure foundation. The power contemplated is regulative and not prohibitory, although it does involve a power to prevent transactions which are inconsistent with the tenor of the scheme. But the exercise of the power will be limited and in no respect arbitrary. In every case it will be conditioned by considerations as to how best to give effect to the purposes of the Mandate. Any control contemplated will be fenced with due safeguards to secure as little interference as possible with the free transfer of land. The centralized control will take effect as from such date only as the authority charged with the duty of carrying out the policy of land development shall begin to operate. The High Commissioner will, pending

the establishment of such centralized control, have full powers to take all steps necessary to protect the tenancy and occupancy rights, including the rights of squatters, throughout Palestine.

13. Further, the statement of policy of his Majesty's Government did not imply a prohibition of acquisition of additional land by Jews. It contains no such prohibition, nor is any such intended. What it does contemplate is such temporary control of land disposition and transfers as may be necessary not to impair the harmony and effectiveness of the scheme of land settlement to be undertaken. His Majesty's Government feel bound to point out that they alone of the Governments which have been responsible for the administration of Palestine since the acceptance of the Mandate have declared their definite intention to initiate an active policy of development which it is believed will result in substantial and lasting benefit to both Jews and Arabs.

IMMIGRATION

14. Cognate to this question is the control of immigration. It must, first of all, be pointed out that such control is not in any sense a departure from previous policy. From 1920 onwards, when the original Immigration Ordinance came into force, regulations for the control of immigration have been issued from time to time, directed to prevent elicit entry and to define and facilitate authorized entry. This right of regulation has at no time been challenged.

15. But the intention of his Majesty's Government appears to have been represented as being that "no further immigration of Jews is to be permitted as long as it might prevent any Arab from obtaining employment." His Majesty's Government never proposed to pursue such a policy. They were concerned to state that, in the regulation of Jewish immigration, the following principles should apply — namely, that "it is essential to ensure that the immigrants should not be a burden upon the people of Palestine as a whole, and that they should not deprive any section of the present population of their employment" (White Paper, 1922). In the one aspect his Majesty's Government have to be mindful of their obligations to facilitate Jewish immigration under suitable conditions, and to encourage close settlement of Jews on the land; in the other aspect they have to be equally mindful of their duty to ensure that no prejudice

results to the rights and position of the non-Jewish community. It is because of this apparent conflict of obligations
that his Majesty's Government have felt bound to emphasize
the necessity of the proper application of the absorptive capacity principle. That principle is vital to any scheme of
development, the primary purpose of which must be the
settlement both of Jews and of displaced Arabs upon the
land. It is for that reason that his Majesty's Government
have insisted, and are compelled to insist, that Government
control of immigration must be maintained and that immigration regulations must be properly applied. The considerations relevant to the limits of absorptive capacity are
purely economic considerations.

16. His Majesty's Government did not prescribe and
do not contemplate any stoppage or prohibition of Jewish
immigration in any of its categories. The practice of
sanctioning a "Labour Schedule" of wage-earning
immigrants will continue. In each case consideration will
be given to anticipated labour requirements for works
which, being dependent on Jewish or mainly Jewish capital,
would not be or would not have been undertaken unless
Jewish labour was made available. With regard to public and
municipal works falling to be financed out of public funds,
the claim of Jewish labour to a due share of the employment
available, taking into account Jewish contributions to public
revenue, shall be taken into consideration. As regards other
kinds of employment, it will be necessary in each case to
take into account the factors bearing upon the demand for
labour including the factor of unemployment among both
the Jews and the Arabs. Immigrants with prospects of
employment other than employment of a purely ephemeral
character will not be excluded on the sole ground that the
employment cannot be guaranteed to be of unlimited
duration.

JEWISH EMPLOYMENT

17. In determining the extent to which immigration
at any time may be permitted, it is necessary also to have regard to the declared policy of the Jewish Agency to the effect that in "all the works or undertakings carried out or
furthered by the Agency it shall be deemed to be a matter of
principle that Jewish labour shall be employed." His
Majesty's Government do not in any way challenge the right
of the Agency to formulate or approve and endorse such a

policy.   The principle of preferential and, indeed, exclusive employment of Jewish labour in Jewish organizations is a principle which the Jewish Agency are entitled to affirm. But it must be pointed out that if in consequence of this policy Arab labour is displaced or existing employment becomes aggravated, that is a factor in the situation to which the Mandatory is bound to have regard.

18.   His Majesty's Government desire to say finally, as they have repeatedly and unequivocally affirmed, that the obligations imposed upon the Mandatory, by its acceptance of the Mandate, are solemn international obligations, from which there is not now, nor has there been at any time, any intention to depart.   To the tasks imposed by the Mandate his Majesty's Government have set their hand, and they will not withdraw it.   But if their efforts are to be successful there is need for cooperation, confidence, readiness on all sides to appreciate the difficulties and complexities of the problem, and, above all, there must be a full and unqualified recognition   that no solution can be satisfactory or permanent which is not based upon justice, both to the Jewish people and to the non-Jewish community of Palestine.

I am, &c
[Signed] J. Ramsay MacDonald

10 Downing Street
Feb. 13.

Peel Commission Report, 1937

Despite Lord Passfield's claim that the Prime Minister's letter of interpretation did not change a thing in his "Statement of Policy," it was received with satisfaction by Dr. Chaim Weizmann, although he was attacked by the Zionist Congress for accepting it in lieu of a new White Paper. He later wrote:

But whether I was right or not in my acceptance may be judged by a simple fact: it was under MacDonald's letter to me that the change came about in the Government's attitude, and in the attitude of the Palestine administration, which enabled us to make the magnificent gains of the ensuing years. It was under MacDonald's letter that Jewish immigration into Palestine was permitted to reach figures like forty thousand for 1934 and sixty-two thousand for 1935, figures undreamed of in 1930. [Vladimir] Jabotinsky, the extremist, testifying before the Shaw Commission,

Source: Great Britain. Parliamentary Papers. *Palestine Royal Commission Report. Presented by the Secretary of State for the Colonies to Parliament by Command of His Majesty, July, 1937.* London: His Majesty's Stationery Office, 1937). Cmd. 5479. The text of the document reproduced are the recommendations to be found on pages 370-96. Reprinted by permission of the Controller of Her Majesty's Stationery Office.

had set thirty thousand a year as a satisfactory figure.[1]

Furthermore, he claims that he was specifically consulted upon the appointment of the new high commissioner for Palestine.

The six year's immediately following the issuance of the 1930 White Paper witnessed other areas of the Near East coming out from under mandate rule, or promises made for independence: by 1929 Trans-Jordan had already received representative institutions and the Arabs there enjoyed a certain measure of independence; the Mandate over Iraq was replaced by a treaty in 1932; in 1936 a treaty was finally signed between Britain and Egypt allowing for the establishment of the monarchy; and even the French had concluded a treaty (although it was never ratified) with the Syrians in that same year designed to bring an end to the Mandate. Palestine, however, remained without any representative body and still under military occupation. In November 1935, the disparate Arab parties within the country temporarily united in an attempt to pressure the government to grant some semblance of democratic leadership, prohibit all further transfers of land to the Jews, and cease all further Jewish immigration until the absorptive capacity of the country could be determined. All of these demands were rejected. In April 1936 the collective leadership, terming itself the "Arab Higher Committee," under the leadership of the more radical Grand Mufti of Jerusalem, Amin al-Husaini called for a general strike throughout the country. This, unfortunately, was accompanied by violence. The leaders of the surrounding states now began to interest themselves in what had certainly become the "Palestine Problem" and appealed to the committee to call off the strike in return for their

---

[1] Chaim Weizmann. *Trial and Error; the Autobiography of Chaim Weizmann*, vol. 2 (Philadelphia: The Jewish Publication Society of America, 5709-1949) 335.

attempt   to   mediate   with   the   British
Government.   In response, the strike was ended
the   following   October.   Stung   by   the
widespread   nature   of   the   strike,   the   government in London decided in May to send yet another   commission   of   inquiry   in   an   attempt   to
uncover   the   reasons   for   the   outbreak   and   to
make   recommendations   for   the   settlement   of
the "Problem."   A six-member committee was
appointed   under   the   chairmanship   of   Lord
Peel, twice Secretary of State for India, to investigate   the   situation   after   the   strike   had
ended.   The   commissioners   arrived   in
Jerusalem   and   began   their   hearings   on   12
November.   The resultant   report, completed on
22 June   and published the following 7 July
1937, is   the most detailed examination of the
situation   in   Palestine   attempted;   within   the
first 369 pages virtually every aspect of life
was   discussed,   the   remaining   27   pages   [those
reprinted   here]   are   devoted   to   their   radical   solution — partition.
        Within   this   report   an   official   govern-
ment   body   finally   admitted   for   the   first   time
that   which   had   been   predicted   by   the   King-
Crane   Commission   in   1919:   "This   conflict   was
inherent   in   the   situation   from   the   outset.   The
terms   of   the   Mandate   tended   to   confirm   it."
[page   371].

CHAPTER XX.

THE FORCE OF CIRCUMSTANCES.

        1.   Before submitting the proposals we have to offer
for its drastic treatment we will briefly restate the problem
of Palestine.

        2.   Under the stress of the World War the British
Government made promises to Arabs and Jews in order to
obtain their support.   On the strength of those promises both
parties formed certain expectations.

3.   The application to Palestine of the Mandate System in general and of the specific Mandate in particular implied the belief that the obligations thus undertaken towards the Arabs and the Jews respectively would prove in course of time to be mutually compatible owing to the conciliatory effect on the Palestinian Arabs of the material prosperity which Jewish immigration would bring to Palestine as a whole.   That belief has not been justified, and we see no hope of its being justified in the future.

4.   On that account it might conceivably be argued that Britain is now entitled to renounce its obligations.   But we have no doubt that the British people would repudiate any such suggestion.   The spirit of good faith forbids it.   And quite apart from past commitments we have a present duty to discharge.   If there had been no promises or expectations, if there were no Mandate, the existing circumstances in Palestine would still demand the most strenuous efforts we could make to deal with them.   We are responsible for the welfare of the country.   Its government is in our hands.   We are bound to strive to the utmost to do justice and make peace.

5.   What are the existing circumstances?
An irrepressible conflict has arisen between two national communities within the narrow bounds of one small country.   About 1,000,000 Arabs are in strife, open or latent, with some 400,000 Jews.   There is no common ground between them.   The Arab community is predominantly Asiatic in character, the Jewish community predominantly European.   They differ in religion and in language.   Their cultural and social life, their ways of thought and conduct, are as incompatible as their national aspirations.   These last are the greatest bar to peace.   Arabs and Jews might possibly learn to live and work together in Palestine if they would make a genuine effort to reconcile and combine their national ideals and so build up in time a joint or dual nationality.   But this they cannot do.   The War and its sequel have inspired all Arabs with the hope of reviving in a free and united Arab world the traditions of the Arab golden age.   The Jews similarly are inspired by their historic past.   They mean to show what the Jewish nation can achieve when restored to the land of its birth.   National assimilation between Arabs and Jews is thus ruled out.   In the Arab picture the Jews could only occupy the place they occupied in Arab Egypt or Arab Spain.   The Arabs would be as much outside

the Jewish picture as the Canaanites in the old land of Israel. The National Home, as we have said before, cannot be half-national.   In   these   circumstances   to   maintain   that Palestinian citizenship has any more meaning is a mis-chievous pretence.   Neither Arab nor Jew has any sense of service to a single State.

6.   This conflict was inherent in the situation from the outset.   The terms of the Mandate tended to confirm it.   If the Government had adopted a more rigorous and consistent policy it might have repressed the conflict for a time, but it could not have resolved it.

7.   The conflict has grown steadily more bitter.   It has been marked by a series of five Arab outbreaks, culminating in the rebellion of last year.   In the earlier period hostility to the Jews was not widespread among the *fellaheen*.   It is now general.   The first three outbreaks, again, were directed only against the Jews.   The last two were directed against the Government as well.

8.   This intensification of the conflict will continue. The estranging force of conditions inside Palestine is growing year by year.   The educational systems, Arab and Jewish, are schools of nationalism, and they have only ex-isted for a short time.   Their full effect on the rising gen-eration has yet to be felt.   And patriotic "youth-movements", so familiar a feature of present-day politics in other coun-tries of Europe or Asia, are afoot in Palestine.   As each com-munity grows, moreover, the rivalry between them deepens. The more numerous and prosperous and better-educated the Arabs become, the more insistent will be their demand for national independence and the more bitter their hatred of the obstacle that bars the way to it.   As the Jewish National Home grows older and more firmly rooted, so will grow its self-confidence and political ambition.

9.   The conflict is primarily political, though the fear of economic subjection to the Jews is also in Arab minds. The Mandate, it is supposed, will terminate sooner or later. The Arabs would hasten the day, the Jews retard it, for obvi-ous reasons in each case.   Meanwhile the whole situation is darkened by uncertainty as to the future.   The conflict, in-deed, is as much about the future as about the present.   Every intelligent Arab and Jew is forced to ask the question "Who in the end will govern Palestine?"   This uncertainty is

doubtless aggravated by the fact that Palestine is a mandated territory; but, in the light of nationalist movements elsewhere, we do not think the situation would be very different if Palestine had been a British Colony.

10.   Meantime the "external factors" will continue to play the part they have played with steadily increasing force from the beginning.   On the one hand, Saudi Arabia, the Yemen, 'Iraq and Egypt are already recognized as sovereign states, and Trans-Jordan as an "independent government."   In less than three years' time Syria and the Lebanon will attain their national sovereignty.   The claim of the Palestinian Arabs to share in the freedom of all Asiatic Arabia will thus be reinforced.   Before the War they were linked for centuries past with Syria and the Lebanon.   They already exceed the Lebanese in numbers.   That they are as well qualified for self-government as the Arabs of neighbouring countries has been admitted.

11.   On the other hand, the hardships and anxieties of the Jews in Europe are not likely to grow less in the near future.   The pressure on Palestine will continue and might at any time be accentuated.   The appeal of the good faith and humanity of the British people will lose none of its force. The Mandatory will be urged unceasingly to admit as many Jews into Palestine as the National Home can provide with a livelihood and to protect them when admitted from Arab attacks.

12.   Thus, for internal and external reasons, it seems probable that the situation, bad as it now is, will grow worse. The conflict will go on, the gulf between Arabs and Jews will widen.

13.   It remains to consider the position of the third party involved in the matter -- the Mandatory Power and its agents in Palestine.   The Government of Palestine is of the Crown Colony type, unsuitable in normal circumstances for governing educated Arabs or democratic Jews.   But it cannot evolve, as it has elsewhere evolved, into a system of self-government, since there is no such system which could ensure justice both to the Arabs and to the Jews or in which both the Arabs and the Jews would agree to participate.   The establishment of a Legislative Council or even of an enlarged Advisory Council in which both races would co-operate is thus impracticable.   Nor are other methods of con-

sultation and collaboration with the representatives of both races feasible. Jewish co-operation, it is true, is required by the Mandate, and is forthcoming sometimes to an embarrassing extent. But Arab co-operation, in any regular and continuous form, is unobtainable. Thus a bureaucratic Government must continue in being, unmodified by any representative institutions on a national scale, and unable to dispel the conflicting grievances of the dissatisfied and irresponsible communities it governs. Nor will the Government be able to count on any inborn sense of allegiance to the Crown. It is the national leaders, not the Mandatory Government, who make the first claim on the loyalty of their compatriots.

14. In these circumstances, we are convinced that peace, order and good government can only be maintained in Palestine for any length of time by a rigorous system of repression. Throughout this Report we have been careful not to overstate the facts as we see them: but understatement is no less reprehensible; and we should be failing in our duty if we said anything to encourage a hopeful outlook for the future peace of Palestine under the existing system or anything akin to it. The optimism which naturally prevailed at the outset of the enterprise was chilled by the series of Arab outbreaks, but never extinguished. In each case it soon revived, and in each case it proved false. The lesson is plain, and nobody, we think, will now venture to assert that the existing system offers any real prospect of reconciliation between the Arabs and the Jews. Hence the Government are faced with the unpleasant necessity of maintaining security-services at a very high cost, with the result that they are unable to improve and expand, and may even have to curtail, the services directed to "the well-being and development" of the population which, in the words of the Covenant, constitute their "sacred trust". If "disturbances", moreover, should recur on a similar scale to that of last year's rebellion, the cost of military operations must soon exhaust the revenues of Palestine and ultimately involve the British Treasury to an incalculable extent. The moral objections to maintaining a system of government by constant repression are self-evident. Nor is there any need to emphasize the undesirable reactions of such a course of policy on opinion outside Palestine.

15. And the worst of it is that such a policy leads nowhere. However vigorously and consistently maintained,

it will not solve the problem. It will not allay, it will exacerbate the quarrel between the Arabs and the Jews. The establishment of a single self-governing Palestine will remain just as impracticable as it is now. It is not easy to pursue the dark path of repression without seeing daylight at the end of it.

16.   Those, in our judgment, are the circumstances which Your Majesty's Government have to face in Palestine. We do not, of course, mean to suggest by anything we have said that the British people would flinch from bearing the burden of governing Palestine under the existing system if they were in honour bound to bear it. They lack neither the power nor the will. But they would be justified in asking if there is no other way in which their duty can be done.

17.   Nor do we suggest that the obligations Britain undertook towards the Arabs and the Jews some twenty years ago have lost in moral or legal weight through what has happened since. The trouble is that they have proved irreconcilable; and, as far ahead as we can see, they must continue to conflict. To put it in one sentence, we cannot — in Palestine as it now is —both concede the Arab claim to self-government and secure the establishment of the Jewish National Home. And this conflict between the two obligations is the more unfortunate because each of them, taken separately, accords with British sentiment and British interest. On the one hand, the application of the Mandate System to Arab Palestine as a means of advancement to self-government was in harmony with British principles -- the same principles as have been put into practice since the War in different circumstances in India, "Iraq and Egypt. British public opinion is wholly sympathetic with Arab aspirations towards a new age of unity and prosperity in the Arab world. Conversely, the task of governing without the consent or even the acquiescence of the governed is one for which, we believe, the British people have little heart. On the other hand, there is a strong British tradition of friendship with the Jewish people. Nowhere have Jews found it easier to live and prosper than in Britain. Nowhere is there a more genuine desire to do what can be done to help them in their present difficulties. Nowhere, again, was Zionism better understood before the War or given such practical proofs of sympathy. From the earliest days of the British connexion with India and beyond, the peace of the Middle East has been a cardinal principle of our foreign policy; and for the

maintenance of that peace British statesmanship can show
an almost unbroken record of friendship with the Arabs.   It
is no less desirable now than it has always been that this
friendship should not be impaired.   On the other hand, it is
clearly a British interest to retain, as far as may be, the
confidence of the Jewish people wherever they are.   We val-
ued it highly in the War and we cannot disdain it in peace.

18.   In these last considerations lies a final argument
for seeking a way out, at almost any cost, from the existing
deadlock in Palestine.   For a continuance or rather an ag-
gravation — for this is what continuance will be — of the
present situation cannot be contemplated without the
gravest misgivings.   It will mean constant unrest and dis-
turbance in peace and potential danger in the event of war.
It will mean a steady decline in our prestige.   It will mean
the gradual alienation of two peoples who are traditionally
our friends: for already the Arabs of Palestine have been
antagonized and the patience of their kinsmen throughout
the Arab world is being strained; and already the Jews, particularly, we understand, in the United States, are questioning the sincerity with which we are fulfilling the promises
we made and suggesting that negligence or weakness on our
part is the real cause of all the trouble.   That is a state of affairs which, we submit, must be stopped from going on and
getting worse if there is any just and practicable means of
stopping it.

19.   Manifestly the problem cannot be solved by giving either the Arabs or the Jews all they want.   The answer
to the question "Which of them in the end will govern
Palestine?" must surely be "Neither".   We do not think that
any fair-minded statesman would suppose, now that the hope
of harmony between the races has proved untenable, that
Britain ought either to hand over to Arab rule 400,000 Jews,
whose entry into Palestine has been for the most part facilitated by the British Government and approved by the League
of Nations; or that, if the Jews should become a majority, a
million or so of Arabs should be handed over to their rule.
But, while neither race can justly rule all Palestine, we see
no reason why, if it were practicable, each race should not
rule part of it.

20.   No doubt the idea of Partition as a solution of the
problem has often occurred to students of it, only to be dis-
carded.   There are many who would have felt an instinctive

dislike to cutting up the Holy Land.   The severance of Trans-Jordan, they would have thought, from historic Palestine was bad enough.   On that point we would suggest that there is little moral value in maintaining the political unity of Palestine at the cost of perpetual hatred, strife and blood-shed, and that there is little moral injury in drawing a polit-ical line through Palestine if peace and goodwill between the peoples on either side of it can thereby in the long run be attained.   Others may have felt that Partition would be a confession of failure.   One of the finest and most character-istic features of the British Commonwealth, they have   ar-gued, has been the manner in which the conflicting claims of nationality have been reconciled within its borders; and the hope of achieving a similar result in Palestine should not   lightly be abandoned.   To that we would reply that, where the conflict of nationalities has been overcome and unity achieved — in Britain itself, in Canada, in South Africa — one of the parties concerned was English or British, and that, where that has not been so, as in the schism between the Northern and Southern Irish or between Hindus and Moslems in India, the quarrel, though it is centuries old, has not yet been composed.   Others, again, if they thought of Partition, dismissed it, no doubt, as impossible.   The practical difficulties seemed too great.   And great they unquestionably are.   The closer the question is examined, the clearer they stand out.   We do not underestimate them.   They cannot be brushed aside.   Nevertheless, when one faces up to them, those difficulties do not seem so insuperable as the difficul-ties inherent in the continuance of the Mandate or in any other alternative arrangement which has been proposed to us or which we ourselves could devise.   Partition seems to of-fer at least a chance of ultimate peace.   We can see none in any other plan.

CHAPTER XXI.

CANTONISATION.

1.   The political division of Palestine could be effected in   a   less   final   and   thorough-going   manner   than   by Partition.   It could be divided as federal States are divided into provinces or cantons; and this method has been so often mentioned   and   so   ably   advocated   under   the   name   of "Cantonisation" as a means of solving the Palestine problem

that it is incumbent on us to discuss it before setting out the plan for Partition which we ourselves have to propose.

2.   The essence of the Cantonisation scheme is, in the words of one of its principal advocates,

> "that areas should be officially defined within which Jewish acquisition of land and close settlement would be permitted and encouraged in discharge of the positive obligation under the Mandate regarding the National Home, and without which the land would be reserved for the needs of the indigenous population."[*]

3.   The scheme may be formulated in a variety of ways; but in general it envisages the division of Palestine into a Jewish and an Arab canton (the former corresponding to the areas of densest Jewish settlement -- more particularly the plain of Esdraelon, the coastal plain north of Tel Aviv and the old-established settlements centred on Rishon le Tsiyon and Rehovot), while the Holy Places of Jerusalem and Bethlehem with the port of Haifa would be retained in enclaves under direct Mandatory administration. It has been proposed that the area round Tiberias, Safad and Huleh might constitute a third "mixed" canton.   The Arab canton, it is suggested, might embrace not only the predominantly Arab areas of Palestine, proper, but also the whole of the present territory of Trans-Jordan.

4.   It is contemplated that each canton would have its own Government, completely autonomous in such matters as public works, health, education and general administration (including control of land sales and immigration), while the central (Mandatory) Government, with the assistance presumably of advice from representatives of the cantons, would retain control over such matters as foreign relations, defence, customs, railways, posts and telegraphs and the like, and would continue to collect customs and postal and

----

[*] Cantonisation: a Plan for Palestine, by Mr. Archur Cust, Journal of the Royal Central Asian Society, Vol. XXIII, page 206. [original footnote].

any other federal revenues.   Choice of official languages would be left to the cantons.

5.   On behalf of such an arrangement it is claimed that it would solve the three major problems of land, immigration and self-government.   There would, of course, be many difficult points to settle under each of these heads, but it can be argued that the scheme would give the Jews in their canton the right to buy as much land as they wished (subject no doubt to certain safeguards in the interests of existing non-Jewish owners) and to admit as many immigrants as they themselves determined, while the Arab canton within its own boundaries would be free to impose any restrictions it pleased on the further extension of Zionist settlement.   Each canton would attain self-government in all but the "federal" sphere.

6.   As against those apparent advantages there are certain obvious difficulties in the scheme.   In the first place, the drafting of federal constitutions is never easy. Complicated questions are involved in the structure of the central government and the division of function between it and the component units.   There are constant dangers of overlapping and of rival claims on the same field of authority.   In "cantonised" Switzerland and most other federations, federation was the act of a number of separate units which bound themselves together for the furtherance of common objects.   In such federations the community of interest or tradition which has supplied the motive for union will also supply that element of reasonableness and goodwill by which compromises may be arranged and friction overcome. In Palestine no such element is present.   The "interference" of the central Government would always be resented by both Arabs and Jews and, we fear, wherever possible hindered, as an alien and unwanted intrusion.

7.   Difficulties would arise, in particular, in the financial relations between the central Government and the cantons.   Whether in the distribution between the cantons of an excess of federal revenue or in the collection of contributions towards a federal deficit every assessment would give rise to fierce argument and bitter recrimination.   The financial consequences, moreover, of unfettered Jewish control of immigration into the Jewish canton might be extremely embarrassing to the federal Government, called upon to provide federal services for a population increasing

at a far more rapid rate than what it might itself consider reasonable. Thus Cantonisation, though it would mitigate the difficulties caused by Jewish immigration, would by no means eliminate them. They would still have to be considered to some extent by the Mandatory Government at the centre, and would keep alive the feud between Arabs and Jews. Only, in fact, by Partition can the problem of immigration be solved.

8. There is another drawback in the present situation which Cantonisation would do little or nothing to remedy. We have pointed out in Chapter VII how difficult and costly is the task of maintaining law and order and providing public security in Palestine. It would prove impossible, we think, to delegate that duty to the cantonal Government except to a limited extent. The major responsibility for keeping the peace would still fall on the Mandatory Government.

9. In any scheme of dividing Palestine the primary difficulty lies in the fact that no line can be drawn which would separate all the Arabs from all the Jews. Both under Cantonisation and under Partition a minority of each race remains in an area controlled by a majority of the other. That is the cardinal problem, and for its effective treatment the boldest and most far-seeing statesmanship is needed. But the sort of measures which, as we shall explain in the next chapter, ought in our view to be adopted, would not be worth the hardship and the cost they would entail unless they opened up the prospect of a final and lasting settlement of the Palestine problem. And that, we believe, Partition does, and Cantonisation manifestly does not.

10. For Cantonisation does not settle the question of national self-government. Cantonal autonomy would not satisfy for a moment the demands of Arab nationalism; it would not raise the status of Palestinian Arabs to the level of that enjoyed or soon to be enjoyed by Arabs in the neighbouring countries. Nor would it give the Jews the full freedom they desire to build up their National Home in their own way at their own pace, nor offer them the prospect of realizing on a small territorial scale all that Zionism means. And in the background, still clouding and disturbing the situation from year to year, still intensifying the antagonism between the races, would remain the old uncertainty as to the future destiny of Palestine.

11.   Cantonisation, in sum, presents most, if not all, of the difficulties presented by Partition without Partition's one supreme advantage — the possibility it offers of eventual peace.

CHAPTER XXII.

A PLAN OF PARTITION.

1.   We return, then, to Partition as the only method we are able to propose for dealing with the root of the trouble.

2.   At the time of our appointment, while the gravity of the situation in Palestine was to some extent, though not to its full extent, appreciated in this country, we think that the continuance of the Mandate was generally taken for granted, and our terms of reference implied the hope that we should be able to make recommendations which, if adopted, would in our opinion make it possible to bring about a lasting settlement without abandoning the Mandate.   But, as our inquiry proceeded, we became more and more persuaded that, if the existing Mandate continued, there was little hope of lasting peace in Palestine, and at the end we were convinced that there was none.   It was   clear to us that only drastic methods of dealing with the problem offered any prospect of success and that one such method, very difficult though it evidently was, should not be regarded as impossible.   In those circumstances we felt that we should be failing in our duty if we did no more than demonstrate, as we have tried to do in earlier chapters of this Report, that the situation in Palestine has reached a deadlock.   We believe that Your Majesty's Government would wish us to submit to them any suggestions we may be in a position to make as to how that deadlock might possibly be overcome.   It is true that the bulk of the evidence we have heard was not directly concerned with Partition, but in view of the fact that most of it was relevant, directly or indirectly, for forming a judgment on that issue, and in the light of other information we have obtained as to past and present conditions in Palestine, we feel justified in recommending that Your Majesty's Government should take the appropriate steps for the termination of the present Mandate on the basis of Partition.

3.   While we do not think Your Majesty's Government
would expect us to embark on the further protracted inquiry
which would be needed for working out a scheme of
Partition in full detail, it would be idle to put forward the
principle of Partition and not to give it any concrete shape.
Clearly we must show that an actual plan can be devised
which meets the main requirements of the case.   There seem
to us to be three essential features of such a plan.   It must be
practicable.   It must conform to our obligations.   It must do
justice to the Arabs and the Jews.

1. A Treaty System.

4.   The Mandate for Palestine should terminate and be
replaced by a Treaty System in accordance with the precedent set in Iraq and Syria.

5.   A new Mandate for the Holy Places should be instituted to fulfil the purposes defined in Section 2 below.

6.   Treaties of Alliance should be negotiated by the
Mandatory with the Government of Trans-Jordan and the
representatives of the Arabs of Palestine on the one hand
and with the Zionist Organisation on the other.   These
Treaties would declare that, within as short a period as may
be convenient, two sovereign independent States would be
established — the one an Arab State, consisting of Trans-
Jordan united with that part of Palestine which lies to the
east and south of a frontier such as we suggest in Section 3
below; the other a Jewish State consisting of that part of
Palestine which lies to the north and west of that frontier.

7.   The Mandatory would undertake to support any requests for admission to the League of Nations which the
Governments of the Arab and the Jewish States might make
in accordance with Article I of the Covenant.

8.   The Treaties would include strict guarantees for the
protection of minorities in each State, and the financial and
other provisions to which reference will be made in subsequent Sections.

9.   Military Conventions would be attached to the
Treaties, dealing with the maintenance of naval, military
and air forces, the upkeep and use of ports, roads and railways, the security of the oil pipe line and so forth.

2. The Holy Places.

10.   The partition of Palestine is subject to the overriding necessity of keeping the sanctity of Jerusalem and Bethlehem inviolate and of ensuring free and safe access to them for all the world.   That, in the fullest sense of the mandatory phrase, is "a sacred trust of civilization" — a trust on behalf not merely of the peoples of Palestine but of multitudes in other lands to whom those places, one or both, are Holy Places.

11.   A new Mandate, therefore, should be framed with the execution of this trust as its primary purpose.   An enclave should be demarcated extending from a point north of Jerusalem to a point south of Bethlehem, and access to the sea should be provided by a corridor extending to the north of the main road and to the south of the railway, including the towns of Lydda and Ramle, and terminating at Jaffa.

12.   We regard the protection of the Holy Places as a permanent trust, unique in its character and purpose, and not contemplated by Article 22 of the Covenant of the League of Nations.   We submit for consideration that, in order to avoid misunderstanding, it might frankly be stated that this trust will only terminate if and when the League of Nations and the United States desire it to do so, and that, while it would be the trustee's duty to promote the well-being and development of the local population concerned, it is not intended that in course of time they should stand by themselves as a wholly self-governing community.

13.   Guarantees as to the rights of the Holy Places and free access thereto (as provided in Article I3 of the existing Mandate), as to transit across the mandated area, and as to non-discrimination in fiscal, economic and other matters should be maintained in accordance with the principles of the Mandate System.   But the policy of the Balfour Declaration would not apply; and no question would arise of balancing Arab against Jewish claims or *vice versa*.   All the inhabitants of the territory would stand on an equal footing. The only "official language" would be that of the Mandatory Administration.   Good and just government without regard for sectional interests would be its basic principle.

14.   We think it would accord with Christian sentiment in the world at large if Nazareth and the Sea of Galilee (Lake

Tiberias) were also covered by this Mandate. We recommend that the Mandatory should be entrusted with the administration of Nazareth and with full powers to safeguard the sanctity of the waters and shores of Lake Tiberias.

15. The Mandatory should similarly be charged with the protection of religious endowments and of such buildings, monuments and places in the Arab and Jewish States as are sacred to the Jews and the Arabs respectively.

16. For the upkeep of the Mandatory Government, a certain revenue should be obtainable, especially from the large and growing urban population in its charge, both by way of customs-duties and by direct taxation; but it might prove insufficient for the normal cost of the administration. In that event, we believe that, in all the circumstances, Parliament would be willing to vote the money needed to make good the deficit.

3. The Frontier.

17. The natural principle for the Partition of Palestine is to separate the areas in which the Jews have acquired land and settled from those which are wholly or mainly occupied by Arabs. As shown in Map No. 4 at the end of this Report, the Jewish lands and colonies are mostly to be found in the/Maritime Plain between Al Majdal and Mount Carmel, in the neighbourhood of Haifa, in the Plain of Esdraelon and the Valley of Jezreel, and in the east of Galilee, i.e., south of Tiberias, on the shores of the Lake, near Safad, and in the Huleh Basin. The rest of Galilee[*] and the northern part of the plain of Acre are almost wholly in Arab occupation. So also is the central hill-country of old Samaria and Judaea — except for Jerusalem and its vicinity. The towns of Nablus, Jenin and Tulkaram, the last an outpost on the edge of the Maritime Plain, are centres of Arab nationalism. Except in and near Jerusalem and at Hebron, there are practically no Jews between Jenin and Beersheba. This Arab block extends eastwards to the River Jordan between the

---

[*]

We use the term "Galilee" to include the Sub-Districts of Acre, Safad, Tiberias and Nazareth. [original footnote].

Dead Sea and Beisan. In the area stretching south and south-east of Beersheba to the Egyptian frontier, the Jews have bought some isolated blocks of land but the population is entirely Arab.

18. This existing separation of the area of Jewish land and settlement from that of wholly or mainly Arab occupation seems to us to offer a fair and practicable basis for Partition, provided that, in accordance with the spirit of our obligations, (I) a reasonable allowance is made with the boundaries of the Jewish State for the growth of population and colonization, and (2) reasonable compensation is given to the Arab State for the loss of land and revenue. This last is one of the reasons we give in paragraph 23 below for suggesting the payment of a subvention by the Jewish State to the Arab State in the event of Partition coming into force.

19. Any proposal for Partition would be futile if it gave no indication, however rough, as to how the most vital question in the whole matter might be determined. With the information at our command, we are not in a position to assert that the proposal we have to make in this matter is the only solution of an obviously difficult problem. But as one solution of it, which in our judgment would be both practicable and just, we submit the following frontier, based on the principle stated above. It is not possible for us to draw a precise line: for that purpose we would recommend the appointment of a Frontier Commission.

20. Starting from Ras an Naqura, it follows the existing northern and eastern frontier of Palestine to Lake Tiberias and crosses the Lake to the outflow of the River Jordan whence it continues down the river to a point a little north of Beisan. It then cuts across the Beisan Plain and runs along the southern edge of the Valley of Jezreel and across the Plain of Esdraelon to a point near Megiddo, whence it crosses the Carmel ridge in the neighbourhood of the Megiddo road. Having thus reached the Maritime Plain, the line runs southwards down its eastern edge, curving west to avoid Tulkarm, until it reaches the Jerusalem-Jaffa corridor near Lydda. South of the Corridor it continues down the edge of the Plain to a point about I0 miles south of Rehovot, whence it turns west to the sea.*

---

*

See Map No. 8 [not included in this collection].

21.   In terms of the present administrative divisions of Palestine this frontier would mean the inclusion in the Jewish Area of the Sub-Districts of Acre, Safad, Tiberias, Nazareth and Haifa and parts of the Sub-Districts of Jenin, Tulkarm, Beisan, Jaffa and Ramle; and the inclusion in the Arab Area of the Sub-Districts of Nablus, Ramallah, Jericho, Hebron, Gaza and Beersheba, and parts of the Sub-Districts of Beisan, Jenin, Tulkarm, Jaffa, Ramle, Jerusalem and Bethlehem.

22.   We make the following observations and recommendations with regard to the proposed frontier and to questions arising from it:--

(i) No frontier can be drawn which separates all Arabs and Arab-owned land from all Jews and Jewish-owned land.

(ii) The Jews have purchased substantial blocks of land in the Gaza Plain and near Beersheba and obtained options for the purchase of other blocks in this area. The proposed frontier would prevent the utilization of those lands for the southward expansion of the Jewish National Home. On the other hand, the Jewish lands in Galilee, and in particular the Huleh basin (which, as we have explained in an earlier chapter, offers a notable opportunity for development and colonization), would be in the Jewish Area.

(iii) The proposed frontier necessitates the inclusion in the Jewish Area of the Galilee highlands between Safad and the Plain of Acre. It will be remembered that this is the part of Palestine in which the Jews have retained a foothold almost if not entirely without a break from the beginning of the Diaspora to the present day, and that the sentiment of all Jewry is deeply attached to the "holy cities" of Safad and Tiberias.[†] Until quite recently, moreover, the Jews in Galilee have lived on friendly terms with their Arab neighbours; and throughout

---

† See pages 11 and 12 above [not included in this collection].

the series of "disturbances" the *fellaheen* of Galilee have shown themselves less amenable to political incitement than those of Samaria and Judaea, where the centres of Arab nationalism are located. At Tiberias, on the other hand (which contains 6,150 Jews and 3,550 Arabs) and at Safad (which contains 2,000 Jews and 7,900 Arabs) the outbreak of last year has led to serious friction. There has been trouble also, though not so acute, in the two other "mixed" towns in the Jewish Area -- Haifa (about 50,000 Jews and 48,000 Arabs) and Acre (8,500 Arabs and 250 Jews). We believe that it would greatly promote the successful operation of Partition in its early stages and in particular help to ensure the execution of the Treaty guarantees for the protection of minorities, if those four towns were kept for a period under Mandatory administration.

(iv) Jaffa is an essentially Arab town in which the Jewish minority has recently been dwindling. We suggest that it should form part of the Arab State. The question of its communication with the latter presents no difficulty, since transit through the Jaffa-Jerusalem Corridor would be open to all. The Corridor, on the other hand, requires its own access to the sea, and for this purpose a narrow belt of land should be acquired and cleared on the north and south sides of the town. This would also solve the problem, sometimes said to be insoluble, created by the contiguity of Jaffa with Tel Aviv in the north and the nascent Jewish town to the south. If necessary, Mandatory police could be stationed on this belt. This arrangement may seem artificial, but it is clearly practicable.

(v) While the Mediterranean would be accessible to the Arab State at Jaffa and at Gaza, we think that in the interests of Arab trade and industry the Arab State should also have access for commercial purposes to Haifa, the only existing deep-water port on the coast. We recommend, therefore, that the Jewish Treaty should provide for the free transit of goods in bond between the Arab State and Haifa.

The Arab Treaty, similarly, should provide for the free transit of goods in bond over the railway between the Jewish State and the Egyptian frontier.

The same principle applies to the question of access for commercial purposes to the Red Sea. The use of that exit to the East might prove in course of time of great advantage to both Arab and Jewish trade and industry, and we understand that the construction of a railway down the Wadi Araba has been contemplated. Having regard to these possibilities we suggest that an enclave on the north-west coast of the Gulf of Aqaba should be retained under Mandatory administration, and that the Arab Treaty should provide for the free transit of goods between the Jewish State and this enclave.

The Treaties should provide for similar facilities for the transit of goods between the Mandated Area and Haifa, the Egyptian frontier and the Gulf of Aqaba.

4.   Inter-State   Subvention.

23.   As we have explained in an earlier chapter, the Jews contribute more *per capita* to the revenues of Palestine than the Arabs, and the Government has thereby been enabled to maintain public services for the Arabs at a higher level than would otherwise have been possible. Partition would mean, on the one hand, that the Arab Area would no longer profit from the taxable capacity of the Jewish Area. On the other hand, (I) the Jews would acquire a new right of sovereignty in the Jewish Area: (2) that Area, as we have defined it, would be larger than the existing area of Jewish land and settlement: (3) the Jews would be freed from their present liability for helping to promote the welfare of Arabs outside of that Area. It seems to us, therefore, not unreasonable to suggest that the Jewish State should pay a subvention to the Arab State when Partition comes into effect. There have been recent precedents for equitable financial arrangements of this kind in those connected with the separation of Sind from Bombay and of Burma from the Indian Empire; and in accordance with those precedents we recommend that a Finance Commission should be appointed to consider and report as to what the amount of the subvention should be.

24. The Finance Commission should, also, consider and report on the proportion in which the Public Debt of Palestine, which now amounts to about £4,500,000, should be divided between the Arab and the Jewish States, and on the manner in which any other "financial obligations legitimately incurred by the Administration of Palestine during the period of the Mandate" should be honoured in accordance with Article 28 thereof. The Commission should also deal with the financial questions involved in the administration of the railways, ports and telegraph and telephone systems in the event of Partition.

5.   British   Subvention.

25. The Inter-State Subvention would adjust the financial balance in Palestine; but it must be remembered that the plan we are submitting involves the inclusion of Trans-Jordan in the Arab State.   The taxable capacity of Trans-Jordan is very low and its revenues have never sufficed to meet the cost of its administration.   From 1921 to the present day it has received grants-in-aid from the United Kingdom, which have amounted to a total sum of £1,253,000 or an average of about £78,000 a year.   Grants have also been made towards the cost of the Trans-Jordan Frontier Force, and loans to the amount of £60,575, of which about £30,000 has been repaid, have been provided for earthquake-relief and the distribution of seed.

26. The Mandate for Trans-Jordan ought not in our opinion to be relinquished without securing, as far as possible, that the standard of administration should not fall too low through lack of funds to maintain it; and it is in this matter, we submit, that the British people might fairly be asked to do their part in facilitating a settlement. The continuance of the present Mandate, as we have more than once pointed out, would almost inevitably involve a recurrent and increasing charge on the British Treasury. If peace can be promoted by Partition, money spent on helping to bring it about and making it more effective for its purpose would surely be well spent. And apart from any such considerations we think that the British people, great as their financial burdens now are, would agree to a capital payment in lieu of their present annual liability, as a means towards honouring their obligations and making peace in Palestine.

27. We recommend, therefore, that in the event of the Treaty System coming into force, Parliament should be asked to make a grant of £2,000,000 to the Arab State.

6.   Tariffs   and   Ports.

28. The Arab and Jewish States, being sovereign in-dependent States, would determine their own tariffs. Subject to the terms of the Mandate, the same would apply to the Mandatory Government.

29. We recognize the crux arising from the fact that the tariff-policies of the Arab and Jewish States are likely to conflict. The prevention of smuggling might be difficult and costly. It would greatly ease the position and it would promote the interests of both the Arab and Jewish States if they could agree to impose identical customs-duties on as many articles as possible, and if the Mandatory Government, likewise, could assimilate its customs-duties as far as might be with those of one or both of the two States.

We regard it as an essential part of the proposed Treaty System that a commercial convention should be con-cluded with a view to establishing a common tariff over the widest possible range of imported articles and to facilitating the freest possible interchange of goods between the three territories   concerned.

It would simplify the situation at one point if it were provided in the commercial convention that the town of Jaffa, while treated for all other purposes as an outlying part of the Arab State, should be treated for tariff purposes as part of the mandated Jaffa-Jerusalem Corridor. The cus-toms-duties paid on goods destined for Jaffa would accrue to the Arab State, but the rates of duty would be those fixed for goods destined for the Mandated Area.

30. It would promote, we think the smooth working of Partition at the outset if the collection of customs at the ports were entrusted for a period to the Mandatory Government. We suggest, therefore, that not only at Haifa and Acre, which we have proposed should in any case remain for a time under Mandatory administration, but also at Jaffa and Tel Aviv and, if it should be found necessary, at other points, the Mandatory Government should collect the customs-duties and remit the sums paid on imports destined for the Arab State, the Jewish State and the Mandated Area to their re-spective Treasuries.

31. We should regard it as highly undesirable that the provision recently made for loading and landing goods at Tel Aviv should be expanded into a substantial harbour quite detached from Jaffa. If the need for a second deep-water port beside Haifa be established, we recommend the adoption of the plan for a joint port for Jaffa and Tel Aviv. In the event of Partition such a port should be controlled by a Joint Harbour Board, composed of representatives of the Arab and Jewish States and presided over by an officer of the Mandatory Government.

7.   Nationality.

32. All persons domiciled in the Mandated area (including Haifa, Tiberias, Safad, and the enclave on the Gulf of Aqaba, as long as they remain under Mandatory administration) who now possess the status of British protected persons would retain it; but apart from this all Palestinians would become the nationals of the States in which they are domiciled.

8.   Civil Services.

33. It seems probable that, in the event of Partition, the services of the Arab and Jewish officials in the pre-existing Mandatory Administration would to a large extent be required by the Governments of the Arab and Jewish States respectively, whereas the number of British officials would be substantially reduced. The rights of all of them, including rights to pensions or gratuities, must be fully honoured in accordance with the provisions of Article 28 of the existing Mandate, it being borne in mind that, under any plan of Partition, there will be three Governments in place of the single Government of Palestine which is contemplated in that Article as being established in the event of the termination of the Mandate. This matter should be dealt with by the Finance Commission.

9.   Industrial Concessions.

34. In the event of Partition agreements entered into by the Government of Palestine for the development and security of industries (e.g., the agreement with the Palestine Potash Company) should be taken over and carried out by the Governments of the Arab and Jewish States. Guarantees to that effect should be given in the Treaties. The security of

the Electric Power Station at Jisr el Majami should be similarly guaranteed.

10. Exchange of Land and Population.

35. We have left to the last the two-fold question which, after that of the Frontier, is the most important and most difficult of all the questions which Partition in any shape involves.

36. If Partition is to be effective in promoting a final settlement it must mean more than drawing a frontier and establishing two States. Sooner or later there should be a transfer of land and, as far as possible, an exchange of population.

37. As regards land, the Jews on the one hand may wish to dispose of some or all of the lands now owned by them which lie within the boundaries of the Arab State, and their Jewish occupants may wish to move into the Jewish State and resume their life on the land therein. The Arabs on the other hand may likewise be willing to sell the land they own within the boundaries of the Jewish State. But what is to become, in that case, of the its occupants, whether owners or tenants or labourers? Whether they remain in the Jewish State or move into the Arab State, where there is under present conditions no cultivable land to spare, there is a manifest risk of their becoming a "landless proletariat".

38. The Treaties should provide that, if Arab owners of land in the Jewish State or Jewish owners of land in the Arab State should wish to sell their land and any plantations or crops thereon, the Government of the State concerned should be responsible for the purchase of such land, plantations and crops at a price to be fixed, if required, by the Mandatory Administration. We suggest that for this purpose a loan should, if required, be guaranteed for a reasonable amount.

39. The political aspect of the land-problem is still more important. Owing to the fact that there has been no census since 1931 it is impossible to calculate with precision the distribution of population between the proposed Arab and Jewish areas, but, according to an approximate estimate supplied to us, in the area allocated in our plan to the Jewish State (excluding the urban districts which we suggest should

be retained for a period under Mandatory administration)
there are now about 225,000 Arabs.   In the area allotted to
the Arab State there are only some 1,250 Jews: but in
Jerusalem and Haifa there are about 125,000 Jews as against
85,000 Arabs.   The existence of these minorities clearly
constitutes the most serious hindrance to the smooth and
successful operation of Partition.   The "Minority Problem"
has become only too familiar in recent years, whether in
Europe or in Asia.   It is one of the most troublesome and in-
tractable products of post-war nationalism; and nationalism
in Palestine, as we have seen, is at least as intense a force as
it is anywhere else in the world.   We believe that   Partition,
once effected, might ultimately moderate and appease it as
nothing else could.   But it is, of course, too much to hope that
after Partition there would be no friction at all between
Arabs and Jews, no "incidents", no recriminations, keeping
open the wound which Partition must inflict.   If then the
settlement is to be clean and final, this question of the minorities must be boldly faced and firmly dealt with.   It calls
for the highest statesmanship on the part of all concerned.

40.   An instructive precedent is afforded, as it hap-
pens, by the exchange effected between the Greek and
Turkish populations on the morrow of the Greco-Turkish
War of 1922.   On the initiative of Dr. Nansen a convention
was signed by the Greek and Turkish Governments at the
beginning of 1923, providing that Greek nationals of the
Orthodox religion living in Turkey should be compulsorily
removed to Greece, and Turkish nationals of the Moslem religion living in Greece to Turkey.   To control the operation a
Mixed Commission and a group of sub-commissions were
established, consisting of representatives of the Greek and
Turkish Governments and of the League of Nations.   The
numbers involved were high — no less than some 1,300,000
Greeks and some 400,000 Turks.   But so vigorously and effectively was the task accomplished that within about eighteen
months from the spring of 1923 the whole exchange was
completed.   Dr. Nansen was sharply criticized at the time for
the inhumanity of his proposal, and the operation manifestly imposed the gravest hardships on multitudes of people.   But the courage of the Greek and Turkish statesmen
concerned has been justified by the result.   Before the operation the Greek and Turkish minorities had been a constant irritant.   Now the ulcer has been clean cut out, and
Greco-Turkish relations, we understand, are friendlier than
they have ever been before.

41.   Unfortunately for our purposes the analogy
breaks down at one essential point.   In Northern Greece a
surplus of cultivable land was available or could rapidly be
made available for the settlement of the Greeks evacuated
from Turkey.   In Palestine there is at present no such surplus.   Room exists or could soon be provided within the proposed boundaries of the Jewish State for the Jews now living
in the Arab Area.   It is the far greater number of Arabs who
constitute the major problem; and, while some of them could
be re-settled on the land vacated by the Jews, far more land
would be required for the re-settlement of all of them.   On
earlier pages of this Report we drew attention to the lack of
adequate evidence on this question, but such information as
was available seemed to us, as we said, to justify the hope that
the execution of large-scale plans for irrigation, water-stor-
age, and development in Trans-Jordan — and the same applies to Beersheba and the Jordan Valley — would make provision for a much larger population than exists there at the
present   time.

42.   The immediate need, therefore, is for those areas
to be surveyed and an authoritative estimate made of the
practical possibilities of irrigation and development.   This,
we suggest, should be undertaken at once, and the requisite
staff and funds provided for its completion in the shortest
possible time.   If, as a result, it is clear that a substantial
amount of land could be made available for the re-settlement
of Arabs living in the Jewish area, the most strenuous efforts should be made to obtain an agreement for the exchange of land and population.   The provision of new land
would bring the position in Palestine and Trans-Jordan
closer to what it was in 1923 in Turkey and Greece, and the
number of people involved would be very much smaller.   In
view of the present antagonism between the races and of the
manifest advantage to both of them of reducing the opportunities of future friction to the utmost, it is to be hoped that
the Arab and Jewish leaders might show the same high
statesmanship as that of the Turks and the Greeks and make
the same bold decision for the sake of peace.   If an agreement on the question were secured, provisions should be inserted in or added to the Treaties for the transfer, under the
supervision and control of the Mandatory Government, of
land and population to the extent to which new land is, or
may within a reasonable period become, available for re-
settlement.

43.   We think that in the event of Partition friction would be less likely to occur in the hill-country of North Galilee with its wholly Arab population than in the plain-lands where the population is mixed.   In the former area, therefore, it might not be necessary to effect a greater ex-change of land and population than could be effected on a voluntary basis.   But as regards the Plains, including Beisan, and as regards all such Jewish colonies as remained in the Arab State when the Treaties came into force, it should be part of the agreement that in the last resort the exchange would be compulsory.

44.   The cost of the proposed irrigation and develop-ment scheme would be heavier than the Arab State could, in our opinion, be expected to bear.   Here again we believe that the British people would be willing to help to bring about a settlement; and we recommend that, if an arrangement could be made for the transfer, voluntary or otherwise, of land and population, Parliament should be asked to make a grant to meet the cost of the aforesaid scheme.

45.   If the results of the survey were favourable, the execution of the scheme would take a considerable time, and in all probability the proposed Treaty System would come into operation before it was completed.   It should therefore be laid down in the Treaties that the full control of this work, as also of any such operations for the exchange of land and population as may be agreed on, should continue to be exercised by the Mandatory Government until its com-pletion.

46.   If irrigation and development should prove prac-ticable on such a scale as may be hoped, it is clear that the work should be carried out with the least possible delay.   The Palestine Government as at present constituted could not be expected to cope with it.   It would try beyond its strength an already overtried administration.   We think, moreover, that some of the ordinary rules of Crown Colony government should be modified to meet this exceptional case.   We suggest that a new Partition Department should be established at Jerusalem to deal with the irrigation and development work and such exchange-operations as may follow on it.   The Department should be directly under the High Commissioner; the head of it should have the same status as the Chief Secretary; and it should possess a reasonable mea-sure of independence in its administration of the funds

voted by Parliament. It seems to us essential that some special arrangement should be made to prevent the inevitable and often protracted delay which would arise if every item of expenditure, however small, had to be referred either to the British or the Palestine Treasury for sanction. The appointment of a representative of the British Treasury as Financial Director of the proposed Department might perhaps meet the case.

47.   Such is the plan of Partition which we submit to the consideration of Your Majesty's Government. We believe that it fulfils the essential conditions of Partition and demonstrates that, if Palestine ought to be divided, it can be divided.

48.   It remains to deal briefly with the main points that would arise in the immediate future if it should be agreed to terminate the Mandate and establish a Treaty System on a basis of Partition. The new regime could not, of course, be introduced before the new Mandate and the Treaties came into force, and during this period the existing Mandate would continue to be the governing instrument of the Palestine Administration. But the recommendations we made in Part II of this Report as to what should be done under the existing Mandate presupposed its continuance for an indefinite time. Clearly they would not as a whole apply to so changed a situation as the prospect of Partition would bring about. The character of that situation would largely depend on the kind of scheme adopted; but under any scheme certain main questions would arise, and we think Your Majesty's Government would wish us to express our opinion as to how those questions should be settled.

49.   The following, then, are our recommendations for the period of transition.

(1) *Land.*

Steps should be taken to prohibit the purchase of land by Jews within the Arab Area (i.e., the area of the projected Arab State) or by Arabs within the Jewish Area (i.e., the area of the projected Jewish State).

The settlement of the plain-lands of the Jewish Area should be completed within two years.

(2) *Immigration*.

Instead of the political "high-level" recommended in Chapter X, paragraph 97, there should be a territorial restriction on Jewish immigration. No Jewish immigration into the Arab Area should be permitted. Since it would therefore not affect the Arab Area and since the Jewish State would soon become responsible for its results, the volume of Jewish immigration should be determined by the economic absorptive capacity of Palestine less the Arab Area.

(3) *Trade*.

Negotiations should be opened without delay to secure the amendment of Article 18 of the Mandate and to place the external trade of Palestine upon a fairer basis.

(4) *Advisory Council*.

The Advisory Council should, if possible, be enlarged by the nomination of Arab and Jewish representatives; but, if either party refused to serve, the Council should continue as at present.

(5) *Local Government*.

The municipal system should be reformed on expert advice as recommended in Chapter XVII, paragraph 31.

(6) *Education*.

A vigorous effort should be made to increase the number of Arab schools. The "mixed schools" situated in the area to be administered under the new Mandate should be given every support, and the possibility of a British University should be considered (as recommended in Chapter XVI, paragraph 28), since those institutions might play an important part after Partition in helping to bring about an ultimate reconciliation of the races.

CHAPTER XXIII.

CONCLUSION.

1.   "Half a loaf is better than no bread" is a peculiarly English proverb; and, considering the attitude which both the Arab and Jewish representatives adopted in giving evidence before us, we think it improbable that either party will be satisfied at first sight with the proposals we have submitted for the adjustment of their rival claims.   For Partition means that neither will get all it wants.   It means that the Arabs must acquiesce in the exclusion from their sovereignty of a piece of territory, long occupied and once ruled by them.   It means that the Jews must be content with less than the Land of Israel they once ruled and have hoped to rule again.   But it seems to us possible that on reflection both parties will come to realize that the drawbacks of Partition are outweighed by its advantages.   For, if it offers neither party all it wants, if [sic] offers each what it wants most, namely freedom and security.

2.   The advantages to the Arabs of Partition on the lines we have proposed may be summarized as follows:—

(i)   They obtain their national independence and can co-operate on an equal footing with the Arabs of the neighbouring countries in the cause of Arab unity and progress.

(ii)   They are finally delivered from the fear of being "swamped" by the Jews and from the possibility of ultimate subjection to Jewish rule.

(iii)   In particular, the final limitation of the Jewish National Home within a fixed frontier and the enactment of a new Mandate for the protection of the Holy Places, solemnly guaranteed by the League of Nations, removes all anxiety lest the Holy Places should ever come under Jewish control.

(iv)   As a set-off to the loss of territory the Arabs regard as theirs, the Arab State will receive a subvention from the Jewish State.   It will also, in view of the backwardness of Trans-Jordan, obtain a grant of £2,000,000 from the British Treasury; and, if an arrangement can be made for the exchange of land and population, a further grant will be made for the conversion, as far as may prove possible, of uncultivable land in the Arab State into productive land from which the cultivators and the State alike will profit.

3.   The advantages of Partition to the Jews may be summarized as follows:—

(i)   Partition secures the establishment of the Jewish National Home and relieves it from the possibility of its being subjected in the future to Arab rule.

(ii)   Partition enables the Jews in the fullest sense to call their National Home their own: for it converts it into a Jewish State. Its citizens will be able to admit as many Jews into it as they themselves believe can be absorbed. They will attain the primary objective of Zionism — a Jewish nation, planted in Palestine, giving its nationals the same status in the world as other nations give theirs. They will cease at last to live a "minority life."

4.   To both Arabs and Jews Partition offers a prospect— and we see no such prospect in any other policy — of obtaining the inestimable boon of peace. It is surely worth some sacrifice on both sides if the quarrel which the Mandate started could be ended with its termination. It is not a natural or old-standing feud. An able Arab exponent of the Arab case told us that the Arabs throughout their history have not only been free from anti-Jewish sentiment but have also shown that the spirit of compromise is deeply rooted in their life. And he went on to express his sympathy with the fate of the Jews in Europe. "There is no decent-minded person," he said, "who would not want to do everything humanly possible to relieve the distress of those persons," provided that it was "not at the cost of inflicting a corresponding distress on another people." Considering what the possibility of finding a refuge in Palestine means to many thousands of suffering Jews, we cannot believe that the "distress" occasioned by Partition, great as it would be, is more than Arab generosity can bear. And in this, as in so much else connected with Palestine, it is not only the peoples of that country that have to be considered. The Jewish Problem is not the least of the many problems which are disturbing international relations at this critical time and obstructing the path to peace and prosperity. If the Arabs at some sacrifice could help to solve that problem, they would earn the gratitude not of the Jews alone but of all the Western World.

5.   There was a time when Arab statesmen were willing to concede little Palestine to the Jews, provided that the rest of Arab Asia were free.   That condition was not fulfilled then, but it is on the eve of fulfilment now.   In less than three years' time all the wide Arab area outside Palestine between the Mediterranean and the Indian Ocean will be independent, and, if Partition is adopted, the greater part of Palestine will be independent too.

6.   There is no need to stress the advantage to the British people of a settlement in Palestine.   We are bound to honour to the utmost of our power the obligations we undertook in the exigencies of war towards the Arabs and the Jews.   When those obligations were incorporated in the Mandate, we did not fully realize the difficulties of the task it laid on us.   We have tried to overcome them, not always with success.   They have steadily become greater till now they seem almost insuperable.   Partition offers a possibility of finding a way through them, a possibility of obtaining a final solution of the problem which does justice to the rights and aspirations of both the Arabs and the Jews and discharges the obligations we undertook towards them twenty years ago to the fullest extent that is practicable in the circumstances of the present time.

7.   Nor is it only the British people, nor only the nations which conferred the Mandate or approved it, who are troubled by what has happened and is happening in Palestine.   Numberless men and women all over the world would feel a sense of deep relief if somehow an end could be put to strife and bloodshed in a thrice hallowed land.

The report was submitted to the Permanent Mandates Commission at its meeting held in Geneva, 30 July-18 August 1937, which found that the Mandate had become unworkable once the government had publicly so stated, but objected to the immediate creation of two independent states.   The Arab leadership totally rejected the division of the country and called for the immediate establishment of a single Arab government.   On the whole, the Zionist leaders were, understandably, in favor of the formation of an independent Jewish state.

Faced with uncertainties and divided world opinion, the British Government postponed a final decision by appointing a technical commission to work out a detailed scheme of partition based upon the recommendations of the Peel Commission. This, the so-called "Woodhead Commission" was comprised of Sir John Woodhead, chairman, Sir Alison Russell, A. P. Waterfield, and T. Reid. In their report, published in October 1938,[2] they could not agree as to how to divide Palestine to avoid leaving Arabs in the Jewish state or Jews in the Arab state. They did, however, suggest economic federalism should partition be effected [p. 244]. Considering the difficulties involved and the necessity of providing an annual subsidy to any proposed Arab state, the government the following November issued a new statement of policy in which they stated:

4.   His Majesty's Government, after careful study of the Partion Commissions' report, have reached the conclusion that this further examination has shown that the political, administrative and financial difficulties involved in the proposal to create independent Arab and Jewish States inside Palestine are so great that this solution of the problem is impracticable.[3]

---

[2] Great Britain. Parliamentary Papers. *Palestine Partition Report — October 1938* (London: His Majesty's Stationery Office, 1938).   Cmd. 5854

[3] Great Britain. Parliamentary Papers. *Palestine. Statement by His Majesty's Government in the United Kingdom. November 1938* (London: His Majesty's Stationery Office, 1938).   Cmd. 5893. Reprinted by permission of the Controller of Her Majesty's Stationery Office.

1939 White Paper, 1939

The political and financial difficulties inherent within any scheme of partition, as reported by the Woodhead Commission, quickly dulled the earlier enthusiasm for partition as a means of settling the ongoing conflict within Palestine following the submission of the Peel Commission White Paper. As noted privously, a Statement of Policy (Cmd. 5893) was issued simultaneously with the report of Woodhead rejecting any further consideration of this concept. In order to devise a coherent policy for Palestine Malcolm MacDonald, the Secretary of State for the Colonies, called for a London Conference with representatives from the Jewish Agency and of the Palestinian and other Arabs. The meetings extended through February and March of 1939 without reaching an agreement. Despite this setback in attempting to directly involve both the Arabs and the Jews in formulating a new direction, the government, on 17 May 1939 published its final proposals that had been presented towards the end of the conference. This new Statement of Policy, a radical departure from those that had

Source: Great Britain. Parliamentary Papers. *Palestine: Statement of Policy* (London: His Majesty's Stationery Office, 1939). Cmd. 6019. Reprinted by permission of the Controller of Her Majesty's Stationery Office.

been formulated over the nearly twenty years of the Mandate, called for: 1) the creation of a united independent Palestine State at the end of a ten-year transition period, 2) a limitation upon Jewish immigration to a total of an additional 75,000 people during a five-year period effective the preceding April, and 3) giving the high commissioner wide powers to prohibit and regulate transfers of land.

In the Statement on Palestine, issued on 9th November, 1938 [Cmd. 5893], His Majesty's Government announced their intention to invite representatives of the Arabs of Palestine, of certain neighbouring countries and of the Jewish Agency to confer with them in London regarding future policy. It was their sincere hope that, as a result of full, free and frank discussion, some understanding might be reached. Conferences recently took place with Arab and Jewish delegations, lasting for a period of several weeks, and served the purpose of a complete exchange of views between British Ministers and the Arab and Jewish representatives. In the light of the discussions as well as of the situation in Palestine and of the Reports of the Royal Commission [Cmd. 5479] and the Partition Commission [Cmd. 5854], certain proposals were formulated by His Majesty's Government and were laid before the Arab and Jewish delegations as the basis of an agreed settlement. Neither the Arab nor the Jewish delegations felt able to accept these proposals, and the conferences therefore did not result in an agreement. Accordingly His Majesty's Government are free to formulate their own policy, and after careful consideration they have decided to adhere generally to the proposals which were finally submitted to, and discussed with, the Arab and Jewish delegations.

2. The Mandate for Palestine, the terms of which were confirmed by the Council of the League of Nations in 1922, has governed the policy of successive British Governments for nearly 20 years. It embodies the Balfour Declaration and imposes upon the Mandatory four main obligations. These obligations are set out in Articles 2, 6 and 13 of the Mandate. There is no dispute regarding the interpretation of one of these obligations, that touching the protection of and access to the Holy Places and religious buildings or sites. The other

three main obligations are generally as follows:—

(i) To place the country under such political, administrative and economic conditions as will secure the establishment in Palestine of a national home for the Jewish people, to facilitate Jewish immigration under suitable conditions, and to encourage, in co-operation with the Jewish Agency, close settlement by Jews on the land.

(ii) To safeguard the civil and religious rights of all the inhabitants of Palestine irrespective of race and religion, and, whilst facilitating Jewish immigration and settlement, to ensure that the rights and position of other sections of the population are not prejudiced.

(iii) To place the country under such political, administrative and economic conditions as will secure the development of self-governing institutions.

3.   The Royal Commission and previous Commissions of Enquiry have drawn attention to the ambiguity of certain expressions in the Mandate, such as the expression "a national home for the Jewish people", and they have found in this ambiguity and the resulting uncertainty as to the objectives of policy a fundamental cause of unrest and hostility between Arabs and Jews.   His Majesty's Government are convinced that in the interest of the peace and well-being of the whole people of Palestine a clear definition of policy and objectives is essential.   The proposal of partition recommended by the Royal Commission would have afforded such clarity, but the establishment of self-supporting independent Arab and Jewish States within Palestine has been found to be impracticable.   It has therefore been necessary for His Majesty's Government to devise an alternative policy which will, consistently with their obligations to Arabs and Jews, meet the needs of the situation in Palestine.   Their views and proposals are set forth below under the three heads, (I) The Constitution, (II) Immigration, and (III) Land.

I. - THE CONSTITUTION

4.   It has been urged that the expression "a national home for the Jewish people" offered a prospect that Palestine might in due course become a Jewish State or Commonwealth.   His Majesty's Government do not wish to contest the view, which was expressed by the Royal Commission, that the Zionist leaders at the time of the issue

of the Balfour Declaration recognised that an ultimate Jewish State was not precluded by the terms of the Declaration.   But, with the Royal Commission, His Majesty's Government believe that the framers of the Mandate in which the Balfour Declaration was embodied could not have intended that Palestine should be converted into a Jewish State against the will of the Arab population of the country. That Palestine was not to be converted into a Jewish State might be held to be implied in the passage from the Command Paper of 1922 [Cmd. 1700] which reads as follows:--

> "Unauthorised statements have been made to the effect that the purpose in view is to create a wholly Jewish Palestine.   Phrases have been used such as that 'Palestine is to become as Jewish as England is English'.   His Majesty's Government regard any such expectation as impracticable and have no such aim in view.   Nor have they at any time contemplated ..... the disappearance or the subordination of the Arabic population, language or culture in Palestine.   They would draw attention to the fact that the terms of the (Balfour) Declaration referred to do not contemplate that Palestine as a whole should be converted into a Jewish National Home, but that such a Home should be founded *in Palestine*".

But this statement has not removed doubts, and His Majesty's Government therefore now declare unequivocally that it is not part of their policy that Palestine should become a Jewish State.   They would indeed regard it as contrary to their obligations to the Arabs under the Mandate, as well as to the assurances which have been given to the Arab people in the past, that the Arab population of Palestine should be made the subjects of a Jewish State against their will.

5.   The nature of the Jewish National Home in Palestine was further described in the Command Paper of 1922 as follows:—

> "During the last two or three generations the Jews have recreated in Palestine a community, now numbering 80,000, of whom about one-fourth are farmers or workers upon the land.   This community has its own political organs; an elected assembly for the direction of its domestic concerns; elected councils in the towns; and an organisation for the control of its schools.   It has its elected Chief Rabbinate and

Rabbinical Council for the direction of its religious affairs. Its business is conducted in Hebrew as a vernacular language, and a Hebrew press serves its needs. It has its distinctive intellectual life and displays considerable economic activity. This community, then, with its town and country population, its political, religious and social organisations, its own language, its own customs, its own life, has in fact 'national' characteristics. When it is asked what is meant by the development of the Jewish National Home in Palestine, it may be answered that it is not the imposition of a Jewish nationality upon the inhabitants of Palestine as a whole, but the further development of the existing Jewish community, with the assistance of Jews in other parts of the world, in order that it may become a centre in which the Jewish people as a whole may take, on grounds of religion and race, an interest and a pride. But in order that this community should have the best prospect of free development and provide a full opportunity for the Jewish people to display its capacities, it is essential that it should know that it is in Palestine as of right and not on sufferance. That is the reason why it is necessary that the existence of a Jewish National Home in Palestine should be internationally guaranteed, and that it should be formally recognised to rest upon ancient historic connection".

6. His Majesty's Government adhere to this interpretation of the Declaration of 1917 and regard it as an authoritative and comprehensive description of the character of the Jewish National Home in Palestine. It envisaged the further development of the existing Jewish community with the assistance of Jews in other parts of the world. Evidence that His Majesty's Government have been carrying out their obligation in this respect is to be found in the facts that, since the statement of 1922 was published, more than 300,000 Jews have immigrated to Palestine, and that the population of the National Home has risen to some 450,000, or approaching a third of the entire population of the country. Nor has the Jewish community failed to take full advantage of the opportunities given to it. The growth of the Jewish National Home and its achievements in many fields are a remarkable constructive effort which must command the admiration of the world and must be, in particular, a source of pride to the Jewish people.

7.   In the recent discussions the Arab delegations have repeated the contention that Palestine was included within the area in which Sir Henry McMahon, on behalf of the British Government, in October, 1915, undertook to recognise and support Arab independence.   The validity of this claim, based on the terms of the correspondence which passed between Sir Henry McMahon and the Sharif of Mecca, was thoroughly and carefully investigated by British and Arab representatives during the recent conferences in London.   Their Report, which has been published [Cmd. 5974], states that both the Arab and the British representatives endeavoured to understand the point of view of the other party but that they were unable to reach agreement upon an interpretation of the correspondence.   There is no need to summarise here the arguments presented by each side.   His Majesty's Government regret the misunderstandings which have arisen as regards some of the phrases used. For their part they can only adhere, for the reasons given by their representatives in the Report, to the view that the whole of Palestine west of the Jordan was excluded from Sir Henry McMahon's pledge, and they therefore cannot agree that the McMahon correspondence forms a just basis for the claim that Palestine should be converted into an Arab State.

8.   His Majesty's Government are charged as the Mandatory authority "to secure the development of self-governing institutions" in Palestine.   Apart from this specific obligation, they would regard it as contrary to the whole spirit of the Mandate system that the population of Palestine should remain for ever under Mandatory tutelage.   It is proper that the people of the country should as early as possible enjoy the rights of self-government which are exercised by the people of neighbouring countries.   His Majesty's Government are . unable at present to foresee the exact constitutional forms which government in Palestine will eventually take, but their objective is self-government, and they desire to see established ultimately an independent Palestine State.   It should be a State in which the two peoples in Palestine, Arabs and Jews, share authority in government in such a way that the essential interests of each are secured.

9.   The establishment of an independent State and the complete relinquishment of Mandatory control in Palestine would require such relations between the Arabs and the Jews as would make good government possible.   Moreover,

the growth of self-governing institutions in Palestine, as in other countries, must be an evolutionary process. A transitional period will be required before independence is achieved, throughout which ultimate responsibility for the Government of the country will be retained by His Majesty's Government as the Mandatory authority, while the people of the country are taking an increasing share in the Government, and understanding and co-operation amongst them are growing. It will be the constant endeavour of His Majesty's Government to promote good relations between the Arabs and the Jews.

10. In the light of these considerations His Majesty's Government make the following declaration of their intentions regarding the future government of Palestine:—

(1) The objective of His Majesty's Government is the establishment within ten years of an independent Palestine State in such treaty relations with the United Kingdom as will provide satisfactorily for the commercial and strategic requirements of both countries in the future. This proposal for the establishment of the independent State would involve consultation with the Council of the League of Nations with a view to the termination of the Mandate.

(2) The independent State should be one in which Arabs and Jews share in government in such a way as to ensure that the essential interests of each community are safe-guarded.

(3) The establishment of the independent State will be preceded by a transitional period throughout which His Majesty's Government will retain responsibility for the government of the country. During the transitional period the people of Palestine will be given an increasing part in the government of their country. Both sections of the population will have an opportunity to participate in the machinery of government, and the process will be carried on whether or not they both avail themselves of it.

(4) As soon as peace and order have been sufficiently restored in Palestine steps will be taken to carry out this policy of giving the people of Palestine an increasing part in the government of their country, the objective being to place Palestinians in charge of all the Departments of Government, with the assistance of British advisers and subject to the control of the High Commissioner. With this object in

view His Majesty's Government will be prepared immediately to arrange that Palestinians shall be placed in charge of certain Departments, with British advisers.   The Palestinian heads of Departments will sit on the Executive Council, which advises the High Commissioner.   Arab and Jewish representatives will be invited to serve as heads of Departments approximately in proportion to their respective populations. The number of Palestinians in charge of Departments will be increased as circumstances permit until all heads of Departments are Palestinians, exercising the administrative and advisory functions which are at present performed by British officials.   When that stage is reached consideration will be given to the question of converting the Executive Council into a Council of Ministers with a consequential change in the status and functions of the Palestinian heads of Departments.

(5) His Majesty's Government make no proposals at this stage regarding the establishment of an elective legislature.   Nevertheless they would regard this as an appropriate constitutional development, and, should public opinion in Palestine hereafter show itself in favour of such a development, they will be prepared, provided that local conditions permit, to establish the necessary machinery.

(6) At the end of five years from the restoration of peace and order, an appropriate body representative of the people of Palestine and of His Majesty's Government will be set up to review the working of the constitutional arrangements during the transitional period and to consider and make recommendations regarding the constitution of the independent Palestine State.

(7) His Majesty's Government will require to be satisfied that in the treaty contemplated by sub-paragraph (1) or in the constitution contemplated by sub-paragraph (6) adequate provision has been made for:—

> (a) the security of, and freedom of access to, the Holy Places, and the protection of the interests and property of the various religious bodies.
>
> (b) the protection of the different communities in Palestine in accordance with the obligations of His Majesty's Government to both Arabs and Jews and for the special position in Palestine of

the Jewish National Home.

(c) such requirements to meet the strategic situation as may be regarded as necessary by His
Majesty's Government in the light of the circumstances then existing.

His Majesty's Government will also require to be
satisfied that the interests of certain foreign countries in Palestine, for the preservation of which they
are at present responsible, are adequately safeguarded.

(8) His Majesty's Government will do everything
in their power to create conditions which will enable
the independent Palestine State to come into being
within ten years.   If, at the end of ten years, it appears to His Majesty's Government that, contrary to
their hope, circumstances require the postponement
of the establishment of the independent State, they
will consult with representatives of the people of
Palestine, the Council of the League of Nations and the
neighbouring Arab States before deciding on such a
postponement.   If His Majesty's Government come to
the conclusion that postponement is unavoidable,
they will invite the co-operation of these parties in
framing plans for the future with a view to achieving
the desired objective at the earliest possible date.

11.   During the transitional period steps will be
taken to increase the powers and responsibilities of
municipal corporations and local councils.

II. - IMMIGRATION.

12.   Under Article 6 of the Mandate, the
Administration of Palestine, "while ensuring that the rights
and position of other sections of the population are not prejudiced", is required to "facilitate Jewish immigration under
suitable conditions".   Beyond this, the extent to which Jewish
immigration into Palestine is to be permitted is nowhere defined in the Mandate.   But in the Command Paper of 1922 it
was laid down that for the fulfilment of the policy of establishing a Jewish National Home

"it is necessary that the Jewish community in
Palestine should be able to increase its numbers by
immigration.   This immigration cannot be so great in
volume as to exceed whatever may be the economic
capacity of the country at the time to absorb new ar-

rivals. It is essential to ensure that the immigrants should not be a burden upon the people of Palestine as a whole, and that they should not deprive any section of the present population of their employment."

In practice, from that date onwards until recent times, the economic absorptive capacity of the country has been treated as the sole limiting factor, and in the letter which Mr. Ramsay MacDonald, as Prime Minister, sent to Dr. Weizmann in February 1931 it was laid down as a matter of policy that economic absorptive capacity was the sole criterion. This interpretation has been supported by resolutions of the Permanent Mandates Commission. But His Majesty's Government do not read either the Statement of Policy of 1922 or the letter of 1931 as implying that the Mandate requires them, for all time and in all circumstances, to facilitate the immigration of Jews into Palestine subject only to consideration of the country's economic absorptive capacity. Nor do they find anything in the Mandate or in subsequent Statements of Policy to support the view that the establishment of a Jewish National Home in Palestine cannot be effected unless immigration is allowed to continue indefinitely. If immigration has an adverse effect on the economic position in the country, it should clearly be restricted; and equally, if it has a seriously damaging effect on the political position in the country, that is a factor that should not be ignored. Although it is not difficult to contend that the large number of Jewish immigrants who have been admitted so far have been absorbed economically, the fear of the Arabs that this influx will continue indefinitely until the Jewish population is in a position to dominate them has produced consequences which are extremely grave for Jews and Arabs alike and for the peace and prosperity of Palestine. The lamentable disturbances of the past three years are only the latest and most sustained manifestation of this intense Arab apprehension. The methods employed by Arab terrorists against fellow-Arabs and Jews alike must receive unqualified condemnation. But it cannot be denied that fear of indefinite Jewish immigration is widespread amongst the Arab population and that this fear has made possible disturbances which have given a serious setback to economic progress, depleted the Palestine exchequer, rendered life and property insecure, and produced a bitterness between the Arab and Jewish populations which is deplorable between citizens of the same country. If in these circumstances immigration is continuted up to the economic absorptive capacity of the country, regardless of all other considerations, a fatal enmity between the two peoples will be perpetuated, and the situation in Palestine may become a permanent source of friction amongst all peoples in the Near and Middle East. His Majesty's Government cannot take the view that either their obligations under the Mandate, or considerations of common sense and justice, require that they should ignore these circumstances in framing immigration policy.

13. In view of the Royal Commission, the association of the policy of the Balfour Declaration with the Mandate system implied the belief that Arab hostility to the former would sooner or later be overcome. It has been the hope of the British Governments every since the Balfour Declaration was issued that in time the Arab population, recognizing the advantages to be derived from Jewish settlement and development in Palestine, would become reconciled to the further growth of the Jewish National Home. This hope has not been fulfilled. The alternatives before His Majesty's Government are either (i) to seek to expand the Jewish National Home indefinitely by immigration, against the strongly expressed will of the Arab people of the country; or (ii) to permit further expansion of the Jewish National Home by immigration only if the Arabs are prepared to acquiesce in it. The former policy means rule by force. Apart from other considerations, such a policy seems to His Majesty's Government to be contrary to the whole spirit of Article 22 of the Covenant of the League of Nations, as well as to their specific obligations to the Arabs in the Palestine Mandate. Moreover, the relations between the Arabs and the Jews in Palestine must be based sooner or later on mutual tolerance and goodwill; the peace, security and progress of the Jewish National Home itself require this. Therefore His Majesty's Government, after earnest consideration, and taking into account the extent to which the growth of the Jewish National Home has been facilitated over the last twenty years, have decided that the time has come to adopt in principle the second of the alternatives referred to above.

14. It has been urged that all further Jewish immigration into Palestine should be stopped forthwith. His Majesty's Government cannot accept such a proposal. It would damage the whole of the financial and economic system of Palestine and thus affect adversely the interests of Arabs and Jews alike. Moreover, in the view of His Majesty's

Government, abruptly to stop further immigration would be unjust to the Jewish National Home. But, above all, His Majesty's Government are conscious of the present unhappy plight of large numbers of Jews who seek a refuge from certain European countries, and they believe that Palestine can and should make a further contribution to the solution of this pressing world problem. In all these circumstances, they believe that they will be acting consistently with their Mandatory obligations to both Arabs and Jews, and in the manner best calculated to serve the interests of the whole people of Palestine, by adopting the following proposals regarding immigration:—

(1) Jewish immigration during the next five years will be at a rate which, if economic absorptive capacity permits, will bring the Jewish population up to approximately one-third of the total population of the country. Taking into account the expected natural increase of the Arab and Jewish populations, and the number of illegal Jewish immigrants now in the country, this would allow of the admission, as from the beginning of April of this year, of some 75,000 immigrants over the next five years. These immigrants would, subject to the criterion of economic absorptive capacity, be admitted as follows:—

(a) For each of the next five years a quota of 10,000 Jewish immigrants will be allowed, on the understanding that a shortage in any one year may be added to the quotas for subsequent years, within the five-year period, if economic absorptive capacity permits.

(b) In addition, as a contribution towards the solution of the Jewish refugee problem, 25,000 refugees will be admitted as soon as the High Commissioner is satisfied that adequate provision for their maintenance is ensured, special consideration being given to refugee children and dependants.

(2) The existing machinery for ascertaining economic absorptive capacity will be retained, and the High Commissioner will have the ultimate responsibility for deciding the limits of economic capacity. Before each periodic decision is taken, Jewish and Arab representatives will be consulted.

(3) After the period of five years no further

Jewish immigration will be permitted unless the Arabs of Palestine are prepared to acquiesce in it.

(4) His Majesty's Government are determined to check illegal immigration, and further preventive measures are being adopted. The numbers of any Jewish illegal immigrants who, despite these measures, may succeed in coming into the country and cannot be deported will be deducted from the yearly quotas.

15. His Majesty's Government are satisfied that, when the immigration over five years which is now contemplated has taken place, they will not be justified in facilitating, nor will they be under any obligation to facilitate, the further development of the Jewish National Home by immigration regardless of the wishes of the Arab population.

III.- LAND.

16. The Administration of Palestine is required, under Article 6 of the Mandate, "while ensuring that the rights and position of other sections of the population are not prejudiced", to encourage "close settlement by Jews on the land", and no restriction has been imposed hitherto on the transfer of land from Arabs to Jews. The Reports of several expert Commissions have indicated that, owing to the natural growth of the Arab population, and the steady sale in recent years of Arab land to Jews, there is now in certain areas no room for further transfers of Arab land, whilst in some other areas such transfers of land must be restricted if Arab cultivators are to maintain their existing standard of life and a considerable landless Arab population is not soon to be created. In these circumstances, the High Commissioner will be given general powers to prohibit and regulate transfers of land. These powers will date from the publication of this statement of policy and the High Commissioner will retain them throughout the transitional period.

––––––––

18. In framing these proposals His Majesty's Government have sincerely endeavoured to act in strict accordance with their obligations under the Mandate to both the Arabs and the Jews. The vagueness of the phrases employed in some instances to describe these obligations has led to controversy and has made the task of interpretation

difficult.   His Majesty's Government cannot hope to satisfy the partisans of one party or the other in such controversy as the Mandate has aroused.   Their purpose is to be just as between the two peoples in Palestine whose destinies in that country have been affected by the great events of recent years, and who, since they live side by side, must learn to practice mutual tolerance, goodwill and co-operation.   In looking to the future, His Majesty's Government are not blind to the fact that some events of the past make the task of creating these relations difficult; but they are encouraged by the knowledge that at many times and in many places in Palestine during the recent years the Arab and Jewish inhabitants have lived in friendship together.   Each community has much to contribute to the welfare of their common land, and each must earnestly desire peace in which to assist in increasing the well-being of the whole people of the country.   The responsibility which falls on them, no less than upon His Majesty's Government, to co-operate together to ensure peace is all the more solemn because their country is revered by many millions of Moslems, Jews and Christians throughout the world who pray for peace in Palestine and for the happiness of her people.

As its authors had expected this new Statement of Policy satisfied neither the Arabs nor the Jews; the Arabs disliked it because it did not halt further Jewish immigration immediately, and the Jewish Agency in Jerusalem claimed that it was a " breach of faith."   In its statement, issued the same date as the White Paper, 17 May, the Agency stated, in part:

1.   The effect of the new policy for Palestine laid down by the Mandatory Government ..., is to deny to the Jewish people the right to reconstitute their National Home in their ancestral country.   It is a policy which transfers authority over Palestine to the present Arab majority, puts the Jewish population at the mercy of that majority, decrees the stoppage of Jewish immigration as soon as the Jewish inhabitants form one-third of the total, and sets up a territorial ghetto for the Jews in their own homeland.[1]

---

[1] Jewish Agency for Palestine. *Book of Documents Submitted to the General Assembly of the United Nations to the Establishment of the*

With the outbreak of the war on 3
September 1939 the proposal for the establishment of an independent Palestinian State at the
end of the ten year period was put into
abeyance, although the limitations imposed
upon further immigration and land transfers
were attempted. To give effect to the latter, the
Government, on the 28th of February, 1940, addressed a letter to the Secretary-General of the
League of Nations advising the Council of the
League and the Permanent Mandates
Commission of the limitations that were to be
placed upon further land transfers and the
manner in which this was to be accomplished.[2]

National Home for the Jewish People (New York: The Jewish Agency
for Palestine, May, 1947) 137.

[2] Great Britain. Parliamentary Papers. *Palestne. Miscellaneous No.
2 (1940). Palestine Land Transfers Registration. Letter to the
Secretary-General of the League of Nations London. February 28,
1940. Presented by the Secretary of State for Foreign Affairs to
Parliament by Command of His Majesty February 1940* (London: His
Majesty's Stationery Office, 1940).   Cmd. 6180.

Congressional Resolutions, 1944

Even before the White Paper of 1939 could be implemented, particularly those parts that limited both wide-scale Jewish immigration into Palestine and land transfers, political pressure began to be made upon the governments of both Great Britain and the United States to scuttle this new policy. The opposition to it was particularly strong in the United States. As a result of numerous letters and petitions presented to Congress from Zionist and Jewish organizations, both the Senate and the House of Representatives reacted sharply in the days following the publication of the White Paper. Hamilton Fish, a representative from the State of New York who had introduced the pro-

---

Source: The two identical resolutions presented to the House (H. Res. 418 and H. Res. 419) have been printed in: United States. Congress of the United States. *Hearings Before the Committee on Foreign Affairs, House of Representatives, Seventy-eighth Congress, Second Session on H. Res. 418 and H. Res. 419. Resolutions Relative to the Jewish National Home in Palestine* (Washington, D.C.: Government Printing Office, 1944) 1. That jointly presented to the Senate by Senators Wagner and Taft is to be found in: United States. Congress of the United States. *United States of America. Congressional Record. Proceedings and Debates of the 78th Congress, Second Session* vol. 90, part 1 (Washington, D.C.: United States Government Printing Office, 1944) 963.

Zionist Joint Resolution of Congress in 1922, brought before the House on 25 May a petition signed by 15 members of the Committee on Foreign Affairs addressed to the Secretary of State requesting him "... to advise the British Government that the contemplated action, if carried out, will be regarded as a violation of the British—American Convention and will be viewed with disfavor by the American people."1 The argument put forth in this petition against the new British policy was that it repudiated the Balfour Declaration, the mandate of the League of Nations, and Article 7 of the the Anglo-American convention of 3 December 1924 (this may have been an intentional misinterpretation of that article).

The outbreak of the war in Europe in September of 1939 did not lessen the demands of the Zionists in Britain and the United States that the gates of Palestine be opened to unlimited Jewish immigration, but, in fact, intensified them because of the large numbers of Jewish refugees fleeing German persecution. The fear of an Axis invasion of the Near East brought yet another demand from these same leaders, that the Jewish inhabitants of Palestine be permitted to establish solely Jewish regiments for their own protection, although Britain continued to maintain troops within the country. To the Arabs, not only in Palestine, but throughout the Near East, the fear of armed Jews was an even greater threat than German troops. Axis propaganda, and particularly that from Germany, played upon this fear and was seen as undermining the efforts of the Allied powers, not only in the Near East, but throughout the Muslim world. In the draft of a letter dated 2 June 1942, prepared for Secretary of State Sumner Wells addressed to President Franklin Roosevelt, the Advisor on

---

1 United States. Congress of the United States. *United States of American Congressional Record. Proceedings and Debates of the 76th Congress. First Session*, vol. 84, part 6 (Washington, D.C.: United States Government Printing Office) 6167.

Political Relations in the Department of State,
Wallace Murray, wrote:

> The agitation for the formation of a Jewish
> army in Palestine is having such alarming effects in
> the Near and Middle East that I am impelled to draw
> your attention to the matter. ... [The Muslims] are be-
> coming more and more hostile to the United Nations'
> cause due to the fear that their fellow Moslems in
> Palestine will be overridden. As the result of contin-
> uous agitation by the Zionists of their ambitions in
> Palestine, the Axis propagandists have been broad-
> casting, with good effect from their viewpoint, that the
> United States intends to turn Palestine over to the
> Jews despite the opposition of the Moslem majority in
> that country. Of course, this agitation, which has re-
> cently taken the form of full-page advertisements in
> the metropolitan press advocating the formation of a
> Jewish army to defend Palestine, and a widely publi-
> cized dinner here in Washington, give the Axis powers
> additional oil to pour on the fire, which is already
> dangerously high. We have just learned that the Axis
> powers have promised the Arabs their independence
> and the elimination of the Jewish national home in
> Palestine.[2]

Two months prior to this letter an
"Extraordinary Zionist Conference," held at the
Biltmore Hotel in New York City, on 11 May
adopted what was later to be termed the
"Biltmore Declaration." Included within this
statement was a demand that further alarmed
the Arab Palestinians: "... that Palestine be
established as a *Jewish Commonwealth* integrated in the structure of the new democratic
world."[3] The remainder of 1942 and all of 1943

---

[2] United States. Department of State. *Foreign Relations of the
United States. Diplomatic Papers: 1943. Volume IV: The Near East
and Africa* (Washington, D.C.: Government Printing Office, 1963)
539-40.

[3] Jewish Agency for Palestine. *Book of Documents submitted to the
General Assembly of the United Nations Relating to the Establishment
of the National Home for the Jewish People* (New York: The Jewish
Agency for Palestine, 1947) 226-27. [emphasis added].

witnessed continued political agitation on the part of individuals and organizations in both Great Britain and the United States for the abrogation of the 1939 White Paper, unlimited Jewish immigration, continued and unrestricted land purchases by the Jewish Agency in Palestine and other groups, and the establishment of the Jewish state in Palestine immediately following the conclusion of the war; all accompanied by widespread terrorist activities throughout Palestine by the infamous Stern Gang and the Irgun.

These demands came to play an even more important rôle at the beginning of 1944, both a presidential and a congressional election year. On 27 January Representatives James A. Wright of Pennsylvania and Ranulf Compton of Connecticut introduced identical resolutions into the House of Representatives calling for free entry into Palestine of Jews and the ultimate constitution of Palestine "... as a free and democratic Jewish commonwealth." Five days later, 1 February, an identical resolution was brought before the Senate by Robert F. Wagner of New York and Robert A. Taft of Ohio.

Whereas the Sixty-seventh Congress of the United States on June 30, 1922, unanimously resolved "that the United States of America favors the establishment in Palestine of a national home for the Jewish people, it being clearly understood that nothing shall be done which may prejudice the civil and religious rights of Christian and all other non-Jewish communities in Palestine, and that the holy places and religious buildings and sites in Palestine shall be adequately protected"; and

Whereas the ruthless persecution of the Jewish people in Europe has clearly demonstrated the need for a Jewish homeland as a haven for the large numbers who have become homeless as a result of this persecution: Therefore be it

Resolved, That the United States shall use its good offices and take appropriate measures to the end that the doors of Palestine shall be opened for free entry of Jews into that country, and that there shall be full opportunity for colonization so that the Jewish people may ultimately reconsti-

tute Palestine as a free and democratic Jewish commonwealth.

The introduction of these resolutions
into both Houses of Congress and their immediate assignment to the respective committees
on foreign affairs for hearings was of immediate concern to the administration, particularly those responsible for the conduct of the
war — Henry L. Stimson, Secretary of War, and
General George C. Marshall, Chief of Staff. As
they had expected, the news of these resolutions was quickly transmitted to the Near East,
causing great consternation as to the policy of
the United States in advocating the establishment of a Jewish state in Palestine. In a letter
dated 7 February, addressed to Senator John B.
Connally, chairman of the Senate Committee on
Foreign Relations, Secretary Stimson wrote:

The subject of this resolution is a matter of
deep military concern to the War Department. I feel
that the passage of this resolution at the present time,
or even any public hearings thereon, would be apt to
provoke dangerous repercussions in areas where we
have many vital military interests. Any conflict between Jews and Arabs would require the retention of
troops in the affected areas and thus reduce the total
forces that could otherwise be placed in combat
against Germany. The consequent unrest in other
portions of the Arab world would keep United Nations
resources away from the combat zone. I believe
therefore that our war effort would be seriously prejudiced by such action.[4]

Despite this expressed concern regard-
ing the resolution in both the Senate and the
House of Representatives, Congressman Sol
Bloom, chairman of the House Committee on
Foreign Affairs, held hearings on the House

---

[4] United States. Department of State. *Foreign Relations of the
United States: Diplomatic Papers 1944. Vol. V: The Near East and
Africa. The Far East* (Washington, D.C.: Government Printing Office,
1965) 563.

resolutions 8, 9, 15, and 16 February. It was not until 17 March, following a further letter from Secretary Stimson, did the committee issue a brief statement: "Advice and information given to us by those responsible for the conduct of the war, have convinced the Committee that action upon the resolutions at this time would be unwise."[5] Thus neither resolution was reported out of the respective committees. The political agitation for the passage of the resolution, as to be seen in the pages of *The New York Times*, did not cease, and was manifested in the political platforms adopted by the Republican national convention on 28 June and the Democratic national convention on 21 July, both of which called for unrestricted Jewish immigration into Palestine and the establishment of Palestine as "a free and democratic Jewish commonwealth."[6]

Immediately following the election in November the American Zionist leaders pushed to have the resolutions reintroduced in Congress, despite the warning from President Roosevelt, who was himself in favor of the Zionist program for Palestine, that it would be unwise. Nontheless, the resolutions were revived and were defeated only by the personal appearance of Secretary of State Edward R. Stettinius, Jr., before the Senate Foreign Relations Committee.

---

[5]   Ibid., 591.

[6] The complete text of the Republican platform was printed in *The New York Times*, 28 June 1944, p. 14; that of the Democratic platform on 21 July 1944, p. 12.

24

Pact of the Arab League, 1945

As a direct result of the division of the Near East at the end of the first World War by Great Britain and France the League of Arab States was formed. Interestingly, it was the British Government, one of the leading proponents of that division and the establishment of the mandates, that suggested this unitary movement. On two separate occasions, in 1941 and again in 1943, Anthony Eden, the foreign secretary, stated that His Majesty's Government would view with sympathy and give full support to such a scheme. Because of their joint support on behalf of the Palestinians since 1936 and, perhaps, a recognition of the need for collective action in the post-war world, the political leaders of Iraq, Transjordan, and Egypt, in early 1943, cautiously began to put forth ideas which could lead to an "Arab League." As a result of the initiative of the Egyptian prime

Source: League of Arab States. *League of Arab States Treaty Series: Agreements and Conventions concluded between member States within the framework of the Arab League* (Cairo: League of Arab States, n.d.) 1-9. Courtesy of the League of Arab States. The original text was, of course, written in Arabic. The English translation employed here is that approved and published by the League. Portions of the text have been omitted in this compilation which do not pertain to the Arab-Israeli conflict.

minister a "Preparatory Committee," meeting in Alexandria 25 September-7 October 1944, signed the "Alexandria Protocol" by which the states agreed to establish a league of Arab states. On 22 March 1945 the final form of the Pact of the League of Arab States was approved and signed by the heads of state of Egypt, Iraq, Lebanon, Saudi Arabia, Syria, Transjordan, and the Yemen. The basic philosophy behind the formation of the League is succinctly set forth in the Prologue to the Pact:

With a view to strengthen the close relations and numerous ties which bind the Arab States,

And out of concern for the cementing and reinforcing of these bonds on the basis of respect for the independence and sovereignty of these States,

And in order to direct their efforts toward the goal of the welfare of all the Arab States, their common weal, the guarantee of their future and the realization of their aspirations,

And in response to Arab public opinion in all the Arab countries,

Have agreed to conclude a pact to this effect... .

Mindful of their earlier concern for the fate of their fellow Arabs in Palestine. the framers of the Pact from the outset were determined to include them within the League, which was accomplished by adjoining to the document the "Annex on Palestine."

Article 1. — The League of Arab State[s] shall be composed of the independent Arab States that have signed this Pact.

Every Independent Arab State shall have the right to adhere to the League. Should it desire to adhere, it shall present an application to this effect which shall be filed with the permanent General Secretariat and submitted to the Council at is [sic] first meeting following the presentation of the application.

Article 2. — The purpose of the League is to draw closer the relations between member States and co-ordinate their political activities with the aim of realizing a close collaboration between them, to safeguard their independence and sovereignty, and to consider in a general way the affair and interests of the Arab countries. ... .

Article 3. — The League shall have a Council composed of the representatives of the member States.   Each State shall have one vote, regardless of the number of its representatives.

The Council shall be entrusted with the function of realizing the purpose of the League and of supervising the execution of the agreements concluded between the member States on matters referred to in the preceding article or on other matters.

It shall also have the function of determining the means whereby the League will collaborate with the international organizations which may be created in the future to guarantee peace and security and organize economic and social relations.

Article 5. — The recourse to force for the settlement of disputes between two or more member States shall not be allowed.   Should there arise among them a dispute that does not involve the independence of a State, its sovereignty or its territorial integrity, and should the two contending parties apply to the Council for the settlement of this dispute, the decision of the Council shall then be effective and obligatory.

In this case, the States among whom the dispute has arisen shall not participate in the deliberations and decisions of the Council.

The Council shall mediate in a dispute which may lead to war between two member States or between a member State and another State in order to conciliate them.

The decisions relating to arbitration and mediation shall be taken by a majority vote.

Article 6. — In case of aggression or threat of aggression by a State against a member State, the attacked or threatened with attack may request an immediate meeting of the Council.

The Council shall determine the necessary measures to repel this aggression.   Its decision shall be taken unanimously.   If the aggression is committed by a member State the vote of that State will not be counted in determining unanimity.

If the aggression is committed in such a way as to render the Government of the State attacked unable to communicate with the Council, the representative of that State in the Council may request the Council to convene for the purpose set forth in the preceding paragraph. If the representative is unable to communicate with the Council, it shall be the right of any member State to request a meeting of the Council.

Article 7. — The decisions of the Council taken by a unanimous vote shall be binding on all the member States of the League; those that are reached by a majority vote shall bind only those that accept them.

In both cases the decisions of the Council shall be executed in each State in accordance with the fundamental structure of that State.

Article 8. — Every member State of the League shall respect the form of government obtaining in the other States of the League, and shall recognize the form of government obtaining as one of the rights of those States, and shall pledge itself not to take any action tending to change that form. ... .

Article 17. — The member States of the League shall file with the General Secretariat copies of all treaties and agreements which they have concluded or will conclude with any other State, whether a member of the League or otherwise.

ANNEX ON PALESTINE

At the end of the last Great War, Palestine together with the other Arab States was separated from the Ottoman Empire. She became independent, not belonging to any other State.

The Treaty of Lausanne proclaimed that their fate should be decided by the parties concerned in Palestine.

Even though Palestine was not able to control her own destiny, it was on the basis of the recognition of her independence that the Covenant of the League of Nations determined a system of government for her.

Her existence and her independence among the nations can, therefore, no more be questioned (de jure) [than] the independence of any of the other Arab States.

Even though the outward signs of this independence have remained veiled as a result of (force majeure,) it is not fitting that this should be an obstacle to the participation of Palestine in the work of the League.

Therefore, the State[s] signatory to the Pact of the Arab League consider that in view of Palestine's special circumstances, the Council of the League should designate an Arab delegate from Palestine to participate in its work until this country enjoys actual independence.

25

Anglo-American Commission
of Inquiry, 1946

Throughout the war Prime Minister Winston Churchill and President Franklin Roosevelt, both favorable to the Zionist cause, had repeatedly stated in writing and in speeches that no decision regarding the future of Palestine would be made without consulting both the Arabs and the Jews. Nontheless, both leaders had also repeatedly stated that they favored unrestricted Jewish immigration and the establishment of a Jewish state in Palestine; as a consequence the highest members of the Department of State had serious difficulty in attempting to explain official policy regarding the Near East, even questioning if one actually existed. (This problem for them is to be found repeatedly discussed in the pages of the *Foreign Relations of the United States: Diplomatic Papers* for the relevant years).

Source: United States. Congress of the United States. *Senate Documents. 79th Congress, 2nd Session. Document No. 182. Admission of Jews into Palestine: Statement of the President of the United States together with The Report of the Anglo-American Commission of Inquiry on Palestine as submitted to the President and to the Government of the United Kingdom* (Washington, D.C.: United States Government Printing Office, 1946). In order to conserve space in this reprinting of the Report the lengthy "Comments" accompanying each recommendation have been omitted.

Upon the sudden death of President Roosevelt in Warm Springs, Georgia, on 12 April 1945 Vice-President Harry S. Truman automatically assumed the presidency. Aside from having served nearly two terms in the Senate, the new president had no governmental experience, and certainly no knowledge of foreign affairs; although in May of 1944 he had already indicated his willingness to aid the Zionist cause. Six days later the Secretary of State, Edward R. Stettinius, Jr., felt it necessary to write a personal and confidential letter to the new president advising him: "It is very likely that efforts will be made by some of the Zionist leaders to obtain from you at an early date some commitments in favor of the Zionist program which is pressing for unlimited Jewish immigration into Palestine and the establishment there of a Jewish state. ... The question of Palestine is, however, a highly complex one and involves questions which go far beyond the plight of the Jews of Europe."[1] As expected, Rabbi Stephen S. Wise, co-chairman of the American Zionist Emergency Council, was enabled to obtain an appointment with Truman on 20 April at which he urged the new administration's support for the Jewish state. Eleven days later, on 1 May , the Acting Secretary of State, Joseph C. Grew, found it necessary to write a memorandum to Truman reminding him of the letter previously sent by Stettinius and of the earlier declarations made by Roosevelt that no decision regarding Palestine would be made without full consultations with both Jews and Arabs. In preparing for the Potsdam Conference ("Big 3" — Churchill, Stalin, and Truman), to be held 16 July — 2 August, Grew advised the president that the Zionists would urge him to "... insist upon a settle-

---

[1] United States. Department of State. *Foreign Relations of the United States. Diplomatic Papers: 1945. Volume VIII: The Near East and Africa* (Washington, D.C.: United States Government Printing Office, 1969) 704-5.

ment of the question in their favor."[2] As he had anticipated, in the weeks preceding the conference Truman received numerous letters from Zionist leaders and politicians, and on the 5th of July a petition signed by thirty-seven governors was sent to the White House urging that unlimited Jewish immigration and the establishment of a Jewish commonwealth in Palestine be brought up at the conference. As a result of his own predelictions and this extraordinary political pressure, on 24 July, during the course of the conference, Truman wrote a memorandum to Churchill urging the British Government to lift the restrictions upon large-scale Jewish immigration imposed by the White Paper.[3] However, as a result of the British elections, Churchill's government had been voted out of office so that he was replaced at the Potsdam Conference by the head of the new Labour government, Clement R. Attlee. His response to Truman's memorandum was that his government would have to consider the matter. Taking advantage of the new Secretary of States James F. Byrnes's visit to London, Truman wrote a letter to Attlee on 31 August pressing for the immediate admission into Palestine of 100,000 Jews. In his response, contained in separate letters dated the 14th and the 16th of September, Attlee stated that the 1,500 certificates for immigration into Palestine for September had not even been taken up, that the admission of so many additional Jews into the country at one time would be extremely detrimental to Britain's position, not only in the Near East, but also in India, and further, that this continued pressure from Truman "... could not fail to do grievous harm to relations between our two countries."[4] In response to a request of the State Department, the

---

2 Ibid., 709. "Memorandum by the Acting Secretary of State to President Truman," dated 16 June 1945.

3 Ibid., 716-17.

4 Ibid., 739.

Department of War estimated that it would require the presence of 400,000 soldiers, including American, in Palestine to quell the disturbances should a large number of Jews be permitted to enter the country in a relatively short time.

Because of Truman's continued involvement in British policy regarding Palestine, on 19 October Attlee's government decided to have the United States participate more actively by proposing the immediate appointment of a joint Anglo—American Committee of Enquiry to Europe and Palestine to investigate the Jewish refugee problem and to recommend a course of action.   On 10 December the two governments, after protracted negotiations over its terms of reference and composition, appointed the Anglo-American Committee composed of six Americans and six British, with joint chairmen.

PREFACE

We were appointed by the Governments of the United States and of the United Kingdom, as a joint body of American and British membership, with the following terms of reference:

1.   To examine political, economic, and social conditions in Palestine as they bear upon the problem of Jewish immigration and settlement therein and the well-being of the peoples now living therein.

2.   To examine the position of the Jews in those countries in Europe where they have been the victims of Nazi and Fascist persecution, and the practical measures taken or contemplated to be taken in those countries to enable them to live free from discrimination and oppression and to make estimates of those who wish or will be impelled by their conditions to migrate to Palestine or other countries outside Europe.

3.   To hear the views of competent witnesses and to consult representative Arabs and Jews on the problems of Palestine as such problems are affected by conditions subject to examination under paragraphs 1 and 2 above and by other relevant facts and circumstances, and to make recommendations to His Majesty's Government and the Government of the United States

for ad interim handling of these problems as well as for their permanent solution.

4. To make such other recommendations to His Majesty's Government and the Government of the United States as may be necessary to meet the immediate needs arising from conditions subject to examination under paragraph 2 above, by remedial action in the European countries in question or by the provision of facilities for emigration to and settlement in countries outside Europe.

The Governments urged upon us the need for the utmost expedition in dealing with the subjects committed to us for investigation, and requested to be furnished with our report within 120 days of the inception of our inquiry. We assembled in Washington on Friday, January 4, 1946, and began our public sessions on the following Monday. We sailed from the United States on January 18 and resumed our public sessions in London on January 25. We left for Europe on February 4 and 5, and, working in subcommittees, proceeded to our investigations in Germany, Poland, Czechoslovakia, Austria, Italy, and Greece. On February 28 we flew to Cairo and, after sessions there, reached Jerusalem on March 6. In Palestine, our sessions were interspersed with personal visits to different parts of the country, during which we sought to acquaint ourselves at first hand with its various characteristics and the ways of life of its inhabitants. Subcommittees visited the capitals of Syria, Lebanon, Iraq, Saudi Arabia and Trans-Jordan to hear the views of the Arab governments and representatives of bodies concerned with the subjects before us. We left Palestine on March 28 and have concluded our deliberations in Switzerland. ... We now submit the following report:

CHAPTER I. RECOMMENDATIONS AND COMMENTS

THE EUROPEAN PROBLEM

Recommendation No. 1

We have to report that such information as we received about countries other than Palestine gave no hope of substantial assistance in finding homes for Jews wishing or impelled to leave Europe.

But Palestine alone cannot meet the emigration needs of the Jewish victims of Nazi and Fascist persecution; the whole world shares responsibility for them and indeed for the resettlement of all "displaced persons."

We therefore recommend that our governments, together and in association with other countries, should endeavor immediately to find new homes for all such "displaced persons," irrespective of creed or nationality, whose ties with their former communities have been irreparably broken.

Though emigration will solve the problems of some victims of persecution, the overwhelming majority, including a considerable number of Jews, will continue to live in Europe. We recommend, therefore, that our governments endeavor to secure that immediate effect is given to the provision of the United Nations Charter calling for "universal respect for, and observance of, human rights and fundamental freedoms for all without distinction as to race, sex, language, or religion."

REFUGEE IMMIGRATION INTO PALESTINE

Recommendation No. 2

We recommend (*a*) that 100,000 certificates be authorized immediately for the admission into Palestine of Jews who have been the victims of Nazi and fascist [*sic*] persecution, (*b*) that these certificates be awarded as far as possible in 1946 and that actual immigration be pushed forward as rapidly as conditions will permit.

PRINCIPLES OF GOVERNMENT: NO ARAB, NO JEWISH STATE

Recommendation No. 3

In order to dispose, once and for all, of the exclusive claims of Jews and Arabs to Palestine, we regard it as essential that a clear statement of the following principles should be made:

I. That Jew shall not dominate Arab and Arab shall not dominate Jew in Palestine. II. That Palestine shall be neither a Jewish state nor an Arab state. III. That the form of government ultimately to be established, shall, under international guarantees, fully protect and preserve the interests in the Holy Land of Christendom and of the Moslem and Jewish faiths.

Thus Palestine must ultimately become a state which guards the rights and interests of Moslems, Jews, and

Christians alike: and accords to the inhabitants, as a whole, the fullest measure of self-government, consistent with the three paramount principles set forth above.

MANDATE AND UNITED NATIONS TRUSTEESHIP

Recommendation No. 4

We have reached the conclusion that the hostility between Jews and Arabs and, in particular, the determination of each to achieve domination, if necessary by violence, make it almost certain that, now and for some time to come, any attempt to establish either an independent Palestinian state or independent Palestinian states would result in civil strife such as might threaten the peace of the world. We therefore recommend that, until this hostility disappears, the government of Palestine be continued as at present under mandate pending the execution of a trusteeship agreement under the United Nations.

EQUALITY OF STANDARDS

Recommendation No. 5

Looking toward a form of ultimate self-government, consistent with the three principles laid down in Recommendation No. 3, we recommend that the mandatory or trustee should proclaim the principle that Arab economic, educational, and political advancement in Palestine is of equal importance with that of the Jews; and should at once prepare measures designed to bridge the gap which now exists and raise the Arab standard of living to that of the Jews; and so bring the two peoples to a full appreciation of their common interest and common destiny in the land where both belong.

FUTURE IMMIGRATION POLICY

Recommendation No. 6

We recommend that pending the early reference to the United Nations and the execution of a trusteeship agreement, the mandatory should administer Palestine according to the mandate which declares with regard to immigration that "the administration of Palestine, while insuring that the rights and position of other sections of the population are not prejudiced, shall facilitate Jewish immigration under suitable conditions."

LAND POLICY

Recommendation No. 7

(a) We recommend that the Land Transfers Regulations of 1940 be rescinded and replaced by regulations based on a policy of freedom in the sale, lease, or use of land, irrespective of race, community or creed; and providing adequate protection for the interests of small owners and tenant cultivators. (b) We further recommend that steps be taken to render nugatory and to prohibit provisions in conveyances, leases, and agreements relating to land which stipulate that only members of one race, community, or creed may be employed on or about or in connection therewith. (c) We recommend that the Government should exercise such close supervision over the holy places and localities such as the Sea of Galilee and its vicinity as will protect them from desecration and from uses which offend the conscience of religious people; and that such laws are required for this purpose be enacted forthwith.

ECONOMIC DEVELOPMENT

Recommendation No. 8

Various plans for large-scale agricultural and industrial development in Palestine have been presented for our consideration; these projects, if successfully carried into effect, could not only greatly enlarge the capacity of the country to support an increasing population, but also raise the living standards of Jew and Arab alike.

We are not in a position to assess the soundness of these specific plans; but we cannot state too strongly that, however technically feasible they may be, they will fail unless there is peace in Palestine. Moreover their full success requires the willing cooperation of adjacent Arab states, since they are not merely Palestinian projects. We recommend therefore that the examination, discussion and execution of these plans be conducted from the start and throughout, in full consultation and cooperation not only with the Jewish agency but also with the governments of the neighboring Arab states directly affected.

EDUCATION

Recommendation No. 9

We recommend that, in the interests of the concilia-tion of the two peoples and of general improvement of the Arab standard of living, by the educational system of both Jews and Arabs be reformed including the introduction of compulsory education within a reasonable time.

THE NEED FOR PEACE IN PALESTINE

Recommendation No. 10

We recommend that, if this report is adopted, it should be made clear beyond all doubt to both Jews and Arabs that any attempt from either side, by threats of violence, by ter-rorism, or by the organization or use of illegal armies to prevent its execution, will be resolutely suppressed.

Furthermore, we express the view that the Jewish Agency should at once resume active cooperation with the mandatory in the suppression of terrorism and of illegal immigration, and in the maintenance of that law and order throughout Palestine which is essential for the good of all, including the new immigrants.

> [The remaining 34 pages of the report com-prise, together with the "Comments" following each Recommendation, a detailed report about the Jews in Europe and the situation in Palestine as it appeared to the members of the Commission in 1946.]

Signed at Lausanne, Switzerland, on April 20, 1946.

26

The Grady-Morrison Plan, 1946

Without definitively stating so, the Anglo-American Committee unanimously recommended the revocation of the 1939 White Paper with its restrictions upon both immigration and land transfers. Both governments agreed that the recommendations of the committee should not be regarded as necessarily the policy of either, but were to serve as the bases for discussion between the two. They each submitted the report to the Jewish Agency, the Arab League, the Arab governments, and various Jewish organizations for comment to satisfy their long-standing promises that both the Arabs and the Jews would be consulted before any decision was reached. President Harry Truman, who had assumed personal responsibility for the determination of U.S. policy in respect to Palestine following his succession to the presidency, in June 1946, established a

Source: United States. Department of State. *Foreign Affairs of the United States 1946. Volume VII: The Near East and Africa* (Washington, D.C.: United States Government Printing Office, 1969) 652-68. The British version, with slight additions, is printed in: Great Britain. Parliamentary Papers. *Proposals for the Future of Palestine. July, 1946-February, 1947* (London: His Majesty's Stationery Office, 1947). Cmd. 7044. The plan is also referred to as "The Morrison Plan" or "The Provincial Autonomy Plan."

"Cabinet Committee on Palestine and Related Problems" composed of the Secretaries of State, War, and Treasury, with the Secretary of State as chairman.   On his part, Prime Minister Clement Attlee also appointed a high-level committee, composed of representatives from the Foreign Service, the Colonial Office, Treasury, and the Services.   By these actions both governments considered the situation in Palestine to be one of extraordinary importance.

In their early examination of the report the British Government stated that over a ten-year period the financial cost of admitting the additional 100,000 Jews would be between £115,000,000 and £125,000,000 for housing and fitting them into the economy of the country and an armed force of between 300,000 and 400,000 men to keep the peace, costs which Britain alone could not bear.   "The British are convinced that they would not be in a position to put the report into operation without substantial financial and military contributions from the US Govt."[1] In response to a request from the State—War—Navy Coordinating Committee charged with examining the military aspects of the Committee's recommendations, on 21 June the Joint Chiefs of Staff wrote: "We urge that no US armed forces be involved in carrying out the Committee's recommendations. We recommend that in implementing the report, the guiding principle be that no action should be taken which will cause repercussions in Palestine which are beyond the capabilities of British troops to control."[2] In keeping with their earlier commitments in originally appointing the Anglo-American Committee of Enquiry Attlee and Truman appointed a joint six member committee to examine the recommendations and arrive at "broad principles" for the determination, hopefully, of

[1] Top secret and urgent telegram from Secretary of State Byrnes to President Truman, Paris, 9 May 1946.   Reprinted in ibid. pp. 601-2.
[2] Ibid., p. 632.

a unified policy.   The chief of the American
group was Henry F. Grady, a career diplomat;
for the British, Herbert S. Morrison, Lord
President of the Council and Leader of the
House of Commons.   On 24 July 1946, the so-
called "Grady-Morrison Plan" was submitted to
the two governments.   These recommendations
were approved by the British Cabinet the following day.

1.   The British and United States Delegations have
now examined as a whole the recommendations of the
Anglo-American Committee of Enquiry and have arrived at a
common viewpoint on the broad principles of a policy for
carrying out these recommendations.   The following
summary of these general principles is submitted for
consideration by the two Governments.

DISPLACED PERSONS AND THE POSITION OF EUROPEAN JEWS

2.   There are two aspects to this problem — (I) resettlement in Europe and (II) emigration to countries outside
Europe.
The Anglo-American Committee recognized that the
overwhelming majority of displaced persons, including a
considerable number of Jews, will continue to live in
Europe.   One of our objectives should, therefore, be to create
conditions favourable to the re-settlement of a substantial
number of displaced persons in Europe.
3.   The only areas in Europe in which our two
Governments can directly control these conditions are the
British and United States [occupation] zones of Germany and
Austria.
In these areas, they are prepared to assist native Jews
to resettle once more in German and Austrian communities.
All available means are being used to eradicate anti-
Semitism.   Concentration camp survivors receive special
treatment as to rations, financial assistance, housing and
employment.   Moreover, both American and British authorities are pressing for an early decision on plans, at present under quadripartite examination, for the restitution of
property confiscated by the Nazis.   We recommend that all
further practicable steps should be taken to make possible
the resettlement of displaced persons in those zones.

4.   Italy and the four ex-enemy satellite states will be required by the peace treaties to secure to all persons under their jurisdiction human rights and the fundamental freedoms, and it may be hoped that this will promote in these countries conditions favourable to the re-settlement of displaced persons.

5.   Elsewhere in Europe our two Governments must rely on action through the United Nations to give practical effect to the provisions on human rights in the Charter. They should support the establishment of a commission for human rights and, also such measure of implementation as the United Nations may adopt to ensure the protection of these rights to the fullest extent practicable.   Through their support of the efforts of the United Nations to re-establish political and economic stability in Europe, our Governments will continue to contribute to the restoration of those basic conditions which will make possible the reintegration in Europe of a substantial number of displaced persons, including Jews.

6.   Though substantial numbers of displaced persons may be resettled in Europe, new homes must be found elsewhere for many of those, including Jews, whose ties with their former communities have been irreparably broken. As the Anglo-American Committee pointed out, Palestine alone cannot provide for the emigration needs of all Jewish victims of Nazi and Fascist persecution.   The two Governments should, therefore, proceed at once with measures designed to aid the re-settlement elsewhere of other Jews and displaced persons.   These will include the following:

(a)   Continuing support, through the United Nations, for the establishment of the international refugee organization which will be capable of dealing effectively with the problem of refugees and displaced persons as a whole.

(b)   Strong support for the appeal to be made at the forthcoming General Assembly of the United Nations calling on all member governments to receive in territories under their control a proportion of the displaced persons in Europe, including Jews.   In doing so, it should be emphasised that the United Kingdom Government has already accepted a commitment to promote the re-settlement of about 235,000 Polish troops and civilians and their dependents.

In addition, a large proportion of the refugees admitted during the period of Nazi persecution have remained in

the United Kingdom. Of these, approximately 70,000 are
Jews. With respect to the United States, 275,000 refugees
have been permanently resettled there, including 180,000
Jews. On resumption of the normal flow of immigration to
the United States some 53,000 quota and non-quota immigrants from those European countries from which the displaced persons are drawn will be able to enter as permanent
residents every year. It may be assumed that in the fiscal
year ending June 30, 1947, the large majority of these immigrants will be Jews and other displaced persons. The
President of the United States is prepared to seek the approval of Congress for special legislation for the entry into
the United States of 50,000 displaced persons, including Jews.

(c) Simultaneous, though separate approaches to
the governments of the British Dominions, who should be
informed of the action taken and proposed, and should be invited to support the appeal to member governments of the
United Nations and to receive a number of displaced persons
in territories under their control. Both governments, in
their approach, would emphasise the weight of the influence which could be exerted by the example of action by the
Dominions, the United Kingdom and the United States, in in-
ducing other United Nations to correspondingly liberal action. The United Kingdom Government would further stress
the relations between the settlement of displaced persons
and the problem of Jewish immigration into Palestine. The
United States Government would indicate that the arrangements it could undertake for an emergency quota would be
favourably influenced if assurances had been given that a
number of displaced persons would be re-settled in the
British Commonwealth.

(d) Continued active support to the Intergovern-
mental Committee on Refugees and, through it, to the re-settlement of as many refugees and displaced persons as
practicable. Active consideration is already being given to a
promising proposal for the transfer of displaced persons to
Brazil. The number to be re-settled there is estimated at
200,000 or more. Similar proposal relating to other South
American countries are also being explored.

7. We recommend that simultaneously with the announcement of the new policy for Palestine, our two
Governments should make a statement on the lines indicated
in paragraphs 2-6 above. Arab opposition to the admission
of 100,000 Jews to Palestine will be much stronger if this
movement begins before any indication has been given that

steps are being taken to promote the re-settlement of Jews and other displaced persons in Europe and to secure that other countries receive a share of those for whose emigration provision must be made.

8. We accept the principles laid down in recommendation 3 of the report of the Anglo-American Committee, that Palestine as a whole can be neither a Jewish nor an Arab state, that neither of the two communities in Palestine should dominate the other, and that the form of government should be such as to safeguard the interests in the Holy Land of the three great monotheistic religions. We recommend that any form of government adopted should be based on these principles. We also endorse the ultimate objective, set forth in the report, of securing self-government for the inhabitants.

The various alternatives to proceeding with the implementation of the recommendations of the Anglo-American Committee have been considered. It is our view that some alteration in the present governmental situation in Palestine has to be made and made speedily. To attempt to continue the present situation would involve the imposition of a policy by the exertion of military force and against the resistance of either or both of the two peoples of Palestine.

In the present situation in Palestine the imposition of a system of government by external authority could only be avoided either (a) by the termination of the mandate and withdrawal of British troops, which would lead to such internecine warfare by the Jews and Arabs as to make such a course unthinkable, or (b) by agreement among the Jews and Arabs themselves, of which there seems to be no present prospect.

Since some degree of compulsion will probably have to be employed it should be employed in setting in motion a system of government based on recommendation 3. The degree of such compulsion may be minimized and perhaps even acquiescence secured by wise and practical implementation of that recommendation.

The crux of the governmental problem in Palestine is to find a constitutional system which while observing the principles of recommendation 3 will best make possible progress towards self-government. The report puts forward no detailed suggestions for this purpose and our main task has therefore been to devise a method for its attainment.

We have considered an instrument of government on unitary bi-national lines based on parity between the two peoples in its legislative and executive functions, with pro-

vision for emergency action by the administering authority
in the event of absence of willingness on the part of the two
peoples to participate in the functioning of such a plan, or
in the event of a deadlock in such governmental machinery.

In view, however, of the expressed reaction of the two
peoples to the report of the Anglo-American Committee, we
believe that the following plan
is more practicable and that effect could be given to it with
less difficulty.

PLAN FOR PROVINCIAL AUTONOMY

9. *Territorial areas.* The plan envisages the division
of Palestine into four areas: an Arab province, a Jewish
province, a district of Jerusalem and a district of the Negev.
The Jewish province will include Eastern Galilee, most the
Plains of Esdraelon and Jezreel, the Beisan area, Haifa, the
Plain of Sharon (excluding the town of Jaffa) and a portion
of the southern coastal plain. The Jerusalem district will
include Jerusalem, Bethlehem and their immediate environs.
The Negev district will consist of the uninhabited triangle of
waste land in the south of Palestine beyond the present limit
of cultivation. The Arab province will include the remainder of Palestine.

The population of these areas will be approximately as
follows:

	Arabs	Jews
Arab province	815,000	15,000
Jewish province	301,000	451,000
Jerusalem district	96,000	102,000
Negev district	—	—

The provincial boundaries will be purely administrative boundaries, defining the area within which a local legislature is empowered to legislate on certain subjects and a
local executive to administer its laws. They will in no sense
for [be] frontiers and they will consequently have no
significance   as   regards   defence,   customs   or
communications. In our view, however, it is of great
importance to make it clear that, once settled, these
boundaries will not be susceptible of change except by
agreement between the two provinces. We recommend that
a provision to this effect be embodied in any trusteeship

agreement and in any instrument bringing the plan into operation.[3]

10. *Division of powers.* The provincial governments will have power of legislation and administration within their provincial areas with regard to municipal and village administration, agriculture, fisheries, forest, land registration, land sales, land settlement, land purchase and expropriation, education, public health and other social services, trade and industry, and local roads, irrigation, development and public works.   They will also have power to limit the number and determine the qualifications of persons who may take up permanent residence in their territories, after the date of the introduction of the plan.   The provincial governments will be required by the instrument of government which establishes the fundamental law to provide for the guarantee of civil rights and equality before the law for all residents.   They shall not, in their legislation or administration, impose obstacles to free inter-territorial transit, trade or commerce.

For the purpose of carrying out these functions the provincial governments will have power to appropriate funds, to levy taxes, excluding customs and excise, to borrow within the province and, with the consent of the central government, to borrow abroad.

Control of foreign exchange and currency shall, for the time being, be a function of the central government. The central government shall also for the time being be responsible for the licensing of imports.   It shall allocate licenses equitably between the two provinces after consultation with their representatives.   Within two years of the introduction of the provincial autonomy plan (unless a later date is agreed to by the provinces and the central government) a broad allocation of the value of import licenses between the two provinces shall be made from time to time by the central government, in consultation with the provinces. Thereafter the provinces shall have the right to obtain for their residents licenses up to the amount of the allocation and to decide to what classes of goods such licenses shall be allocated.   At a date not later than 31 December, 1946, import licensing shall be on a non-discriminatory basis as between sources of supply.

---

[3] The British version includes the sentence: "The details of the boundaries   proposed are shown in the map reproduced in Appendex A."   The map was not reproduced in the U.S. version.

If Palestine becomes a member of the United Nations or any specialized agencies thereof (including the International Monetary Fund, the International Bank, or the proposed International Trade Organization) the provincial governments must deal with all relevant matters within their jurisdiction in a manner consistent with the obligations of Palestine as a member of these bodies.

There will be reserved to the central government exclusive authority as to defence, foreign relations and customs and excise. In addition there will be reserved initially to the central government exclusive authority as to police, prisons, courts, railway facilities and Haifa harbour, posts and telegraphs, civil aviation, broadcasting and antiquities, though certain of these powers will be transferred in whole or in part to the provincial governments as soon as it becomes practicable. The central government will in addition have power to borrow money, to make financial grants to the provinces, to provide for inter-territorial and international irrigation and development projects, to facilitate inter-territorial and international trade and commerce and communications, and to provide for arterial highways. It will be empowered to examine and verify municipal and provincial accounts, to prescribe suitable and uniform methods of accounting, to prescribe the uses of any funds granted by it to the provinces, and to examine proposed budgets of provincial expenditures, and to make recommendations with respect to them.

Immigration will be administered by the central government. So far as the provinces are concerned, the central government will authorise the immigration desired by the respective provincial governments, to the extent to which the economic absorptive capacity of the province will not thereby be exceeded. It shall not have power to authorise immigration into either province in excess of any limitations imposed by the provincial government.

All powers not expressly granted to the provincial governments will be reserved to the central government.

11. *Provincial governments.* An elected legislative chamber will be established in each province. During the first 5 years of the plan the presiding officers of those chambers will be appointed by the High Commissioner. Thereafter they will be elected by the chambers from among their members. Bills passed by the legislative chambers will become law only after they have received the assent of the High Commissioner, representing the administering au-

thority, but assent will be denied only if such bills are inconsistent with the instrument of government.

A provincial legislature may provide that any residents of the Jerusalem district designated by it may be represented in the provincial legislature if they so desire.

An executive consisting of a chief minister and a council of ministers will be appointed in each province by the High Commissioner from among the members of the legislative chamber after consultation with its leaders.

If a provincial government fails to perform a proper governmental function or exceeds its proper authority the High Commissioner will have authority to exercise emergency powers within the province for the performance of that function or to prevent such excess.

12. *The Central government.* The executive and legislative functions of the central government will initially be exercised by a High Commissioner appointed by the administering authority. He will be assisted by a nominated executive council composed of the heads of the major executive departments. Certain of these departments will be headed, as soon as the High Commissioner deems practicable, by Palestinians.

A development planning board will be established by the High Commissioner comprising the heads of the appropriate central executive departments, and representatives of each of the provinces. This board will initiate plans for the general economic development of Palestine and will supervise the implementation of such plans. A tariff board will also be established on similar lines to advise on customs and excise policy and on the rates of duty to be imposed.

13. *The Jerusalem district.* In the Jerusalem district there will be established a council with powers similar to those of a municipal council. The majority of its members will be elected, but there will be certain members designated by the High Commissioner.

As [the] central government, in respect of the Jerusalem district, will have the same powers to limit the number and determine the qualifications of persons who may take up permanent residence in that district as are conferred on the provincial governments in respect of their provinces.

Powers not delegated to the district council will be exercised in the Jerusalem district by the central government.

14. *The Negev district.* The Negev district will be held under direct administration by the central government

pending a survey of its development possibilities. Within 5 years and upon the completion of this survey, the administering authority shall submit to the appropriate organ of the United Nations recommendations, arrived at after consultation with the Arab and Jewish provinces, concerning the disposition of the area.

15. *Considerations in the adoption of the provincial plan.* The following are the main advantages of the plan for provincial autonomy:

The plan offers to the Jews an opportunity to exercise a wide measure of control over immigration into one part of Palestine and to forward in the Jewish province the development of the Jewish national home. At the same time it offers to the majority of the Arabs of Palestine their own political institutions in an Arab province and freedom from fear of further Jewish immigration into that province without their consent. It makes it possible to give practical [effect] to the principles of government enunciated in recommendation 3 of the Anglo-American Committee; and it offers a prospect of development towards self-government of which there is less home in a unitary Palestine. It provides a means of segregating Jew and Arab to an extent which should substantially reduce the risk of a continuation of widespread violence and disorder in Palestine. In the long term, the plan leaves the way open for constitutional development either towards partition or towards federal unity. The association of representatives of the two provinces in the administration of central subjects may lead ultimately to a fully developed federal constitution. On the contrary, if the centrifugal forces prove too strong, the way is open towards partition. The provincial plan does not prejudge this issue either way. The administering authority will be prepared to hand over the government to the people of the country as soon as the two communities express a common desire to that end and present an agreed scheme which will ensure its stable administration.

In arriving at the provincial autonomy plan as preferable on grounds of practicability to the unitary binational plan, we are not unmindful of the fact that there are inherent in it certain difficulties:

(1) The plan calls for immediate decision on the highly controversial matter of the boundaries of the respective provinces. It is one on which feelings on both sides are apt to run high.

(2) The Jewish and Arab populations are so interlaced in the area out of which a Jewish province would have to be

created that a very serious minority problem would arise in that province which would not be involved in the proposed Arab province. The argument may be made by the Arabs that if it is proper to submit such a large segment of the Arab population to a majority rule by the Jews in the Jewish province those same considerations would support their own contention that a Palestinian state be set up in which there would be a majority of the Arabs and a minority of the Jews. Under the proposed system, however, there would be effective protection for the Arab minority in the Jewish province.

(3)   The proposed boundaries are such that the land and other economic resources in the Jewish area are superior to those in the Arab area. The Jewish area would be well able to support the requisite government services of the provincial government. The Arab area would not now be able to support even the present level of services, much less the improved services which the recommendations of the Anglo-American report urge as necessary to raise the Arab standard of living. This difficulty is met by the general power given to the central government to make grants to provinces and by the specific provisions in a later paragraph for meeting the anticipated deficiencies in the budget of the Arab province during the earlier years of the autonomy plan.

After considering the foregoing difficulties, we feel that the provincial autonomy plan is the preferable one for meeting recommendation 3.[4]

HOLY PLACES

16.   It will be the duty of the central government to safeguard the Moslem, Jewish and Christian holy places. An inter-denominational council will be set up to advise the

---

[4] The British version contains the following additional section, numbered 15A: *"Further Details of Provincial Autonomy Plan.* The United States Delegation have submitted a preliminary draft for the heads of an instrument of government to give effect to this Plan. This draft, which is reproduced in Appendix B [not included in this collection], gives some further details of the constitution proposed. The draft has not been examined by the two Delegations jointly; but it is a valuable contribution which will serve as a basis for further work on the preparation of the draft constitution."

central government on all matters relating to the Christian holy places.

LAND POLICY

17.   In putting the provincial autonomy plan into effect the administratering authority will rescind the land transfer regulations of 1940.   The prohibition or frustration of provisions in leases stipulating that only members of one race, community or creed may be employed on or in connection with the land leased will be a matter for action by the provincial authorities.

IMMIGRATION

18.   Under the provincial autonomy plan immigration will be administered by the central government separately for the Arab province, the Jewish province, and the Jerusalem and Negev districts.   In effect immigration into the provinces will be regulated by the provincial governments, subject only to the power of the central government which may impose limitations upon immigration in accordance with the economic absorptive capacity of either province.   These provisions will probably mean the complete exclusion of Jewish immigrants from the Arab province, but will result, under ordinary circumstances, in immigration into the Jewish province on whatever scale is desired by its government.   The grounds on which the central government could curtail the immigration quotas proposed by the provinces will be defined in the instrument of government and in any trusteeship agreement or other instrument approved by the United Nations.   The provincial authorities will, therefore, be able to appeal to the United Nations against any decision in respect of immigration which they consider to be in contravention of the terms of such instruments.

On the assumption that our proposals for provincial autonomy are adopted as the policy of our two Governments, we recommend the acceptance of recommendations 2 and 6 of the Anglo-American Committee.

19.   We have considered the memorandum embodying the results of the preliminary discussions held in London from 17th to 27th June on recommendation 2 of the Anglo-American report, and we endorse the outline plan for the movement of 100,000 Jews to Palestine.   We recommend that

this plan be initiated immediately if it is decided to put the constitutional proposals into effect.

We recommend that every effort should be made to complete the operation within 12 months of the date on which the emigration begins. We recommend that the necessary immigration certificates should be issued as rapidly as possible. As regards the rate of movement, shipment will proceed at the maximum rate consistent with the clearance of the transit camps in Palestine.

For the purpose of checking illegal immigration any Jews entering Palestine illegally after the plan has been initiated will be counted against the 100,000.

THE ARAB PROGRAMME

20. We accept recommendations 5 and 9 of the Anglo-American Committee that the economic and educational standards of the Arabs should be raised, subject to the proviso that the pace at which such development can be undertaken will have to be limited by practical considerations, such as the provision of trained personnel and the capacity of the economy of the area to absorb a large spending programme. A tentative plan has been worked out by Palestine Government which can form the basis of the programme.

(a) *Health and social services.* We endorse the proposals for a health service for the Arabs of a standard similar to that established for the Jews. We also contemplate the establishment of social services ancillary to education and health, e.g. institutions for the care of mothers, children and the old, school feeding, playgrounds, unemployment assistance, the teaching of handicrafts, youth and cultural organizations.

(b) *Education.* The immediate provision of compulsory education for the Arabs is not practicable, but universal primary education could be achieved in 10 years, except as regards girls in the smaller villages. Immediate steps should be taken to improve primary, secondary and university education in the Arab community.

(c) *Economic measures.* Improved facilities for education and for health and other social services will not alone bridge the gap between the standards of living of the two communities; a wide economic advancement must accompany them.

The greatest part of the Arab rural community, which constitutes 66% of the whole Arab population, consists of a peasantry living at about bare subsistence level. There are few village industries and Arab industry in general provides very little employment. Measures to improve Arab economic conditions must be directed primarily to the agricultural population, but should also include measure to promote the development of light industries. The principal measures envisaged are the following:

(I)   Agrarian reorganization to rationalize and consolidate land holdings.

(II)   Improvement in the use of land: promotion of regional development: prevention of erosion: agricultural research.

(III)   Promotion of light industries and development of local crafts and industries.

(IV)   Provision of cheap credit.

(V)   Expansion of labour organizations.

(VI)   Promotion of the cooperative movement.

(*d*) *Living conditions*. We also recommend the following measures for improving living conditions in the Arab community:

(I)   Improvements in housing and promotion of housing schemes.

(II)   Survey and town planning with a view to improvement schemes.

(III)   Improvement of water supplies.

21.   The cost of the foregoing proposals is discussed in later paragraphs.

DEVELOPMENT PROJECTS

22.   We believe that the need for economic development in Palestine should be recognized as merely a part of the broader situation with respect to economic development in the countries of the Middle East. In any statement which is made to the interested parties or to the public, it should be emphasized that our Governments have assisted and welcomed the advent of the states of the Middle East into full political equality. They have observed with interest the examination by those states of their possibilities for economic development, which appear to be great. If it is the desire of any of those states to resort to international agencies for aid by loan or otherwise in exploring and effectuating such projects, as for example in the reclaiming or improvement

of great areas by water control and irrigation, they will receive sympathetic support.

Certainly most substantial Palestinian development should be linked with developments in Transjordan and probably in Syria and Lebanon.

We recommend that a survey of the water resources of Palestine and, with the consent of the Government of Transjordan, of water resources common to the two areas should be undertaken as soon as possible by consulting engineers of international repute. They should further be invited, if adequate data for the purpose is available, to draw up an outline project indicating the best use of the water available. This project should be considered, and action on it taken, by the central government in consultation with the development board to which, for this purpose, the Government of Transjordan, and of any other neighboring state affected, would be invited to send representatives.

23.   Long term development schemes which are wholly within one province will be financed by borrowing internally or abroad by the provincial government or an appropriate organization in the province. In the event that the borrowing is from abroad it is possible that the loans will have to be guaranteed by the central government. Long-term development schemes which involve both provinces or perhaps neighboring countries will require participation by the central government but it will be desirable for the provincial governments to take as much responsibility as is practicable in day-to-day administration and particularly in finance. The financial support of such projects should ultimately be made the responsibility of the provinces in proportion to the benefits which they derive. Schemes financed by loans should be self-liquidating and, as such, they can be secured on revenues from the projects, reinforced when necessary by a general charge on provincial revenues.

FINANCE

24.   We have considered various estimates of the cost of carrying out the measures set out above. We have also considered the effect on the Palestine budget of introducing the proposed scheme of provincial autonomy. We have based our conclusions on two assumptions; first, that the cost of living index will not rise in Palestine, and, secondly, that there will be no increased expenditure on law and order

coupled with loss of revenue due to disorders and non-cooperation.

On the first of the points, it is clear that the programmes envisaged will constitute an inflationary influence, but against this a large part of expenditures will be for imported goods financed with external money. In addition substantial borrowing of savings within Palestine may be assumed and increasing supplies of imported goods at lower prices should become available. Should our assumption be incorrect, it is not possible to estimate the effect on the Palestine budget but cost of living subsidies involving expenditure of up to £4,000,000 might be necessary. Equally, disorders and non-cooperation might add significantly to expenditures and reduce revenues.

25. *The Jewish programme.* According to our studies the total costs of the immigration of the 100,000 Jews can be put at approximately £70,000,000, made up as follows:

Transitional assistance, £6,000,000.

Housing, £14,000,000.

Capital investment to provide employment, £50,000,000.

Since it is essential to complete the programme as soon as possible, we assume that the whole £70,000,000 will be spent within 2 years. The maximum expectation from reparations available for Palestine is £5,000,000; from contributions by world Jewry £20,000,000; and from loans to be raised in Palestine (whether in Palestine pounds or in sterling) £35,000,000. This would give a total of £60,000,000 for the Jewish programme, leaving a deficit of £10,000,000, which can be met by self-liquidating loans.

26. The Jewish Agency has publicly accepted responsibility for costs connected with the immigration of 100,000 Jews to Palestine. This financial responsibility should be confirmed, but there would be no need to ask the Agency to agree to any of our specific estimates. In due course the responsibility in question will be transferred to the government of the Jewish province.

Our studies indicate that £10 million of required capital cannot be provided from Jewish sources within the next 2 years. As, however, this deficiency is for purposes suitable for self-liquidating loans, it can be met by loans under the $250 million credit provided for in paragraph 29.

27. *Financial effects of provincial autonomy.* A rough distribution of existing expenditures and revenues on the basis of the division of responsibility among the central

government, the two provinces, and the Jerusalem district indicates that:

(*a*)   The central government will continue to incur more than half of the present expenditures of the Palestine Government.   It will have an estimated surplus in the order of perhaps £1,000,000.

(*b*)   Revenues of the Jewish province will be substantially in excess of expenditures, giving rise to a surplus of £1,400,000.

(*c*)   Expenditures of the Arab province will be substantially in excess of revenues, giving rise to a deficit of £2,100,000.

Since expenditures in the programme for the benefit of the Arabs would be concentrated entirely in the Arab province, the deficit of £2,100,000 in that province will be increased by an amount which might run to £1,000,000 annually as an average in the first 5 years.

From this total recurrent deficit of roundly £3,000,000 there may be deducted possibly as much as £1,000,000 representing excess revenues of the central government subject to grants to the province.   There will remain currently a net deficit in the neighbourhood of £2,000,000.   The United Kingdom Delegation proposes to recommend to His Majesty's Government to ask Parliament to assume of [the] ultimate responsibility for recurring deficits up [to] the time when increased revenues permit it to be met out of Arab provincial or central government funds.

28. *Cost of the Arab program[me]*.   We have attempted to estimate the cost of a practicable program[me], using as a guide the estimate of costs made in a survey by the Palestine Government.   That survey was made on the basis of a program[me] spread over the whole of Palestine.   The concentration of the program[me] in the Arab area would in any case make it necessary to revise these estimates.   We have allowed for this, and also for such limitations as the provision of trained personnel and the capacity of the Arab economy to absorb a large spending program[me].   Allowing for such considerations we think that a spending program[me] of up to £15 million to £20 million over 10 years should be regarded as fully adequate to implement the recommendations for improved education, health, and economic services of the Anglo-American Committee.   In addition, £10 million should be provided for credit facilities.   There are, however, so many unknown factors in the carrying out of such a program[me] that it would be most unwise to commit ourselves

to any public statement as to the amount of the program[me]s to be undertaken.   Of the Arab program[me] £10
million for credit facilities could be secured from local bank
credits.   Of the remainder of the program[me], only a small
portion would be suitable for the self-liquidating loans dealt
with under paragraph 29.   Provision of an additional
£12,500,000 at this time will, it is believed, care for expenditure sufficient to ensure that the program[me] will be effectively carried forward to the period when means of additional financing may be found.   The United States Delegation
has therefore agreed, as a part of its contribution to the
general program[me], to propose to the President of the
United States that he recommend legislation granting
£50,000,000[5] to the Government of Palestine for the purpose
of financing development schemes not suitable for self-liquidating loans and for assisting in the meeting of extraordinary expenses during the difficulties of the transitional period.

   29. *Capital for development.*   A large portion of the
capital needed for the self-sustaining projects mentioned in
paragraph 22 must come from outside sources.   It is possible
that Palestine could obtain a loan from the International
Bank if she should become a member.   The United States
Delegation proposes, in the event that finance from other
sources such as the International Bank is not available, to
recommend that the President seek legislation authorizing
the making of loans through an appropriate agency for the
development of the Middle East region, including Palestine,
up to £250[6] million.

   30. *Public order.*   It is clear that the difficulties of introducing the policy which we have outlined will be greatly
enhanced so long as there are in existence armed organizations, Arab and Jewish, determined in the last resort to oppose by force any solution which is not to their liking.   We
agree that private armies constitute a danger to the peace of
the world and ought not to exist, and that attempts to prevent
by violence the execution of the policy once it has been put
into effect should be resolutely suppressed.   We agree that to
this end it is necessary that armed organisations which are
not prepared to submit themselves to the full control of the
central government should be dissolved and that the illegal

---

[5] The British Command Paper reads "dollars."
[6] "Dollars" in the British version.

holding of arms and explosives should be vigorously combatted.

31. *Future procedure*. We recognise that, in view of the existing situation in Palestine, any policy for that country will probably have to be introduced without the willing consent of either community. On the other hand, there is a degree of sustained and determined resistance of either Jews or Arabs beyond which no policy could be enforced. An effort to obtain at least a measure of acquiescence from the Arabs and Jews would therefore be an essential preliminary to the introduction of the above proposals. We therefore recommend that, if these proposals are adopted by our two Governments, they should be presented to Arab and Jewish representatives as a basis for negotiations at a conference to be convened by the United Kingdom Government.

32. In accordance with recommendation 4 of the Anglo-American Committee, we propose that the new policy should be embodied in a trusteeship agreement for Palestine. The conference with Arab and Jewish representatives should therefore be convened in time for its results to be available before the opening of the second part of the first session of the General Assembly of the United Nations. If the results of the conference were such as to suggest that the new policy would meet with a sufficient degree of acceptance in Palestine, the Government of the United Kingdom would proceed to put the plan into effect and would inform the General Assembly that practical considerations required this to be done under the existing mandate, but that they would press on as quickly as possible with a trusteeship agreement and would hope to lay a draft before the General Assembly at its next (1947) session. It would then be possible simultaneously to inaugurate the policy in Palestine and to undertake the consultations provided for in article 79 of the United Nations Charter.

33. We are not able at this stage to make recommendations regarding the course to be adopted if the conference with Arab and Jewish representatives led to the conclusion that the introduction of the policy proposed would be so violently resisted by one or both of the two peoples in Palestine that it could not be enforced. In that situation further consultation between our two Governments would be necessary.

27

British Letter to the United Nations, 1947

The proposals set forth in the "Grady-Morrison Plan" were almost immediately leaked, believed at the time by Dr. Nahum Goldmann, an American member of the Executive of the Jewish Agency, then in London. There was an immediate outcry on the part of the Zionist leaders in the United States, the most vociferous being Rabbi Abba Hillel Silver of Cleveland, Ohio, the extremist president of the Zionist Organization of America, who had the ear of Senator Robert A. Taft, of Ohio. On 30 July Harry Truman had a long meeting with his cabinet regarding the proposals, in which he was warned that the plan was "loaded with political dynamite," and consulted with members of both houses of Congress, including Senator Taft. In addition, the newspapers were filled with letters and columns attacking the plan and the president received numerous letters and petitions. As a result, he felt that he could not obtain "... the support necessary to fulfill the proposals. ... In view of the extreme intensity of feeling in centers of Jewish population in this country

Source: United Nations. *Official Records of the First Special Session of the General Assembly. Vol. I: Plenary Meetings of the General Assembly. Verbatum Record: 28 April- 15 May 1947.* (Lake Success, New York: United Nations, 1947) Annex 1, p. 183 (Document A/286).

neither political party would support this program at the present time ..."[1] Upon being informed of Truman's decision, by the American Ambassador in London on the 31st, Clement Attlee on 7 August, in a personal letter addressed to President Truman, expressed his great disappointment and confusion as to what his government's position regarding the plan should now be. Meanwhile, the terrorist activities in Palestine continued, and the Jewish Agency adamantly refused to assist the government in helping to put an end to the bloodshed.

On 5 August the Executive of the Jewish Agency announced that the proposals were "... unacceptable as a basis for discussion" and demanded:

" *a*) the immediate grant of 100,000 certificates and the immediate beginning of the transportation of the 100,000 to Palestine;
"*b*) the grant of immediate full autonomy (in appointing its administration and in the economic field) to that area of Palestine to be designated to become a Jewish State;
"*c*) the grant of the right of control of immigration to the administration of that area in Palestine designated to be a Jewish State."[2]

The reaction from the Conference of Arab Foreign Ministers, meeting in Alexandria, was just as strong in condemning the plan, rejecting any form of partition and demanding that Palestine be given its immediate independence. The British Government, however, felt that it could not abandon the plan, at least as a basis for discussion, as it had been reached in good faith and had been

---

[1] Memorandum of a conversation between Acting Secretary of State Dean Acheson and Lord Halifax, the British Ambassador, 30 July 1946. United States. Department of State. *Foreign Relations of the United States: 1946* , 7 (Washington, D.C., United States Government Printing Office, 1969) 673-4.
[2] Ibid., 680.

accepted by the cabinet.   Foreign Minister
Ernest Bevan and   Prime Minister Attlee were
determined to proceed with the predetermined
discussions with representatives of the Arab
states and the executive of the Jewish Agency.
The Conference on Palestine began on 10
September at Lancaster House in London, with
the Arabs and the Zionists meeting separately
with Bevan and the colonial secretary, as they
refused to sit together, began on 10 September
at Lancaster House in London.   It temporarily
adjourned on 2 October so that the British
Government could study the proposals put forth
by the Arab delegation.   Although it had been
hoped to reopen the talks in the middle of
December, it was not until 21 January 1947 that
the conference was reconvened.   By the 14th of
February the talks had completely broken
down.   Britain was unable to find a compromise
between the opposing demands of the Arabs
and the Jews, the former pressing for the
immediate end to the mandate and the
establishment of an independent state
comprising the whole of Palestine, the latter
proposing the partitioning of Palestine   that
would lead to "a viable Jewish state" in the
western half of the country.   At a cabinet
meeting held on 14 February it was agreed that
"the right course was now to submit the whole
problem to the United Nations, ...   If the
settlement suggested by the United Nations
were not acceptable to us, we should be at
liberty then to surrender the Mandate and
leave the United Nations to make other
arrangements for the future administration of
Palestine."[3] In a speech before the House of
Commons on 25 February Foreign Minister
Bevan charged that intervention in Britain's
attempts to find a solution to the Palestine
problem on the part of the U.S. administration
had led to the impasse.   "I really must point
out," he said, "that in international affairs I

---

[3] CAB 128/9(47), quoted in: T. G. Fraser, *The Middle East, 1914-1979* (New York: St. Martin's Press, 1980) 39.

cannot settle things if my problem is made the subject of [American] local elections."[4]

As a result of the decision of the cabinet the British Ambassador to the United Nations, Sir Alexander Cadogan, was instructed to deliver the following letter to the Secretary-General of the United Nations placing the Palestine problem before the General Assembly.

United Kingdom delegation
to the United Nations

New York
2 April 1947

Dr. Victor Chi Tsai Hoo,
Assistant Secretary-General of the United Nations,
Lake Success

Sir,

I have received the following message from my Government:

"His Majesty's Government in the United Kingdom request the Secretary-General of the United Nations to place the question of Palestine on the agenda of the General Assembly at its next regular annual session. They will submit to the Assembly an account of their administration of the League of Nations mandate and will ask the Assembly to make recommendations, under Article 10 of the Charter, concerning the future government of Palestine.

"In making this request, His Majesty's Government draw the attention of the Secretary-General to the desirability of an early settlement in Palestine and to the risk that the General Assembly might not be able to decide upon its recommendations at its next regular annual session unless some preliminary study of the question had previously been made under the auspices of the United Nations. They therefore request the Secretary-General to summon, as soon as possible, a special session of the General Assembly for the purpose of constituting and instructing a special committee to prepare for the consideration, at the

---

[4] Great Britain. *Parliamentary Debates: House of Commons*, 5th series, vol. 433, col. 1901.

regular session of the Assembly, of the question referred to in the preceding paragraph."

I have the honour to be

(*Signed*) Alexander Cadogan

28

United Nations Partition Plan for Palestine, 1947

In accordance with the request of the British Government [#27], Trygve Lie, the secretary-general of the United Nations, called a special meeting of the General Assembly, which convened on 28 April 1947. The sole item on the agenda was to constitute and instruct a special committee to consider the question of Palestine; the General Committee disallowed the request of Egypt, Iraq, Syria, Lebanon, and Saudi Arabia to have also placed upon the agenda: "The termination of the Mandate over Palestine and the declaration of its independence."[1] On 15 May, on a vote of forty-five to seven, with one abstention, the Assembly adopted resolution 106 (S-1) establishing the United Nations Special Committee on Palestine (UNSCOP). Those states opposing the resolution were: Afghanistan, Egypt, Iraq, Lebanon, Saudi Arabia, Syria, and Turkey; Siam abstained.

Source: United Nations. *Official Records of the Second Session of the General Assembly. Resolutions 18 September-29 November 1947.* (Lake Success, New York: United Nations, 1947) 131-50. Double column with opposing English and French texts.

[1] United Nations. *Official Records of the Second Session of the General Assembly: Supplement No. 11. United Nations Special Committee on Palestine. Report to the General Assembly.* (Lake Success, New York: United Nations, 1947) 1.

Representatives on the committee were to be drawn from Australia, Canada, Czechoslovakia, Guatemala, India, Iran, Netherlands, Peru, Sweden, Uruguay, and Yugoslavia. By article 2 of the resolution the committee was to "... have the widest powers to ascertain and record facts, and to investigate all questions and issues relevant to the problem of Palestine;... ." Under its terms of reference the committee was permitted only three and one-half months in which to conduct its investigations and prepare its final report, for by article 7 :"The Special Committee's report shall be communicated to the Secretary-General not later than 1 September 1947, in order that it may be circulated to the Members of the United Nations in time for consideration by the second regular session of the General Assembly;... ."[2] From the date of its first meeting on 26 May until the signing of the report on 31 August, the committee held sixteen public meetings and thirty-six private meetings at Lake Success, New York, Jerusalem, Beirut, and Geneva. In its final report the committee presented the plan for the partitioning of Palestine by a majority vote, with the representatives from Australia, Guatemala, India, Uruguay, and Yugoslavia, expressing grave reservations to the recommendation in whole or in part. Understandably, the Arab states, and those with close relations to them, rejected the idea of partitioning, while the Jews and Zionists were very much in favor, for it would provide through an international organization that which they had been seeking for many years. Within the United States Government there was a division of opinion, with President Truman and many members of Congress in favor of the resolution whilst the State Department was opposed, fearful of its impact upon U.S. relations with the Arab states. From the time of the submission of UNSCOP's report and the final

---

[2] The full text of the resolution is printed on pp. 2-2 of the above report.

vote by the General Assembly on 29 November, the White House was deluged by pro-Zionist mail and petitions; in addition, the leaders of the Democratic party were concerned that if Truman ordered the U.S. delegation to vote against partition, Jewish campaign contributions might very well dry up. Once again Palestine had intruded upon domestic U.S. politics. In the days preceding the vote in the United Nations various members of the U.S. Government, including some in Congress, and leading American Zionists began to exert extraordinary pressure upon a number of the smaller states, including the Philippines, Haiti, Liberia, Cuba, China, Ecuador, Honduras, Paraguay, and Greece to either vote in favor of the resolution or to abstain.[3] On 29 November the General Assembly, by a vote of 33 to 13, with 10 abstentions (slightly more than the required two-thirds majority) voted in favor of partition.

The resolution thus passed provided for the termination of the British mandate no later that 1 August 1948; called for the establishment of Arab and Jewish states within the borders established by UNSCOP no later than 1 October 1948 and an internationalized City of Jerusalem under the authority of the United Nations; the appointment of a five member United Nations Palestine Commission[4] ; and, as if it would be possible for the two intractible enemies to co-operate after twenty-seven years of conflict, the formation of a ten-year Economic Union of Palestine with responsibility for a customs union, joint currency, joint operation of the

---

[3] The political maneuvering within the U.S. Government at this time has been well documented in Robert J. Donovan's excellent account of Truman's presidency, *Conflict and Crisis: The Presidency of Harry S. Truman 1945-1948* (New York: W. W. Norton & Company, 1977), 324-31.

[4] The Commission was relieved of its duties by General Assembly Resolution 186 (S-2), dated 14 May 1948, with the appointment of a United Nations Mediator.

railways, posts, telegraph, ports, and airports, and joint economic development.

RESOLUTION ADOPTED ON THE REPORT OF THE *AD HOC* COMMITTEE ON THE PALESTINIAN QUESTION

181 (II) Future government of Palestine

A

The General Assembly,

Having met in special session at the request of the mandatory Power to constitute and instruct a special committee to prepare for the consideration of the question of the future government of Palestine at the second regular session;

Having constituted a Special Committee and instructed it to investigate all questions and issues relevant to the problem of Palestine, and to prepare proposals for the solution of the problem, and

Having received and examined the report of the Special Committee (document A/364)[5] including a number of unanimous recommendations and a plan of partition with economic union approved by the majority of the Special Committee,

Considers that the present situation in Palestine is one which is likely to impair the general welfare and friendly relations among nations;

Takes note of the declaration by the mandatory Power that it plans to complete its evacuation of Palestine by 1 August 1948;

Recommends to the United Kingdom, as the mandatory Power for Palestine, and to all other Members of the United Nations the adoption and implementation, with regard to the future government of Palestine, of the Plan of Partition with Economic Union set out below;

Requests that

(a) The Security Council take the necessary measures as provided for in the plan for its implementation;

---

[5] "See *Official Records of the second session of the General Assembly*, Supplement No. 11, Volumes I-IV." [Original footnote in text].

(*b*) The Security Council consider, if circumstances during the transitional period require such consideration, whether the situation in Palestine constitutes a threat to the peace. If it decides that such a threat exists, and in order to maintain international peace and security, the Security Council should supplement the authorization of the General Assembly by taking measures, under Articles 39 and 41 of the Charter, to empower the United Nations Commission, as provided in this [132] resolution, to exercise in Palestine the functions which are assigned to it by this resolution;

(*c*) The Security Council determine as a threat to the peace, breach of the peace or act of aggression, in accordance with Article 39 of the Charter, any attempt to alter by force the settlement envisaged by this resolution;

(*d*) The Trusteeship Council be informed of the responsibilities envisaged for it in this plan;

Calls upon the inhabitants of Palestine to take such steps as may be necessary on their part to put this plan into effect;

Appeals to all Governments and all peoples to refrain from taking any action which might hamper or delay the carrying out of these recommendations, and

Authorizes the Secretary-General to reimburse travel and subsistence expenses of the members of the Commission referred to in Part I, Section B, paragraph 1 below, on such basis and in such form as he may determine most appropriate in the circumstances, and to provide the Commission with the necessary staff to assist in carrying out the functions assigned to the Commission by the General Assembly.

B[6]

The General Assembly

Authorizes the Secretary-General to draw from the Working Capital Fund a sum not to exceed $2,000,000 for the purposes set forth in the last paragraph of the resolution on the future government of Palestine.

Hundred and twenty-eighth plenary meeting,

29 November 1947.

---

[6] "This resolution was adopted without reference to a Committee." [Original footnote in text].

At its hundred and twenty-eighth plenary meeting on 29 November 1947 the General Assembly, in accordance with the terms of the above resolution, elected the following members of the United Nations Commission on Palestine:
BOLIVIA, CZECHOSLOVAKIA, DENMARK, PANAMA and PHILIPPINES.

PLAN OF PARTITION WITH ECONOMIC UNION

PART I

Future constitution and government of Palestine

A. TERMINATION OF MANDATE, PARTITION AND INDEPENDENCE

1. The Mandate for Palestine shall terminate as soon as possible but in any case not later than 1 August 1948.
2. The armed forces of the mandatory Power shall be progressively withdrawn from Palestine, the withdrawal to be completed as soon as possible but in any case not later than 1 August 1948.

The mandatory Power shall advise the Commission, as far in advance as possible, of its intention to terminate the Mandate and to evacuate each area.

The mandatory Power shall use its best endeavours to ensure that an area situated in the territory of the Jewish State, including a seaport and hinterland adequate to provide facilities for a substantial immigration, shall be evacuated at the earliest possible date and in any event not later than 1 February 1948.

3. Independent Arab and Jewish States and the Special International Regime for the City of Jerusalem, set forth in part III of this plan, shall come into existence in Palestine two months after the evacuation of the armed forces of the mandatory Power has been completed but in any case not later than 1 October 1948. The boundaries of the Arab State, the Jewish State, and the City of Jerusalem shall be as described in parts II and III below.

4. The period between the adoption by the General Assembly of its recommendation on the question of Palestine and the establishment of the independence of the Arab and Jewish States shall be a transitional period.

B. STEPS PREPARATORY TO INDEPENDENCE

1.   A Commission shall be set up consisting of one representative of each of five Members States.   The Members represented on the Commission shall be elected by the General Assembly on as broad a basis, geographically and otherwise, as possible.

2.   The administration of Palestine shall, as the mandatory Power withdraws its armed forces, be progressively turned over to the Commission, which shall act in conformity with the recommendations of the General Assembly, under the guidance of the Security Council.   The mandatory Power shall to the fullest possible extent co-ordinate its plans for withdrawal with the plans of the Commission to take over and administer areas which have been evacuated.

In the discharge of this administrative responsibility the Commission shall have authority to issue necessary regulations and take other measures as required.

The mandatory Power shall not take any action to prevent, obstruct or delay the implementation by the Commission of the measures recommended by the General Assembly.

3.   On its arrival in Palestine the Commission shall proceed to carry out measures for the establishment of the frontiers of the Arab and Jewish States and the City of Jerusalem in accordance with the general lines of the recommendations of the General Assembly on the partition of Palestine.   Nevertheless, the boundaries as described in part II of this plan are to be modified in such a way that village areas as a rule will not be divided by state boundaries unless pressing reasons make that necessary.

4.   The Commission, after consultation with the democratic parties and other public organizations of the Arab and Jewish States, shall select and establish in each State as rapidly as possible a Provisional Council of Government.   The activities of both the Arab and Jewish Provisional Councils of Government shall be carried out under the general direction of the Commission.

If by 1 April 1948 a Provisional Council of Government cannot be selected for either of the States, or, if selected, cannot carry out its functions, the Commission shall communicate that fact to the Security Council for such action with respect to that State as the Security Council may deem proper, and to the Secretary-General for communication to the Members of the United Nations.

5.   Subject to the provisions of these recommendations, during the transitional period the Provisional Councils of Government, acting under the Commission, shall have full authority in the Areas under their control, including authority over matters of immigration and land regulation.

6.   The Provisional Council of Government of each State, acting under the Commission, shall progressively receive from the Commission full responsibility for the administration of that State in the period between the termination of the Mandate and the establishment of the State's independence.

7.   The Commission shall instruct the Provisional Councils of Government of both the Arab and Jewish States, after their formation, to proceed to the establishment of administrative organs of government, central and local.

8.   The Provisional Council of Government of each State shall, within the shortest time possible, recruit an armed militia from the residents of that
State, sufficient in number to maintain internal order and to prevent frontier clashes.

This armed militia in each State shall, for operational purposes, be under the command of Jewish or Arab officers resident in that State, but general political and military control, including the choice of the militia's High Command, shall be exercised by the Commission.

9.   The Provisional Council of Government of each State shall, not later than two months after the withdrawal of the armed forces of the mandatory Power, hold elections to the Constituent Assembly which shall be conducted on democratic lines.

The election regulations in each State shall be drawn up by the Provisional Council of Government and approved by the Commission.   Qualified voters for each State for this election shall be persons over eighteen years of age who are: (a) Palestinian citizens residing in that State and (b) Arabs and Jews residing in the State, although not Palestinian citizens, who, before voting, have signed a notice of intention to become citizens of such State.

Arabs and Jews residing in the City of Jerusalem who have signed a notice of intention to become citizens, the Arabs of the Arab State and the Jews of the Jewish State, shall be entitled to vote in the Arab and Jewish States respectively.

Women may vote and be elected to the Constituent Assemblies.

During the transitional period no Jew shall be permitted to establish residence in the area of the proposed Arab State, and no Arab shall be permitted to establish residence in the area of the proposed Jewish State, except by special leave of the Commission.

10. The Constituent Assembly of each State shall draft a democratic constitution for its State and choose a provisional government to succeed the Provisional Council of Government appointed by the Commission. The constitutions of the States shall embody chapters 1 and 2 of the Declaration provided for in section C below and include *inter alia* provisions for:

(*a*) Establishing in each State a legislative body elected by universal suffrage and by secret ballot on the basis of proportional representation, and an executive body responsible to the legislature;

(*b*) Settling all international disputes in which the State may be involved by peaceful means in such a manner that international peace and security, and justice, are not endangered;

(*c*) Accepting the obligations of the State to refrain in its international relations from the threat or use of force against the territorial integrity or political independence of any State, or in any other manner inconsistent with the purposes of the United Nations;

(*d*) Guaranteeing to all persons equal and non-discriminatory rights in civil, political, economic and religious matters and the enjoyment of human rights and fundamental freedoms, including freedom of religion, language, speech and publication, education, assembly and association;

(*e*) Preserving freedom of transit and visit for all residents and citizens of the other State in Palestine and the City of Jerusalem, subject to considerations of national security, provided that each State shall control residence within its borders.

11. The Commission shall appoint a preparatory economic commission of three members to make whatever arrangements are possible for economic co-operation, with a view to establishing, as soon as practicable, the Economic Union and the Joint Economic Board, as provided in section D below.

12. During the period between the adoption of the recommendations on the question of Palestine by the General Assembly and the termination of the Mandate, the mandatory Power in Palestine shall maintain full responsibility for administration in areas from which it has not

withdrawn its armed forces. The Commission shall assist the mandatory Power in the carrying out of these functions. Similarly the mandatory Power shall co-operate with the Commission in the execution of its functions.

13. With a view to ensuring that there shall be continuity in the functioning of administrative services and that, on the withdrawal of the armed forces of the mandatory Power, the whole administration shall be in the charge of the Provisional Councils and the Joint Economic Board, respectively, acting under the Commission, there shall be a progressive transfer, from the mandatory Power to the Commission, of responsibility for all the functions of government, including that of maintaining law and order in the areas from which the forces of the mandatory Power have been withdrawn.

14. The Commission shall be guided in its activities by the recommendations of the General Asembly and by such instructions as the Security Council may consider necessary to issue.

The measures taken by the Commission, within the recommendations of the General Assembly, shall become immediately effective unless the Commission has previously received contrary instructions from the Security Council.

The Commission shall render periodic monthly progress reports, or more frequently if desirable, to the Security Council.

15. The Commission shall make its final report to the next regular session of the General Assembly and to the Security Council simultaneously.

C. DECLARATION

A declaration shall be made to the United Nations by the provisional government of each proposed State before independence. It shall contain *inter alia* the following clauses:

GENERAL PROVISION

The stipulations contained in the declaration are recognized as fundamental laws of the State and no law, regulation or official action shall conflict or interfere with these stipulations, nor shall any law, regulation or official action prevail over them.

CHAPTER 1

Holy Places, religious buildings and sites

1. Existing rights in respect of Holy Places and religious buildings or sites shall not be denied or impaired.

2. In so far as Holy Places are concerned, the liberty of access, visit and transit shall be guaranteed, in conformity with existing rights, to all residents and citizens of the other State and of the City of Jerusalem, as well as to aliens, without distinction as to nationality, subject to requirements of national security, public order and decorum.

Similarly, freedom of worship shall be guaranteed in conformity with existing rights, subject to the maintenance of public order and decorum.

3. Holy Places and religious buildings or sites shall be preserved. No act shall be permitted which may in any way impair their sacred character. If at any time it appears to the Government that any particular Holy Place, religious building or site is in need of urgent repair, the Government may call upon the community or communities concerned to carry out such repair. The Government may carry it out itself at the expense of the community or communities concerned if no action is taken within a reasonable time.

4. No taxation shall be levied in respect of any Holy Place, religious building or site which was exempt from taxation on the date of the creation of the State.

No change in the incidence of such taxation shall be made which would either discriminate between the owners or occupiers of Holy Places, religious buildings or sites, or would place such owners or occupiers in a position less favourable in relation to the general incidence of taxation than existed at the time of the adoption of the Assembly's recommendations.

5. The Government of the City of Jerusalem shall have the right to determine whether the provisions of the Constitution of the State in relation to Holy Places, religious buildings and sites within the borders of the State and the religious rights appertaining thereto, are being properly applied and respected, and to made decisions on the basis of existing rights in cases of disputes which may arise between the different religious communities or the rites of a religious community with respect to such places, buildings and

sites. He shall receive full co-operation and such privileges and immunities as are necessary for the exercise of his functions in the State.

CHAPTER 2

Religious and minority rights

1.   Freedom of conscience and the free exercise of all forms of worship, subject only to the maintenance of public order and morals, shall be ensured to all.

2.   No discrimination of any kind shall be made between the inhabitants on the ground of race, religion, language or sex.

3.   All persons within the jurisdiction of the State shall be entitled to equal protection of the laws.

4.   The family law and personal status of the various minorities and their religious interests, including endowments, shall be respected.

5.   Except as may be required for the maintenance of public order and good government, no measure shall be taken to obstruct or interfere with the enterprise of religious or charitable bodies of all faiths or to discriminate against any representative or member of these bodies on the ground of his religion or nationality.

6.   The State shall ensure adequate primary and secondary education for the Arab and Jewish minority, respectively, in its own language and it own cultural traditions.

The right of each community to maintain its own schools for the education of its own members in its own language, while conforming to such educational requirements of a general nature as the State may impose, shall not be denied or impaired. Foreign educational establishments shall continue their activity on the basis of their existing rights.

7.   No restriction shall be imposed on the free use by any citizen of the State of any language in private intercourse, in commerce, in religion, in the Press or in publications of any kind, or at public meetings.[7]

---

7   "The following stipulation shall be added to the declaration concerning the Jewish State: 'In the Jewish State adequate facilities shall be given to Arabic-speaking citizens for the use of their language, either orally or in writing, in the legislature, before the Courts and in the administration.'"   [Original footnote in the text].

8.   No expropriation of land owned by an Arab in the Jewish State (by a Jew in the Arab State)[8]   shall be allowed except for public purposes.   In all cases of expropriation full compensation as fixed by the Supreme Court shall be paid previous to dispossession.

CHAPTER 3

Citizenship, international conventions and financial obligations

1.   *Citizenship.*   Palestinian citizens residing in Palestine outside of the City of Jerusalem, as well as Arabs and Jews who, not holding Palestinian citizenship, reside in Palestine outside the City of Jerusalem shall, upon the recognition of independence, become citizens of the State in which they are resident and enjoy full civil and political rights.   Persons over the age of eighteen years may opt, within one year from the date of recognition of independence of the State in which they reside, for citizenship of the other State, providing that no Arab residing in the area of the proposed Arab State shall have the right to opt for citizenship in the proposed Jewish State and no Jew residing in the proposed Jewish State shall have the right to opt for citizenship in the proposed Arab State.   The exercise of this right of option will be taken to include the wives and children under eighteen years of age of persons so opting.
    Arabs residing in the area of the proposed Jewish State and Jews residing in the area of the proposed Arab State who have signed a notice of intention to opt for citizenship of the other State shall be eligible to vote in the elections to the Constituent Assembly of that State, but not in the elections to the Constituent Assembly of the State in which they reside.
    2.   *International conventions.*   (*a*) The State shall be bound by all international agreements and conventions, both general and special, to which Palestine has become a party.   Subject to any right of denunciation provided for therein, such agreements and conventions shall be respected by the State throughout the period for which they were concluded.

---

[8] "In the declaration concerning the Arab State, the words 'by an Arab in the Jewish State' should be replaced by the words 'by a Jew in the Arab State'."   [Original footnote in the text].

(*b*) Any dispute about the applicability and continued validity of international conventions or treaties signed or adhered to by the mandatory Power on behalf of Palestine shall be referred to the International Court of Justice in accordance with the provisions of the Statute of the Court.

3. *Financial obligations.* (*a*) The State shall respect and fulfil all financial obligations of whatever nature assumed on behalf of Palestine by the mandatory Power during the exercise of the Mandate and recognized by the State. This provision includes the right of public servants to pensions, compensation or gratuities.

(*b*) These obligations shall be fulfilled through participation in the Joint Economic Board in respect of those obligations applicable to Palestine as a whole, and individually in respect of those applicable to, and fairly apportioned between, the State.

(*c*) A Court of Claims, affiliated with the Joint Economic Board, and composed of one member appointed by the United Nations, one representative of the United Kingdom and one representative of the State concerned, should be established. Any dispute between the United Kingdom and the State respecting claims not recognized by the latter should be referred to that Court.

(*d*) Commercial concessions granted in respect of any part of Palestine prior to the adoption of the resolution by the General Assembly shall continue to be valid according to their terms, unless modified by agreement between the concession-holder and the State.

CHAPTER 4

Miscellaneous provisions

1. The provisions of chapters 1 and 2 of the declaration shall be under the guarantee of the United Nations, and no modifications shall be made in them without the assent of the General Assembly of the United Nations. Any Member of the United Nations shall have the right to bring to the attention of the General Assembly any infraction or danger of infraction of any of these stipulations, and the General Assembly may thereupon make such recommendations as it may deem proper in the circumstances.

2. Any dispute relating to the application or the interpretation of this declaration shall be referred, at the re-

quest of either party, to the International Court of Justice, unless the parties agree to another mode of settlement.

D. ECONOMIC UNION AND TRANSIT

1. The Provisional Council of Government of each State shall enter into an undertaking with respect to Economic Union and Transit. This undertaking shall be drafted by the Commission provided for in section B, paragraph 1, utilizing to the greatest extent possible the advice and co-operation of representative organizations and bodies from each of the proposed States. It shall contain provisions to establish the Economic Union of Palestine and provide for other matters of common interest. If by 1 April 1948 the Provisional Council of Government have not entered into the undertaking, the undertaking shall be put into force by the Commission.

The Economic Union of Palestine

2. The objectives of the Economic Union of Palestine shall be:

(*a*) A customs union;

(*b*) A joint currency system providing for a single foreign exchange rate;

(*c*) Operation in the common interest on a non-discriminatory basis of railways; inter-State highways; postal, telephone and telegraphic services, and ports and airports involved in international trade and commerce;

(*d*) Joint economic development, especially in respect of irrigation, land reclamation and soil conservation;

(*e*) Access for both States and for the City of Jerusalem on a non-discriminatory basis to water and power facilities.

3. There shall be established a Joint Economic Board, which shall consist of three representatives of each of the two States and three foreign members appointed by the Economic and Social Council of the United Nations. The foreign members shall be appointed in the first instance for a term of three years; they shall serve as individuals and not as representatives of States.

4. The functions of the Joint Economic Board shall be to implement either directly or by delegation the measures necessary to realize the objectives of the Economic Union. It shall have all powers of organization and administration necessary to fulfil its functions.

5.   The States shall bind themselves to put into effect the decisions of the Joint Economic Board.   The Board's decisions shall be taken by a majority vote.

6.   In the event of a failure of a State to take the necessary action the Board may, by a vote of six members, decide to withhold an approriate [sic] portion of that part of the customs revenue to which the State in question is entitled under the Economic Union.   Should the State persist in its failure to co-operate, the Board may decide by a simple majority vote upon such further sanctions, including disposition of funds which it has withheld, as it may deem appropriate.

7.   In relation to economic development, the functions of the Board shall be the planning, investigation and encouragement of joint development projects, but it shall not undertake such projects except with the assent of both States and the City of Jerusalem, in the event that Jerusalem is directly involved in the development project.

8.   In regard to the joint currency system the currencies circulating in the two States and the City of Jerusalem shall be issued under the authority of the Joint Economic Board, which shall be the sole issuing authority and which shall determine the reserves to be held against such currencies.

9.   So far as is consistent with paragraph 2 (b) above, each State may operate its own central bank, control its own fiscal and credit policy, its foreign exchange receipts and expenditures, the grant of import licenses, and may conduct international financial operations on its own faith and credit.   During the first two years after the termination of the Mandate, the Joint Economic Board shall have the authority to take such measures as may be necessary to ensure that — to the extent that the total foreign exchange revenues of the two States from the export of goods and services permit, and provided that each State take appropriate measures to conserve its own foreign exchange resources — each State shall have available, in any twelve months' period, foreign exchange sufficient to assure the supply of quantities of imported goods and services for consumption in its territory equivalent to the quanitities of goods and services consumed in that territory in the twelve months' period ending 31 December 1947.

10.   All economic authority not specifically vested in the Joint Economic Board is reserved to each State.

11. There shall be a common customs tariff with complete freedom of trade between the States, and between the States and the City of Jerusalem.

12. The tariff schedules shall be drawn up by a Tariff Commission, consisting of representatives of each of the States in equal numbers, and shall be submitted to the Joint Economic Board for approval by a majority vote. In case of disagreement in the Tariff Commission, the Joint Economic Board shall arbitrate the points of difference. In the event that the Tariff Commission fails to draw up any schedule by a date to be fixed, the Joint Economic Board shall determine the tariff schedule.

13. The following items shall be a first charge on the customs and other common revenue of the Joint Economic Board:

(a) The expenses of the customs service and of the operation of the joint services;

(b) The administrative expenses of the Joint Economic Board;

(c) The financial obligations of the Administration of Palestine consisting of:

(i) The service of the outstanding public debt;

(ii) The cost of superannuation benefits, now being paid or falling due in the future, in accordance with the rules and to the extent established by paragraph 3 of chapter 3 above.

14. After these obligations have been met in full, the surplus revenue from the customs and other common services shall be divided in the following manner: not less than 5 per cent and not more than 10 per cent to the City of Jerusalem; the residue shall be allocated to each State by the Joint Economic Board equitably, with the objective of maintaining a sufficient and suitable level of government and social services in each State, except that the share of either State shall not exceed the amount of that State's contribution to the revenues of the Economic Union by more than approximately four million pounds in any year. The amount granted may be adjusted by the Board according to the price level in relation to the prices prevailing at the time of the establishment of the Union. After five years, the principles of the distribution of the joint revenues may be revised by the Joint Economic Board on a basis of equity.

15. All international conventions and treaties affecting customs tariff rates, and those communications services under the jurisdiction of the Joint Economic Board, shall be entered into by both States. In these matters, the

two States shall be bound to act in accordance with the majority vote of the Joint Economic Board.

16. The Joint Economic Board shall endeavour to secure for Palestine's exports fair and equal access to world markets.

17. All enterprises operated by the Joint Economic Board shall pay fair wages on a uniform basis.

Freedom of transit and visit

18. The undertaking shall contain provisions preserving freedom of transit and visit for all residents or citizens of both States and the City of Jerusalem, subject to security considerations; provided that each State and the City shall control residence within its borders.

Termination, modification and interpretation of the undertaking

19. The undertaking and any treaty issuing therefrom shall remain in force for a period of ten years. It shall continue in force until notice of termination, to take effect two years thereafter, is given by either of the parties.

20. During the initial ten-year period, the undertaking of any treaty issuing therefrom may not be modified except by consent of both parties and with the approval of the General Assembly.

21. Any dispute relating to the application or the interpretation of the undertaking and any treaty issuing therefrom shall be referred, at the request of either party, to the International Court of Justice, unless the parties agree to another mode of settlement.

E. ASSETS

1. The movable assets of the Administration of Palestine shall be allocated to the Arab and Jewish States and the City of Jerusalem on an equitable basis. Allocations should be made by the United Nations Commission referred to in section B, paragraph 1, above. Immovable assets shall become the property of the government of the territory in which they are situated.

2. During the period between the appointment of the United Nations Commission and the termination of the Mandate, the mandatory Power shall, except in respect of ordinary operations, consult with the Commission on any

measure which it may contemplate involving the liquidation, disposal or encumbering of the assets of the Palestine
Government, such as the accumulated treasury surplus, the
proceeds of Government bond issues, State lands or any
other asset.

F. ADMISSION TO MEMBERSHIP IN THE UNITED NATIONS

When the independence of either the Arab or the
Jewish State as envisaged in this plan has become effective
and the declaration and undertaking, as envisaged in this
plan, have been signed by either of them, sympathetic consideration should be given to its application for admission to
membership in the United Nations in accordance with
Article 4 of the Charter of the United Nations.

PART II

Boundaries[9]

A. THE ARAB STATE

The area of the Arab State in Western Galilee is
bounded on the west by the Mediterranean and on the north
by the frontier of the Lebanon from Ras en Naqura to a
point north of Saliha. From there the boundary proceeds
southwards, leaving the built-up area of Saliha in the Arab
State, to join the southernmost point of this village. Thence
it follows the western boundary line of the villages of 'Alma,
Rihaniya and Teitaba, thence following the northern
boundary line of Meirun village to join the Acre-Safad sub-
district boundary line. It follows this line to a point west of
Es Sammu'i village and joins it again at the northernmost
point of Farradiya. Thence it follows the sub-district boundary line to the Acre-Safad main road. From here it follows
the western boundary of Kafr I'nan village until it reaches
the Tiberias-Acre sub-district boundary line, passing to the
west of the junction of the Acre-Safad and Lubiya-Kafr

---

[9] "The boundary lines described in part II are indicated in Annex A
[not reproduced here]. The base map used in marking and describing
this boundary is 'Palestine 1:250,000' published by the Survey of
Palestine, 1946." [Original footnote in text].

I'nan roads.   From the south-west corner of Kafr I'nan village the boundary line follows the western boundary of the
Tiberias sub-district to a point close to the boundary line
between the villages of Maghar and Eilabun, thence bulging
out to the west to include as much of the eastern part of the
plain of Battuf as is necessary for the reservoir proposed by
the Jewish Agency for the irrigation of lands to the south
and east.

   The boundary rejoins the Tiberias sub-district boundary at a point on the Nazareth-Tiberias road south-east of
the built-up area of Tur'an; thence it runs southwards, at
first following the sub-district boundary and then passing
between the Kadoorie Agricultural School and Mount Tabor,
to a point due south at the base of Mount Tabor.   From here it
runs due west, parallel to the horizontal grid line 230, to the
north-east corner of the village lands of Tel Adashim.   It
then runs to the north-west corner of these lands, whence it
turns south and west so as to include in the Arab State the
sources of the Nazareth water supply in Yafa village.   On
reaching Ginneiger it follows the eastern, northern and
western boundaries of the lands of this village to their
south-west corner, whence it proceeds in a straight line to a
point on the Haifa-Afula railway on the boundary between
the villages of Sarid and El Mujeidil.   This is the point of intersection.

   The south-western boundary of the area of the Arab
State in Galilee takes a line from this point, passing northwards along the eastern boundaries of Sarid and Gevat to the
north-eastern corner of Nahalal, proceeding thence across
the land of Kefar ha Horesh to a central point on the southern boundary of the village of 'Ilut, thence westwards along
that village boundary to the eastern boundary of Beit Lahm,
thence northwards and north-eastwards along its western
boundary to the north-eastern corner of Waldheim and
thence north-westwards across the village lands of Shafa
'Amr to the south-eastern corner of Ramat Yohanan.   From
here it runs due north-north-east to a point on the Shafa
'Amr-Haifa road, west of its junction with the road to I'Billin.
From there it proceeds north-east to a point on the southern
boundary of I'Billin situated to the west of the I'Billin-Birwa
road.   Thence along that boundary to its westernmost point,
whence it turns to the north, follows across the village land
of Tamra to the north-western corner and along the western
boundary of Julis until it reaches the Acre-Safad road.   It
then runs westwards along the southern side of the Safad-

Acre road to the Galilee-Haifa District boundary, from which point it follows that boundary to the sea.

The boundary of the hill country of Samaria and Judea starts on the Jordan River at the Wadi Malih south-east of Beisan and runs due west to meet the Beisan-Jericho road and then follows the western side of that road in a north-westerly direction to the junction of the boundaries of the sub-districts of Beisan, Nablus, and Jenin. From that point it follows the Nablus—Jenin sub-district boundary westwards for a distance of about three kilometres and then turns north-westwards, passing to the east of the built-up areas of the villages of Jalbun and Faqqu'a, to the boundary of the sub-districts of Jenin and Beisan at a point north-east of Nuris. Thence it proceeds first north-westwards to a point due north of the built-up area of Zir'in and then westwards to the Afula-Jenin railway, thence north-westwards along the district boundary line to the point of intersection on the Hejaz railway. From here the boundary runs south-west-wards, including the built-up area and some of the land of the village of Kh.Lid in the Arab State to cross the Haifa-Jenin road at a point on the district boundary between Haifa and Samaria west of El Mansi. It follows this boundary to the southernmost point of the village of El Buteimat. From here it follows the northern and eastern boundaries of the village of Ar'ara, rejoining the Haifa-Samaria district boundary at Wadi 'Ara, and thence proceeding south-south-westwards in an approximately straight line joining up with the western boundary of Qaqun to a point east of the railway line on the eastern boundary of Qaqun village. From here it runs along the railway line some distance to the east of it to a point just east of the Tulkarm railway station. Thence the boundary follows a line half-way between the railway and the Tulkarm-Qalqiliya-Jaljuliya and Ras el Ein road to a point just east of Ras el Ein station, whence it proceeds along the railway some distance to the east of it to the point on the railway line south of the junction of the Haifa-Lydda and Beit Nabala lines, whence it proceeds along the southern border of Lydda airport to its south-west corner, thence in a south-westerly direction to a point just west of the built-up area of Sarafand el 'Amar, whence it turns south, passing just to the west of the built-up area of Abu el Fadil to the north-east corner of the lands of Beer Ya'Aqov. (The boundary line should be so demarcated as to allow direct access from the Arab State to the airport.) Thence the boundary line follows the western and southern boundaries of Ramle village, to the north-east corner of El Na'ana village, thence in a straight line to the southernmost point of El Barriya, along the eastern boundary of that village and the southern boundary of 'Innaba village. Thence it turns north to follow the southern side of the Jaffa-Jerusalem road until El Qubab, whence it follows the road to the boundary of Abu Shusha. It runs along the eastern boundaries of Abu Shusha, Seidun, Hulda to the southernmost point of Hulda, thence westwards in a straight line to the north-eastern corner of Umm Kalkha, thence following the northern boundaries of Umm Kalkha, Qazaza and the northern and western boundaries of Mukhezin to the Gaza District boundary and thence runs across the village lands of El Mismiya, El Kabira, and Yasur to the southern point of intersection, which is midway between the built-up areas of Yasur and Batani Sharqi.

From the southern point of intersection the boundary lines run north-westwards between the village of Gan Yavne and Barqa to the sea at a point half way between Nabi Yunis and Minat el Qila, and south-eastwards to a point west of Qastina, whence it turns in a south-westerly direction, passing to the east of the built-up areas of Es Sawafir, Esh Sharqiya and Ibdis. From the south-east corner of Ibdis village it runs to a point south-west of the built-up area of Beit 'Affa, crossing the Hebron-El Majdal road just to the west of the built-up area of Iraq Suweidan. Thence it proceeds southwards along the western village boundary of El Faluja to the Beersheba sub-district boundary. It then runs across the tribal lands of 'Arab el Jubarat to a point on the boundary between the sub-districts of Beersheba and Hebron north of Kh. Khuweilifa, whence it proceeds in a south-westerly direction to a point on the Beersheba-Gaza main road two kilometres to the north-west of the town. It then turns south-eastwards to reach Wadi Sab' at a point situated one kilometre to the west of it. From here it turns north-eastwards and proceeds along Wadi Sab' and along the Beersheba-Hebron road for a distance of one kilometre, whence it turns eastwards and runs in a straight line to Kh. Huseifa to join the Beersheba-Hebron sub-district boundary. It then follows the Beersheba-Hebron boundary eastwards to a point north of Ras Ez Zuweira, only departing from it so as to cut across the base of the indentation between vertical grid lines 150 and 160.

About five kilometres north-east of Ras ez Zuweira it turns north, excluding from the Arab State a strip along the coast of the Dead Sea not more than seven kilometres in depth, as far as Ein Geddi, whence it turns due east to join the Transjordan frontier in the Dead Sea.

The northern boundary of the Arab section of the coastal plain runs from a point between Minat el Qila and Nabi Yunis, passing between the built-up areas of Gan Yavne and Barqa to the point of intersection. From here it turns south-westwards, running across the lands of Batani Sharqi, along the eastern boundary of the lands of Beit Daras and across the lands of Julis, leaving the built-up areas of Batani Sharqi and Julis to the westwards, as far as the north-west corner of the lands of Beit Tima. Thence it runs east of El Jiya across the village lands of El Barbara along the eastern boundaries of the villages of Beit Jirja, Deir Suneid and Dimra. From the south-east corner of Dimra the boundary passes across the lands of Beit Hanun, leaving the Jewish lands of Nir-Am to the eastwards. From the south-east corner of Beit Hanun the line runs south-west to a point south of the parallel grid line 100, then turns north-west for two kilometres, turning again in a south-westerly direction and continuing in an almost straight line to the north-west corner of the village lands of Kirbet Ikhza'a. From there it follows the boundary line of this village to its southernmost point. It then runs in a southerly direction along the vertical grid line 90 to its junction with the horizontal grid line 70. It then turns south-eastwards to Kh. el Ruheiba and then proceeds in a southerly direction to a point known as El Baha, beyond which it crosses the Beersheba-El 'Auja main road to the west of Kh. el Mushrifa. From there it joins Wadi El Zaiyatin just to the west of El Subeita. From there it turns to the north-east and then to the south-east following this wadi and passes to the east of 'Abda to join Wadi Nafkh. It then bulges to the south-west along Wadi Nafkh, Wadi Airim and Wadi Lassan to the point where Wadi Lassan crosses the Egyptian frontier.

The area of the Arab enclave of Jaffa consists of that part of the town-planning area of Jaffa which lies to the west of the Jewish quarters lying south of Tel-Aviv, to the west of the continuation of Herzl street up to its junction with the Jaffa-Jerusalem road, to the south-west of the section of the Jaffa-Jerusalem road lying south-east of that junction, to the west of Miqve Yisrael lands, to the north-west of Holon local council area, to the north of the line linking up the north-west corner of Holon with the north-east corner of Bat Yam local council area and to the north of Bat Yam local council area. The question of Karton quarter will be decided by the Boundary Commission, bearing in mind among other considerations the desirability of includ-ing the smallest possible number of its Arab inhabitants and the largest possible number of its Jewish inhabitants in the Jewish State.

B. THE JEWISH STATE

The north-eastern sector of the Jewish State (Eastern Galilee) is bounded on the north and west by the Lebanese frontier and on the east by the frontiers of Syria and Transjordan.   It includes the whole of the Hula Basin, Lake Tiberias, the whole of the Beisan sub-district, the boundary line being extended to the crest of the Gilboa mountains and the Wadi Malih.   From there the Jewish State extends north-west, following the boundary described in respect of the Arab State.

The Jewish section of the coastal plain extends from a point between Minat et Qila and Nabi Yunis in the Gaza sub-district and includes the towns of Haifa and Tel-Aviv, leaving Jaffa as an enclave of the Arab State.   The eastern boundary of the Jewish State follows the boundary described in respect of the Arab State.

The Beersheba area comprises the whole of the Beersheba sub-district, including the Negeb and the eastern part of the Gaza sub-district, but excluding the town of Beersheba and those areas described in respect of the Arab State.   It includes also a strip of land along the Dead Sea stretching from the Beersheba-Hebron sub-district boundary line to Ein Geddi, as described in respect of the Arab State.

C. THE CITY OF JERUSALEM

The boundaries of the City of Jerusalem are as defined in the recommendations on the City of Jerusalem.   (See Part III, Section B, below).

PART III

City   of   Jerusalem

A. SPECIAL REGIME

The City of Jerusalem shall be established as a *corpus separatum* under a special international regime and shall be administered by the United Nations.   The Trusteeship Council shall be designated to discharge the responsibilities of the Administering Authority on behalf of the United Nations.

B. BOUNDARIES OF THE CITY

The City of Jerusalem shall include the present municipality of Jerusalem plus the surrounding villages and towns, the most eastern of which shall be Abu Dis; the most southern, Bethlehem; the most western, Ein Karim (including also the built-up area of Motsa); and the most northern Shu'fat, as indicated on the attached sketch-map (annex B).

C. STATUTE OF THE CITY

The Trusteeship Council shall, within five months of the approval of the present plan, elaborate and approve a detailed Statute of the City which shall contain *inter alia* the substance of the following provisions:

1. *Government machinery; special objectives.* The Administering Authority in discharging its administrative obligations shall pursue the following special objectives:

(*a*) To protect and to preserve the unique spiritual and religious interests located in the city of the three great monotheistic faiths throughout the world, Christian, Jewish and Moslem; to this end to ensure that order and peace, and especially religious peace, reign in Jerusalem;

(*b*) To foster co-operation among all the inhabitants of the city in their own interests as well as in order to encourage and support the peaceful development of the mutual relations between the two Palestinian peoples throughout the Holy Land; to promote the security, well-being and any constructive measures of the development of the residents, having regard to the special circumstances and customs of the various peoples and communities.

2. *Governor and administrative staff.* A Governor of the City of Jerusalem shall be appointed by the Trusteeship Council and shall be responsible to it. He shall be selected on the basis of special qualifications and without regard to nationality. He shall not, however, be a citizen of either State in Palestine.

The Governor shall represent the United Nations in the City and shall exercise on their behalf all powers of administration, including the conduct of external affairs. He shall be assisted by an administrative staff classed as international officers in the meaning of Article 100 of the Charter and chosen whenever practicable from the residents of the city and of the rest of Palestine on a non-dis-

criminatory basis.   A detailed plan for the organization of
the administration of the city shall be submitted by the
Governor to the Trusteeship Council and duly approved by it.
     3. *Local autonomy.*   (*a*) The existing local
autonomous units in the territory of the city (villages,
townships and municipalities) shall enjoy wide powers of
local government and administration.
     (*b*) The Governor shall study and submit for the con-
sideration and decision of the Trusteeship Council a plan for
the establishment of special town units consisting, respectively, of the Jewish and Arab sections of new Jerusalem.
The new town units shall continue to form part of the present municipality of Jerusalem.
     4. *Security measures.*   (*a*) The City of Jerusalem
shall be demilitarized; its neutrality shall be declared and
preserved, and no para-military formations, exercises or
activities shall be permitted within its borders.
     (*b*) Should the administration of the City of
Jerusalem be seriously obstructed or prevented by the non-
co-operation or interference of one or more sections of the
population, the Governor shall have authority to take such
measures as may be necessary to restore the effective
functioning of the administration.
     (*c*) To assist in the maintenance of internal law and
order and especially for the protection of the Holy Places
and religious buildings and sites in the city, the Governor
shall organize a special police force of adequate strength,
the members of which shall be recruited outside of
Palestine.   The Governor shall be empowered to direct such
budgetary provision as may be necessary for the maintenance of this force.
     5. *Legislative organization.* A Legislative Council,
elected by adult residents of the city irrespective of nationality on the basis of universal and secret suffrage and
proportional representation, shall have powers of legislation and taxation.   No legislative measures shall, however,
conflict or interfere with the provisions which will be set
forth in the Statute of the City, nor shall any law,
regulation, or official action prevail over them.   The Statute
shall grant to the Governor a right of vetoing bills
inconsistent with the provisions referred to in the
preceding sentence.   It shall also empower him to
promulgate temporary ordinances in case the Council fails
to adopt in time a bill deemed essential to the normal
functioning of the administration.

6. *Administration of justice.* The Statute shall provide for the establishment of an independent judiciary system, including a court of appeal. All the inhabitants of the City shall be subject to it.

7. *Economic union and economic regime.* The City of Jerusalem shall be included in the Economic Union of Palestine and be bound by all stipulations of the undertaking and of any treaties issued therefrom, as well as by the decisions of the Joint Economic Board. The headquarters of the Economic Board shall be established in the territory of the City.

The Statute shall provide for the regulation of economic matters not falling within the regime of the Economic Union, on the basis of equal treatment and non-discrimination for all Members of the United Nations and their nationals.

8. *Freedom of transit and visit; control of residents.* Subject to considerations of security, and of economic welfare as determined by the Governor under the directions of the Trusteeship Council, freedom of entry into, and residence within, the borders of the City shall be guaranteed for the residents or citizens of the Arab and Jewish States. Immigration into and residence within, the borders of the city for nationals of other States shall be controlled by the Governor under the directions of the Trusteeship Council.

9. *Relations with the Arab and Jewish States.* Representatives of the Arab and Jewish States shall be accredited to the Governor of the City and charged with the protections of the interests of their States and nationals in connexion with the international administration of the City.

10. *Official languages.* Arabic and Hebrew shall be the official languages of the city. This will not preclude the adoption of one or more additional working languages, as may be required.

11. *Citizenship.* All the residents shall become *ipso facto* citizens of the City of Jerusalem unless they opt for citizenship of the State of which they have been citizens or, if Arabs and Jews, have filed notice of intention to become citizens of the Arab or Jewish State respectively, according to part I, section, B, paragraph 9, of this plan.

The Trusteeship Council shall make arrangements for consular protection of the citizens of the City outside of its territory.

12. *Freedoms of citizens.* (*a*) Subject only to the requirements of public order and morals, the inhabitants of the City shall be ensured the enjoyment of human rights

and fundamental freedoms, including freedom of conscience, religion and worship, language, education, speech and Press, assembly and association, and petition.

(*b*) No discrimination of any kind shall be made between the inhabitants on the grounds of race, religion, language or sex.

(*c*) All persons within the City shall be entitled to equal protection of the laws.

(*d*) The family law and personal status of the various persons and communities and their religious interests, including endowments, shall be respected.

(*e*) Except as may be required for the maintenance of public order and good government, no measure shall be taken to obstruct or interfere with the enterprise of religious or charitable bodies of all faiths or to discriminate against any representative or member of these bodies on the ground of his religion or nationality.

(*f*) The City shall ensure adequate primary and secondary education for the Arab and Jewish communities respectively, in their own languages and in accordance with their cultural traditions.

The right of each community to maintain its own schools for the education of its own members in its own language, while conforming to such educational requirements of a general nature as the City may impose, shall not be denied or impaired. Foreign educational establishments shall continue their activity on the basis of their existing rights.

(*g*) No restriction shall be imposed on the free use by any inhabitant of the city of any language in private intercourse, in commerce, in religion, in the Press or in publications of any kind, or at public meetings.

13. *Holy Places.* (*a*) Existing rights in respect of Holy Places and religious buildings or sites shall not be denied or impaired.

(*b*) Free access to the Holy Places and religious buildings or sites and the free exercise of worship shall be secured in conformity with existing rights and subject to the requirements of public order and decorum.

(*c*) Holy Places and religious buildings or sites shall be preserved. No act shall be permitted which may in any way impair their sacred character. If at any time it appears to the Governor that any particular Holy Place, religious building or site is in need of urgent repair, the Governor may call upon the community or communities concerned to carry out such repair. The Governor may carry it out himself at the expense of the community or communities concerned if no action is taken within a reasonable time.

(*d*) No taxation shall be levied in respect of any Holy Place, religious building or site which was exempt from taxation on the date of the creation of the City. No change in the incidence of such taxation shall be made which would either discriminate between the owners or occupiers of Holy Places, religious buildings or sites, or would place such owners or occupiers in a position less favourable in relation to the general incidence of taxation than existed at the time of the adoption of the Assembly's recommendations.

14. *Special powers of the Governor in respect of Holy Places, religious buildings and sites in the City and in any part of Palestine.* (*a*) The protection of the Holy Places, religious buildings and sites located in the City of Jerusalem shall be a special concern of the Governor.

(*b*) With relation to such places, buildings and sites in Palestine outside the city, the Governor shall determine, on the ground of powers granted to him by the Constitutions of both States, whether the provisions of the Constitutions of the Arab and Jewish States in Palestine dealing therewith and the religious rights appertaining thereto are being properly applied and respected.

(*c*) The Governor shall also be empowered to make decisions on the basis of existing rights in cases of disputes which may arise between the different religious communities or the rites of a religious community in respect of the Holy Places, religious buildings and sites in any part of Palestine.

In this task he may be assisted by a consultative council of representatives of different denominations acting in an advisory capacity.

D. DURATION OF THE SPECIAL REGIME

The Statute elaborated by the Trusteeship Council on the aforementioned principles shall come into force not later than 1 October 1948. It shall remain in force in the first instance for a period of ten years, unless the Trusteeship Council finds it necessary to undertake a re-examination of these provisions at an earlier date. After the expiration of this period the whole scheme shall be subject to re-examination by the Trusteeship Council in the light of the experience acquired with its functioning. The residents of the City shall be then free to express by means of a refer-

endum their wishes as to possible modifications of the
regime of the City.

PART IV

Capitulations

States whose nationals have in the past enjoyed in
Palestine the privileges and immunities of foreigners, including the benefits of consular jurisdiction and protection,
as formerly enjoyed by capitulation or usage in the Ottoman
Empire, are invited to renounce any right pertaining to
them in the re-establishment of such privileges and immunities in the proposed Arab and Jewish States and the City
of Jerusalem.

29

Termination of the Mandate, 1948

Opposed as they were to the partitioning of
Palestine, and desirous of evacuating Palestine
as soon as practicable, the British Government
determined that the mandatory government
would end at one minute past midnight on 15
May 1948, four and one-half months prior to
the date established by the General Assembly
under its resolution.

The passage of the resolution resulted
almost immediately in armed conflict between
the Palestinian Arabs and the Jews, with the
British authorities not always successful in
maintaining order. Because of the chaos arising out of the civil strife, the refusal of the
British Government to assist in the implementation of partitioning, and the Security Council
having failed to provide UNSCOP with any
means by which to enforce the resolution (in
fact, the commission never left New York), the
final withdrawal of the Palestine Government
on 15 May meant that Palestine would be left
without any government. Fifteen hours prior
to the expected end of the mandate the Union

Source: Great Britain. *British and Foreign State Papers 'with which
is incorporated Hertslet's Commercial Treaties, 1948 Part I, Vol. 150*
(London: Her Majesty's Stationery Office, 1956) 278-81. Reprinted
by permission of the Controller of Her Majesty's Stationery Office.

Jack was lowered over Government House in Jerusalem at 9.00 A.M. on the 14th of May and the high commissioner and the military commander left for Haifa to board a British cruiser, thus officially terminating the mandate.

ACT OF PARLIAMENT to make provision with respect to the termination of His Majesty's jurisdiction in Palestine, and for purposes connected therewith. [11 & 12 Geo. 6. c. 27.] - 29th April, 1948

BE it enacted by the King's Most Excellent Majesty, by and with the advice and consent of the Lords Spiritual and Temporal, and Commons, in this present Parliament assembled, and by the authority of the same, as follows:-

1.-(1) On the fifteenth day of May, nineteen hundred and forty-eight, or such earlier date as His Majesty may by Order in Council declare to be the date on which the mandate in respect of Palestine accepted by His Majesty on behalf of the League of Nations will be relinquished (in this Act referred to as "the appointed day"), all jurisdiction of His Majesty in Palestine shall determine, and His Majesty's Government in the United Kingdom shall cease to be responsible for the government of Palestine.

(2) Nothing in this Act shall affect the jurisdiction of His Majesty, or any powers of the Admiralty, the Army Council or the Air Council, or of any other authority, in relation to any of His Majesty's forces which may be in Palestine on or after the appointed day.

2.-(1) Any appeal to His Majesty in Council which, on the appointed day, is pending from any court in Palestine, not being a prize court constituted under the Prize Acts, 1854 to 1944, shall abate on that day.

(2) No proceeding, whether civil or criminal, shall be instituted in any court to which this subsection applies in respect of anything done, whether within or outside of Palestine, by any person in the service of His Majesty or by any person acting under the authority of any such person,

if done in good faith and done or purported to be done in the execution of his duty-

> (*a*) before the appointed day, or the maintenance of peace or order in Palestine, or other wise for the good government thereof;
> (*b*) whether before, on or after that day, for the purpose of or in connexion with the termination of His Majesty's jurisdiction in Palestine or the withdrawal from Palestine of any of His Majesty's forces or of any stores or other property belonging to His Majesty or to any such forces, or the protection of any such forces, stores or property; or
> (*c*) on or after that day and before the withdrawal from Palestine of the said forces, for the protection in Palestine of the life or property of any British subject:

Provided that nothing in this subsection shall prevent the institution of any proceedings in respect of anything done before the 26th day of February, 1948, or the institution of any proceedings on behalf of His Majesty.

(3) The courts to which the last foregoing subsection applies are British courts, not being courts martial, exercising jurisdiction either within or outside the United Kingdom, except courts in a Dominion, in Southern Rhodesia, or in any territory administered by the government of a Dominion.

(4) For the purposes of this section, a certificate by a Secretary of State or the Admiralty that anything was done under the authority of a person in the service of His Majesty, or was done by any person in the execution of his duty, shall be sufficient evidence of the matter so certified; and anything done by or under the authority of a persons in the service of His Majesty shall be deemed to have been done in good faith unless the contrary is proved.

(5) In this section the expression "Dominion" means a Dominion within the meaning of the Statute of Westminster, 1931 ([1]), India, Pakistan and Ceylon; and references in this section to anything done shall be construed as including references to anything omitted to be done.

---

[1] " Vol. 134, page 167." [Original footnote in text].

3.-(1)   The enactments specified in the First Schedule to this Act [not reproduced] are hereby repealed to the extent specified in the third column of that Schedule.

(2)   Subject to the provisions of this section, any other enactment of the Parliament of the United Kingdom which, immediately before the appointed day, applies or extends to Palestine, whether by virtue of Order in Council or otherwise, shall cease on the appointed day to apply or extend to Palestine:

Provided that-
(a) nothing in this subjection shall be construed as preventing the continuance in force of any such enactment after the appointed day as part of the law of Palestine; and
(b) subsection (2) of section thirty-eight of the Interpretation Act, 1889(^{2}) (which relates to the effect of repeals), shall have effect in relation to any such enactment as if it had been repealed by this Act.

(3)   The transitional provisions contained in the Second Schedule to this Act [not reproduced] shall have effect in relation to the enactments mentioned in that Schedule; and His Majesty may by Order in Council direct that any other enactment to which the last foregoing subsection applies shall (subject to such modifications, if any, as may be specified in the Order) have effect, in relation to anything done before the appointed day, as if that subsection had not been enacted.

(4)   His Majesty may by Order in Council make provision-
(a) for the disposal or application of any property vested in or belonging to the Government of Palestine or any public authority constituted under any law in force in Palestine before the appointed day;
(b) for applying any enactment relating to superannuation in relation to any person who holds office in the service of the Government of Palestine immediately before the appointed day, as if he continued to hold office during such period after that day as may be determined by or under the Order;

2   "52 & 53 Vict. c. 63." [Original footnote in text].

(*c*) for any other purpose which appears to His Majesty to be necessary or expedient in consequence of the termination of his jurisdiction in Palestine.

4.-(1) Any Order in Council made under the last foregoing section after the appointed day may be made so as to take effect as from that day or as from such later date as may be specified therein.

(2) Any Order in Council made under the last foregoing section may be varied or revoked by a subsequent Order in Council.

(3) Any such Order in Council as aforesaid shall be subject to annulment in pursuance of a resolution of either House of Parliament.

5. This Act may be cited as the Palestine Act, 1948.

30

Proclamation of the State of Israel, 1948

The passage of the resolution partitioning Palestine, which the Arab member states and certain of their friends had bitterly opposed, was met with armed conflict on the part of the Palestinian Arabs, supported by most of the surrounding Arab regimes. The Palestine Commission reported that during the brief period 30 November 1947 to 3 April 1948 1,977 Arabs, British, and Jews were killed and 4,210 were wounded (with the Arab civilians suffering the greatest losses in both categories).[1] The vehemence of the opposition to partition surprised some of the strongest supporters of the resolution so that a number, including the United States, began to question the wisdom of the action of the United Nations.

The representatives of the states (Bolivia, Czechoslovakia, Denmark, Panama, and Philippines) that had been appointed to the Palestine Commission by the secretary-general recognized that if the partition plan was to be effected it required the advice and

Source: Courtesy of the Embassy of Israel. There are a few slight differences between this text issued by the Government of Israel and the proclamation as it was published in the *Palestine Post* 16 May 1948, pp. 1-2.
[1] United Nations.

assistance of Great Britain, the Jewish Agency,
and the Arab Higher Committee. The first two
did designate representatives to the proposed
cunsultative committee. The Arab Higher
Committee declined to participate because of its
rejection of the resolution. Much to the dismay
of the members of the commission Sir
Alexander Cadogan, the British representative,
who was also his country's ambassador to the
United Nations, at the commission's meeting
on 14 January 1948, stated "... that his
Government 'will endeavour to give the
Commission the benefit of their experience and
knowledge of the situation in Palestine, subject
always to their decision that they are unable to
take part in the implementation of the United
Nations plan. ... we could not alone implement
any plan not accepted by both sides; and that as
regards joining in any implementation, that
would depend on two conditions. The
Commission will remember that one was the
inherent justice of the plan, and the other was
the degree of force requisite for its
implementation.'"[2] Not only, therefore, did the
mandatary power categorically state that she
would not participate in the forcible
partitioning of Palestine, but perhaps more
importantly, she would not permit the
commission to enter Palestine earlier than two
weeks before the termination of the mandate
on 15 May 1948. In its report to the General
Assembly, dated 10 April 1948, the members of
the commission bitterly attacked Great Britain
for these decisions, stating: "The [U.N.]
Palestine Administration has accordingly been
unable to take any steps or to pursue any measures which would be designed to prepare the
ground for the Plan."[3]
    The commission, faced with armed resis-
tance to the partition plan, realized that it
could only be effected, following the
withdrawal of the British troops, by military

[2] Ibid., 6-7.
[3] Ibid., 9.

force drawn from other sources. Appeals to the Security Council to provide this assistance were rebuffed; the United States, upon the advice of the Defense Department, adamantly refused to provide military assistance, as did a number of other states.

Considering that the United Nations could not enforce its own resolution, and with the Zionists' closest ally, the United States, seriously reconsidering its own position in support of partition, the Jewish leaders in Palestine became fearful that the objective for which they had fought so hard since the First World War — an independent Jewish state — could easily be lost. The Jewish Agency Executive determined that they would have to seize the initiative and declare the establishment of the State of Israel upon the formal dissolution of the mandate. Despite the doubts of some of his colleagues, David Ben-Gurion, chairman of the executive, at 4.00 P.M. on 14 May 1948, eight hours before the expiration of the mandate, read over the radio from the Tel Aviv Museum the following Proclamation of the State of Israel.

In a meeting at the White House on 14 May between the president, members of the White House staff, Secretary of State General George C. Marshall and other members of the Department of State, to discuss the Palestine situation, President Harry Truman was informed that it was the intention of the Jewish Agency in Jerusalem to establish a sovereign state on 16 May. During the course of this meeting Clark M. Clifford, special counsel to the president, urged that prompt recognition be given to the provisional Jewish government following the termination of the mandate. Secretary of State Marshall retorted that: "This is just straight politics."[4] The Act of Independence creating the State of Israel became effective at

[4] United States of America. *Foreign Relations of the United States 1948. Volume V: The Near East, South Asia and Africa. Part 2* (Washington, D.C.: United States Government Printing Office, 1976) 976.

one minute past 6.00 P.M., Washington time. At 6.11 President Truman, without previously informing the secretary of state or the U.S. ambassador to the United Nations, then in session, issued the following statement:

> This Government has been informed that a Jewish state has been proclaimed in Palestine, and recognition has been requested by the provisional government thereof.
> The United States recognizes the provisional government as the *de facto* authority of the new State of Israel.[5]

The Land of Israel was the birthplace of the Jewish people. Here their spiritual, religious and national identity was formed. Here they achieved independence and created a culture of national and universal significance. Here they wrote and gave the Bible to the world.

Exiled from Palestine, the Jewish people remained faithful to it in all the countries of their dispersion, never ceasing to pray and hope for their return and the restoration of their national freedom.

Impelled by this historic association, Jews strove throughout the centuries to go back to the land of their fathers and regain their statehood. In recent decades they returned in masses. They reclaimed the wilderness, revived their language, built cities and villages, and established a vigorous and ever-growing community, with its own economic and cultural life. They sought peace yet were prepared to defend themselves. They brought the blessings of progress to all inhabitants of the country.

In the year 1897 the First Zionist Congress, inspired by Theodor Herzl's vision of the Jewish State, proclaimed the right of the Jewish people to national revival in their own country.

This right was acknowledged by the Balfour Declaration of November 2, 1917, and re-affirmed by the Mandate of the League of Nations, which gave explicit international recognition to the historic connection of the Jewish people with Palestine and their right to reconstitute their National Home.

---

5 Ibid., 992.

The Nazi holocaust, which engulfed millions of Jews in Europe, proved anew the urgency of the re-establishment of the Jewish State, which would solve the problem of Jewish homelessness by opening the gates to all Jews and lifting the Jewish people to equality in the family of nations.

The survivors of the European catastrophe, as well as Jews from other lands, proclaiming their right to a life of dignity, freedom and labor, and undeterred by hazards, hardships and obstacles, have tried unceasingly to enter Palestine.

In the Second World War the Jewish people in Palestine made a full contribution in the struggle of the freedom-loving nations against the Nazi evil. The sacrifices of their soldiers and the efforts of their workers gained them title to rank with the peoples who founded the United Nations.

On November 29, 1947, the General Assembly of the United Nations adopted a Resolution for the establishment of an independent Jewish State in Palestine, and called upon the inhabitants of the country to take such steps as may be necessary on their part to put the plan into effect.

This recognition by the United Nations of the right of the Jewish people to establish their independent State may not be revoked. It is, moreover, the self-evident right of the Jewish people to be a nation, as all other nations, in its own sovereign State.

ACCORDINGLY, WE, the members of the National Council, representing the Jewish people in Palestine and the Zionist movement of the world, met together in solemn assembly today, the day of termination of the British Mandate for Palestine, by virtue of the natural and historic right of the Jewish people and of the Resolution of the General Assembly of the United Nations,

HEREBY PROCLAIM the establishment of the Jewish State in Palestine, to be called ISRAEL.

WE HEREBY DECLARE that as from the termination of the Mandate at midnight, this night of the 14th to 15th May, 1948, and until the setting up of the duly elected bodies of the State in accordance with a Constitution, to be drawn up by a Constituent Assembly not later than the first day of October, 1948, the present National Council shall act as the provisional administration, shall constitute the Provisional Government of the State of Israel.

THE STATE OF ISRAEL will be open to the immigration of Jews from all countries of their dispersion; will promote the development of the country for the benefit of all its inhabitants; will be based on the precepts of liberty, justice and peace taught by the Hebrew Prophets; will uphold the full social and political equality of all its citizens, without distinction of race, creed or sex; will guarantee full freedom of conscience, worship, education and culture; will safeguard the sanctity and inviolability of the shrines and Holy Places of all religions; and will dedicate itself to the principles of the Charter of the United Nations.

THE STATE OF ISRAEL will be ready to cooperate with the organs and representatives of the United Nations in the implementation of the Resolution of the Assembly of November 29, 1947, and will take steps to bring about the Economic Union over the whole of Palestine.

We appeal to the United Nations to assist the Jewish people in the building of its State and to admit Israel into the family of nations.

In the midst of wanton aggression, we yet call upon the Arab inhabitants of the State of Israel to return to the ways of peace and play their part in the development of the State, with full and equal citizenship and due representation in all its bodies and institutions — provisional or permanent.

We offer peace and unity to all the neighboring states and their peoples, and invite them to cooperate with the independent Jewish nation for the common good of all.

Our call goes out to the Jewish people all over the world to rally to our side in the task of immigration and development and to stand by us in the great struggle for the fulfillment of the dream of generations — the redemption of Israel.

With trust in Almighty God, we set our hand to this Declaration, at this Session of the Provisional State Council, in the city of Tel Aviv, on this Sabbath eve, the fifth of Iyar, 5708, the fourteenth day of May, 1948.

[Signatures]

31

United Nations Conciliation Commission, 1948

In consideration of the widespread hostilities in Palestine and the opposition of the Arab Higher Committee towards the U.N. General Assembly partition resolution, thus ensuring that partitioning could only be effected by use of force, various officials within the U.S. Government began to doubt their earlier enthusiasm for the resolution. In early December 1947, the National Security Council in the White House requested the Department of State to prepare a position paper. On 19 January the Policy Planning Staff presented to the Secretary of State a "Top Secret" detailed paper in which it argued that: "We should take no further initiative in implementing or aiding partition. We should oppose sending armed forces into Palestine by the UN or any member thereof for the purpose of implementing partition." It was further suggested that the U.S. could work towards a trusteeship over Palestine

---

Source: United Nations. *Official Records of the Third Session of the General Assembly, Part 1. 21 September-12 December 1948: Resolutions* (Paris: Palais de Chaillot, [1948] 21-5. Double column with facing English and French texts.

by the United Nations.[1] It was feared in this paper, and would remain so during the ensuing months, that should the United States continue to press for partition it could seriously weaken the United Nations, further strain relations with the Arab states, and allow for increased Soviet influence within the Near East. On 19 March the U.S. representative to the United Nations proposed to the Security Council the establishment of a temporary trusteeship over Palestine pending a political settlement. However, because of opposition to this as a strong advocate of partition, the Soviet Union blocked consideration of this suggestion by the Security Council. By 11 May the United States, together with several other states, including Great Britain, had given up on the establishment of a trusteeship, but were still concerned regarding what would occur with the end of the mandate. On 14 May the General Assembly adopted, with changes, an American draft resolution [Resolution 186 (S-2)] allowing for the appointment of a United Nations Mediator to:

(i) Arrange for the operation of common services necessary to the safety and well-being of the population of Palestine;
(ii) Assure the protection of the Holy Places, religious buildings and sites in Palestine;
(iii) Promote a peaceful adjustment of the future situation of Palestine;... .[2]

The Swedish diplomat, Count Folke Bernadotte, was appointed to serve as the mediator on 20 May, with the American Dr. Ralph Bunche as his assistant. On 17 September 1948 Bernadotte was fatally shot while riding in his car within the Jewish sector of new Jerusalem by two men dressed in Israeli Army uniforms. The Jewish military authorities, the U.N. ob-

---

[1] United States. *Foreign Relations of the United States 1948. Volume V: The Near East, South Asia, and Africa* (Washington, D.C.: United States Government Printing Office, 1976) 553-54.
[2] Ibid., 994-95.

server group, and the U.S. Consul General believed that the assassination had been carried
out by members of the terrorist organization
known as the Stern Gang, which had been operating in Palestine for many years.   Within
twenty-four hours 190 members of the group
were arrested and the gang outlawed by the
new Israeli government.

The fighting that had broken out between the Jews and the Palestinian Arabs following the passage of the partition resolution
in November, while devastating, was very un-
even.   The Jews were, on the whole, well organized and armed, but the Arabs lacked adequate
centralized leadership, modern equipment, and
were ill-trained,   so that the former were enabled to extend their hold on territories beyond
those which had been allotted to them under
the partition resolution.   Therefore, the political and military leaders of the surrounding
Arab states, Egypt, Iraq, Lebanon, Saudi Arabia,
Syria, Transjordan, and the Yemen, under
pressure from their own populations, attacked
Israel on 15 May with approximately 25,000
troops.   These were, in fact, no better prepared
than had been the Palestinian Arabs.   To meet
this threat to world peace the Security Council
passed the first of a number of   truce resolutions on 29 May, during which time both sides
were enabled to improve their military capabilities.

With the proclamation of the State of
Israel and the subsequent fighting, thousands
of Arabs, particularly women and children, began to flee Palestine to escape both the rule of
the new Jewish state and the warfare.   They
headed for the neighbouring Arab countries.
In his last progress report to the U.N., dated 16
September, Count Bernadotte stated: "As a result
of the conflict in Palestine there are approximately 330,000 Arab refugees and 7,000 Jewish
refugees requiring aid in that country and adjacent States.   Large numbers of these are in-
fants, children, pregnant women and nursing
mothers.   Their condition is one of destitution
and they are 'vulnerable groups' in the

medical and social sense."3 In his opinion their relief should be assumed by the United Nations, the local states, and other international organizations until such time that they could be repatriated or resettled. He further proposed that: (1) the existing indefinite truce should be superseded by a formal peace or armistice under U.N. supervision; (2) the frontiers should be established by the United Nations; (3) the Arab portions of Palestine should be merged with Transjordan; (4) the City of Jerusalem should be placed under "effective United Nations control"; (5) a Palestine conciliation should commission be established; and (6) payment of adequate compensation for the property of those refugees not wishing to return should be supervised by the U.N. Bernadotte's proposals were, however, opposed by both the Arabs and the Jews and their respective supporters, except Great Britain, with whom his ideas closely coincided. On 4 December the British representative submitted a draft resolution to the General Assembly calling for the formation of a conciliation commission, together with many of the suggestions made by Bernadotte. After much emendation the General Assembly passed the following resolution on 11 December by a vote of thirty-five to fifteen, with eight abstentions.

By this resolution the General Assembly: (1) replaced the office of mediator with a three-member conciliation commission; (2) reemphasized the necessity of the internationalization of Jerusalem and its surrounding areas; and (3) called for the repatriation or compensation of the refugees, a theme that was to be returned to throughout the following years.

---

3 United Nations. *Official Records of the General Assembly, Third Session. Supplement No. 11 (A/648)*

The General Assembly

Having considered further the situation in Palestine,

1. *Expresses* its deep appreciation of the progress achieved through the good offices of the late United Nations Mediator in promoting a peaceful adjustment of the future situation of Palestine, for which cause he sacrificed his life; and

Extends its thanks to the Acting Mediator and his staff for their continued efforts and devotion to duty in Palestine;

2. *Establishes* a Conciliation Commission consisting of three States Members of the United Nations which shall have the following functions:

(*a*) To assume, in so far as it considers necessary in existing circumstances, the functions given to the United Nations Mediator on Palestine by resolution 186 (S-2) of the General Assembly of 14 May 1948;

(*b*) To carry out the specific functions and directives given to it by the present resolution and such additional functions and directives as may be given to it by the General Assembly or by the Security Council;

(*c*) To undertake, upon the request of the Security Council, any of the functions now assigned to the United Nations Mediator on Palestine or to the United Nations Truce Commission by resolutions of the Security Council; upon such request to the Conciliation Commission by the Security Council with respect to all the remaining functions of the United Nations Mediator on Palestine under Security Council resolutions, the office of the Mediator shall be terminated;

3. *Decides* that a Committee of the Assembly, consisting of China, France, the Union of Soviet Socialist Republics, the United Kingdom and the United States of America, shall present, before the end of the first part of the present session of the General Assembly, for the approval of the Assembly, a proposal concerning the names of the three States which will constitute the Conciliation Commission;

4. *Requests* the Commission to begin its functions at once, with a view to the establishment of contact between the parties themselves and the Commission at the earliest possible date;

5. *Calls upon* the Governments and authorities concerned to extend the scope of the negotiations provided for in the Security Council's resolution of 16 November 1948 and to seek agreement by negotiations conducted either with the Conciliation Commission for directly, with a view to the final settlement of all questions outstanding between them;

6. *Instructs* the Conciliation Commission to take steps to assist the Governments and authorities concerned to achieve a final settlement of all questions outstanding between them;

7. *Resolves* that the Holy Places — including Nazareth — religious buildings and sites in Palestine should be protected and free access to them assured, in accordance with existing rights and historical practice; that arrangements to this end should be under effective United Nations supervision; that the United Nations Conciliation Commission, in presenting to the fourth regular session of the General Assembly its detailed proposals for a permanent international regime for the territory of Jerusalem, should include recommendations concerning the Holy Places in that territory; that with regard to the Holy Places in the rest of Palestine the Commission should call upon the political authorities of the areas concerned to give appropriate formal guarantees as to the protection of the Holy Places and access to them; and that these undertakings should be presented to the General Assembly for approval;

8. *Resolves* that, in view of its association with three world religions, the Jerusalem area, including the present municipality of Jerusalem *plus* the surrounding villages and towns, the most eastern of which should be Abu Dis; the most southern, Bethlehem; the most western, Ein Karim (including also the built-up area of Motsa); and the most northern, Shu'fat, should be accorded special and separate treatment from the rest of Palestine and should be placed under effective United Nations control;

Requests the Security Council to take further steps to ensure the demilitarization of Jerusalem at the earliest possible date;

Instructs the Conciliation Commission to present to the fourth regular session of the General Assembly detailed proposals for a permanent international regime for the Jerusalem area which will provide for the maximum local autonomy for distinctive groups consistent with the special international status of the Jerusalem area;

The Conciliation Commission is authorized to appoint a United Nations representative, who shall co-operate with the local authorities with respect to the interim administration of the Jerusalem area;

9. *Resolves* that, pending agreement on more detailed arrangements among the Governments and authorities concerned, the freest possible access to Jerusalem by road, rail or air should be accorded to all inhabitants of Palestine;

Instructs the Conciliation Commission to report immediately to the Security Council, for appropriate action by that organ, any attempt by any party to impede such access;

10. *Instructs* the Conciliation Commission to seek arrangements among the Governments and authorities concerned which will facilitate the economic development of the area, including arrangements for access to ports and airfields and the use of transportation and communication facilities;

11. *Resolves* that the refugees wishing to return to their homes and live at peace with their neighbours should be permitted to do so at the earliest practicable date, and that compensation should be paid for the property of those choosing not to return and for loss of or damage to property which, under principles of international law or in equity, should be made good by the Governments or authorities responsible;

Instructs the Conciliation Commission to facilitate the repatriation, resettlement and economic and social rehabilitation of the refugees and the payment of compensation, and to maintain close relations with the Director of the United Nations Relief for Palestine Refugees and, through him, with the appropriate organs and agencies of the United Nations;

12. *Authorizes* the Conciliation Commission to appoint such subsidiary bodies and to employ such technical experts, acting under its authority, as it may find necessary for the effective discharge of its functions and responsibilities under the present resolution;

The Conciliation Commission will have its official headquarters at Jerusalem. The authorities responsible for maintaining order in Jerusalem will be responsible for taking all measures necessary to ensure the security of the Commission. The Secretary-General will provide a limited number of guards for the protection of the staff and premises of the Commission;

13. *Instructs* the Conciliation Commission to render progress reports periodically to the Secretary-General for transmission to the Security Council and to the Members of the United Nations;

14. *Calls upon* all Governments and authorities concerned to co-operate with the Conciliation Commission and to take all possible steps to assist in the implementation of the present resolution;

15. *Requests* the Secretary-General to provide the necessary staff and facilities and to make appropriate arrangements to provide the necessary funds required in carrying out the terms of the present resolution.

Hundred and eighty-sixth plenary meeting,
11 December 1948.

*
* *

At the 186th plenary meeting on 11 December 1948, a committee of the Assembly consisting of the five States designated in paragraph 3 of the above resolution proposed that the following three States should constitute the Conciliation Commission:
FRANCE, TURKEY, UNITED STATES OF AMERICA.

The proposal of the Committee having been adopted by the General Assembly at the same meeting, the Conciliation Commission is therefore composed of the above-mentioned three States.

32

Admission of Israel to United Nations, 1949

On 15 May 1948 the Israeli political leaders, desirous of international recognition of the new state and the ability to actively participate in discussions regarding the grave situation in Palestine, telegraphed the secretary-general applying for membership in the United Nations. As yet only the United States had officially recognized the Provisional Government; Soviet recognition was not to be accorded until 18 May, and the British Government was of the opinion that recognition by any state was premature. United Nations' procedure required that applications for membership had to be transmitted by the secretary-general to the Security Council for consideration, which had to pass upon the application with a minimum of seven affirmative votes before it could be sent to the Political Committee of the General Assembly in which the necessary resolution would be formulated for presentation to the Assembly for vote.

Although the United States favored early membership for Israel, no action was taken in the Security Council regarding Israel's appli-

Source: United Nations. *Official Records of the Third Session of the General Assembly, Part 11. 5 April-18 May 1949. Resolutions* (Lake Success, New York: United Nations [1949] 18.

cation because of the deteriorating situation within Palestine.[1] With the concurrence of the United States, Israel reapplied for membership on 29 November. When it was taken up by the Security Council on 17 December only the United States and the Soviet Union voted in the affirmative, Syria opposed, and Belgium, Canada, China, France, and the United Kingdom abstained, thus effectively killing the proposal, apparently because of the continued presence of Israeli troops in Lebanon. The disappointment over failure to obtain membership in the United Nations strengthened the position of the Israeli military in the conflict with the Arab states and the belief "... that UN may not arrive at any satisfactory solution... ."[2] It was not until 24 February 1949 that Israel again reapplied for membership. When it came before the Security Council on 4 March, supported with a draft resolution by the United States, it was passed by nine affirmative votes with only Great Britain abstaining.

273 (III). Admission of Israel to membership in the United Nations.

Having received the report of the Security Council on the application of Israel for membership in the United Nations,[3]

Noting that, in the judgment of the Security Council, Israel is a peace-loving State and is able and willing to carry out the obligations contained in the Charter,

Noting that the Security Council has recommended to

---

[1] The entire second part of the *Foreign Relations of the United States 1948, Volume V: The Near East, South Asia, and Africa* (Washington, D.C.: United States Government Printing Office, 1976) is devoted to U.S. relations with Israel (1,730 pages).

[2] Ibid., 1680, secret telegram from the U.S. Special Representative in Israel to the Acting Secretary of State, dated 21 December 1948.

[3] "See document A/818." [Original footnote in text].

the General Assembly that it admit Israel to membership in
the United Nations,

Noting furthermore the declaration of the State of
Israel that it "unreservedly accepts the obligations of the
United Nations Charter and undertakes to honour them from
the day which it becomes a Member of the United Nations",[4]

Recalling its resolutions of 29 November 1947[5] and 11
December 1948[6] and taking note of the declarations and ex-
planations made by the representative of the Government of
Israel[7] before the *ad hoc* Political Committee in respect of
the implementation of the said resolutions,

The General Assembly,

Acting in discharge of its functions under Article 4
of the Charter and rule 125 of its rules of procedure,

1. *Decides* that Israel is a peace-loving State which
accepts the obligations contained in the Charter and is able
and willing to carry out those obligations;

2. *Decides* to admit Israel to membership in the United
Nations.

*Two hundred and seventh plenary meeting.   11 May
1949.*

---

[4] "See document S/1093."   [Original footnote in text].
[5] "See *Resolutions adopted by the General Assembly* during its
recent session, ppages 131-132."   [Original footnote in text].
[6] "See *Resolutions adopted by the General Assembly* during Part I of
its third session, pages 21-25."   [Original footnote in text].
[7] "See documents A/AC.24/SR.45-48, 50 and 51."   [Original footnote
in text].

33

United Nations Assistance to Palestinian Refugees, 1949

By the early spring of 1949 the number of Christian and Muslim Arab refugees who had fled from the battle areas or had been expelled from the newly conquered Israeli territories had greatly increased, with the estimates of their numbers varying from 700,000 to 950,000 according to the U.S. and British Governments, the higher number reported by the U.N. Palestine Conciliation Commission. To the officials of both governments so many refugees living under the most abysmal conditions, demoralized and starving, became of great concern both for humanitarian and political reasons. Among many officials in the U.S. Department of State appeared a feeling of responsibility, although officially denied, that so many previously productive persons had been so abruptly denied their livelihoods. As a result, a new post of Special Assistant to the Secretary of State on Palestine Refugee Matters was created in early March. The main concerns were: 1) to provide as quickly as possible financial support for the feeding and housing of the refugees, 2) to establish projects so as to

Source: United Nations. *Official Records of the Fourth Session of the General Assembly. Resolutions 30 September - 10 December 1949.* (Lake Success, New York: United Nations, 1949) 23-5.

permit the able-bodied (estimated at approximately 25 percent of the total) to find useful employment, 3) to persuade Israel to repatriate approximately 200,000 of the refugees and to compensate those who did not wish to return to their homes for the loss of their properties or whose assets had been expropriated by the Israeli Government, and, 4) to resettle the remainder in non-Israeli Palestine and in the surrounding Arab states.

Despite international concern little financial assistance was forthcoming, with most governments, including those most responsible for the partitioning of Palestine, contributing only token amounts, if any. According to the Department of State, between the spring and the first of December of 1948, the Arab governments contributed the most, $11 million in cash or in kind. "This sum, in light of the very slender budgets of most of these Governments, is relatively enormous. The total direct relief offered the Arab refugees by the Israeli Government to date [15 March 1949] consists of 500 cases of oranges."[1] A secret State Department paper of this date reported that: ". . . , the Representatives of the Provisional Government of Israel have clearly indicated that Israel has no intention of taking back more than a portion of the refugees. . . . Furthermore, Israeli authorities have followed a systematic program of destroying Arab houses in such cities as Haifa and in village communities in order to build modern habitations for the influx of Jewish immigrants from DP camps in Europe. There are, thus, in many instances, literally no houses for the refugees to return to. In other cases incoming Jewish immigrants have occupied Arab dwellings and will most certainly not relinquish them in favor of the refugees."[2] The Israeli leaders

---

[1] United States. *Foreign Relations of the United States 1949. Volume VI: The Near East, South Asia, and Africa* (Washington, D.C.: United States Government Printing Office, 1977) 835.

[2] Ibid., 837.

maintained that the Arab refugees were not their problem as they had come into being because of the action of the surrounding Arab states. Furthermore, neither repatriation or compensation would be considered, they argued, until peace treaties had been signed.

Unable to convince Israel to carry out any repatriation, even the often- proposed 200,000, the highest members of the Department of State began to propose, in May 1949, the establishment of an economic survey group by the Palestine Conciliation Commission with representatives from the United States, the United Kingdom, and France to investigate how best to provide for the refugees on a long-term basis. After protracted negotiations between the governments to be involved the Economic Survey Mission was created by the PCC the following August. In its "Terms of Reference" the Mission was instructed:

... to examine the economic situation in the countries affected by the recent hostilities, and to make recommendations to the Commission for an integrated programme:

(a) To enable the Governments concerned to further such measures and development programmes as are required to overcome economic dislocations created by the hostilities;

(b) To facilitate the repatriation, resettlement and economic and social rehabilitation of the refugees and the payment of compensation pursuant to the provisions of paragraph eleven of the General Assembly's resolution of 11 December 1948, in order to reintegrate the refugees into the economic life of the area on a self-sustaining basis within a minimum period of time;

(c) To promote economic conditions conducive to the maintenance of peace and stability in the area.[3]

---

[3] Ibid., 1346-47, reprinted from GA(IV), *Ad Hoc Political Committee, Annex*, vol. 1, 1949, 29.

The Mission's report found that the refugee problem had become so vast that assistance to them required international co-operation, which could only be achieved through the United Nations.

302   (IV).   Assistance to Palestine Refugees

The General Assembly,

Recalling its resolutions 212 (III)[4] 19 November 1948 and 194 (III)[5] of 11 December 1948, affirming in particular the provisions of paragraph 11 of the latter resolution,

Having examined with appreciation the first interim report[6] of the United Nations Economic Mission for the Middle East and the report[7] of the Secretary-General on assistance to Palestine refugees,

1. *Expresses* its appreciation to the Governments which have generously responded to the appeal embodied in its resolution 212 (III), and to the appeal of the Secretary-General, to contribute in kind or in funds to the alleviation of the conditions of starvation and distress among the Palestine refugees;

2. *Expresses* also its gratitude to the International Committee of the Red Cross, to the League of Red Cross Societies and to the American Friends Service Committee for the contribution they have made to this humanitarian cause by discharging, in the face of great difficulties, the responsibility they voluntarily assumed for the distribution of relief supplies and the general care of the refugees; and welcomes the assurance they have given the Secretary-General that they will continue their co-operation with the United

---

4 "*Official Records of the third session of the General Assembly, Part I. Resolutions*. 66." [Original footnote in text].

5 "*Ibid*, p. 21." [Original footnote in text].

6 "See *Official Documents of the fourth session of the General Assembly, Annex to the Ad Hoc Political Committee*, document A/1106." [Original footnote in text].

7 "*Ibid*, documents A/1060/Add.1." [Original footnote in text].

Nations until the end of March 1950 on a mutually accept-able basis;

3. *Commends* the United Nations International Children's Emergency Fund for the important contribution which it has made towards the United Nations programme of assistance; and commends those specialized agencies which have rendered assistance in their respective fields, in par-ticular the World Health Organization, the United Nations Educational, Scientific and Cultural Organization and the International Refugee Organization;

4. *Expresses* its thanks to the numerous religious, charitable and humanitarian organizations which have materially assisted in bringing relief to Palestine refugees;

5. *Recognizes* that, without prejudice to the provi-sions of paragraph II of General Assembly resolution 194 (III) of 11 December 1948, continued assistance for the relief of the Palestine refugees is necessary to prevent conditions of starvation and distress among them and to further condi-tions of peace and stability, and that constructive measures should be undertaken at an early date with a view to the termination of international assistance for relief;

6. *Considers* that, subject to the provisions of paragraph 9 (*a*) of the present resolution, the equivalent of approximately $33,700,000 will be required for direct relief and works programmes for the period 1 January to 31 December 1950 of which the equivalent of $20,200,000 is required for direct relief and $13,500,000 for works programmes; that the equivalent of approximately $21,200,000 will be required for works programmes from 1 January to 30 June 1951, all inclusive of administrative expenses; and that direct relief should be terminated not later than 31 December 1950 unless otherwise determined by the General Assembly at its fifth regular session.

7. *Establishes* the United Nations Relief and Works Agency for Palestine Refugees in the Near East:
(*a*) To carry out in collaboration with local govern-ments the direct relief and works programmes as recom-mended by the Economic Survey Mission;
(*b*) To consult with the interested Near Eastern Governments concerning measures to be taken by them

preparatory to the time when international assistance for
relief and works projects is no longer available;

8. *Establishes* an Advisory Commission consisting
of representatives of France, Turkey, the United Kingdom of
Great Britain and Northern Ireland and the United States of
America, with power to add not more than three additional
members from contributing Governments, to advise and assist the Director of the United Nations Relief and Works
Agency for Palestine Refugees in the Near East in the execution of the programme; the Director and Advisory
Commission shall consult with each Near Eastern
Government concerned in the selection, planning and exe-
cution of projects;

9. *Requests* the Secretary-General to appoint the
Director of the United Nations Relief and Works Agency for
Palestine Refugees in the Near East in consultation with the
Governments represented on the Advisory Commission:
(*a*) The Director shall be the chief executive officer
of the United Nations Relief and Works Agency for Palestine
Refugees in the Near East responsible to the General
Assembly for the operation of the programme;
(*b*) The Director shall select and appoint his staff in
accordance with general arrangements make in agreement
with the Secretary-General,
(*c*) The Director shall, in consultation with the
Secretary-General and the Advisory Committee on
Administrative and Budgetary Questions, establish financial
regulations for the United Nations Relief and Works Agency
for Palestine Refugees in the Near East;
(*d*) Subject to the financial regulations established
pursuant to clause (*c*) of the present paragraph, the
Director, in consultation. with the Advisory Commission,
shall apportion available funds between direct relief and
works projects in their discretion, in the event that the estimates in paragraph 6 require revision.

10. *Requests* the Director to convene the Advisory
Commission at the earliest practicable date for the purpose
of developing plans for the organization and administration
of the programme, and adopting rules of procedure;

11. *Continues* the United Nations Relief for
Palestine Refugees as established under General Assembly
resolution 212 (III) until 1 April 1950, or until such date

thereafter as the transfer referred to in paragraph 12 is effected, and requests the Secretary-General in consultation with the operating agencies to continue the endeavour to reduce the numbers of rations by progressive stages in the light of the findings and recommendations of the Economic Survey Mission;

12. *Instructs* the Secretary-General to transfer to the United Nations Relief and Works Agency for Palestine Refugees in the Near East the assets and liabilities of the United Nations Relief for Palestine Refugees by 1 April 1950, or at such date as may be agreed by him and the Director of the United Nations Relief and Works Agency for Palestine Refugees in the Near East;

13. *Urges* all Members of the United Nations and non-members to make voluntary contributions in funds or in kind to ensure that the amount of supplies and funds required is obtained for each period of the programme as set out in paragraph 6; contributions in funds may be made in currencies other than the United States dollar in so far as the programme can be carried out in such currencies;

14. *Authorizes* the Secretary-General, in consultation with the Advisory Committee on Administrative and Budgetary Questions, to advance funds deemed to be available for this purpose and not exceeding $5,000,000 from the Working Capital Fund to finance operations pursuant to the present resolution, such sum to be repaid not later than 31 December 1950 from the voluntary governmental contributions requested under paragraph 13 above;

15. *Authorizes* the Secretary-General, in consultation with the Advisory Committee on Administrative and Budgetary Questions, to negotiate with the International Refugee Organization for an interest-free loan in an amount not to exceed the equivalent of $2,800,000 to finance the programme subject to mutually satisfactory conditions for repayment;

16. *Authorizes* the Secretary-General to continue the Special Fund established under General Assembly resolution 212 (III) and to make withdrawals therefrom for the operation of the United Nations Relief for Palestine Refugees and, upon the request of the Director, for the

operations of the United Nations Relief and Works Agency for Palestine Refugees in the Near East;

17. *Calls upon* the Governments concerned to accord to the United Nations Relief and Works Agency for Palestine Refugees in the Near East the privileges, immunities, exemptions and facilities which have been granted to the United Nations Relief for Palestine Refugees, together with all other privileges, immunities, exemptions and facilities necessary for the fulfilment of its functions;

18. *Urges* the United Nations International Children's Emergency Fund, the International Refugee Organization, the World Health Organization, the United Nations Educational, Scientific and Cultural Organization, the Food and Agriculture Organization and other appropriate agencies and private groups and organizations, in consultation with the Director of the United Nations Relief and Works Agency for Palestine Refugees in the Near East, to furnish assistance within the framework of the programme;

19. *Requests* the Director of the United Nations Relief and Works Agency for Palestine Refugees in the Near East:
(*a*) To appoint a representative to attend the meeting of the Technical Assistance Board as observer so that the technical assistance activities of the United Nations Relief and Works Agency for Palestine Refugees in the Near East may be co-ordinated with the technical assistance programme of the United Nations and specialized agencies referred to in Economic and Social Council resolution 222 (IX) A[8] of 15 August 1949;
(*b*) To place at the disposal of the Technical Assistance Board full information concerning any technical assistance work which may be done by the United Nations Relief and Works Agency for Palestine Refugees in the Near East, in order that it may be included in the reports submitted by the Technical Assistance Board to the Technical Assistance Committee of the Economic and Social Council;

20. *Directs* the United Nations Relief and Works Agency for Palestine Refugees in the Near East to consult

---

[8] "See *Official Records of the Economic and Souial Councit* , Fourth Year, Ninth Session, Resolutions, page 4." [Original footnote in text].

with the United Nations Conciliation Commission for Palestine in the best interests of their respective tasks, with particular reference to paragraph II of General Assembly resolution 194 (III) of 11 December 1948;

21. *Requests* the Director to submit to the General Assembly of the United Nations an annual report on the work of the United Nations Relief and Works Agency for Palestine Refugees in the Near East, including an audit of funds, and invites him to submit to the Secretary-General such other reports as the United Nations Relief and Works Agency for Palestine Refugees in the Near East may wish to bring to the attention of Members of the United Nations, or its appropriate organs;

22. *Instructs* the United Nations Conciliation Commission for Palestine to transmit the final report of the Economic Survey Mission, with such comments as it may wish to make, to the Secretary-General for transmission to the Members of the United Nations and to the United Nations Relief and Works Agency for Palestine Refugees in the Near East.

273rd plenary meeting,
8 December 1949.

34

Security Council Resolutions
242 and 338, 1967

As a result of the successful Israeli military actions during the course of the 1948 war, and
the inability of the United Nations to enforce
its numerous truce and cease-fire agreements,
the territories of the new state were greatly expanded over those accorded to Israel by partition.   In most of the surrounding Arab countries the war had been devastating economically and in the morale of the armed forces.
Beginning with Egypt in February of 1949, and
during   the   course   of   the   following   five
months, a series of armistice agreements were
signed between Israel and Lebanon, Jordan,
and   Syria.   As   time   progressed,   however,
relations   between   Israel   and   her   neighbors
deteriorated   with   infiltrations,   raids,   and
counterraids.   Particularly disturbing to Israeli
political leaders was the Egyptian revolution in
1952 that brought to power Jamal 'abd al-Nasir,
who, in the following years, laid claim to the
leadership of the Arab national movement and,

Source: **Res. 242:** United Nations. *Resolutions and Decisions of
the Security Council 1967.   Security Council Official Records:
Twenty-second Year.*   (New York: United Nations, 1967) 8-9.   **Res.
338:** United Nations. *Resolutions and Decisions of the Security
Council 1973.   Security Council Official Records: Twenty-eighth
Year* (New York: United Nations, 1974) 10.

in July 1956, nationalized the Suez Canal, thus
effectively cutting off Israeli contact to the
south.   In that same year, 'Abd al-Nasir
concluded military agreements with Syria and
Saudi Arabia.   On 29 October 1956 Israeli forces
invaded the Sinai Peninsula, thus initiating the
so-called "Suez War" in which she was joined
by Great Britain and France.   Under the auspices of a United Nations resolution, which
established the United Nations Emergency
Force (UNEF), the three nations completed the
withdrawal of their forces from Egyptian territory and the Gaza Strip on 9 March 1957.
Basically, the only long-lasting effects of the
war were the further deterioration of British
influence in the Near East and the strengthening of 'Abd al-Nasir's position as the leader of
Arab nationalism.

'Abd al-Nasir had allowed the stationing
of UNEF forces on the Egyptian side of the border with Israel as well as along the eastern
coast of the Sinai Peninsula, although Israel
adamantly refused to permit them to be placed
on her side of the border, thus placing Egypt in
a position of inequality with her enemy to the
east.   Stung by the continual taunts by the
other Arab states for the position into which
he placed Egypt, 'Abd al-Nasir, on 28 May 1967,
demanded that the United Nations troops be removed and shortly thereafter announced that
the Straits of Tiran — connecting the Gulf of
Aqaba to the Red Sea at the south-eastern end
of the Sinai Peninsula — would be blockaded to
Israeli shipping (her only route to South
Africa with the Suez Canal closed to her following the Suez War of 1956).   Although the block-
ade was never enforced, the government and
military leaders of Israel considered both these
actions provocative and on 5 June launched a
surprise attack upon Egypt by air and by land.
The Egyptian air force was almost immediately
virtually destroyed and Israeli forces seized
control of not only the Gaza Strip (which had
been under Egyptian protection since 1948) but
all of the Sinai Peninsula to the Suez Canal.   By
virtue of long-standing military agreements

between Egypt, Jordan, Syria, and Iraq the latter three states were dragged into a war that none had anticipated. Although King Husayn of Jordan, by virtue of the British legacy, had the best organized army, it was met with such Israeli ferocity that East Jerusalem (the "Old City") and the entire West Bank of the Jordan River, which had been annexed to Jordan following the 1948 war, were quickly occupied by Israeli forces. Iraq had not time to mobilize before most of her air force was destroyed. As in 1948, there was a complete lack of co-ordination between the Syrian and Egyptian forces so that Syrian participation in the war was negligible. After the proclamation of the first cease-fire by the United Nations, Israeli forces moved into and occupied the Syrian Golan Heights. The victories of the Israelis were extraordinary and the defeats of the Arab armies were ignominous.

Following the conclusion of the war, which had resulted in greatly enlarged territories for the State of Israel, the international community recognized the need for some action on the part of the United Nations if another war within the Near East was to be averted, possibly involving the two Super Powers. Numerous draft resolutions were brought up in both the General Assembly and the Security Council, but none could satisfy either the belligerent states or the Soviet Union or the United States. The United Nations itself appeared to be at a standstill. Lord Caradon, the British ambassador to the United Nations and sponsor of Resolution 242 that was finally passed, succinctly described the impass:

All the previous summer in the United Nations General Assembly there had been a long, fruitless and frustrating debate with no indication and apparently no possibility of agreement. Various resolutions had been proposed in the Assembly, but it never appeared that there would be an agreement. In the end the Soviet Resolution was voted down clause by clause until there was nothing left to vote on, and the United States had no hope of putting forward a resolution which had any prospect of the two-thirds majority required in the Assembly. . . . It seemed that the Middle East was doomed to continue the centre of a bitter and deep-seated and irreconcilable dispute which would divide the world and lead on in the end to another conflict on a far wider scale.

We, the Members of the United Nations, had not only failed to resolve the international dispute, we had intensified and prolonged it.[1]

After lengthy discussions Caradon was enabled to bring to the Security Council the following brief and intentionally ambiguous resolution that was subsequently passed unanimously by the fifteen members of the Council, precisely because of its ambiguity.

Resolution 242 (1967) of 22 November 1967

The Security Council,

Expressing its continuing concern with the grave situation in the Middle East,

Emphasizing the inadmissibility of the acquisition of territory by war and the need to work for a just and lasting peace in which every State in the area can live in security,

Emphasizing further that all Member States in their acceptance of the Charter of the United Nations have undertaken a commitment to act in accordance with Article 2 of the Charter,[2]

---

1 Georgetown University. *U.N. Security Council Resolution 242: a case study in diplomatic ambiguity.* (Washington, D.C.: Institute for the Study of Diplomacy, Edmund A. Walsh School of Foreign Service, Georgetown University, 1981) 3-4.

2 "**Article 2** - The organization and its members, in pursuit of the purposes stated in Article 1, shall act in accordance with the following principles:

  1. The organization is based on the principle of the sovereign equality of all its members.

1.   *Affirms*   that the fulfillment of the Charter principles requires the establishment of a just and lasting peace in the Middle East which should include the application of both the following principles:

(i) Withdrawal of Israeli armed forces from territories occupied in the recent conflict;

(ii) Termination of all claims or states of belligerency and respect for and acknowledgement of the sovereignty, territorial integrity and political independence of every State in the area and their right to live in peace with secure and recognized boundaries free from threats or acts of force:

2.   *Affirms further*   the necessity

(*a*) For guaranteeing freedom of navigation through international waterways in the area;

(*b*) For guaranteeing the territorial inviolability and political independence of every State in the area through measures including the establishment of demilitarized zones;

3.   *Requests*   the Secretary-General to designate a Special Representative to proceed to the Middle East to establish and maintain contacts with the States concerned in order to promote agreement and assist efforts to achieve a peaceful and accepted settlement in accordance with the provisions and principles in this resolution;

4.   *Requests*   the Secretary-General to report to the Security Council on the progress of the efforts of the Special Representative as soon as possible.

> *Adopted unanimously at   the*
> *1382nd   meeting.*

---

2.   All members, in order to insure to all of them the rights and benefits resulting from membership, shall fulfill in good faith the obligations assumed by them in accordance with the present charter."   [Footnote added].

Egypt, Jordan, and Syria accepted the resolution with British and U.S. assurances regarding the preamble ". . . the inadmissibility of the acquisition of territory by war. . . ." It was not until 31 July 1970 did Israel accept it with major reservations, including: 1) that the "withdrawal of forces" should not signify total evacuation, 2) final boundaries should be left to direct negotiation, and, 3) it should lead to a comprehensive peace plan.

Resolution 338 (1973)
of 22 October 1973

On 28 September 1970 the long-term President of Egypt, Jamal 'abd al-Nasir, collapsed and died from a heart attack. He was immediately succeeded by an early companion and fellow member of the Free Officers Society, Vice-President Anwar al-Sadat. His accession to the position was confirmed by the National Assembly on the 7th of October and subsequently by popular vote. From the outset the new president began to veer from the extremist positions of 'Abd al-Nasir in both internal affairs and foreign policy, leading to a new liberalism and a determination to find a solution to the Arab-Israeli conflict, so costly to the Egyptian economy and continued Israeli occupation of Egyptian soil in the Sinai Peninsula. On 8 February 1971 the special envoy of the United Nations, Ambassador Gunnar Jarring of Sweden, presented simultaneous memoranda to the Egyptian and Israeli Governments asking each to abide by Resolution 242. Although Egypt had already accepted the resolution, Jarring particularly asked al-Sadat if Egypt was prepared to 1) accept the existence of Israel, 2) agree to abandon the state of belligerency between the two countries, and 3) acknowledge the necessity of secure boundaries for Israel. To these al-Sadat agreed. Armed with these additional concessions, Ambassador Jarring asked Israeli Prime Minister Golda Meir if

Israel would accept Resolution 242 and withdraw from the newly occupied territories under its terms. To this Meir replied in the negative, stating that it was "not in the national interest."

With this rebuff, and even unable to obtain U.S. assistance in pursuading Israel to accept fully Resolution 242, particularly withdrawal from the occupied territories, al-Sadat
was determined to obtain the sophisticated
weaponry for his armed forces, and expected to
receive, from the Soviet Union under the fif-
teen-year treaty of friendship and co-operation signed on 27 May 1971. Al-Sadat sought to
bring to an end the "no-war-no-peace" stalemate which he realized could, in time, only lead
to *de facto* international recognition of the
Israeli occupation of lands taken during the
1967 conflict. The Israelis had, in fact, established eight Jewish settlements and five airfields in the Sinai.

On 6 October Egyptian forces launched a
surprise attack upon the Israeli military line
on the eastern bank of the Suez Canal while coordinating Syrian forces attacked the Israeli
positions in the Golan Heights. Coming as it did
during the Muslim holy month of Ramadan and
the Yom Kippur holiday, the Israelis were
caught completely off guard so that both the
Egyptians and the Syrians were originally enabled to make surprisingly important military
advances against the superior Israeli forces.
Not only were personnel losses on both sides
considerable, but also were those in military
supplies. As a result, the Egyptians and the
Syrians called upon the Soviet Union for renewed armaments, which were rushed to them,
and the Israelis requested relief from the
United States, which were airlifted from both
the United States and stockpiles in Europe.
There was international consternation that, as
had long been feared, the Near Eastern conflict
could erupt into a major war between the two
Super Powers on behalf of their respective
clients. On the 16th al-Sadat called for a cease-
fire based upon Israeli withdrawal from all oc-

cupied territories, which, of course, was re-fused. The Security Council, had learned from its failure to act in a decisive manner six years earlier, and in order to ease the tension, on 22 October quickly passed Resolution 338, pre-sented jointly by the Soviet Union and the United States, re-emphasizing its resolution of 1967. In this manner both resolutions became the basis for all subsequent efforts to secure peace in the Middle East.

The Security Council

1.   *Calls upon*   all parties to the present fighting to cease all firing and terminate all military activity immedi-ately, no later than 12 hours after the moment of the adop-tion of this decision, in the positions they now occupy;

2.   *Calls   upon*   the parties concerned to start immediately after the cease-fire the implementation of Security Council Resolution 242 (1967) in all of its parts;

3.   *Decides*   that, immediately and concurrently with the cease-fire, negotiations start between the parties con-cerned under appropriate auspices airmed at establishing a just and durable peace in the Middle East.

Adopted at the 1747th meet-ing by 14 votes to none.
[China did not participate in the voting]

35

The Palestinian National Covenant, 1968

The "Pact of the League of Arab States" (Document 24), included an "Annex on Palestine" by which the signatories to the Pact permitted the Council of the League to ". . . designate an Arab delegate from Palestine to participate in its work until this country enjoys actual independence." In September 1948 the Council formed an "All-Palestinian Government," recognized by all member states except Jordan, which was headed by Ahmad Hilmi, the Palestinian delegate to the League, until his death in September 1963. This "Government," however, failed to capture the imagination of the Palestinians, so that the Egyptian Government, in 1959, proposed the formation of a different "Palestinian entity" that was placed under study. Upon the death of Hilmi, the one-time assistant secretary-general of the League, Ahmad Shukairy, became the Palestinian representative on the Council and was delegated to formulate the proposed "entity." In the following months Shukairy and his staff worked on the draft of a national charter and a constitution of the organization

Source: Official translation of the Palestine Liberation Organization. Courtesy of the Palestine Liberation Organization United Nations Observer Office, New York.

he and they envisaged — the Palestine Liberation Organisation. As Theodor Herzl had done in the formation of the World Zionist Organization in 1896, Shukairy called for a meeting of 388 representatives of the Palestinians in Jerusalem on 28 May 1964. On 2 June this Palestine National Congress adopted the "Palestine National Covenant," which established the Palestine Liberation Organisation under Article 23. Meeting in Cairo 10-17 July 1968 the Fourth Palestine National Assembly adopted revised forms of both the Charter and the Constitution.

1. This Charter shall be known as "the Palestine National Charter."

Articles of the Charter:

Article 1. Palestine, the homeland of the Palestinian Arab people; is an inseparable part of the greater Arab homeland, and the Palestinian people are a part of the Arab Nation.

Article 2. Palestine, within the frontiers that existed under the British mandate, is an indivisible territorial unit.

Article 3. The Palestinian Arab people alone have legitimate rights to their homeland, and shall exercise the right of self-determination after the liberation of their homeland, in keeping with their wishes and entirely of their own accord.

Article 4. The Palestinian identity is an authentic, intrinsic and indissoluble quality that is transmitted from father to son. Neither the Zionist occupation nor the dispersal of the Palestinian Arab people as a result of the afflictions they have suffered can efface this Palestinian identity.

Article 5. Palestinians are Arab citizens who were normally resident in Palestine until 1947. This includes both those who were forced to leave or who stayed in Palestine.

Anyone born to a Palestinian father after that date, whether inside or outside Palestine, is a Palestinian.

Article 6. Jews who were normally resident in Palestine up to the beginning of the Zionist invasion are Palestinians.

Article 7. Palestinian identity, and material, spiritual and historical links with Palestine are immutable realities. It is a national obligation to provide every Palestinian with a revolutionary Arab upbringing, and to instil in him a profound spiritual and material familiarity with his homeland and a readiness both for armed struggle and for the sacrifice of his material possessions and his life, for the recovery of the homeland. All available educational means of guidance must be enlisted to that end, until liberation is achieved.

Article 8. The Palestinian people is at the stage of national struggle for the liberation of its homeland. For that reason, differences between Palestinian national forces must give way to the fundamental difference that exists between Zionism and imperialism on the one hand, and the Palestinian Arab people on the other. On that basis, the Palestinian masses, both as organizations and as individuals, whether in the homeland or in such places as they now live as refugees, constitute a single national front working for the recovery and liberation of Palestine through armed struggle.

Article 9. Armed struggle is the only way of liberating Palestine, and is thus strategic, not tactical. The Palestinian Arab people hereby affirm their unwavering determination to carry on the armed struggle and to press on towards popular revolution for the liberation of and return to their homeland. They also affirm their right to a normal life in their homeland, to the exercise of their right of self-determination therein and to sovereignty over it.

Article 10. Commando action constitutes the nucleus of the Palestinian popular war of liberation. This requires that commando action should be escalated, expanded and protected and that all the resources of the Palestinian masses and all scientific potentials available to them should be mobilized and organized to play their part in the armed Palestinian revolution. It also requires solidarity in national struggle among the different groups within the Palestinian people and between that people and the Arab masses, to ensure the continuity of the escalation and victory of the revolution.

Article 11. Palestinians shall have three slogans: national unity, national mobilisation and liberation.

Article 12. The Palestinian Arab people believe in Arab unity. To fulfil their role in the achievement of that objective, they must, at the present stage of their national struggle, retain their Palestinian identity and all that it involves, work for increased awareness of it and oppose all measures liable to weaken or dissolve it.

Article 13. Arab unity and the liberation of Palestine are complementary objectives; each leads to the attainment of the other. Arab unity will lead to the liberation of Palestine; and the liberation of Palestine will lead to Arab unity. To work for one is to work for both.

Article 14. The destiny of the Arab nation, indeed the continued existence of the Arabs, existence itself, depends on the fate of the Palestinian cause. This interrelationship is the point of departure of the Arab endeavour to liberate Palestine. The Palestinian people are the vanguard of the movement to achieve this sacred national objective.

Article 15. The liberation of Palestine is a national obligation for the Arabs. It is their duty to repel the Zionist and imperialist invasion of the greater Arab homeland and to liquidate the Zionist presence in Palestine. The full responsibility for this belongs to the peoples and governments of the Arab nation and to the Palestinian people first and foremost.

For this reason, the task of the Arab nation is to enlist all the military, human, moral and material resources at its command to play an effective part, along with the Palestinian people, in the liberation of Palestine. Moreover, it is the task of the Arab nation, particularly at the present stage of the Palestinian armed revolution, to offer the Palestinian people all possible aid, material and manpower support, and to place at their disposal all the means and opportunities that will enable them to continue to perform their role as the vanguard of their armed revolution until the liberation of their homeland is achieved.

Article 16. On the spiritual plane, the liberation of Palestine will establish in the Holy Land an atmosphere of peace and tranquility in which all religious institutions will be safeguarded and freedom of worship and the right of visit guaranteed to all without discrimination or distinction of race, colour, language or creed.   For this reason, the people of Palestine look to all spiritual forces in the world for support.

Article 17. On the human plane, the liberation of Palestine will restore to the Palestinians their dignity, integrity and freedom.   For this reason, the Palestinian Arab people look to all those who believe in the dignity and freedom of man for support.

Article 18. On the international plane, the liberation of Palestine is a defensive measure dictated by the requirements of self-defence.   This is why the Palestinian people, who seek to win the friendship of all peoples, look for the support of all freedom, justice and peace-loving countries in restoring the legitimate state of affairs in Palestine, establishing security and peace in it and enabling its people to exercise national sovereignty and freedom.

Article 19. The partition of Palestine, which took place in 1947, and the establishment of Israel, are fundamentally invalid, however long they last, for they contravene the will of the people of Palestine and their natural right to their homeland and contradict the principles of the United Nations Charter, foremost among which is the right of self-determination.

Article 20. The Balfour Declaration, the Mandate Instrument, and all their consequences, are hereby declared null and void.   The claim of historical or spiritual links between the Jews and Palestine is neither in conformity with historical fact nor does it satisfy the requirements for statehood.   Judaism is a revealed religion; it is not a separate nationality, nor are the Jews a single people with a separate identity; they are citizens of their respective countries.

Article 21. The   Palestinian Arab people, expressing themselves through the   Palestinian armed revolution,   reject all alternatives to the total liberation of Palestine. They also reject all proposals for the liquidation or internationalisation of the Palestinian problem.

Article 22. Zionism is a political movement that is organically linked with world imperialism and is opposed to all liberation movements or movements for progress in the world. The Zionist movement is essentially fanatical and racialist; its objectives involve aggression, expansion and the establishment of colonial settlements, and its methods are those of the Fascists and the Nazis. Israel acts as cat's paw for the Zionist movement, a geographic and manpower base for world imperialism and a springboard for its thrust into the Arab homeland to frustrate the aspirations of the Arab nation to liberation, unity and progress. Israel is a constant threat to peace in the Middle East and the whole world. Inasmuch as the liberation of Palestine will eliminate the Zionist and imperialist presence in that country and bring peace to the Middle East, the Palestinian people look for support to all liberals and to all forces of good, peace and progress in the world, and call on them, whatever their political convictions, for all possible aid and support in their just and legitimate struggle to liberate their homeland.

Article 23. The demands of peace and security and the exigencies of right and justice require that all nations should regard Zionism as an illegal movement and outlaw it and its activities, out of consideration for the ties of friendship between peoples and for the loyalty of citizens to their homelands.

Article 24. The Palestinian Arab people believe in justice, freedom, sovereignty, self-determination, human dignity and the right of peoples to enjoy them.

Article 25. In pursuance of the objectives set out in this charter, the Palestine Liberation Organization shall perform its proper role in the liberation of Palestine to the full.

Article 26. The Palestine Liberation Organisation, as the representative of the forces of the Palestinian revolution, is responsible for the struggle of the Palestinian Arab people to regain, liberate and return to their homeland and to exercise the right of self-determination in that homeland, in the military, political and financial fields, and for all else

that the Palestinian cause may demand, both at Arab and
international levels.

Article 27. The Palestine Liberation Organisation
shall cooperate with all Arab countries, each according to its
means, maintaining a neutral attitude vis-`a-vis these coun-
tries in accordance with the requirements of the battle of
liberation, and on the basis of that factor.   The Organisation
shall not interfere in the internal affairs of any Arab state.

Article 28. The Palestinian Arab people hereby affirm the authenticity and independence of their national
revolution and reject all forms of interference, tutelage   or
dependency.

Article 29. The Palestinian Arab people have the legitimate and prior right to liberate and recover their
homeland, and shall define their attitude to all countries and
forces in accordance with the attitude adopted by such
countries and forces to the cause of the Palestinian people
and with the extent of their support for that people in their
revolution to achieve their objectives.

Article 30. Those who fight or bear arms in the battle
of liberation form the nucleus of the popular army which
will shield the achievements of the Palestinian Arab people.

Article 31. The Organisation shall have a flag, an oath
of allegiance and an anthem, to be decided upon in accordance with appropriate regulations.

Article 32. Regulations, to be known as Basic Regulations for the Palestine Liberation Organisation, shall be appended to this Charter.   These regulations shall define the
structure of the Organisation, its bodies and institutions, and
the powers, duties and obligations of each of them, in accordance with this Charter.

Article 33. This Charter may only be amended with a
majority of two thirds of the total number of members of the
National Assembly of the Palestine Liberation Organisation
at a special meeting called for that purpose.

The Palestine Liberation Organisation
was recognized as the sole legitimate represen-

tative of the Palestinian people at the fifth
Arab Summit meeting of heads of state in Al-
giers, Algeria, in November of 1973 and Yasir
Arafat was accorded a seat on the Council of the
League of Arab States.   This decision was   reinforced even more specifically by a   resolution
passed unanimously by the heads of state of six
North   African   and   Near   Eastern   countries
(Algeria, Egypt, Jordan, Morocco, Sa'udi Arabia,
and Syria) at the sixth Summit held in Rabat,
Morocco, on 28 October 1974.   In this resolution
the Arab states: 1) affirmed the right of the
Palestinians to return to their homeland and to
self-determination; 2) recognized the PLO as
the sole legitimate representative of the Palestinian people and the establishment of an independent "national authority" under its leadership over any liberated territory; 3) declared
their   countries'   support   of   the   PLO   in
"exercising its national and international responsibilities; 4) appointed Jordan, Egypt,
Syria, and the PLO to co-ordinate their relations
and to implement the preceding decisions; and,
5) called upon all Arab countries to consolidate
the national Palestinian unity and to avoid intervention in the actions of the PLO.

36

Constitution of the Palestine Liberation Organization, 1968

Following the passage of the covenant that established, under Article 23, the Palestine Liberation Organisation, the representatives attending the congress in Jerusalem thereupon adopted the "General Principles of a Fundamental Law," a Constitution, also prepared by Ahmad Shuqairy and his group. In accordance with Article 5 of the Constitution this first congress became, in effect, the National Assembly or "parliament" of the PLO. From amongst those in attendance Shuqairy selected the members of the Executive Committee and assumed its chairmanship.

Together with the National Charter, the Constitution also underwent slight changes in its wording during the course of the meeting of the Council in Cairo in July 1968.

CHAPTER I

General Principles

Article 1. The Palestinians, in accordance with the provisions of this Constitution, form themselves into an or-

Source: Courtesy of the Palestine Liberation Organization Observer Office, New York.

ganisation to be known as the Palestine Liberation Organisation.

Article 2. The Palestine Liberation Organisation shall exercise its responsibilities in accordance with the principles of the National Charter, the provisions of this Constitution, and such rules, provisions and resolutions as may be issued in conformity with these principles and provisions.

Article 3. Relationships within the Organisation shall be based on commitment to struggle and to national action, the different levels of the Organisation, from its base up to its collective leadership, being closely linked together on a basis of the following principles: the minority shall defer to the will of the majority, confidence of the people shall be won through persuasion, the movement of Palestinian struggle shall be continued, the armed Palestinian revolution shall be supported, and every possible effort shall be made to ensure that it continues and escalates, so that the impetus of the masses towards liberation may take its course until victory is achieved.

In implementation of this principle, the Executive Committee shall draft constitutions for the Organisation's subsidiary bodies, due regard being paid to the circumstances of Palestinians in all places where they are concentrated, to the circumstances of the Palestinian revolution, and to the realisation of the objectives of the Charter and the Constitution.

Article 4. All Palestinians are natural members of the Palestine Liberation Organisation, performing their duty to liberate their country in accordance with their abilities and qualifications. The Palestinian people is the base of this Organisation.

CHAPTER II

The National Assembly

Article 5. The members of the National Assembly shall be elected by the Palestinian people by direct ballot, in accordance with a system to be devised for this purpose by the Executive Committee.

Article 6. (a) Should it be impossible to hold an election to the Assembly, the National Assembly shall continue to sit until circumstances permit of the holding of elections.

(b) If, for some reason, one or more seats in the National Assembly fall vacant, the Assembly shall appoint a member or members to fill the vacant seats.

Article 7. (a) The National Assembly is the supreme authority of the Liberation Organisation. It drafts the policy, planning and programmes of the Organisation.

(b) Jerusalem is the seat of the Palestine Liberation Organisation.

Article 8. The National Assembly is elected for three years,[1] and it shall be convened in regular session once every six months by its President or, should extraordinary sessions be necessary, by the President at the request of the Executive Committee, or of a quarter of its members. It shall meet in Jerusalem, Gaza, or any other place, depending on circumstances. Should the President not call such a session, the session shall convene automatically in such place and at such time as are designated in the request submitted by its members or by the Executive Committee.

Article 9. The National Assembly shall have a President's Office, consisting of the President, two Vice-Presidents, and a Secretary, elected by the National Assembly when it first meets.

Article 10. The National Assembly in ordinary session shall consider:

(a) The annual report submitted by the Executive Committee on the achievements of the Organisation and its subsidiary bodies.

(b) The annual report of the National Fund and budget allocations.

(c) Proposals submitted by the Executive Committee and recommendations of Assembly committees.

(d) Any other question submitted to it.

---

[1] The term of office for members of the National Assembly was reduced to two years in 1968.

Article 11. The National Assembly shall form such committees as it deems necessary to assist it in the performance of its duties.

These committees shall submit their reports and recommendations to the National Assembly, which shall debate them and issue its decisions as regards them.

Article 12. Attendance by two-thirds of the members of the Assembly shall constitute a quorum.   Decisions shall be taken by a majority vote of those present.

CHAPTER III

The Executive Committee

Article 13. (a) All members of the Executive Committee shall be elected by the National Assembly.

(b) The Chairman of the Executive Committee shall be elected by the Committee itself.

(c) The Executive Committee shall be elected from the National Assembly.

Article 14. The Executive Committee shall consist of eleven members, including the Chairman of the Board of Directors of the Palestine National Fund.

Should vacancies occur on the Executive Committee, for any reason, when the National Assembly is not sitting, they shall be filled as follows:

(a) If the vacancies are less than a third of the total membership, they shall not be filled until the first session of the National Assembly.

(b) If the vacancies amount to a third or more of the total membership of the Executive Committee, the National Assembly shall fill them at a session convened for the purpose in not more than thirty days.

(c) Should it be impossible, for valid reasons, to convene the National Assembly in extraordinary session, vacancies arising in either of the above cases shall be filled by the Executive Committee, the Assembly's Bureau and such members of the Assembly as are able to attend, at a joint assembly formed for this purpose.   The new members shall be chosen by a majority vote of those present.

Article 15. The Executive Committee is the highest executive authority of the Organisation.   It shall remain in permanent session, its members devoting themselves exclusively to their work.   It shall be responsible for executing the policy, programmes and planning approved by the National Assembly, to which it shall be responsible, collectively and individually.

Article 16. The Executive Committee shall assume responsibility for:

(a) Representing the Palestinian people.

(b) Supervising the Organisation's subsidiary bodies.

(c) Issuing regulations and instructions, and taking decisions on the Organisation's activities, provided these are not incompatible with the Charter or the Constitution.

(d) Implementing the Organisation's financial policy and drafting its budget.

In general, the Executive Committee shall assume all the responsibilities of the Liberation Organisation, in accordance with the general policies and resolutions adopted by the National Assembly.

Article 17. The permanent headquarters of the Executive Committee shall be in Jerusalem.[2]   It shall also be entitled to hold its meetings in any other place it sees fit.

Article 18. The Executive Committee shall establish the following departments:

(a) A Military Department.

(b) A Department for Political and Information Affairs.

(c) A Palestine National Fund Department.

(d) A Department for Research and Specialised Institutes.

(e) A Department for Administrative Affairs.

(f) Any other department the Committee considers necessary.

Each department shall have a Director-General and the rquisite staff.   The authority of each department shall be

---

[2] Following the conquest of East Jerusalem by the Israelis in 1973 the headquarters of the Committee was moved to Beirut, Lebanon. Upon the withdrawal of the PLO from Beirut in 1983 the Executive Committee established its new headquarters in Tunis, Tunisia, where they remain today.

defined by special regulations drawn up by the Executive Committee.

Article 19. The Executive Committee shall establish close relations and coordinate activities between the Organisation and all Arab and international organisations, federations and institutions which agree with its aims, or which help it in the realisation of the Organisation's objectives.

Article 20. The Executive Committee shall continue to exercise its prerogatives as long as it enjoys the confidence of the National Assembly. The Executive Committee shall submit its resignation to the new National Assembly at its first session. It is subject to re-election.

Article 21. Attendances of two thirds of its members shall constitute a quorum, and its resolutions shall be adopted by majority vote of those present.

CHAPTER IV

General Rules

Article 22. The Palestine Liberation Organisation shall form an army of Palestinians, to be known as the Palestine Liberation Army, with an independent command which shall operate under the supervision of the Executive Committee, and carry out its instructions and decisions, both general and particular. Its national duty is to become the vanguard in the battle for the liberation of Palestine.

Article 23. The Executive Committee shall make every effort to enroll Palestinians in Arab military colleges and institutes for military training, to mobilise the potentials and resources of the Palestinians, and to prepare them for the battle of liberation.

Article 24. A fund, to be known as the Palestine National Fund, shall be established to finance the activities of the Organisation, which Fund shall be administered by a board of directors to be formed in accordance with special regulations for the Fund issued by the National Assembly.

Article 25. The Fund's sources of revenues shall be:
(a) An impost on Palestinians imposed and collected in accordance with a special system.

(b) Financial assistance provided by Arab governments and the Arab nation.

(c) The sale of "liberations stamps" which the Arab states will issue for use in postal and other transactions.

(d) Contributions and donations.

(e) Arab loans and aid from Arab countries and friendly peoples.

(f) Any other sources of revenue approved by the Assembly.

Article 26. Committees to be known as "Committees for the Support of Palestine" shall be formed in Arab and friendly countries to collect contributions and support the organisation in its national endeavours.

Article 27. The level at which the Palestinian people is represented in Arab organisations and conferences shall be determined by the Executive Committee. The Executive Committee shall appoint a representative for Palestine to the League of Arab States.

Article 28. The Executive Committee shall be entitled to make such regulations as are necessary for the implementation of the provisions of this constitution.

Article 29. The Organisation's National Assembly shall be empowered to amend, alter, or add to this Constitution by a two thirds majority of its members.

CHAPTER V

Transitional Provisions

Article 30. On July 10, 1968, the National Assembly convened in Cairo shall replace the former Provisional National Assembly of the Palestine Liberation Organisation, and exercise all the prerogatives allotted to it by this Constitution.

Article 31. The National Assembly shall sit for two years as from July 10, 1968. Should it prove impossible to hold elections for its successor, it shall meet and decide either to extend its term for another period or to form a new Assembly in such a manner as it may approve.

Article 32. The National Assembly alone is entitled to co-opt new members from time to time, as it sees fit, should this be desirable in view of the requirements of the battle for liberation and the need to strengthen national unity, in conformity with the provisions of the National Charter, in accordance with regulations to be drafted by the Executive Committee in the coming session.

37

United Nations Observer Status of the PLO, 1974

The question of Palestine and the rights of the Palestinian refugees who had suffered so much during the four Arab-Israeli wars, particularly that of 1967, remained a constant problem before the General Assembly of the United Nations. Indeed, the refugee problem was long recognized as one of the major stumbling blocks to peace in the Near East, for without settling that no long-term solution could be found practicable. With the founding of the Palestine Liberation Organisation in 1964 the dispersed Palestinians believed that they had obtained a voice by which they could speak to the world community, for from virtually the beginning of its existence the PLO was recognized by the vast majority of them as their body — nearly a "government-in-exile." The charter of the Organisation identified them as "the Palestinian people," an entity, so that they firmly believed that they too should be represented in some fashion in the work of the United Nations. The PLO came to be recognized as the official spokesbody for the Palestinians

Source: United Nations. *Resolutions adopted by the General Assembly during its Twenty-ninth Session. Volume I: 17 September-18 December 1974. General Assembly Official Records: Twenty-ninth Session: Supplement No. 31 (A/9631)* (New York: United Nations, 1974) 4.

by the surrounding Arab states and was officially sanctioned by the Council of the League
of Arab States.   Furthermore, the PLO was invited to participate in the work of some of the
specialized agencies of the United Nations.   It
was natural, therefore, that its members, and
their supporters, should wish to have the General Assembly grant to it a special status as
"observer" in the debates of that body.   Both of
the following resolutions leading to the
granting of this position were introduced directly into the agenda of the General Assembly
by the Syrian Arab Republic, thus bypassing
the Political Committee.   After several days of
heated debate both resolutions were passed by a
large majority.   The resolution granting observer status, number 3237, was passed on 22
November 1974 by a vote of 95 to 17, with 19 ab-
sentions.   Among those states in opposition
were Israel, the United Kingdom, and the
United States.

3236 (XXIX).   Question of Palestine

The General Assembly,

Having heard the statement of the Palestine Liberation Organization, the representative of the Palestinian people,

Having also heard other statements made during the debate,

Deeply concerned that no just solution to the problem of
Palestine has yet been achieved and recognizing that the
problem of Palestine continues to endanger international
peace and security,

Recognizing that the Palestine people is entitled to self-determination in accordance with the Charter of the United
Nations,

Expressing its grave concern that the Palestinian people has
been prevented from enjoying its inalienable rights, in
particular its right to self-determination,

Guided by the purposes and principles of the Charter,

Recalling its relevant resolutions which affirm the right of the Palestinain people to self-determination,

1. *Reaffirms* the inalienable rights of the Palestinian people in Palestine, including:

(*a*) The right of self-determination without external interference;

(*b*) The right to national independence and sovereignty;

2. *Reaffirms also* the inalienable right of the Palestinians to return to their homes and property from which they have been displaced and uprooted, and calls for their return;

3. *Emphasizes* that full respect for and the realization of these inalienable rights of the Palestinian people are indispensable for the solution of the question of Palestine;

4. *Recognizes* that the Palestinian people is a principal party in the establishment of a just and lasting peace in the Middle East;

5. *Further recognizes* the right of the Palestinian people to regain its rights by all means in accordance with the purposes and principles of the Charter of the United Nations;

6. *Appeals* to all States and international organizations to extend their support to the Palestinian people in its struggle to restore its rights, in accordance with the Charter;

7. *Requests* the Secretary-General to establish contacts with the Palestine Liberation Organization on all matters concerning the question of Palestine;

8. *Requests* the Secretary-General to report to the General Assembly at its thirtieth session on the implementation of the present resolution;

9. *Decides* to include the item entitled "Question of Palestine" in the provisional agenda of its thirtieth session.

2296th plenary meeting   22 November 1974

3237 (XXIX). Observer status for the Palestine Liberation Organization

The General Assembly,

Having considered the question of Palestine,

Taking into consideration the universality of the United Nations prescribed in the Charter,

Recalling its resolution 3102 (XXVIII) of 12 December 1973,

Taking into account Economic and Social Council resolutions 1835 (LVI) of 14 May 1974 and 1840 (LVI) of 15 May 1974,

Noting that the Diplomatic Conference on the Reaffirmation and Development of International Humanitarian Law Applicable in Armed Conflicts, the World Population Conference and the World Food Conference have in effect invited the Palestine Liberation Organization to participate in their respective deliberations as an observer,

1 *Invites* the Palestine Liberation Organization to participate in the sessions and the work of the General Assembly in the capacity of observer;

2 *Invites* the Palestine Liberation Organization to participate in the sessions and work of all international conferences convened under the auspices of the General Assembly in the capacity of observer;

3. *Considers* that the Palestine Liberation Organization is entitled to participate as an observer in the sessions and the work of all international conferences convened under the auspices of other organs of the United Nations;

4. *Requests* the Secretary-General to take the necessary steps for the implementation of the present resolution.

2296th plenary   meeting   22 November 1974

38

Camp David Accord, 1978

The 1973 conflict with Egypt and Syria against Israel, during which the two Super Powers had supported their respective clients with additional armaments, was considered by even the United States and the U.S.S.R. to be too dangerous to world peace. Having jointly sponsored Security Council Resolution 338, the two decided to convene a peace conference in Geneva under their joint chairmanship in December of 1973. Despite this initial joint effort to bring peace to the Near East, Israel and the United States were suspicious of involving the Soviet Union in the peace process. Furthermore, by this time, President Anwar al-Sadat had become disenchanted with the Soviet Union and, because of U.S. efforts in effecting the partial withdrawal of Israeli forces from the Suez Canal through the Sinai I (18 January 1974) and Sinai II (4 September 1975) agreements, began to draw closer to the United States, believing that only it had any influence over Israel. As a result, the Geneva conference broke down.

Source: United States. Department of State. *The Camp David Summit September 1978* (Washington, D.C.: Department of State, 1978), Department of State Publication 8954, 6-9 [dbl. col.].

In his memoirs, President Jimmy Carter states that his interest in the Near East began in 1973 when, as governor of the state of Georgia, he and his wife toured Israel as the guests of that government.[1] This interest was carried on following his election when during the Spring of 1977 he was enabled to meet most of the Israeli and Arab leaders. Throughout the following months he attempted to reopen the possibility of a Geneva conference, with great difficulty, for not only did he have to face the great divisions between the Israelis and the Arabs, but also the opposition of many in the American Jewish community. Without prior warning al-Sadat, in a speech before the Egyptian parliament on 9 November, announced that his commitment to peace was so determined he was ready to go before the Israeli Knesset. On the 15th the new prime minister of Israel, Menachem Begin, issued a written invitation to al-Sadat through President Carter to visit Jerusalem and address the parliament 19-21 November. Despite al-Sadat's extraordinary initiative, resulting in Egypt's isolation from most of the Arab world, and a private meeting between him and Begin on Christmas Day, the process began to disintegrate. During the latter part of January 1978, after a whirlwind tour of India, the Near East, and Europe, President Carter began to consider the possibility of having both Begin and al-Sadat sit down with him at the presidential retreat at Camp David, Maryland.

The three leaders with their immediate advisors met 5-17 September 1978, and after a great deal of debate, often acrimonious, arrived at a dual frame-work for peace, the first calling for a multilateral treaty regarding the West Bank and the Gaza Strip and the second for a peace treaty between Egypt and Israel.

---

1 Jimmy Carter, *Keeping Faith: Memoires of a President* (New York: Bantom Books, 1982) 273.

A FRAMEWORK FOR PEACE IN THE MIDDLE EAST AGREED AT CAMP DAVID

Muhammad Anwar al-Sadat, President of the Arab Republic of Egypt, and Menachem Begin, Prime Minister of Israel, met with Jimmy Carter, President of the United States of America, at Camp David from September 5 to September 17, 1978, and have agreed on the following framework for peace in the Middle East. They invite other parties to the Arab-Israeli conflict to adhere to it.

Preamble

The search for peace in the Middle East must be guided by the following:

---The agreed basis for a peaceful settlement of the conflict between Israel and its neighbors is United Nations Security Council Resolution 242, in all its parts.[2]

---After four wars during thirty years, despite intensive human efforts, the Middle East, which is the cradle of civilization and the birthplace of three great religions, does not yet enjoy the blessings of peace. The people of the Middle East yearn for peace so that the vast human and natural resources of the region can be turned to the pursuits of peace and so that this area can become a model for coexistence and cooperation among nations.

---The historic initiative of President Sadat in visiting Jerusalem and the reception accorded to him by the Parliament, government and people of Israel, and the reciprocal visit of Prime Minister Begin to Ismailia, the peace proposals made by both leaders, as well as the warm reception of these missions by the peoples of both countries, have created an unprecedented opportunity for peace which must not be lost if this generation and future generations are to be spared the tragedies of war.

---The provisions of the Charter of the United Nations and the other accepted norms of international law and legitimacy now provide accepted standards for the conduct of relations among all states.

---

[2] Both Security Council Resolutions 242 and 338 were reprinted as an Annex to the Framework. These reprintings have not been reproduced here because they have been given in document 34.

---To achieve a relationship of peace, in the spirit of Article 2 of the United Nations Charter, future negotiations between Israel and any neighbor prepared to negotiate peace and security with it, are necessary for the purpose of carrying out all the provisions and principles of Resolutions 242 and 338.

---Peace requires respect for the sovereignty, territorial integrity and political independence of every state in the area and their right to live in peace within secure and recognized boundaries free from threats or acts of force. Progress toward that goal can accelerate movement toward a new era of reconciliation in the Middle East marked by cooperation in promoting economic development, in maintaining stability, and in assuring security.

---Security is enhanced by a relationship of peace and by cooperation between nations which enjoy normal relations. In addition, under the terms of peace treaties, the parties can, on the basis of reciprocity, agree to special security arrangements such as demilitarized zones, limited armaments areas, early warning stations, the presence of international forces, liaison, agreed measures for monitoring, and other arrangements that they agree are useful.

Framework

Taking these factors into account, the parties are determined to reach a just, comprehensive, and durable settlement of the Middle East conflict through the conclusion of peace treaties based on Security Council Resolutions 242 and 338 in all their parts. Their purpose is to achieve peace and good neighborly relations. They recognize that, for peace to endure, it must involve all those who have been most deeply affected by the conflict. They therefore agree that this framework as appropriate is intended by them to constitute a basis for peace not only between Egypt and Israel, but also between Israel and each of its other neighbors which is prepared to negotiate peace with Israel on this basis. With that objective in mind, they have agreed to proceed as follows:

A. *West Bank and Gaza*

1. Egypt, Israel, Jordan and the representatives of the Palestinian people should participate in negotiations on the resolution of the Palestinian problem in all its aspects.

To achieve that objective, negotiations relating to the West Bank and Gaza should proceed in three stages:

(a) Egypt and Israel agree that, in order to ensure a peaceful and orderly transfer of authority, and taking into account the security concerns of all the parties, there should be transitional arrangements for the West Bank and Gaza for a period not exceeding five years. In order to provide full autonomy to the inhabitants, under these arrangements the Israeli military government and its civilian administration will be withdrawn as soon as a self-governing authority has been freely elected by the inhabitants of these areas to replace the existing military government. To negotiate the details of a transitional arrangement, the Government of Jordan will be invited to join the negotiations on the basis of this framework. These new arrangements should give due consideration both to the principle of self-government by the inhabitants of these territories and to the legitimate security concerns of the parties involved.

(b) Egypt, Israel, and Jordan will agree on the modalities for establishing the elected self-governing authority in the West Bank and Gaza. The delegations of Egypt and Jordan may include Palestinians from the West Bank and Gaza or other Palestinians as mutually agreed. The parties will negotiate an agreement which will define the powers and responsibilities of the self-governing authority to be exercised in the West Bank and Gaza. A withdrawal of Israeli armed forces will take place and there will be a redeployment of the remaining Israeli forces into specified security locations. The agreement will also include arrangements for assuring internal and external security and public order. A strong local police force will be established, which may include Jordanian citizens. In addition, Israeli and Jordanian forces will participate in joint patrols and in the manning of control posts to assure the security of the borders.

(c) When the self-governing authority (administrative council) in the West Bank and Gaza is established and inaugurated, the transitional period of five years will begin. As soon as possible, but not later than the third year after the beginning of the transitional period, negotiations will take place to determine the final status of the West Bank and Gaza and its relationship with its neighbors, and to conclude a peace treaty between Israel and Jordan by the end of the transitional period. These negotiations will be conducted among Egypt, Israel, Jordan, and the elected representatives of the inhabitants of the West Bank and Gaza.

Two separate but related committees will be convened, one committee, consisting of representatives of the four parties which will negotiate and agree on the final status of the West Bank and Gaza, and its relationship with its neighbors, and the second committee, consisting of representatives of Israel and representatives of Jordan to be joined by the elected representatives of the inhabitants of the West Bank and Gaza, to negotiate the peace treaty between Israel and Jordan, taking into account the agreement reached on the final status of the West Bank and Gaza.   The negotiations shall be based on all the provisions and principles of UN Security Council Resolution 242.   The negotiations will resolve, among other matters, the location of the boundaries and the nature of the security arrangements.   The solution from the negotiations must also recognize the legitimate rights of the Palestinian people and their just requirements.   In this way, the Palestinians will participate in the determination of their own future through:

1) The negotiations among Egypt, Israel, Jordan and the representatives of the inhabitants of the West Bank and Gaza to agree on the final status of the West Bank and Gaza and other outstanding issues by the end of the transitional period.

2) Submitting their agreement to a vote by the elected representatives of the inhabitants of the West Bank and Gaza.

3) Providing for the elected representatives of the inhabitants of the West Bank and Gaza to decide how they shall govern themselves consistent with the provisions of their agreement.

4) Participating as stated above in the work of the committee negotiating the peace treaty between Israel and Jordan.

2. All necessary measures will be taken and provisions made to assure the security of Israel and its neighbors during the transitional period and beyond. To assist in providing such security, a strong local police force will be constituted by the self-governing authority. It will be composed of inhabitants of the West Bank and Gaza. The police will maintain continuing liaison on internal security matters with the designated Israeli, Jordanian, and Egyptian officers.

3. During the transitional period, representatives of Egypt, Israel, Jordan, and the self-governing authority will constitute a continuing committee to decide by agreement on the modalities of admission of persons

displaced from the West Bank and Gaza in 1967, together with necessary measures to prevent disruption and disorder. Other matters of common concern may also be dealt with by this committee.

4. Egypt and Israel will work with each other and with other interested parties to establish agreed procedures for a prompt, just and permanent implementation of the resolution of the refugee problem.

B. *Egypt-Israel*

1, Egypt and Israel undertake not to resort to the threat or the use of force to settle disputes. Any disputes shall be settled by peaceful means in accordance with the provisions of Article 33 of the Charter of the United Nations.[3]

2. In order to achieve peace between them, the parties agree to negotiate in good faith with a goal of concluding within three months from the signing of this Framework a peace treaty between them, while inviting the other parties to the conflict to proceed simultaneously to negotiate and conclude similar peace treaties with a view to achieving a comprehensive peace in the area. The Framework for the Conclusion of a Peace Treaty between Egypt and Israel will govern the peace negotiations between them. The parties will agree on the modalities and the timetable for the implementation of their obligations under the treaty.

C. *Associated Principles*

1 Egypt and Israel state that the principles and provisions described below should apply to peace treaties between Israel and each of its neighbors — Egypt, Jordan, Syria and Lebanon.

---

[3] **Article 33**-1. The parties to any dispute, the continuance of which is likely to endanger the maintenance of international peace and security, shall, first of all, seek a solution by negotiation, inquiry, mediation, conciliation, abritration, judicial settlement, resort to regional agencies or arrangements, or other peaceful means of their own choice.

2. The Security Council shall, when it deems necessary, call upon the parties to settle their dispute by such means. [editor's footnote].

2. Signatories shall establish among themselves relationships normal to states at peace with one another. To this end, they should undertake to abide by all the provisions of the Charter of the United Nations. Steps to be taken in this respect include:

(a) full recognition;
(b) abolishing economic boycotts;
(c) guaranteeing that under their jurisdiction the citizens of the other parties shall enjoy the protection of the due process of law.

3. Signatories should explore possibilities for economic development in the context of final peace treaties, with the objective of contributing to the atmosphere of peace, cooperation and friendship which is their common goal.

4. Claims Commissions may be established for the mutual settlement of all financial claims.

5. The United States shall be invited to participate in the talks on matters related to the modalities of the implementation of the agreements and working out the timetable for the carrying out of the obligations of the parties.

6. The United Nations Security Council shall be requested to endorse the peace treaties and ensure that their provisions shall not be violated. The permanent members of the Security Council shall be requested to underwrite the peace treaties and ensure respect for their provisions. They shall also be requested to conform their policies and actions with the undertakings contained in this Framework.

For the Government   For the Government
of the Arab Republic of Egypt   of Israel
A. SADAT   M. BEGIN

Witnessed by:
JIMMY CARTER

Jimmy Carter, President
of the United States of America

On the last day of the summit, when it was realized by the three leaders that the proposed paragraph regarding Jerusalem could very well result in no agreement at all, it was decided that there should be an exchange of letters in which each could present his own country's position regarding the city. These letters could then become a part of the official record.

September 17, 1978

DEAR MR. PRESIDENT,

I am writing you to reaffirm the position of the Arab Republic of Egypt with respect to Jerusalem:

1. Arab Jerusalem is an integral part of the West Bank. Legal and historical Arab rights in the City must be respected and restored.

2. Arab Jerusalem should be under Arab sovereignty.

3. The Palestinian inhabitants of Arab Jerusalem are entitled to exercise their legitimate national rights, being part of the Palestinian People in the West Bank.

4. Relevant Security Council Resolutions, particularly Resolutions 242 and 267, must be applied with regard to Jerusalem. All the measures taken by Israel to alter the status of the City are null and void and should be rescinded.

5. All peoples must have free access to the City and enjoy the free exercise of worship and the right to visit and transit to the holy places without distinction or discrimination.

6. The holy places of each faith may be placed under the administration and control of their representatives.

7. Essential functions in the City should be undivided and a joint municipal council composed of an equal number of Arab and Israeli members can supervise the carrying out of these functions. In this way, the City shall be undivided.

Sincerely,

(signed)

Mohamed Anwar El Sadat

His Excellency JIMMY CARTER

President of the United States

17 September 1978

DEAR MR. PRESIDENT,

I have the honor to inform you, Mr. President, that on 28
June 1967 — Israel's Parliament (The Knesset) promulgated
and adopted a law to the effect: "the Government is empowered by a decree to apply the law, the jurisdiction and administration of the State to any part of Eretz Israel (land of
Israel — Palestine), as stated in that decree."
On the basis of this law, the Government of Israel de-
creed in July 1967 that Jerusalem is one city indivisible, the
Capital of the State of Israel.

Sincerely,

(signed)

Menachem Begin

The President
Camp David
Thurmont, Maryland

The signing of the framework was received, on the whole, with approval in Israel,
for its provisions (or non-provisions) were
similar to the peace proposals advanced by Yi-
gal Allon in 1976 and by Begin himself in 1977.
Within the Arab world, on the other hand, the
framework was castigated as a "sellout" by al-
Sadat because it failed to mention the future of
Jerusalem and the Golan Heights, the position

of the Israeli settlements in the occupied territories, and did not mention the Palestine Liberation Organization, and as a reversal by
Carter of his own previously announced position providing for Israeli withdrawal from the
occupied territories and a "homeland" for the
Palestinians, in the spring of 1977.

Considering that it was their future that
was presumably being decided, without any
Palestinian representative having even been
invited to participate in the Camp David discussions, it is not suprising that the most vociferous opposition to the accords should come from
the Palestinians themselves. On 1 October 1978
the mayors of the West Bank and Gaza, together
with the leaders of a number of unions, and
other influential Palestinians, issued a declaration stating their position on the framework:

"We stand as one with all of our Palestinian
people.

"We have reviewed the Camp David Agree-
ments, and we wish to state that we reject them. We do
so because they serve only to strengthen Sadat's policy
of surrender and to defeat the political gains won by
our Palestinian Arab people. Those political gains, it
should be remembered, were achieved by our people
only after great sacrifice and they have been supported by the Algiers and Rabat Summit Conference
and the United Nations General Assembly.

"It is the aim of Sadat to subject the Arab
world to neo-colonialism by defeating the Arab Liberation Movement and by isolating it from its allies in
the international liberation struggle. His policies
will increase tension in the area, and will subject it to
cold war confrontation and to control by neo-colonialism.

"The so-called 'self-government' proposals for
the occupied West Bank and Gaza only legitimize and
strengthen the Israeli occupation. We thus consider it
a plot against our people's inalienable rights to self-
determination and to national independence in an independent Palestinian state under the leadership of
the PLO, the sole, legitimate representative of the
Palestinians.

"Our people have warned more than once that
Sadat's policies of surrender would lead to a separate
Egyptian peace with Israel, to a division in the Arab
ranks, and to a liquidation of the Palestinian cause.
Realizing these facts and being committed to the
Palestinian Arab national responsibility, the Pales-
tinian people in the occupied territories affirm the
following:

1.   The Palestinian people inside and outside occupied
Palestine are one; united through history, destiny and
struggle.

2.   The 'self-government' proposal is totally rejected
in form and content because it strengthens Israeli occupation and perpetuates Israeli oppression of our
people.

3.   The Palestinian people affirm and insist that the
P.L.O. is its sole, legitimate representative and refuse
any trusteeship or alternative, no matter in what form
or shape.

4.   We look forward to a just and lasting peace in the
area, achieved only through our people's exercise of
their right to self-determination and national independence, after total Israeli withdrawal from all the
occupied territories and after establishing an independent Palestinian state.

5.   Arab Palestinian sovereignty must return to Arab
Jerusalem which is an indivisible part of the West
Bank.   This is a historical and spiritual cause which
can not be compromised."[4]

---

[4]   Courtesy of the Palestine Human Rights Campaign, Washington,
D.C., 1978.

39

Egyptian-Israeli Peace Treaty, 1979

Attached to, and signed on the same day, 17
September 1978, was the following "Framework
for the Conclusion of a Peace Treaty between
Egypt and Israel," which was to provide the
basis for the succeeding agreement, primarily
covering the total withdrawal of Israeli forces
from the Sinai Peninsula. Interestingly, the
"Framework" was particularly detailed regarding the stationing of Egyptian, Israeli, and
United Nations peacekeeping forces within the
Sinai and along the eastern border between the
two countries.

FRAMEWORK FOR THE CONCLUSION OF A
PEACE TREATY BETWEEN EGYPT AND ISRAEL

In order to achieve peace between them, Israel and
Egypt agree to negotiate in good faith with a goal of conclud-

Sources: For the "Framework for the Conclusion of a Peace Treaty
Between Egypt and Israel": *The Camp David Summit September 1978*
(Washington, D.C.: Department of State, 1978. Department of State
Publication 8954, pp. 10-11. For the peace treaty: *The Egyptian-
Israeli Peace Treaty. The White House, Monday, March 26, 1979*
(Washington, D.C.: Department of State, 1979). Department of State
Publication 8973.

ing within three months of the signing of this framework a peace treaty between them.

It is agreed that:

The site of the negotiations will be under a United Nations flag at a location or locations to be mutually agreed.

All of the principles of U.N. Resolution 242 will apply in this resolution of the dispute between Israel and Egypt.

Unless otherwise mutually agreed, terms of the peace treaty will be implemented between two and three years after the peace treaty is signed.

The following matters are agreed between the parties:

(a)   the full exercise of Egyptian sovereignty up to the internationally recognized border between Egypt and mandated Palestine;

(b)   the withdrawal of Israeli armed forces from the Sinai;

(c)   the use of airfields left by the Israelis near El Arish, Rafah, Ras en Naqb, and Sharm el Sheikh for civilian purposes only, including possible commercial use by all nations;

(d)   the right of free passage by ships of Israel through the Gulf of Suez and the Suez Canal on the basis of the Constantinople Convention of 1888 applying to all nations; the Strait of Iran and the Gulf of Aqaba are international waterways to be open to all nations for unimpeded and nonsuspendable freedom of navigation and overflight;

(e)   the construction of a highway between the Sinai and Jordan near Elat with guaranteed free and peaceful passage by Egypt and Jordan; and

(f)   the stationing of military forces listed below.

Stationing of Forces

A.   No more than one division (mechanized or infantry) of Egyptian armed forces will be stationed within an area lying approximately 50 kilometers (km) east of the Gulf of Suez and the Suez Canal.

B.   Only United Nations forces and civil police equipped with light weapons to perform normal police functions will be stationed within an area lying west of the international border and the Gulf of Aqaba, varying in width from 20 km to 40 km.

C.   In the area within 3 km east of the international border there will be Israeli limited military forces not to exceed four infantry battalions and United Nations observers.

D.   Border patrol units, not to exceed three battalions, will supplement the civil police in maintaining order in the area not included above.

The exact demarcation of the above areas will be as decided during the peace negotiations.

Early warning stations may exist to insure compliance with the terms of the agreement: (a) in part of the area in the Sinai lying within about 20 km of the Mediterranean Sea and adjacent to the international border, and (b) in the Sharm el Sheikh area to ensure freedom of passage through the Strait of Tiran; and these forces will not be removed unless such removal is approved by the Security Council of the United Nations with a unanimous vote of the five permanent members.

After a peace treaty is signed, and after the interim withdrawal is complete, normal relations will be established between Egypt and Israel, including: full recognition, including diplomatic, economic and cultural relations; termination of economic boycotts and barriers to the free movement of goods and people; and mutual protection of citizens by the due process of law.

Interim   Withdrawal

Between three months and nine months after the signing of the peace treaty, all Israeli forces will withdraw east of a line extending from a point east to El Arish to Ras Muhammad, the exact location of this line to be determined by mutual agreement.

For the Government   For   the   Government
of the Arab   of   Israel:
Republic of Egypt:

A. SADAT   M. BEGIN

Witnessed by:

JIMMY CARTER

Jimmy Carter, President
of the United States of America

Following the signing and approval of the Camp David agreements by the Egyptian and Israeli leaders and their acceptance by the Israeli Knesset, President Carter invited the foreign and defense ministers of the two countries to Washington, in October, to work out with himself and his advisors the details for the peace treaty itself. By the 21st a draft treaty had been completed, but both the Egyptian and Israeli governments continued to have difficulties over important points, mainly arising from the Israeli settlements in Gaza and the West Bank, while, at the same time, Carter was attempting to push forward a more comprehensive peace settlement to include all the disputed territories and the future of the Palestinians. At length, in order to keep the peace prospect alive, if only between the two countries, President Carter flew to Egypt to meet with al-Sadat (8-10 March) and address the People's Assembly (parliament) on 10 March, and then to Jerusalem to meet with Begin (10-13 March) and speak before the Knesset on 12 March.[1] By the time he returned to Washington on the 14th the major elements of the treaty had been agreed upon. The treaty was finally signed at the White House in Washington 26 March 1979.

Treaty of Peace Between
The Arab Republic of Egypt and The State of Israel

The Government of the Arab Republic of Egypt and the Government of the State of Israel:

---

[1] The various welcoming speeches, toasts, and addresses before the two parliaments have been printed in: *President Carter's Trip to the Middle East March 7-14, 1979* (Washington, D.C.: The Department of State, Bureau of Public Affairs, Office of Public Communication, March 1979). "Selected Documents No. 10." Additional, more personal, material is to be found in Carter's *Keeping Faith* (New York: Bantam Books, 1982) 417-26.

PREAMBLE

Convinced of the urgent necessity of the establishment of a just, comprehensive and lasting peace in the Middle East in accordance with Security Council Resolutions 242 and 338:

Reaffirming their adherence to the "Framework for Peace in the Middle East Agreed at Camp David," dated September 17, 1978;

Noting that the aforementioned Framework as appropriate is intended to constitute a basis for peace not only between Egypt and Israel but also between Israel and each of its other Arab neighbors which is prepared to negotiate peace with it on this basis;

Desiring to bring to an end the state of war between them and to establish a peace in which every state in the area can live in security;

Convinced that the conclusion of a Treaty of Peace between Egypt and Israel is an important step in the search for a comprehensive peace in the area and for the attainment of the settlement of the Arab-Israeli conflict in all its aspects;

Inviting the other Arab parties to this dispute to join the peace process with Israel guided by and based on the principles of the aforementioned Framework;

Desiring as well to develop friendly relations and cooperation between themselves in accordance with the United Nations Charter and the principles of international law governing international relations in times of peace;

Agree to the following provisions in the free exercise of their sovereignty, in order to implement the "Framework for the Conclusion of a Peace Treaty Between Egypt and Israel":

ARTICLE I

1. The state of war between the Parties will be terminated and peace will be established between them upon the exchange of instruments of ratification of the Treaty.

2. Israel will withdraw all its armed forces and civilians from the Sinai behind the international boundary between Egypt and mandated Palestine, as provided in the annexed protocol (Annex I), and Egypt will resume the exercise of its full sovereignty over the Sinai.

3. Upon completion of the interim withdrawal provided for in Annex I, the Parties will establish normal and friendly relations, in accordance with Article III (3).

ARTICLE II

The permanent boundary between Egypt and Israel is the recognized international boundary between Egypt and the former mandated territory of Palestine, as shown on the map at Annex II [not duplicated], without prejudice to the issue of the status of the Gaza Strip. The Parties recognize this boundary as inviolable. Each will respect the territorial integrity of the other, including their territorial waters and airspace.

ARTICLE III

1.   The Parties will apply between them the provisions of the Charter of the United Nations and the principles of international law governing relations among states in times of peace. In particular:
       a. They recognize and will respect each other's sovereignty, territorial integrity and political independence;
       b. They recognize and will respect each other's right to live in peace within their secure and recognized boundaries;
       c. They will refrain from the threat or use of force, directly or indirectly, against each other and will settle all disputes between them by peaceful means.

2. Each Party undertakes to ensure that acts or threats of belligerency, hostility, or violence do not originate from and are not committed from within its territory, or by any forces subject to its control or by any other forces stationed on its territory, against the population, citizens or property of the other Party. Each Party also undertakes to refrain from organizing, instigating, inciting, assisting or participating in acts or threats of belligerency, hostility, subversion or violence against the other Party, anywhere, and undertakes to ensure that perpetrators of such acts are brought to justice.

3. The Parties agree that the normal relationship established between them will include full recognition, diplomatic, economic and cultural relations, termination of

economic boycotts and discrimination barriers to the free movement of people and goods, and will guarantee the mutual enjoyment by citizens of the due process of law. The process by which they undertake to achieve such a relationship parallel to the implementation of other provisions of this Treaty is set out in the annexed prototcol (Annex III).

ARTICLE IV

1. In order to provide maximum security for both Parties on the basis of reciprocity, agreed security arrangements will be established including limited force zones in Egyptian and Israeli territory, and United Nations forces and observers, described in detail as to nature and timing in Annex I, and other security arrangements the Parties may agree upon.

2. The Parties agree to the stationing of United Nations personnel in areas described in Annex I. The Parties agree not to request withdrawal of the United Nations personnel and that these personnel will not be removed unless such removal is approved by the Security Council of the United Nations, with the affirmative vote of the five Permanent Members, unless the Parties otherwise agree.

3. A Joint Commission will be established to facilitate the implementation of the Treaty, as provided for in Annex I.

4. The security arrangements provided for in paragraphs 1 and 2 of this Article may at the request of either party be reviewed and amended by mutual agreement of the Parties.

ARTICLE V

1. Ships of Israel, and cargoes destined for or coming from Israel, shall enjoy the right of free passage through the Suez Canal and its approaches through the Gulf of Suez and the Mediterranean Sea on the basis of the Constantinople Agreement of 1888, applying to all nations. Israeli nationals, vessels and cargoes, as well as persons, vessels and cargoes destined for or coming from Israel, shall be accorded non-discriminatory treatment in all matters connected with usage of the canal.

2. The Parties consider the Strait of Tiran and the Gulf of Aqaba to be international waterways open to all nations for unimpeded and non-suspendable freedom of navigation and overflight. The Parties will respect each other's right to navigation and overflight for access to either country through the Strait of Tiran and the Gulf of Aqaba.

ARTICLE VI

1. This Treaty does not affect and shall not be interpreted as affecting in any way the rights and obligations of the Parties under the Charter of the United Nations.

2. The Parties undertake to fulfill in good faith their obligations under this Treaty, without regard to action or inaction of any other party and independently of any instrument external to this Treaty.

3. They further undertake to take all the necessary measures for the application in their relations of the provisions of the multilateral conventions to which they are parties, including the submission of appropriate notification to the Secretary General of the United Nations and other depositories of such conventions.

4. The Parties undertake not to enter into any obligation in conflict with this Treaty.

5. Subject to Article 103 of the United Nations Charter,[2] in the event of a conflict between the obligations of the Parties under the present Treaty and any of their other obligations, the obligations under this Treaty will be binding and implemented.

ARTICLE VII

1. Disputes arising out of the application or interpretation of this Treaty shall be resolved by negotiations.

---

[2] **Article 103** - In the event of a conflict between the obligations of the members of the United Nations under the present charter and any other international obligations to which they are subject, their obligations under the present charter shall prevail. [editor's note].

2. Any such disputes which cannot be settled by negotiations shall be resolved by conciliation or submitted to
arbitration.

ARTICLE VIII

The Parties agree to establish a claims commission for
the mutual settlement of all financial claims.

ARTICLE IX

1. This Treaty shall enter into force upon exchange
of instruments of ratification.

2. This Treaty supersedes the Agreement between
Egypt and Israel of September, 1975.

3. All protocols, annexes, and maps attached to this
Treaty shall be regarded as an integral part hereof.

4. The Treaty shall be communicated to the Secretary
General of the United Nations for registration in accordance
with the provisions of Article 102 of the Charter of the
United Nations.

DONE at Washington, D.C. this 26th day of March, 1979,
in triplicate in the English, Arabic, and Hebrew languages,
each text being equally authentic.
In case of any divergence of interpretation, the English text
shall prevail.

For the Government of the   For the Government
Arab Republic of Egypt: of Israel:

[Anwar el Sadat]   [Menachem Begin]

Witnessed by:
_____
Jimmy Carter, President
of the United States of America

ANNEX I

PROTOCOL CONCERNING ISRAELI
WITHDRAWAL AND SECURITY ARRANGEMENTS

Article I
Concept of Withdrawal

1. Israel will complete withdrawal of all its armed forces and civilians from the Sinai not later that three years from the date of exchange of instruments of ratification of this Treaty.

2. To ensure the mutual security of the Parties, the implementation of phased withdrawal will be accompanied by the military measures and establishment of zones set out in this Annex and in Map 1, hereinafter referred to as "the Zones."

3. The withdrawal from the Sinai will be accomplished in two phases:
   a. The interim withdrawal behind the line from east of El Arish to Ras Muhammed as delineated on Map 2 within nine months from the date of exchange of instruments of ratification of this Treaty.
   b. The final withdrawal from the Sinai behind the international boundary not later than three years from the date of exchange of instruments of ratification of this Treaty.

4. A Joint Commission will be formed immediately after the exchange of instruments of ratification of this Treaty in order to supervise and coordinate movements and schedules during the withdrawal, and to adjust plans and timetables as necessary within the limits established by paragraph 3, above. Details relating to the Joint Commission are set out in Article IV of the attached Appendix. The Joint Commission will be dissolved upon completion of final Israeli withdrawal from the Sinai.

Article II
Determination of Final Lines and Zones

1. In order to provide maximum security for both Parties after the final withdrawal, the lines and the Zones

delineated on Map 1 are to be established and organized as follows:

a. Zone A

(1) Zone A is bounded on the east by line A (red line) and on the west by the Suez Canal and on the east coast of the Gulf of Suez, as shown on Map 1.

(2) An Egyptian armed force of one mechanized infantry division and its military installations, and field fortifications, will be in this Zone.

(3) The main elements of that Division will consist of:

(a) Three mechanized infantry brigades.

(b) One armored brigade.

(c) Seven field artillery battalions including up to 126 artillery pieces.

(d) Seven anti-aircraft artillery battalions including individual surface-to-air missiles and up to 126 anti-aircraft guns of 37 mm and above.

(e) Up to 230 tanks.

(f) Up to 480 armored personnel vehicles of all types.

(g) Up to a total of twenty-two thousand personnel.

b. Zone B

(1) Zone B is bounded by line B (green line) on the east and by line A (red line) on the west, as shown on Map 1.

(2) Egyptian border units of four battalions equipped with light weapons and wheeled vehicles will provide security and supplement the civil police in maintaining order in Zone B. The main elements of the four Border Battalions will consist of up to a total of four thousand personnel.

(3) Land based, short range, low power, coastal warning points of the border units may be established on the coast of this Zone.

(4) There will be in Zone B field fortifications and military installations for the four border battalions.

c. Zone C

(1) Zone C is bounded by line B (green line) on the west and the International Boundary and the Gulf of Aqaba on the east, as shown on Map 1.

(2) Only United Nations forces and Egyptian civil police will be stationed in Zone C.

(3) The Egyptian civil police armed with light weapons will perform normal police functions within this Zone.

(4) The United Nations Force will be deployed within Zone C and perform its functions as defined in Article VI of this Annex.

(5) The United Nations Force will be stationed mainly in camps located within the following stationing areas shown on Map 1, and will establish its precise locations after consultations with Egypt:

(a) In that part of the area in the Sinai lying within about 20 Km. of the Mediterranean Sea and adjacent to the International Boundary.

(b) In the Sharm el Sheikh area.

d. Zone D

(1) Zone D is bounded by line D (blue line) on the east and the international boundary on the west, as shown on Map 1.

(2) In this Zone [within Israel] there will be an Israeli limited force of four infantry battalions, their military installations, and field fortifications, and United Nations observers.

(3) The Israeli forces in Zone D will not include tanks, artillery and anti-aircraft missiles except individual surface-to-air missiles.

(4) The main elements of the four Israeli infantry battalions will consist of up to 180 armored personnel vehicles of all types and up to a total of four thousand personnel.

2. Access across the international boundary shall only be permitted through entry check points designated by each Party and under its control. Such access shall be in accordance with laws and regulations of each country.

3. Only those field fortifications, military installations, forces, and weapons specifically permitted by this Annex shall be in the Zones.

Article III
Aerial Military Regime

1. Flights of combat aircraft and reconnaisance flights of Egypt and Israel shall take place only over Zones A and D, respectively.

2. Only unarmed, non-combat aircraft of Egypt and Israel will be stationed in Zones A and D, respectively.

3. Only Egyptian unarmed transport aircraft will take off and land in Zone B and up to eight such aircraft may [be] maintained in Zone B. The Egyptian border units may be equipped with unarmed helicopters to perform their functions in Zone B.

4. The Egyptian civil police may be equipped with unarmed police helicopters to perform normal police functions in Zone C.

5. Only civilian airfields may be built in the Zones.

6. Without prejudice to the provisions of this Treaty, only thos military aerial activities specifically permitted by this Annex shall be allowed in the Zones and the airspace above their territorial waters.

Article IV
Naval Regime

1. Egypt and Israel may base and operate naval vessels along the coasts of Zones A and D, respectively.

2. Egyptian coast guard boats, lightly armed, may be stationed and operate in the territorial waters of Zone B to assist the border units in performing their functions in this Zone.

3. Egyptian civil police equipped with light boats, lightly armed, shall perform normal police functions within the territorial waters of Zone C.

4. Nothing in this Annex shall be considered as derogating from the right of innocent passage of the naval vessels of either party.

5. Only civilian maritime ports and installations may be built in the Zones.

6. Without prejudice to the provisions of this Treaty, only those naval activities specifically permitted by this Annex shall be allowed in the Zones and in their territorial waters.

Article V
Early Warning Systems

Egypt and Israel may establish and operate early warning systems only in Zones A and D respectively.

Article VI
United Nations Operations

1. The Parties will request the United Nations to provide forces and observers to supervise the implementation of this Annex and employ their best efforts to prevent any violation of its terms.

2. With respect to these United Nations and observers, as appropriate, the Parties agree to request the following arrangements:

> a. Operation of check points, reconnaissance patrols, and observation posts along the international boundary and line B, and within Zone C.
> b. Periodic verification of the implementation of the provisions of this Annex will be carried out not less than twice a month unless otherwise agreed by the Parties.
> c. Additional verifications within 48 hours after the receipt of a request from either Party.
> d. Ensuring the freedom of navigation through the Strait of Tiran in accordance with Article V of the Treaty of Peace.

3. The arrangements described in this article for each zone will be implemented in Zones A, B, and C by the

United Nations Force and in Zone D by the United Nations Observers.

4. United Nations verification teams shall be accompanied by liaison officers of the respective Party.

5. The United Nations Force and observers will report their findings to both Parties.

6. The United Nations Force and Observers operating in the Zones will enjoy freedom of movement and other facilities necessary for the performance of their tasks.

7. The United Nations Force and Observers are not empowered to authorize the crossing of the international boundary.

8. The Parties shall agree on the nations from which the United Nations Force and Observers will be drawn. They will be drawn from nations other than those which are permanent members of the United Nations Security Council.

9. The Parties agree that the United Nations should make those command arrangements that will best assure the effective implementation of its responsibilities.

Article   VII
Liaison   System

1. Upon dissolution of the Joint Commission, a liaison system between the Parties will be established. This liaison system is intended to provide an effective method to assess the progress in the implementation of obligations under the present Annex and to resolve any problem that may arise in the course of implementation, and refer other unresolved matters to the higher military authorities of the two countries respectively for consideration. It is also intended to prevent situations resulting from errors or misinterpretation on the part of either Party.

2. An Egyptian liaison office will be established in the city of El-Arish and an Israeli liaison office will be established in the city of Beer-Sheba. Each office will be headed by an officer of the respective country, and assisted by a number of officers.

3. A direct telephone link between the two offices will be set up and also direct telephone lines with the United Nations command will be maintained by both offices.

Article VIII
Respect for War Memorials

Each Party undertakes to preserve in good condition the War Memorials erected in the memory of soldiers of the other Party, namely those erected by Israel in the Sinai and those to be erected by Egypt in Israel, and shall permit access to such monuments.

Article IX
Interim Arrangements

The withdrawal of Israeli armed forces and civilians behind the interim withdrawal line, and the conduct of the forces of the Parties and the United Nations prior to the final withdrawal, will be governed by the attached Appendix and Maps 2 and 3.

[Attached to the Annex is an Appendix that provides the detailed withdrawal arrangements. This Appendix has not been reprinted because the withdrawal of Israeli forces was completed, except for Taba, on 25 April 1982, and is therefore no longer applicable.]

ANNEX III

PROTOCAL CONCERNING RELATIONS OF THE PARTIES

Article 1
Diplomatic and Consular Relations

The Parties agree to establish diplomatic and consular relations and to exchange ambassadors upon completion of the interim withdrawal.

Article 2
Economic and Trade Relations

1. The Parties agree to remove all discriminatory barriers to normal economic relations and to terminate economic boycotts of each other upon completion of the interim withdrawal.

2. As soon as possible, and not later than six months after the completion of the interim withdrawal, the Parties will enter negotiations with a view to concluding an agreement on trade and commerce for the purpose of promoting beneficial economic relations.

Article 3
Cultural Relations

1. The Parties agree to establish normal cultural relations following completion of the interim withdrawal.

2. They agree on the desirability of cultural exchanges in all fields, and shall, as soon as possible and not later than six months after completion of the interim withdrawal, enter into negotiations with a view to concluding a cultural agreement for this purpose.

Article 4
Freedom of Movement

1. Upon completion of the interim withdrawal, each Party will permit the free movement of the nationals and vehicles of the other into and within its territory according to the general rules applicable to nationals and vehicles of other states. Neither Party will impose discriminatory restrictions on the free movement of persons and vehicles from its territory to the territory of the other.

2. Mutual unimpeded access to places of religious and historical significance will be provided on a nondiscriminatory basis.

Article 5
Cooperation for Development and
Good Neighborly Relations

1. The Parties recognize a mutuality of interest in good neighborly relations and agree to consider means to promote such relations.

2. The Parties will cooperate in promoting peace, stability and development in their region. Each agrees to consider proposals the other may wish to make to this end.

3. The Parties shall seek to foster mutual understanding and tolerance and will, accordingly, abstain from hostile propaganda against each other.

Article 6
Transportation and Telecommunications

1. The Parties recognize as applicable to each other the rights, privileges and obligations provided for by the aviation agreements to which they are both party, particularly by the Convention on International Civil Aviation, 1944 ("The Chicago Convention") and the International Air Services Transit Agreement, 1944.

2. Upon completion of the interim withdrawal any declaration of national emergency by a party under Article 89 of the Chicago Convention will not be applied to the other party on a discriminatory basis.

3. Egypt agrees that the use of airfields left by Israel near El Arish, Rafah, Ras El Nagb and Sharm El Sheikh shall be for civilian purposes only, including possible commercial use by all nations.

4. As soon as possible and not later than six months after the completion of the interim withdrawal, the Parties shall enter into negotiations for the purpose of concluding a civil aviation agreement.

5. The Parties will reopen and maintain roads and railways between their countries and will consider further road and rail links. The Parties further agree that a highway will be constructed and maintained between Egypt, Israel and Jordan near Eilat with guaranteed free and peaceful passage of persons, vehicles and goods between Egypt and Jordan, without prejudice to their sovereignty over that part of the highway which falls within their respective territory.

6. Upon completion of the interim withdrawal, normal postal, telephone, telex, data facsimile, wireless and cable communications and television relay services by cable,

radio and satellite shall be established between the two Parties in accordance with all relevant international conventions and regulations.

7. Upon completion of the interim withdrawal, each Party shall grant normal access to its ports for vessels and cargoes of the other, as well as vessels and cargoes destined for or coming from the other. Such access shall be granted on the same conditions generally applicable to vessels and cargoes of other nations. Article 5 of the Treaty of Peace will be implemented upon the exchange of instruments of ratification of the aforementioned treaty.

Article 7
Enjoyment of Human Rights

The Parties affirm their commitment to respect and observe human rights and fundamental freedoms for all, and they will promote these rights and freedoms in accordance with the United Nations Charter.

Article 8
Territorial Seas

Without prejudice to the provisions of Article 5 of the Treaty of Peace each Party recognizes the right of the vessels of the other Party to innocent passage through its territorial sea in accordance with the rules of international law.

AGREED MINUTES
TO ARTICLES I, IV, V AND VI AND ANNEXES I AND III OF TREATY OF PEACE

ARTICLE I

Egypt's resumption of the exercise of full sovereignty over the Sinai provided for in paragraph 2 of Article I shall occur with regard to each area upon Israel's withdrawal from that area.

ARTICLE IV

It is agreed between the parties that the review provided for in Article IV (4) will be undertaken when requested by either party, commencing within three months of such a request, but that any amendment can be made only with the mutual agreement of both parties.

ARTICLE V

The second sentence of paragraph 2 of Article V shall not be construed as limiting the first sentence of that paragraph. The foregoing is not be be construed as contravening the second sentence of paragraph 2 of Article V, which reads as follows:

"The Parties will respect each other's right to navigation and overflight for access to either country through the Strait of Tiran and the Gulf of Aqaba."

ARTICLE VI (2)

The provisions of Article VI shall not be construed in contradiction to the provisions of the framework for peace in the Middle East agreed at Camp David. The foregoing is not to be construed as contravening the provisions of Article VI (2) of the Treaty, which reads as follows:

"The Parties undertake to fulfill in good faith their obligations under this Treaty, without regard to action or inaction of any other Party and independently of any instrument external to this Treaty."

ARTICLE VI (5)

It is agreed by the Parties that there is no assertion that this Treaty prevails over other Treaties or agreements or that other Treaties or agreements prevail over this Treaty. The foregoing is not to be construed as contravening the provisions of Article VI (5) of the Treaty, which reads as follows:

"Subject to Article 103 of the United Nations Charter, in the event of a conflict between the obligations of the Parties under the present Treaty andany of their other obligations, the obligations under this Treaty will be binding and implemented."

ANNEX I

Article VI, Paragraph 8, of Annex I provides as follows:

"The Parties shall agree on the nations from which the United Nations force and observers will be drawn. They will be drawn from nations other than those which are permanent members of the United Nations Security Council."

The Parties have agreed as follows:

"With respect to the provisions of paragraph 8, Article VI, of Annex I, if no agreement is reached between the Parties, they will accept or support a U.S. proposal concerning the composition of the United Nations force and observers."

ANNEX III

The Treaty of Peace and Annex III thereto provide for establishing normal economic relations between the Parties. In accordance therewith, it is agreed that such relations will include normal commercial sales of oil by Egypt to Israel, and that Israel shall be fully entitled to make bids for Egyptian-origin oil not needed for Egyptian domestic oil consumption, and Egypt and its oil concessionaires will entertain bids made by Israel, on the same basis and terms as apply to other bidders for such oil.

For the Government of   For the Government
the Arab Republic of Egypt   of Israel:
[Anwar el Sadat]   [M. Begin]

Witnessed by

Jimmy Carter, President
of the United States of America

On the day that the treaty was signed, 26 March, President Carter, in duplicate letters addressed to al-Sadat and Begin, virtually guaranteed it by the United States:

I wish to confirm to you that subject to United States Constitutional processes:

In the event of an actual or threatened violation of the Treaty of Peace between Egypt and Israel, the United States will, on request of one or both the

Parties, consult with the Parties with respect thereto and will take such other action as it may deem appropriate and helpful to achieve compliance with the Treaty.

The United States will conduct aerial monitority as requested by the Parties pursuant to Annex I of the Treaty.

The United States believes the Treaty provision for permanent stationing of United Nations personnel in the designated limited force zone can and should be implemented by the United Nations Security Council. The United States will exert its utmost efforts to obtain the requisite action by the Security Council. If the Security Council fails to establish and maintain the arrangements called for in the Treaty, the President will be prepared to take those steps necessary to ensure the establishment and maintenance of an acceptable alternative multinational force.

Secretary of State Cyrus Vance, appearing before the Senate Foreign Relations Committee on 11 April 1979, stated that the United States had made a number of financial and other commitments to both sides to encourage the signing and ratification of the treaty, additional to the then-current basic economic assistance programs, amounting to $4.5 billion over a three year period ($3 billion for Israel and $1.5 billion for Egypt):

1. The Israeli Government estimated that the direct costs of her withdrawal from the Sinai would be between $4 and $5 billion. Of this sum, in the form of foreign military sales, the United States would provide $2.2 billion. The entire $1.5 billion requested for Egypt would be used to help replace obsolete military equipment.

2. During the approximate eleven and a half years of Israeli occupation of the Sinai she had built four military air-bases, at El Arish, Rafah, Ras el-Nagb, and Sharm el-Sheikh. Al-Sadat had insisted that these be destroyed, but Begin was likewise insistent that because they had been so costly to construct Israel wanted either reparations or new ones built on Israeli soil. Therefore, the United States granted $800

million for the construction of two military air-fields in the Negev.

3. An additional $300 million would be requested from Congress for civilian economic assistance to Egypt.

4. For a total of 15 years the United States guaranteed Israel oil supplies. "Israel would turn to the United States only if Israel could not make independent arrangements to meet its own domestic consumption requirements through normal procedures [i.e., open market]."[3] Under "Annex III" of the treaty Egypt agreed that Israel would be an accepted bidder for oil not required for domestic consumption.

In addition to military installations constructed by Israel within the Sinai Peninsula a number of Israeli settlements and coastal resorts had also been established. Under the treaty these also had to be either destroyed or handed over to Egypt, which was accomplished, except for the town and district of Taba, about 250 acres in extent on the northern coast of the Gulf of Aqaba a few miles to the south of the city of Elat. The Israelis maintained that the area had been included within Palestine under a 1906 Ottoman-British agreement, but Egypt stated that it had been a part of her territories prior to the 1967 war. Failing to resolve the dispute amicably the two states agreed to binding arbitration by a panel composed of representatives from Egypt, France, Israel, Sweden, and Switzerland in 1986. Finally, on 29 September 1988, the members of the panel, with only Israel dissenting, ruled in favor of Egypt, leaving it to the two governments to agree upon the final boundary. Finally, under an agreement reached by the two governments Taba was turned over to the Egyptians on 15 March 1989, not, however, without protest by Israeli individuals, including the establishment of a new settlement in the occupied West Bank.

---

3 *U.S. Support for the Egyptian-Israeli Peace Treaty* (Washington, D.C.: The Secretary of State, Bureau of Public Affairs, Office of Public Communication, April 11, 1979) 4 pp.

On 6 October 1981 President Anwar al-Sadat was shot and fatally wounded by members of an Islamic fundamentalist movement calling itself "Jihad." At the same time, and in the ensuing riot, an additional 87 people were killed and 156 wounded. Five members of the organization were hanged and seventeen were sentenced to life imprisonment for complicity in the murder.

40

The Baghdad Resolution, 1979

As mentioned earlier there was opposition to
President Anwar al-Sadat's visit to Jerusalem
and his speech before the Israeli Knesset, particularly from the leaders of the Palestine Liberation Organization and the so-called "hard-
line" Arab states. In early December 1977, the
heads of state and representatives of Algeria,
Iraq, Libya, the PLO, Syria, and South Yemen
met in Tripoli, Libya, to discuss their opposition
to al-Sadat's initiative. The only definitive plan
they reached was to call for a freeze on political and diplomatic relations with Egypt. In return, Egypt broke off diplomatic relations with
these states on 5 December. At their meetings
in 1973 and 1974 the member states of the
League of Arab States had consistently affirmed
their support of the Palestine Liberation Organization in its efforts to establish "a national
entity." Therefore, al-Sadat, in participating in
the Camp David meetings and signing a separate peace treaty with Israel, was undermining
the unity of the Arab states in favor of the
Palestinians and against the "Zionist enemy."
Although there was some acrimony among the
League's members during the Baghdad meeting
27-31 March 1979, which Sudan and Oman had

Source: Courtesy of the League of Arab States.

declined to attend and to which Egypt had not been invited, there was unanimity in agreement to punish the Egyptian Government for its unilateral action. On 27 March, the day following the signing of the Egyptian-Israeli peace treaty, Egypt announced that it was "freezing" its relations with the League. The following resolutions adopted on 31 March by the Council of the League at the level of Arab Ministers for Foreign Affairs, Economy and Finance were, therefore, virtually certain.

. . . .

As the Government of the Republic of Egypt disregarded the resolutions of the Arab summits, in particular the resolutions of the Sixth and Seventh Summits held in Algiers and Rabat, and at the same time disregarded the resolutions of the Ninth Arab Summit, especially the call of the Arab Kings and Heads of State to refrain from signing the peace treaty with the Zionist enemy on the 26th March, 1979, thus defying Arab will and entering into complicity with the United States, it sided with the Zionist enemy and acted unilaterally in the Arab-Zionist dispute. By so doing, the Egyptian Government has violated the rights of the Arab Nation and exposed the Nation's dangers and challenges which threaten it. It has excommunicated itself from its national role to liberate the occupied Arab land, especially Jerusalem, as well as the restoration of full national rights of the Arab people of Palestine, including their return to their homeland and their right to self-determination and the setting up of the Palestinian state on their national soil.

In the interest of Arab solidarity, unity of rank for the sake of defending the Arab cause of destiny and in appreciation of the struggle of the Arab people of Egypt and their sacrifices along the path of Arab issues and implementation of the resolutions of the Ninth Arab Summit held in Baghdad from 2-5 November, 1978, consequently at the invitation of the Government of the Republic of Iraq, the Council of the Arab League met in Baghdad at the level of Foreign, Economy and Finance Ministers from 27-31 March, 1979. The Council, in light of the Ninth Arab Summit, studied the latest developments pertaining to the Arab-Zionist conflict, in particular the signing of the peace treaty by the Egyptian Government with the Zionist enemy on March 26, 1979, the Arab Foreign Ministers resolved the following:

Withdrawal of Arab Ambassadors from Egypt immediately.

Recommending severance of political and diplomatic relations with the Government of Egypt.

Considering suspension of membership of the Egypt Arab Republic from the Arab League, valid as from the date of the signing of the peace treaty between Egypt and the Zionist enemy.

Tunis, capital of the Tunisian Republic, shall be the temporary headquarters of the Arab League.

To work towards suspension of Egypt's member-ship from the Non-Aligned Movement, Islamic Conference Organization and Organization of African Unity, since it has violated the resolutions of these organizations concerning the Arab-Zionist conflict.

To continue dealing with the Arab people of Egypt, except those directly or indirectly collaborating with the Zionist enemy.

Member countries shall undertake to notify all foreign countries about their stand vis-a-vis the Egyptian-Zionist treaty and to call on these countries to refrain from supporting this treaty, since it constitutes an aggression on the rights of the Palestinian people and the Arab nation, and is a threat to peace and security in the world.

To condemn the policy pursued by the United States of America for its role in the Camp David Accords and the Egyptian-Zionist treaty.

The Council of the Arab League, at the level of For-eign, Economic and Finance Ministers, also agreed on the following:

To stop granting any loans, deposits, banking facilities and financial or technical aid by the Arab governments and their establishments within the Arab League to the Egyptian Government and its establishments as from the date of the signing of the treaty.

To refrain from offering economic aid from Arab banks' funds and financial establishments within the Arab League to the Egyptian Government and its establishments.

Consequent to the suspension of Egypt's membership from the Arab League, its membership in the establishment funds and organizations shall also be suspended, and all the benefits Egypt may enjoy from these sources shall also be terminated. In case of these bodies are based in Egypt they shall be transferred to other Arab countries temporarily.

As the Egyptian-Zionist treaty and the annexes attached to it commit Egypt to sell oil to Israel, Arab countries shall refrain from supplying Egypt with oil and its derivatives.

To ban trade exchange with public and private Egyptian establishments that engage in transactions with the Zionist enemy.

A) To apply the Arab boycott laws, principles and provisions on Egyptian companies, establishments and individuals who deal directly or indirectly with the Zionist enemy. The Boycott Bureau shall implement and follow up this resolution.

B) The provisions of paragraph A above cover cultural and artistic works which propagate dealing with the Zionist enemy or have association with its institutions.

C) The Arab countries stress the importance of continuing to deal with the national institutions in Egypt that refrain from dealing with the Zionist enemy and encourage them to work in the Arab countries within the framework of their field of interest.

D) The Arab countries stress the importance of respecting the feelings of Egyptians working and living in the Arab countries.

The United Nations shall be asked to transfer its regional offices which cover the Arab Region from Egypt to any other Arab capital.

These measures taken by the Arab Foreign and Economic Ministers are considered the minimum necessary to face the dangers of the treaty and that the Governments shall have the option to take whatever steps they deem necessary in addition to these resolutions.

In the weeks following the Baghdad Resolution Egypt became virtually isolated within the Arab world through the breaking of diplomatic relations with most of her neighbors and the withdrawal of the headquarters of the League of Arab States from its relatively new building on the banks of the Nile to Tunis, Tunisia.

41

European Community
Declaration, 1980

The members of the European Community had, to a large extent, been locked out by the United States in the various attempts to find a peaceful solution to the Arab-Israeli conflict. In Europe there was a feeling that the United States was too closely allied to Israel and unsympathetic to the Palestinians to be able to serve as an unbiased middleman in any negotiations. In most of the western European states the Palestine Liberation Organization was recognized as the "official" spokesbody for the Palestinians, and was permitted to maintain offices in their respective capitals. In France serious consideration was given in 1979 to granting the PLO diplomatic status. The European leaders received the signing of the Camp David Accords with some reservations, based primarily upon the failure of the Accords to address most of the fundamental problems, although the peace treaty between Egypt and Israel was widely accepted as a great step forward.

In a brief address before the General Assembly of the United Nations on 25 Septem-

---

Source: Bulletin of the European Communities, 13:6, 1980, pp. 10-11. There are a number of differences between the official text of the declaration as published in the *Bulletin* and its publication in the *New York Times*, 14 June 1980, p. 4.

ber 1979 the minister of foreign affairs of the
Republic of Ireland, as the president-in-office
of the European Community, spoke of the Community's concern about a number of the
world's problems. Within this framework he
reiterated the European Community Council's
previously ennunciated principles for peace
within the Near East:

These principles are: first, the inadmissibility
of the acquisition of territory by force; secondly, the
need for Israel to end the territorial occupation which
it has maintained since the conflict of 1967; thirdly,
respect for the sovereignty, territorial integrity and
independence of all States in the area and their right
to live in peace within secure and recognized boundaries; and fourthly, recognition that, in the establishment of a just and lasting peace, account must be taken
of the legitimate rights of the Palestinians.
    The nine countries emphasize that it is essen-
tial that all parties to the negotiation accept the right
of all States in the area to live within secure and recognized boundaries with adequate guarantees.
Equally, of course, it is essential that there be respect
for the legitimate rights of the Palestinian people.
These include the right to a homeland and the right,
through its representatives to play its full part in the
negotiation of a comprehensive settlement. . . .
The nine countries will continue to follow the situation closely and will seek in every way they can to advance the aim of a comprehensive and lasting peace
settlement involving all parties and dealing with all of
the fundamental issues I have mentioned.
    It follows that the nine countries must view,
with the greatest regret any action or statement which
aggravates the present situation or places an obstacle
in the way of a peace settlement. Accordingly, they
strongly deplore continued acts of violence by any of
those involved. They are opposed to the Israeli Government's policy of establishing settlements in occupied territories in contravention of international law;
and they cannot accept claims by Israel to sovereignty
over occupied territories, since this would be incompatible with resolution 242 (1967). The security of
Israel, which they consider essential, can be guaranteed, and the legitimate rights of the Palestinians

given effect, within the framework of a comprehensive settlement.

The nine states are fully aware, too, of the importance of the question of Jerusalem to all parties. They know that an acceptable solution to this problem will be vital to an over-all settlement on the basis I have indicated. They consider, in particular, that any agree-ment on the future status of Jerusalem should guarantee free access by all to the Holy Places; and they do not accept any unilateral moves which claim to change the status of the city.[1]

At the annual meeting of the heads of state and foreign ministers of the European Community Council, held in Venice, the following "Venice Declaration" was passed unanimously by the nine members on 13 June 1980.

1. The Heads of State or Government and the Ministers of Foreign Affairs held a comprehensive exchange of views on all aspects of the present situation in the Middle East, including the state of negotiations resulting from the agreements signed between Egypt and Israel in March 1979. They agreed that growing tensions affecting this region constitute a serious danger and render a comprehensive solution to the Israeli-Arab conflict more necessary and pressing than ever.

2. The nine Member States of the European Community consider that the traditional ties and common interests which link Europe to the Middle East oblige them to play a special role and now require them to work in a more concrete way towards peace.

3. In this regard the nine countries of the Community base on Security Council Resolutions 242 and 338 and the positions which they have expressed on several occasions, notably in their declarations of 29 June 1977, 19 September 1978, 26 March and 18 June 1979, as well as in the speech made on their behalf on 25 September 1979 by the Irish

---

[1] United Nations. *United Nations General Assembly, Thirty-fourth session. Official Records* (New York: United Nations, 1979) 119-22.

Minister of Foreign Affairs at the thirty-fourth United Nations General Assembly.

4. On the bases thus set out, the time has come to promote the recognition and implementation of the two principles universally accepted by the international community: the right to existence and to security of all the States in the region, including Israel, and justice for all the peoples, which implies the recognition of the legitimate rights of the Palestinian people.

5. All of the countries in the area are entitled to live in peace within secure, recognized and guaranteed borders. The necessary guarantees for a peace settlement should be provided by the UN by a decision of the Security Council and, if necessary, on the basis of other mutually agreed procedures. The Nine declare that they are prepared to participate within the framework of a comprehensive settlement in a system of concrete and binding international guarantees, including (guarantees) on the ground.

6. A just solution must finally be found to the Palestinian problem, which is not simply one of refugees. The Palestinian people, who is conscious of existing as such, must be placed in a position, by an appropriate process defined within the framework of the comprehensive peace settlement, to exercise fully their right to self-determination.

7. The achievement of these objectives requires the involvement and support of all the parties concerned in the peace settlement which the Nine are endeavouring to promote in keeping with the principles formulated in the declaration referred to above. These principles apply to all the parties concerned, and thus the Palestinian people, and to the PLO, which will have to be associated with the negotiations.

8. The Nine recognize the special importance of the role played by the question of Jerusalem for all the parties concerned. The Nine stress that they will not accept any unilateral initiative designed to change the status of Jerusalem and that any agreement on the city's status should guarantee freedom of access for everyone to the Holy Places.

9. The Nine stress the need for Israel to put an end to the territorial occupation which it has maintained since the conflict of 1967, as it has done for part of Sinai. They are deeply convinced that the Israeli settlements constitute a serious obstacle to the peace process in the Middle East. The Nine consider that these settlements, as well as modifications in population and property in the occupied Arab territories, are illegal under international law.

10. Concerned as they are to put an end to violence, the Nine consider that only the renunciation of force or the threatened use of force by all the parties can create a climate of confidence in the area, and constitute a basic element for a comprehensive settlement of the conflict in the Middle East.

11. The Nine have decided to make the necessary contacts with all the parties concerned. The objective of these contacts would be to ascertain the position of the various parties with respect to the principles set out in this declaration and in the light of the results of this consultation process to determine the form which such an initiative on their part could take.

The heads of state and foreign ministers of the members of the European Community continued to be concerned about the lack of progress towards a peace settlement, so that during their meeting in Brussels on 23 February 1987 the foreign ministers issued yet another statement in which they again called for an international peace conference to be held under the auspices of the United Nations. Also, expressing their concern about the living conditions of the Palestinians in the occupied territories, the ministers decided to grant aid to the population in the West Bank and Gaza and to give preferential access to the European common market for certain products from those territories.

42

Fahd Peace Plan
("Fez Declaration"), 1981

By failing to address a number of the most serious problems in the continuing Arab-Israeli dispute (repatriation or compensation for the Palestinians; self-government by the Palestinians; the occupation of and movement of the capital of Israel to Jerusalem; and continued Israeli occupation of the West Bank, Gaza, and the Golan Heights, together with the increasing numbers of Israeli settlements in those territories), the Camp David Accord was rejected by even the most moderate of the Arab states. On 8 August 1981 Crown Prince Fahd, in a statement issued by the Saudi press agency, proposed an eight-point proposal for peace based, it was stated, upon resolutions passed by the United Nations. At a later news conference held at the time of the visit to Riyadh by British Foreign Secretary Lord Carrington on 5 November 1981, Prince Sa'ud al-Faysal, Foreign Minister of the Kingdom, was asked if the plan implied the recognition of Israel (8. Recognition by Arabs of "each other's rights"). He replied that "There could be no peace without the recognition by both sides of each other's rights."[1] The Sa'udi Government stated

---

Source: Official translation from the minutes of the Twelfth Arab Summit Conference. Courtesy of the Embassy of the Kingdom of Sa'udi Arabia, Washington, D.C.

[1] United Press International, 5 November 1981.

that Prince Fahd's proposal would be placed before the Arab Summit meeting to be held in Fez, Morocco, 25-27 November 1981.

Because it competed with the Camp David Accord, the U.S. Department of State refused to comment upon the plan. In Israel Defense Minister Ariel Sharon replied that his government would establish eight additional settlements in the West Bank, one for each of Prince Fahd's eight point program.

At the twelfth Arab Summit meeting of heads of state the plan was adopted with certain modifications, particularly the Prince's eighth point.

The Summit has agreed upon the following principles:

1) The withdrawal of Israel from all Arab territories occupied in 1967, including the Arab Al Quds (Jerusalem).

2) The dismantling of settlements established by Israel on the Arab territories after 1967.

3) The guarantee of freedom of worship and practice of religious rites for all religions in the holy shrines.

4) The reaffirmation of the Palestinian people's right to self-determination and the exercise of its imprescriptible and inalienable national rights under the leadership of the Palestine Liberation Organization (PLO), its sole and legitimate representative, and the indemnification of all those who do not desire to return.

5) Placing the West Bank and Gaza Strip under the control of the United Nations for a transitory period not exceeding a few months.

6) The establishment of an independent Palestinian state with Al Quds as its capital.

7) The Security Council guarantees peace among all states of the region including the independent Palestinian state.

8) The Security Council guarantees the respect of these principles.

43

Agreement on PLO Withdrawal from Lebanon, 1982

As a result of the establishment of the state of Israel and the subsequent 1948-49 Arab-Israeli war, between 750,000 and 900,000 Palestinians either fled or were forced to leave their homes, seeking refuge in the surrounding areas. Although the largest percentage of these newly stateless persons found temporary safety in the West Bank (an estimated 38 percent) others moved into both Jordan, southern Lebanon or other surrounding states either settling in older villages or, under the United Nations Relief and Works Agency (UNRWA) auspices, refugee camps. The newly independent Kingdom of Jordan suddenly found its population increased by over a third. With the June War of 1967 the commissioner-general of UNRWA estimated that an additional 300,000 were ". . . rendered homeless or have left their homes as a result of the hostilities."[1] Of neces-

Source: United States. Department of State. *Lebanon: Plan for the PLO Evacuation from West Beirut. Current Policy No. 415* (Washington, D.C.: United States Department of State, Bureau of Public Affairs, August 1982) 8-10.

[1] United Nations. *Report of the Commisioner-General of the United Nations Relief and Works Agency 1 July 1966-30 June 1967. General Assembly Official Records: Twenty-second session. Supplement No. 13 (A/6713)* (New York: United Nations, 1967) "Introduction," p. 1.

sity, large numbers of these new refugees
joined their brethren in Jordan and Lebanon,
thereby compounding an already difficult situation within those countries.

From almost the beginning small, disor-
ganized Palestinian groups began to carry on
guerrilla activities against Israeli targets.
However, it was not until the formation of al-
Fatah as a result of the Suez War in 1956, that
"national struggle" on a wide scale became the
rallying cry of the Palestinians. Al-Fatah's
first successful military operation on 31 December 1964 proved the necessity of leadership
in armed operations. With the great influx of
additional refugees into Jordan following the
disastrous defeat of the Arab armies in 1967,
leading to the occupation of the Gaza Strip and
the West Bank, the *fedayeen* organizations
grew both in numbers and in size so that they
began to militarily challenge the authority of
the Government of Jordan. In addition, by carrying on their attacks within both Israel and
the occupied West Bank from Jordan, they invited strong counterattacks by the Israeli
army, often leading to the destruction of entire
villages. King Husayn of Jordan determined
that he must eliminate the threat to his regime
by the Palestinian guerillas and the very great
possibility of an Israeli invasion. Therefore,
throughout the latter part of 1970 and the first
of 1971 his revitalized military forces drove the
fedayeen into Syria and Lebanon, where they
were retrained, regrouped, and enlarged from
the local refugee camps. Southern Lebanon
now became the base from which al-Fatah and
the other military forces of the Palestinians
made their attacks into northern Israel and, in
return, it felt the brunt of often ferocious
reprisal raids by land, sea, and air.

On 4 June 1982 the Israeli ambassador to
the Court of St. James, Shlomo Argov, was criti-
cally wounded by gunmen in London. Israel
attributed the attack to the PLO, although its
leadership denied responsibility. Nevertheless, the following day Israeli American-made
jet aircraft attacked PLO positions in southern

Lebanon and even Beirut itself. This was followed on 6 June by a massive invasion of Lebanon, originally meant only to force the Palestinian armed groups 25 miles north of the border, according to Israeli Prime Minister Menachem Begin. However, the invading forces continued to advance far beyond the stated limit to Beirut itself. In the following weeks Israeli air and artillery forces savagely bombarded both military and civilian targets, including hospitals, in the Lebanese capital, and the Israeli army blockaded west Beirut, preventing the entry of food and water. The General Assembly and the Security Council of the United Nations repeatedly passed resolutions calling for the withdrawal of the Israeli forces from Lebanon, with the United States either abstaining from voting or, in the Security Council, vetoing most of these resolutions.

After tremendous effort President Ronald Reagan's personal emissary to Lebanon, Ambassador Philip C. Habib, was enabled, on 19 August 1982, to obtain an agreement between the Government of Lebanon, the PLO leadership, the Israelis, and the Syrian forces in the country for the evacuation of PLO "leaders, offices, and combatants" in Beirut and for the deployment of a multinational force from the United States, France, and Italy to oversee this withdrawal. Under this agreement members of the PLO military factions were scattered to Jordan, Iraq, Tunisia, North Yemen, South Yemen, Syria, Sudan, and Algeria.

Although the withdrawal was completed according to plan, the "Schedule of Departures" also has been reproduced here because of its own intrinsic interest.

PLAN FOR THE DEPARTURE FROM LEBANON OF THE PLO
LEADERSHIP,
OFFICES, AND COMBATANTS IN BEIRUT

1. Basic Concept. All the PLO leadership, offices, and combatants in Beirut will leave Lebanon peacefully for pre-arranged destinations in other countries, in accord with the departure schedules and arrangements set out in this plan. The basic concept in this plan is consistent with the objective of the Government of Lebanon that all foreign military forces withdraw from Lebanon.

2. Cease-fire. A cease-fire in place will be scrupulously observed by all in Lebanon.

3. U.N. Observers. The U.N. Observer Group stationed in the Beirut area will continue its functioning in that area.

4. Safeguards. Military forces present in Lebanon—whether Lebanese, Israeli, Syrian, Palestinian, or any other— will in no way interfere with the safe, secure, and timely departure of the PLO leadership, offices, and combatants. Law-abiding Palestinian noncombatants left behind in Beirut, including the families of those who have departed, will be subject to Lebanese laws and regulations. The Governments of Lebanon and the United States will provide appropriate guarantees of safety in the following ways.

• The Lebanese Government will provide its guarantees on the basis of having secured assurances from armed groups with which it has been in touch.
• The United States will provide its guarantees on the basis of assurances received from the Government of Israel and from the leadership of certain Lebanese groups with which it has been in touch.

5. "Departure Day" is defined as the day on which advance elements of the multinational force (MNF) deploy in the Beirut area, in accordance with arrangements worked out in advance among all concerned, and on which the initial group or groups of PLO personnel commence departure from Beirut in accord with the planned schedule.

6. The Multinational Force. A temporary multinational force, composed of units from France, Italy, and the United States, will have been formed—at the request of the Lebanese Government—to assist the Lebanese Armed Forces in carrying out their responsibilities in this operation. The Lebanese Armed Forces will assure the departure from Lebanon of the PLO leadership, offices, and combatants, from whatever organization in Beirut, in a manner which will:

   (A) Assure the safety of such departing PLO personnel;
   (B) Assure the safety of other persons in the Beirut area; and
   (C) Further the restoration of the sovereignty and authority of the Government of Lebanon over the Beirut area.

   7. Schedule of Departures and Other Arrangements. The attached schedule of departures is subject to revision as may be necessary because of logistical requirements and because of any necessary shift in the setting of Departure Day. Details concerning the schedule will be forwarded to the Israeli Defense Forces through the Liaison and Coordination Committee. Places of assembly for the departing personnel will be identified by agreement between the Government of Lebanon and the PLO. The PLO will be in touch with governments receiving personnel to coordinate arrival and other arrangements there. If assistance is required the PLO should notify the Government of Lebanon.
   8. MNF Mandate. In the event that the departure from Lebanon of the PLO personnel referred to above does not take place in accord with the agreed and predetermined schedule, the mandate of the MNF will terminate immediately and all MNF personnel will leave Lebanon forthwith.
   9. Duration of MNF. It will be mutually agreed between the Lebanese Government and the governments contributing forces to the MNF that the forces of the MNF will depart Lebanon not later than 30 days after arrival, or sooner at the request of the Government of Lebanon or at the direction of the individual government concerned, or in accord with the termination of the mandate of the MNF provided for above.
   10. The PLO leadership will be responsible for the organization and management of the assembly and the final departure of PLO personnel, from beginning to end, at which time the leaders also will all be gone. Departure ar-

rangements will be coordinated so that departures from Beirut take place at a steady pace, day by day.

11. Lebanese Armed Forces Contribution. The Lebanese Army will contribute between seven and eight army battalions to the operation, consisting of between 2,500-3,500 men. In addition, the internal security force will contribute men and assistance as needed.

12. ICRC. The International Committee of the Red Cross (ICRC) will be able to assist the Government of Lebanon and Lebanese Armed Forces in various ways, including in the organization and management of the evacuation of wounded and ill Palestinian and Syrian personnel to appropriate destinations, and in assisting in the chartering and movement of commercial vessels for use in departure by sea to other countries. The Liaison and Coordination Committee will insure that there will be proper coordination with any ICRC activities in this respect.

13. Departure by Air. While present plans call for departure by sea and land, departures by air are not foreclosed.

14. Liaison and Coordination:

• The Lebanese Armed Forces will be the primary point of contact for liaison with the PLO as well as with other armed groups and will provide necessary information.

• The Lebanese Armed Forces and MNF will have formed prior to Departure Day a Liaison and Coordination Committee, composed of representatives of the MNF participating governments and the Lebanese Armed Forces. The committee will carry out close and effective liaison with, and provide continuous and detailed information to, the Israeli Defense Forces (IDF). On behalf of the committee, the Lebanese Armed Forces will continue to carry out close and effective liaison with the PLO and other armed groups in the Beirut area. For convenience, the Liaison and Coordination Committee will have two essential components:

(A)   Supervisory liaison; and
(B)   Military and technical liaison and coordination.

The Liaison and Coordination Committee will act collectively; however, it may designate one or more of its members for primary liaison contact who would of course act on behalf of all.

• Liaison arrangements and consultations will be conducted in such a way as to minimize misunderstandings and to forestall difficulties. Appropriate means of communications between the committee and other groups will be developed for this purpose.

• The Liaison and Coordination Committee will continually monitor and keep all concerned currently informed regarding the implementation of the plan, including any revisions to the departure schedule as may be necessary because of logistical requirements.

15. Duration of Departure. The departure period shall be as short as possible and, in any event, no longer than 2 weeks.

16. Transit Through Lebanon. As part of any departure arrangement, all movements of convoys carrying PLO personnel must be conducted in daylight hours. When moving overland from Beirut to Syria, the convoys should cross the border into Syria with no stops en route. In those instances when convoys of departing PLO personnel pass through positions of the Israeli Defense Forces, whether in the Beirut area or elsewhere in Lebanon, the Israeli Defense Forces will clear the route for the temporary period in which the convoy is running. Similar steps will be taken by other armed groups located in the area of the route the convoy will take.

17. Arms Carried by PLO Personnel. On their departure, PLO personnel will be allowed to carry with them one individual side weapon (pistol, rifle, or submarine [*sic*] gun) and ammunition.

18. Heavy and Spare Weaponry and Munitions. The PLO will turn over to the Lebanese Armed Forces as gifts all remaining weaponry in their possession, including heavy, crew-served, and spare weaponry and equipment, along with all munitions left behind in the Beirut area. The Lebanese Armed Forces may seek the assistance of elements of the MNF in securing and disposing of the military equipment. The PLO will assist the Lebanese Armed Forces by providing, prior to their departure, full and detailed information as to the location of this military equipment.

19. Mines and Booby Traps. The PLO and the Arab Deterrent Force (ADF) will provide to the Lebanese Armed Forces and the MNF (through the Lebanese Armed Forces) full and detailed information on the location of mines and booby traps.

20. Movement of PLO Leadership. Arrangements will be made so that departing PLO personnel will be accompanied by a proportionate share of the military and political leadership throughout all stages of the departure operation.

21. Turnover of Prisoners and Remains. The PLO will, through the ICRC, turn over to the Israeli Defense Forces, all Israeli nationals whom they have taken in custody, and the remains, or full and detailed information about the location of the remains, of all Israeli soldiers who have fallen. The PLO will also turn over to the Lebanese Armed Forces all other prisoners whom they have taken in custody and the remains, or full and detailed information about the location of the remains, of all other soldiers who have fallen. All arrangements for such turnovers shall be worked out with the ICRC as required prior to Departure Day.

22. Syrian Military Forces. It is noted that arrangements have been made between the Governments of Lebanon and Syria for the deployment of all military personnel of the Arab Deterrent Force from Beirut during the departure period. These forces will be allowed to take their equipment with them, except for that—under mutual agreement between the two governments—which is turned over to the Lebanese Armed Forces. All elements of the Palestine Liberation Army, whether or not they now or in the past have been attached to the Arab Deterrent Force, will withdraw from Lebanon.

SCHEDULE OF DEPARTURES

August 21, 1982—Departure Day

The advance elements of the MNF (approximately 350 men) land at the Port of Beirut at about 0500 and deploy in the Beirut port area in preparation for the initial departures of PLO groups by sea.

Meanwhile, the Lebanese Armed Forces deploy to previously agreed positions in the Beirut area, primarily in the so-called demarcation line area, to assist in the departure of PLO personnel. The Lebanese Armed Forces will take over positions occupied by the PLO.

The PLO will insure that National Movement Forces [collection of Lebanese militias] which had occupied these positions jointly with the PLO shall also withdraw.

As the day proceeds, the Lebanese Armed Forces will take up such other positions as necessary to assist in the departure of PLO personnel.

Meanwhile, the initial group of PLO personnel assemble in preparation for departure by sea later in the day (or on August 22). The vessel or vessels to be used for this purpose will arrive at pier on August 21.

The initial groups could include the wounded and ill, who would be transported in accordance with agreed arrangements—by sea or land, or both—to their destinations in other countries.

The initial group or groups of PLO personnel destined for Jordan and Iraq would move from their assembly point to the waiting commercial vessel or vessels for onward transport by sea.

August 22

All groups destined for Jordan or Iraq will have boarded ship and will have sailed from Beirut.

Duplicating the model followed on August 21, PLO groups destined for Tunisia assemble and move to the Port of Beirut for departure by sea.

August 23

All PLO personnel destined for Tunisia complete their assembly and embark on commercial vessel for Tunisia.

PLO personnel destined for South Yemen assemble and move to a vessel for departure then or on August 24.

August 24—25

Assembly and departure by sea of PLO personnel destined for North Yemen.

August 25

Provided that satisfactory logistical arrangements have been completed, the initial groups of PLO personnel destined for Syria assemble and move overland via the Beirut-Damascus highway to Syria.

The advance French elements of the MNF already in the port area will have taken up such other agreed positions on the land route in the Beirut area as necessary to assist in the overland departure of the PLO personnel for Syria.

The Lebanese Armed Forces join with the French in occupying such positions.

(If it should be agreed that these initial groups should go by sea to Syria rather than by land, this departure schedule also is subject to amendment to assure that logistical requirements are met.)

August 26-28 (Approximately)

The remaining forces of the MNF (from the United States, France, and Italy) arrive in the Beirut area and deploy to agreed locations as determined through the Liaison and Coordinating Committee. This movement may be accompanied by the transfer of the advance French elements previously in the port area and elsewhere to other locations in the Beirut area.

August 26-27-28

PLO groups destined for Syria continue to move—by land or sea—to Syria.

August 22-September 4

Turnover to the Lebanese Armed Forces of PLO weaponry, military equipment, and ammunition in a continuing and orderly fashion.

August 29-30-31

Redeployment [*sic*] out of Beirut of the Syrian elements of the ADF.

September 1-4

Completion of the departure to Syria—by land or sea—of all PLO or Palestine Liberation Army personnel destined for Syria.

September 2-3

Assembly and departure by sea of all PLO personnel destined for Sudan.

Assembly and movement by sea of all PLO personnel destined for Algeria.

September 4-21

The MNF assists the Lebanese Armed Forces in arrangements, as may be agreed between governments concerned, to insure good and lasting security throughout the area of operations.

September 21-26

Departure of MNF.

The withdrawal of the PLO military forces temporarily broke the back of the organized guerilla activities into northern Israel; nonetheless, the Israeli military continued occupation of the southern portion of Lebanon to the Litani River. Yasir Arafat, together with other leaders of the PLO, established new headquarters in Tunis, Tunisia. On 3 April 1988 *The New York Times* reported that the police in Beirut estimated that a majority of the approximately 10,000 PLO members who had been evacuated under the above agreement had returned to the city and its environs and had reestablished themselves in the Palestinian camps and neighborhoods.

44

Reagan Peace Proposal, 1982

Following his successful election, the new future president of the United States, Ronald Reagan, former governor of the State of California,
stated in November 1980 that he would adhere
to the "Camp David Accord" in the search for
peace in the Middle East. He did this despite its
obvious flaws, its nonacceptance by the other
Arab states and the Palestinians, and even by
the European Community. Although he seldom
held televised news conferences, Reagan, a
former broadcaster, fell into the habit of giving a brief address on national and international issues over the radio on Saturdays. The
following "Reagan Plan" was broadcast from
California on 1 September 1982 while on one of
his numerous vacations.

My fellow Americans, today has been a day that should make
us proud. It marked the end of the successful evacuation of
the Palestine Liberation Organization (PLO) from Beirut,
Lebanon. This peaceful step could never have been taken
without the good offices of the United States and, especially,
the truly heroic effort of a great American diplomat, Ambas-

Source: United States. Department of State. *President Reagan: A New Opportunity for Peace in the Middle East. Current Policy No. 417* (Washington, D.C.: United States Department of State, Bureau of Public Affairs, September 1, 1982) 3 pp.

sador Philip Habib. Thanks to his efforts, I am happy to announce that the U.S. Marines contingent helping to supervise the evacuation has accomplished its mission. Our young
men should be out of Lebanon within 2 weeks. They, too,
have served the cause of peace with distinction, and we can
all be very proud of them.

But the situation in Lebanon is only part of the
overall problem of conflict in the Middle East. So, over the
past 2 weeks, while events in Beirut dominated the front
page [of the newspapers], America was engaged in a quiet,
behind-the-scenes effort to lay the groundwork for a
broader peace in the region. For once, there were no premature leaks as U.S. diplomatic missions traveled to Mid-East
capitals, and I met here at home with a wide range of experts
to map out an American peace initiative for the long-suffer-
ing peoples of the Middle East, Arab and Israeli alike.

It seemed to me that, with the agreement in Lebanon,
we had an opportunity for a more far-reaching peace effort
in the region, and I was determined to seize that moment. In
the words of the scripture, the time had come to "follow after
the things which make for peace."

U.S. Involvement

Tonight, I want to report to you on the steps we have taken,
and the prospects they can open up for a just and lasting
peace in the Middle East. America has long been committed
to bring peace to this troubled region. For more than a generation, successive U.S. administrations have endeavored to
develop a fair and workable process that could lead to a true
and lasting Arab-Israeli peace. Our involvement in the
search for Mid-East peace is not a matter of preference, it is
a moral imperative. The strategic importance of the region
to the United States is well known.

But our policy is motivated by more than strategic
interests. We also have an irreversible commitment to the
survival and territorial integrity of friendly states. Nor can
we ignore the fact that the well-being of much of the
world's economy is tied to stability in the strife-torn Middle
East. Finally, our traditional humanitarian concerns dictate
a continuing effort to peacefully resolve conflicts.

When our Administration assumed office in January
1981, I decided that the general framework for our Middle
East policy should follow the broad guidelines laid down by
my predecessors. There were two basic issues we had to address. First, there was the strategic threat to the region

posed by the Soviet Union and its surrogates, best demonstrated by the brutal war in Afghanistan; and, second, the peace process between Israel and its Arab neighbors.   With regard to the Soviet threat, we have strengthened our efforts to develop with our friends and allies a joint policy to deter the Soviets and their surrogates from further expansion in the region and, if necessary, to defend against it. With respect to the Arab-Israeli conflict, we have embraced the Camp David framework as the only way to proceed.   We have also recognized, however, that solving the Arab-Israeli conflict, in and of itself, cannot assure peace throughout a region as vast and troubled as the Middle East.

Our first objective under the Camp David process was to insure the successful fulfillment of the Egyptian-Israeli Peace Treaty.   This was achieved with the peaceful return of the Sinai to Egypt in April 1982.   To accomplish this, we worked hard with our Egyptian and Israeli friends, and eventually with other friendly countries, to create the multinational force which now operates in the Sinai.

Throughout this period of difficult and time-consuming negotiations, we never lost sight of the next step of Camp David: autonomy talks to pave the way for permitting the Palestinian people to exercise their legitimate rights.   However, owing to the tragic assassination of President Sadat and other crises in the area, it was not until January 1982 that we were able to make a major effort to renew these talks. Secretary of State Haig and Ambassador Fairbanks [Richard Fairbanks, Special Negotiator for the Middle East Peace Progress] made three visits to Israel and Egypt early this year to pursue the autonomy talks.   Considerable progress was made in developing the basic outline of an American approach which was to be presented to Egypt and Israel after April.

The successful completion of Israel's withdrawal from Sinai and the courage shown on this occasion by Prime Minister Begin and President Mubarak in living up to their agreements convinced me the time had come for a new American policy to try to bridge the remaining differences between Egypt and Israel on the autonomy process.   So, in May, I called for specific measures and a timetable for consultations with the Governments of Egypt and Israel on the next steps in the peace process.   However, before this effort could be launched, the conflict in Lebanon pre-empted our efforts.   The autonomy talks were basically put on hold while we sought to untangle the parties in Lebanon and still the guns of war.

The Lebanon war, tragic as it was, has left us with a new opportunity for Middle East peace. We must seize it now and bring peace to this troubled area so vital to world stability while there is still time. It was with this strong conviction that over a month ago, before the present negotiations in Beirut had been completed, I directed Secretary of State Schultz to again review our policy and to consult a wide range of outstanding Americans on the best ways to strengthen chances for peace in the Middle East. We have consulted with many of the officials who were historically involved in the process, with Members of the Congress, and with individuals from the private sector; and I have held extensive consultations with my own advisers on the principles I will outline to you tonight.

The evacuation of the PLO from Beirut is now complete. And we can now help the Lebanese to rebuild their war-torn country. We owe it to ourselves, and to posterity, to move quickly to build upon this achievement. A stable and revived Lebanon is essential to all our hopes for peace in the region. The people of Lebanon deserve the best efforts of the international community to turn the nightmares of the past several years into a new dawn of hope.

Resolving the Root Causes of Conflict

But the opportunities for peace in the Middle East do not begin and end in Lebanon. As we help Lebanon rebuild, we must also move to resolve the root causes of conflict between Arabs and Israelis. The war in Lebanon has demonstrated many things, but two consequences are key to the peace process:

First, the military losses of the PLO have not diminished the yearning of the Palestinian people for a just solution of their claims; and

Second, while Israel's military successes in Lebanon have demonstrated that its armed forces are second to none in the region, they alone cannot bring just and lasting peace to Israel and her neighbors.

The question now is how to reconcile Israel's legitimate security concerns with the legitimate rights of the Palestinians. And that answer can only come at the negotiating table. Each party must recognize that the outcome must be acceptable to all and that true peace will require compromises by all.

So, tonight I am calling for a fresh start. This is the moment for all those directly concerned to get involved—or lend their support—to a workable basis for peace. The Camp David agreement remains the foundation of our policy. Its language provides all parties with the leeway they need for successful negotiations.

• I call on Israel to make clear that the security for which she yearns can only be achieved through genuine peace, a peace requiring magnanimity, vision, and courage.

• I call on the Palestinian people to recognize that their own political aspirations are inextricably bound to recognition of Israel's right to a secure future.

• And I call on the Arab states to accept the reality of Israel and the reality that peace and justice are to be gained only through hard, fair, direct negotiation.

In making these calls upon others, I recognize that the United States has a special responsibility. No other nation is in a position to deal with the key parties to the conflict on the basis of trust and reliability.

The time has come for a new realism on the part of all the peoples of the Middle East. The State of Israel is an accomplished fact; it deserves unchallenged legitimacy with the community of nations. But Israel's legitimacy has thus far been recognized by too few countries and has been denied by every Arab state except Egypt. Israel exists; it has a right to exist in peace behind secure and defensible borders; and it has a right to demand of its neighbors that they recognize those facts.

I have personally followed and supported Israel's heroic struggle for survival ever since the founding of the State of Israel 34 years ago. In the pre-1967 borders, Israel was barely 10 miles wide at its narrowest point. The bulk of Israel's nation lived within artillery range of hostile Arab armies. I am not about to ask Israel to live that way again.

The war in Lebanon has demonstrated another reality in the region. The departure of the Palestinians from Beirut dramatizes more than ever the homelessness of the Palestinian people. Palestinians feel strongly that their cause is more than a question of refugees. I agree. The Camp David agreement recognized that fact when it spoke of the legitimate rights of the Palestinian people and their just requirements. For peace to endure, it must involve all those who have been most deeply affected by the conflict. Only through broader participation in the peace process—most immediately by Jordan and by the Palestinians—will Israel be able to rest confident in the knowledge that its security and integrity will be respected by its neighbors. Only through the process of negotiation can all the nations of the Middle East achieve a secure peace.

New Proposals

These then are our general goals. What are the specific new American positions, and why are we taking them?

In the Camp David talks thus far, both Israel and Egypt have felt free to express openly their views as to what the outcome should be. Understandably, their views have differed on many points.

The United States has thus far sought to play the role of mediator; we have avoided public comment on the key issues. We have always recognized—and continue to recognize—that only the voluntary agreement of those parties most directly involved in the conflict can provide an enduring solution. But it has become evident to me that some clearer sense of America's position on the key issues is necessary to encourage wider support for the peace process.

First, as outlined in the Camp David accords, there must be a period of time during which the Palestinian inhabitants of the West Bank and Gaza will have full autonomy over their own affairs. Due consideration must be given to the principle of self-government by the inhabitants of the territories and to the legitimate security concerns of the parties involved.

The purpose of the 5-year period of transition, which would begin after free elections for a self-governing Palestinian authority, is to prove to the Palestinians that they can run their own affairs and that such Palestinian autonomy poses no threat to Israel's security.

The United States will not support the use of any additional land for the purpose of settlements during the transition period. Indeed, the immediate adoption of a settlement freeze by Israel, more than any other action, could create the confidence needed for wider participation in these talks. Further settlement activity is in no way necessary for the security of Israel and only diminishes the confidence of the Arabs that a final outcome can be freely and fairly negotiated.

I want to make the American position well understood: The purpose of this transition period is the peaceful and orderly transfer of authority from Israel to the Palestinian inhabitants of the West Bank and Gaza. At the same time, such a transfer must not interfere with Israel's security requirements.

Beyond the transition period, as we look to the future of the West Bank and Gaza, it is clear to me that peace cannot be achieved by the formation of an independent Palestinian state in those territories. Nor is it achievable on the basis of Israeli sovereignty or permanent control over the West Bank and Gaza.

So the United States will not support the establishment of an independent Palestinian state in the West Bank and Gaza, and we will not support annexation or permanent control by Israel.

There is, however, another way to peace. The final status of these lands must, of course, be reached through the give-and-take of negotiations. But it is the firm view of the United States that self-government by the Palestinians of the West Bank and Gaza in association with Jordan offers the best chance for a durable, just and lasting peace.

We base our approach squarely on the principle that the Arab-Israeli conflict should be resolved through negotiations involving an exchange of territory for peace. This exchange is enshrined in U.N. Security Council Resolution 242, which is, in turn, incorporated in all its parts in the Camp David agreements. U.N. Resolution 242 remains wholly valid as the foundation stone of America's Middle East peace effort.

It is the United States' position that—in return for peace—the withdrawal provision of Resolution 242 applies to all fronts, including the West Bank and Gaza.

When the border is negotiated between Jordan and Israel, our view on the extent to which Israel should be asked to give up territory will be heavily affected by the extent of true peace and normalization and the security arrangements offered in return.

Finally, we remain convinced that Jerusalem must remain undivided, but its final status should be decided through negotiations.

In the course of the negotiations to come, the United States will support positions that seem to us fair and reasonable compromises and likely to promote a sound agreement. We will also put forward our own detailed proposals when we believe they can be helpful. And, make no mistake, the United States will oppose any proposal—from any party and at any point in the negotiating process—that threatens the

security of Israel.   America's commitment to the security of
Israel is ironclad.   And, I might add, so is mine.

        The "Reagan Proposal" was received
positively by the governments of Jordan,
Egypt, Lebanon, Kuwait, and Sa'udi Arabia, as
well within Western Europe.   However, it was
totally rejected by the Israeli cabinet because it
"contradicted" and "deviated" from the Camp
David Accord. Israel reiterated its commitment
to the establishment of further settlements in
the occupied territories.   In a letter dated 5
September, Israeli Prime Minister Menachem
Begin stated that the occupied territories would
never revert to Jordanian control.

45

U.S. Congressional Action
Against the PLO, 1987

Faced with widespread sporadic acts of terrorism against U.S. citizens and diplomatic missions abroad by various underground movements, largely from the Near East, the Reagan
administration became obsessed with
"international terrorism." The 99th Congress
(1986) was highly supportive of this obsession,
enacting thirteen separate bills that dealt
wholly or in part with terrorism, expanding
the definition of terrorism, and increasing the
penalties for carrying out terrorist acts. Frustrated by the extraordinary U.S. financial and
political support of for Israel, the continued
occupation of the West Bank and Gaza leading to
the constant foundation of new Jewish settlements, and the failure to achieve either military victory or a peaceful resolution to the
problem under U.S. leadership, members of the
more extreme of the eight armed groups under
the umbrella of the Palestine Liberation Organization engaged in terrorist activities aimed at
Israeli and American Jews and other U.S. nationals. These actions, combined with statements made in "The Palestinian National

---

Source: United States. Statutes at Large. *Public Law 100-204: Foreign Relations Authorization Act, Fiscal Years 1988 and 1989* (Washington, D.C.: Government Printing Office, 1987).

Covenant," particularly articles 8 and 15, which, in essence, called for the destruction of the State of Israel, and bellicose pronouncements made by various of its leaders, brought odium upon the PLO.

From its very foundation the political leaders of Israel referred to the PLO as a "terrorist organization," not wishing to have it recognized as the collective political and social leader of the Palestinians. This view was readily accepted by U.S. political leadership, so that, in 1975, Secretary of State Henry Kissinger forbad its recognition or for any U.S. official to have conversations with any of the leaders or spokespersons of the PLO, although the organization was accepted as the official body of the Palestinians throughout much of the world and held observer status at the United Nations.

Under this fear of terrorism, combined with the very strong pro-Israeli stance taken by most members of Congress (whose political campaigns were partially financed by pro-Israeli political action committees), Senator Charles Grassley of Iowa on 8 October 1987 introduced an amendment to the appropriation bill for the Department of State then under consideration, the "Anti-Terrorism Act of 1987." The purpose of this bill, co-sponsored by Senators Robert Dole, Frank Lautenberg, Howard Metzenbaum, and Rudy Boschwitz, was to force the closure of the PLO information office in Washington, D.C. and the U.N. observer office in New York. By bringing the amendment up on the floor, Senator Grassley was able to by-pass committee hearings. It was passed upon that day without the Congressional Record recording the vote.[1] The amendment was sent on to the House of Representatives were it was also passed upon and incorporated into Public Law 100-294 and signed by the President on 22 December 1987.

---

[1] The introuction and short debate upon the bill may be found in the *Congressional Record: 100th Congress*, 8 October 1987, (Washington, D.C.: United States Government Printing Office, 1987) pp. S13851-55.

TITLE X—ANTI-TERRORISM ACT OF 1987

SEC. 1001. SHORT TITLE.

This title may be cited as the "Anti-Terrorism Act of 1987".

SEC. 1002. FINDINGS; DETERMINATIONS.

(a) FINDINGS.—The Congress finds that—

(1) Middle East terrorism accounted for 60 percent of total international terrorism in 1985;

(2) the Palestine Liberation Organization (hereafter in this title referred to as the "PLO") was directly responsible for the murder of an American citizen on the Achille Lauro cruise liner in 1985, and a member of the PLO's Executive Committee is under indictment in the United States for the murder of that American citizen;

(3) the head of the PLO has been implicated in the murder of a United States Ambassador overseas;

(4) the PLO and its constituent groups have taken credit for, and been implicated in, the murders of dozens of American citizens abroad;

(5) the PLO covenant specifically states that "armed struggle is the only way to liberate Palestine, thus it is an overall strategy, not merely a tactical phase";

(6) the PLO rededicated itself to the "continuing struggle in all its armed forms" at the Palestine National Council meeting in April 1987; and

(7) the Attorney General has stated that "various elements of the Palestine Liberation Organization and its allies and affiliates are in the thick of international terror".

(b) DETERMINATIONS.—Therefore, the Congress determines that the PLO and its affiliates are a terrorist organization and a threat to the interests of the United States, its allies, and to international law and should not benefit from operating in the United States.

SEC. 1003. PROHIBITIONS REGARDING THE PLO.

It shall be unlawful, if the purpose be to further the interests of the Palestine Liberation Organization or any of its constituent groups, any successor to any of those, or any agents thereof, on or after the effective date of this title—

(1) to receive anything of value except informational material from the PLO or any of its constituent groups, any successor thereto, or any agents thereof;

(2) to expend funds from the PLO or any of its constituent groups, any successor thereto, or any agents thereof; or

(3) notwithstanding any provision of law to the contrary, to establish or maintain an office, headquarters, premises, or other facilities or establishments within the jurisdiction of the United States at the behest or direction of, or with funds provided by the Palestine Liberation Organization or any of its constituent groups, any successor to any of those, or any agents thereof.

SEC. 1004. ENFORCEMENT.

(a) ATTORNEY GENERAL.—The Attorney General shall take the necessary steps and institute the necessary legal action to effectuate the policies and provisions of this title.

(b) RELIEF.—Any district court of the United States for a district in which a violation of this title occurs shall have authority, upon petition of relief by the Attorney General, to grant injunctive and such other equitable relief as it shall deem necessary to enforce the provisions of this title.

SEC. 1005. EFFECTIVE DATE.

(a) EFFECTIVE DATE.—The Attorney General shall take the necessary steps and institute the necessary legal action to effectuate the policies and provisions of this title.

(b) TERMINATION.—The provisions of this title shall cease to have effect if the President certifies in writing to the President pro tempore of the Senate and the Speaker of the House that the Palestine Liberation Organization, its agents, or constituent groups thereof no longer practice or support terrorist actions anywhere in the world.

Prior to the passage of the appropriations bill that included this amendment, the Washington, D.C., office of the PLO was closed by the justice department. The Department of State objected to the law requiring the closure of the PLO's mission office in New York, but the Attorney General's office, acting upon orders from Congress, informed the PLO that its office had to close by 21 March 1988. In an emergency session the General Assembly on 2 March voted overwhelmingly (only Israel cast the one dissenting vote) ordering the U.S. to submit the dispute to binding arbitration. As required by the U.S.-U.N. agreement of 1947 governing the host country's relationship with the international organization the disagreement was submitted to the International Court of Justice in The Hague, Holland. On 26 April 1988 the Court unanimously (with the U.S. justice absenting himself from the proceedings) ruled that the United States must submit the question to the binding arbitration of a three-man tribunal. The Reagan administration responded that there was no disagreement with the United Nations until the U.S. law was carried out and the PLO mission was forced to close, hence the problem was not submitted to arbitration. However, the Department of Justice filed a lawsuit with the Federal District Court in Manhattan to force the closure of the PLO mission office. On 30 June 1988 a federal judge ruled that the United States Government could not enforce the law against the office, stating in his written opinion: "The P.L.O. Mission to the United Nations is an invitee of the United Nations under the Headquarters Agreement and its status is protected by that agreement. The Headquarters Agreement remains a valid and outstanding treaty obligation of the United States."[2]

---

[2] *The New York Times*, 30 June 1988, pp. A1 and A5.

46

Palestinian Declaration of Independence, 1988

After twenty years of military rule and the establishment of 120 Israeli settlements, with approximately 70,000 Jewish settlers, Palestinian youths rebelled on 8 December 1987 in the West Bank and Gaza, at first sporadically and then spreading widely, throwing stones at Israeli military patrols. This popular movement, later known by the Arabic term *intifada,* originally had no leadership until the later formation of the underground "Unified Command of the Uprising" to serve as a bridge between those within the occupied territories and the PLO leadership outside. Israeli Defense Minister Yitzhak Rabin ordered the army to quash the uprising with an "iron fist," a policy that led to the deaths of hundreds and injury to thousands, and worldwide condemnation of Israel. In order to keep pressure on Israel from within the occupied territories, the Arab Persian Gulf nations in June 1988, promised to support the uprising with $128 million annually in addition to $42 million monthly to provide for the activities of the PLO itself.

Source: Official translation of the Palestine National Council, Palestine Liberation Organization. Courtesy of the American Educational Trust.

In response to both the uprising and a
meeting   of the League of Arab States held in
Algiers in May, in which the heads of the Arab
states again reaffirmed the PLO as the sole
representative   of   the   Palestinians,   King
Hussayn   of   Jordan,   in   a   surprise   short
television address on 31 July 1988, announced
that   his   government   was   relinquishing
immediately   all claims to the West Bank, which
his grandfather, 'Abd Allah, had annexed on 1
December 1948 as a result of the first Arab-
Israeli war.   His purpose in doing so, he stated,
was to respect the wishes of the PLO to establish
an   independent   Palestinian   state   on   those
portions of Palestine that they might liberate.
This   action   had   several   widespread
implications: 1) it brought   to an end all
Jordanian support for health, education, and
social welfare programs in the West Bank and
the payment by Jordan of the salaries of the
more than 13,000   Palestinian civil servants in
the occupied land, (which would have been
economically devastating had not the Arab
states promised their financial support); 2) it
gave added impetus to those participating in
the uprising, because they now felt that they
were   fighting   for   their   own   freedom   and
independence; 3) it removed Jordan as the
negotiator for the Palestinians in U.S. peace
proposals, such as that set forth in the Camp
David Accords and accepted by President
Ronald Reagan or Secretary of State George
Schultz's peace mission in early March, and
also probably laid to rest the concept of an
absorption of the West Bank into Jordan; 4) it
galvanized the central leadership of the PLO
into seeking a solution to the forty-year-old
conflict. The sixty member Central Council of
the Organization held an emergency meeting
in Baghdad following the speech to discuss its
implications.
    The Palestinian National Council, the
450-member parliament of the PLO, met in
Algiers, Algeria, 12-15 November 1988. As had
been rumored for several weeks, it issued a
declaration of independence of the State of

Palestine on 15 November. The new state, without a land, was almost immediately recognized by approximately sixty countries, primarily of the "third world."

In the name of God, the Compassionate, the Merciful

DECLARATION OF INDEPENDENCE

Palestine, the land of the three monotheistic faiths, is where the Palestinian Arab people was born, on which it grew, developed and excelled. The Palestinian people was never separated from or diminished in its integral bonds with Palestine. Thus the Palestinian Arab people ensured for itself an everlasting union between itself, its land and its history.

Resolute throughout that history, the Palestinian Arab people forged its national identity, rising even to unimagined levels in its defence, as invasion, the design of others, and the appeal special to Palestine's ancient and luminous place on that eminence where powers and civilizations are joined. All this intervened thereby to deprive the people of its political independence. Yet the undying connection between Palestine and its people secured for the land its character, and for the people its national genius.

Nourished by an unfolding series of civilizations and cultures, inspired by a heritage rich in variety and kind, the Palestinian Arab people added to its stature by consolidating a union between itself and its patrimonial land. The call went out from Temple, Church and Mosque that to praise the Creator, to celebrate compassion and peace was indeed the message of Palestine. And in generation after generation, the Palestinian Arab people gave of itself unsparingly in the valiant battle for liberation and homeland. For what has been the unbroken chain of our people's rebellions but the heroic embodiment of our will for national independence? And so the people was sustained in the struggle to stay and to prevail.

When in the course of modern times a new order of values was declared with norms and values fair for all, it was the

Palestinian Arab people that had been excluded from the destiny of all other peoples by a hostile array of local and foreign powers.   Yet again had unaided justice been revealed as insufficient to drive the world's history along its preferred course.

And it was the Palestinian people, already wounded in its body, that was submitted to yet another type of occupation over which floated the falsehood that "Palestine was a land without people."   This notion was foisted upon some in the world, whereas in Article 22 of the Covenant of the League of Nations (1919) and in the Treaty of Lausanne (1923), the community of nations had recognized that all the Arab territories, including Palestine, of the formerly Ottoman provinces, were to have granted to them their freedom as provisionally independent nations.

Despite the historical injustice inflicted on the Palestinian Arab people resulting in their dispersion and depriving them of their right to self-determination, following upon U.N. General Assembly Resolution 181 (1947), which partitioned Palestine into two states, one Arab, one Jewish, yet it is this Resolution that still provides those conditions of international legitimacy that ensure the right of the Palestinian Arab people to sovereignty.

By stages, the occupation of Palestine and parts of other Arab territories by Israeli forces, the willed dispossession and expulsion from their ancestral homes of the majority of Palestine's civilian inhabitants, was achieved by organized terror; those Palestinians who remained, as a vestige subjugated in its homeland, were persecuted and forced to endure the destruction of their national life.

Thus were principles of international legitimacy violated. Thus were the Charter of the United Nations and its Resolutions disfigured, for they had recognized the Palestinian Arab people's national rights, including the right of Return, the right to independence, the right to sovereignty over territory and homeland.

In Palestine and on its perimeters, in exile distant and near, the Palestinian Arab people never faltered and never abandoned its conviction in its rights of Return and independence.   Occupation, massacres and dispersion achieved no gain in the unabated Palestinian consciousness

of self and political identity, as Palestinians went forward
with their destiny, undeterred and unbowed. And from out
of the long years of trial in evermounting struggle, the
Palestinian political identity emerged further consolidated
and confirmed. And the collective Palestinian national will
forged for itself a political embodiment, the Palestine
Liberation Organization, its sole, legitimate representative
recognized by the world community as a whole, as well as by
related regional and international institutions. Standing on
the very rock of conviction in the Palestinian people's
inalienable rights, and on the ground of Arab national
consensus and of international legitimacy, the PLO led the
campaigns of its great people, molded into unity and
powerful resolve, one and indivisible in its triumphs, even
as it suffered massacres and confinement within and
without its home. And so Palestinian resistance was clarified
and raised into the forefront of Arab and world awareness,
as the struggle of the Palestinian people achieved unique
prominence among the world's liberation movements in the
modern era.

The massive national uprising, the *intifada*, now
intensifying in cumulative scope and power on occupied
Palestinian territories, as well as the unflinching resistance
of the refugee camps outside the homeland, have elevated
awareness of the Palestinian truth and right into still
higher realms of comprehension and actuality. Now at last
the curtain has been dropped around a whole epoch of
prevarication and negation. The *intifada* has set siege to the
mind of official Israel, which has for too long relied
exclusively upon myth and terror to deny Palestinian
existence altogether. Because of the *intifada* and its
revolutionary irreversible impulse, the history of Palestine
has therefore arrived at a decisive juncture.

Whereas the Palestinian people reaffirms most definitely its
inalienable rights in the land of its patrimony:

> Now by virtue of natural, historical and legal rights,
> and the sacrifices of successive generations who gave
> of themselves in defense of the freedom and
> independence of their homeland;

> In pursuance of Resolutions adopted by Arab Summit
> Conferences and relying on the authority bestowed
> by international legitimacy as embodied in the

Resolutions   of   the   United   Nations   Organization   since
1947;

And   in   exercise   by   the   Palestinian   Arab   people   of   its
rights   to   self-determination,   political   independence
and   sovereignty   over   its   territory,

The   Palestine   National   Council,   in   the   name   of   God,
and   in   the   name   of   the   Palestinian   Arab   people,
hereby   proclaims   the   establishment   of   the   State   of
Palestine   on   our   Palestinian   territory   with   its   capital
Jerusalem   (Al-Quds   Ash-Sharif).

The   State   of   Palestine   is   the   state   of   Palestinians   wherever
they   may   be.   The   state   is   for   them   to   enjoy   in   it   their
collective   national   and   cultural   identity,   theirs   to   pursue   in
it   a   complete   equality   of   rights.   In   it   will   be   safeguarded
their   political   and   religious   convictions   and   their   human
dignity   by   means   of   a   parliamentary   democratic   system   of
governance,   itself   based   on   freedom   of   expression   and   the
freedom   to   form   parties.   The   rights   of   minorities   will   duly
be   respected   by   the   majority,   as   minorities   must   abide   by
decisions   of   the   majority.   Governance   will   be   based   on
principles   of   social   justice,   equality   and   non-discrimination
in   public   rights   of   men   or   women,   on   grounds   of   race,
religion,   color   or   sex,   under   the   aegis   of   a   constitution
which   ensures   the   rule   of   law   and   an   independent   judiciary.
Thus   shall   these   principles   allow   no   departure   from
Palestine's   age-old   spiritual   and   civilizational   heritage   of
tolerance   and   religious   coexistence.

The   State   of   Palestine   is   an   Arab   state,   an   integral   and
indivisible   part   of   the   Arab   nation,   at   one   with   that   nation
in   heritage   and   civilization,   with   it   also   in   its   aspiration   for
liberation,   progress,   democracy   and   unity.   The   State   of
Palestine   affirms   its   obligation   to   abide   by   the   Charter   of   the
League   of   Arab   States,   whereby   the   coordination   of   the   Arab
states   with   each   other   shall   be   strengthened.   It   calls   upon
Arab   compatriots   to   consolidate   and   enhance   the   emergence
in   reality   of   our   state,   to   mobilize   potential,   and   to   intensify
efforts   whose   goal   is   to   end   Israeli   occupation.

The   State   of   Palestine   proclaims   its   commitment   to   the
principles   and   purposes   of   the   United   Nations,   and   to   the
Universal   Declaration   of   Human   Rights.   It   proclaims   its

commitment as well to the principles and policies of the Non-Aligned Movement.

It further announces itself to be a peace-loving State, in adherence to the principles of peaceful co-existence. It will join with all states and peoples in order to assure a permanent peace based upon justice and the respect of rights so that humanity's potential for well-being may be assured, an earnest competition for excellence may be maintained, and in which confidence in the future will eliminate fear for those who are just and for whom justice is the only recourse.

In the context of its struggle for peace in the land of Love and Peace, the State of Palestine calls upon the United Nations to bear special responsibility for the Palestinian Arab people and its homeland. It calls upon all peace—and freedom—loving peoples and states to assist it in the attainment of its objectives, to provide it with security, to alleviate the tragedy of its people, and to help it terminate Israel's occupation of the Palestinian territories.

The State of Palestine herewith declares that it believes in the settlement of regional and international disputes by peaceful means, in accordance with the U.N. Charter and resolutions. Without prejudice to its natural right to defend its territorial integrity and independence, it therefore rejects the threat or use of force, violence and terrorism against its territorial integrity or political independence, as it also rejects their use against the territorial integrity of other states.

Therefore, on this day unlike all others, November 15, 1988, as we stand at the threshold of a new dawn, in all honor and modesty we humbly bow to the sacred spirits of our fallen ones, Palestinian and Arab, by the purity of whose sacrifice for the homeland our sky has been illuminated and our Land given life. Our hearts are lifted up and irradiated by the light emanating from the much blessed *intifada*, from those who have endured and have fought the fight of camps, or dispersion, of exile, from those who have borne the standard for freedom, our children, our aged, our youth, our prisoners, detainees and wounded, all those whose ties to our sacred soil are confirmed in camp, village and town. We render special tribute to that brave Palestinian Woman, guardian of sustenance and Life, keeper of our people's perennial flame. To the souls of our sainted martyrs, to the whole of our Palestinian Arab people, to all free and honorable peoples everywhere, we pledge that our struggle shall be continued until the occupation ends, and the foundation of our sovereignty and independence shall be fortified accordingly.

Therefore, we call upon our great people to rally to the banner of Palestine, to cherish and defend it, so that it may forever be the symbol of our freedom and dignity in that homeland, which is a homeland for the free, now and always.

Following this declaration of independence the PNC adopted a political resolution that contained the following points:

1. The necessity of convening an international conference on the Palestine question under the auspices of the United Nations, with the participation of the permanent members of the Security Council and all parties to the conflict, based upon Security Council Resolutions 242 and 338. By this statement the PLO accepted these two resolutions.

2. The withdrawal by Israel from all territories occupied in 1967, including eastern Jerusalem.

3. "The annulment of all measures of annexation and appropriation and the removal of settlements established by Israel in the Palestinian and Arab territories since 1967."

4. Placing the West Bank, the Gaza Strip, and east Jerusalem under the temporary "auspices" of the United Nations for the protection of its inhabitants and to ". . . afford the appropriate atmosphere for the success . . . of the international settlement, . . . and to enable the Palestinian state to exercise its effective authority in these territories."

5. Settlement of the refugee problem in accordance with United Nations resolutions, i.e., repatriation or compensation.

6. Guarantee of the freedom of worship and religious practice for all faiths.

7. "The Security Council to formulate and guarantee arrangements for security and peace between all the states concerned in the region, including the Palestinian state."[1] Thereby, apparently, implicitly recognizing the legal existence of Israel.

At its annual meeting in Brussels the twelve-member European Community Council issued the following declaration on 21 November 1988 approving the recent actions of the Palestine National Council and reiterating the demand for an international peace conference:

The Twelve attach particular importance to the decisions adopted by the Palestine National Council in Algiers, which reflect the will of the Palestinian people to assert their national identity and which include positive steps towards the peaceful settlement of the Arab-Isreali conflict.

They welcome in this respect the acceptance by the PNC of the Security Council Resolutions 242 and 338 as a basis for an international conference, which implies acceptance of the right of existence and of security for all states of the region, including Israel. Respect for this principle goes together with that of justice for the peoples of the region, in particular the right of self-determination of the Palestinian people with all that this implies; for the Twelve it constitutes a necessary condition for the establishment of just, lasting and comprehensive peace in the Near East, as they have repeatedly asserted since the Declaration of Venice. The Twelve also express their satisfaction that the PNC has explicitly condemned terrorism.

The Twelve appeal to all parties concerned, while abstaining from any act of violence and any action which could further aggravate the tense situation in the Near East, to take this opportunity and contribute to the peace process in a positive way, with a view to a just, global and lasting solution to the

---

[1] Translation from the Arabic of the "Political Resolutions of the 19th Palestinian National Congress." Courtesy of the American Educational Trust.

Arab-Israeli conflict. This solution can only be achieved through an International Peace Conference, under the auspices of the United Nations, which represents the suitable framework for the necessary negotiations between the parties directly concerned.

The Twelve are deeply concerned by the deterioration of the situation in the Occupied Territories and the increasing feeling of deception and desperation among the population of those territores which might become worse if there is no prospect of a negotiated solution. They reiterate their commitment to participate actively in all efforts contributing to a negotiated solution.[2]

On 9 November the PLO announced that it had requested a U.S. visa for Yasir Arafat so that he could address the U.N. General Assembly on 30 November, should the National Council approve the proclamation of an independent Palestinian state. Secretary of State George Schultz prior to this announcement had stated that Arafat was not welcome in the United States. It was not, however, until 24 November that Arafat submitted his official request. Two days later the Department of State announced that the PLO chairman had been denied a visa by the personal intervention of the secretary of state because, as the leader of the PLO, Arafat condoned terrorism. The decision was met with derision and outrage in the United States and abroad. In the United Nations the General Assembly passed a resolution overwhelmingly by a vote of 151-2 (opposed only by Israel and the United States, the United Kingdom abstained) condemning the action:

. . .

1. Affirms the right of the Palestine Liberation Organization freely to designate the members of its delegation to participate in the sessions and the work of the General Assembly;

---

2 European Community Council Press Release, Brussels, 21 November 1988.

2. Deplores the failure by the host country to approve the granting of the requested entry visa;

3. Considers that this decision by the Government of the United States of America, the host country, constitutes a violation of the international legal obligations of the host country under the Agreement between the United Nations and the United States of America regarding the Headquarters of the United Nations;

4. Urges the host country to abide scrupulously by the provisions of the agreement and to reconsider and reverse its decision; . . .[3]

Despite this public request that the decision be reconsidered, even by the United States' closest European allies, Schultz remained adamant. Angered by the secretary's obduracy, the members of the General Assembly on 2 December passed a resolution to hold its annual debate on Palestine in the Geneva headquarters of the United Nations 13-15 December. The vote with 154 to 2; the United States and Israel voted against it and three members did not participate.

The General Assembly,

Recalling its resolution 43/48 of 30 November 1988, in which, inter alia, it urged the host country to abide scrupulously by the provisions of the Agreement between the United Nations and the United States of America regarding the Headquarters of the United Nations, dated 26 June 1947 1/ and to reconsider and reverse its decision to deny the visa requested for Mr. Yasser Arafat, Chairman of the Executive Committee of the Palestine Liberation Organization,

Having considered the report of the Secretary-General of 1 December 1988 2/ in which it is stated

---

[3] A/RES/43/48, 65th plenary meeting, 30 November 1988.

that the host country informed him that it saw "no basis for changing our decision",

Affirming the right of persons mentioned in section 11 of the Agreement to enter the United States of America without any impediment for the purpose of transit to or from the headquarters district,

1. Deplores the failure of the host country to respond favourably to the request of the General Assembly contained in its resolution 43/48;

2. Decides, in the present compelling circumstances and without prejudice to normal practice, to consider the question of Palestine, item 37 of the agenda of the forty-third session of the General Assembly, in plenary, at the United Nations Office at Geneva during the period from 13 to 15 December 1988;

3. Requests the Secretary-General to make the necessary arrangements for the implementation of the present resolution, and authorizes him to adjust the schedule of meetings at the United Nations Office at Geneva during those days as required.[4]

On 6 December, under the auspices of the Swedish Minister of Foreign Affairs, Sten Andersson, Yasir Arafat met in Stockholm with a five-member delegation of American Jews to examine the implications of the political statement passed by the Palestine National Council in Algiers, which set forth the new stance of the PLO. Seven days later, on the 13th, Arafat delivered the invited speech before the U.N. General Assembly in Geneva, in which he adopted the Security Council's resolutions 242 and 338, urged the immediate convening under U.N. sponsorship of an international peace conference in Geneva, called for the stationing of U.N. peacekeeping forces in the West Bank and Gaza, and strongly

---

[4] A/RES/43/49, 67th plenary meeting, 2 December 1988.

condemned terrorism.[5] In the eyes of the U.S. Department of State, however, Arafat had still not gone far enough in meeting its demands before it could agree to talk with the PLO. On the 14th, Arafat issued a statement in Geneva in which he stated that the PLO renounced terrorism and explicitly recognized Israel's right to exist, in addition to previously accepting the Security Council's resolutions. Because the PLO had met U.S. demands, the U.S. ambassador to Tunisia, where the PLO maintained its headquarters, was instructed to open a dialogue with the organization's leaders on the 16th, thereby ending a thirteen-year ban on discussions with the PLO. The reaction from Israel was one of shock and anger at the change in U.S. policy. In Geneva, on the last day of its deliberations, 15 December, the General Assembly passed a resolution 138-2 (U.S. and Israel in opposition) calling for an international peace conference and U.N. supervision over the occupied territories. A second resolution, passed by a huge majority, that, although acknowledging the PNC's declaration of an independent Palestinian state but not explicitly recognizing it, called for the exercise of the sovereignty of the Palestinians over the West Bank and Gaza.

On 30 May 1990 sixteen members of the Palestine Liberation Front, under the leadership of Abu Abbas, a member of the PLO Executive Committee, launched a foiled sea attack upon the coast of Israel near Tel Aviv in retaliation for the murder the week previously of seven Palestinian laborers by an Israeli civilian. The Israeli government claimed that the object of the attack was the U.S. Embassy. Yasir Arafat, chairman of the PLO Executive Committee, stated that neither he nor the PLO was involved and that it was an independent action by the group. Using this attempted landing as an excuse, on 20 June, President George Bush, broke off the U.S. talks with the

---

5 Knight-Ridder News Service, *The Denver Post*, 4 December 1988.

PLO until it punished those responsible.   These
talks had been proceding for nearly a year and
a half, and this decision was viewed with alarm
by many of the United States' staunchest allies,
both in Europe and in the Near East, because of
the possiblity of its either slowing further, or
even ending, the stalled peace negotiations.   On
12 July the PLO leaders proposed a compromise,
offering to discipline the PLF once the talks
were resumed and expanded.

47

United Nations Acknowledgment of the State of Palestine, 1989

In Geneva, on the last day of its deliberations on the Palestine Question, 15 December 1988, the General Assembly passed two separate, but related, resolutions in response to the Palestinian Declaration of Independence passed by the Palestine National Council (parliament) exactly one month earlier and to Chairman Yasir Arafat's speech before the Assembly.

The first of these, Resolution 43/176, requested ". . . the Security Council to consider measures needed to convene the International Peace Conference on the Middle East, including the establishment of a preparatory committee, and to consider guarantees for security measures agreed upon by the Conference for all States in the region; . . . " The resolution also:

3. Affirms the following principles for the achievement of comprehensive peace:

(a) The withdrawal of Israel from the Palestinian territory occupied since 1967, including Jerusalem, and from the other occupied Arab territories;

(b) Guaranteeing arrangements for security of all States in the region, including those named in resolu-

---

Source: Courtesy of the Dag Hammarskjöld Library, United Nations.

tion 181 (II) of 29 November 1947, within secure and internationally recognized boundaries;

(c) Resolving the problem of the Palestinian refugees in conformity with General Assembly resolution 194 (III) of 11 December 1948, and subsequent relevant resolutions;

(d) Dismantling the Israeli settlements in the territories occupied since 1967;

(e) Guaranteeing freedom of access to Holy Places, religious buildings and sites; ... .

The resolution was adopted by 138 in favor, 2 opposed (Israel and the United States), and 2 abstentions (Canada and Costa Rica). The representatives of fourteen small nations did not attend this special meeting in Geneva of the General Assembly. The second of these resolutions acknowledged the proclamation of the State of Palestine within the proposed territories of the West Bank and the Gaza Strip. Again only Israel and the United States voted against the resolution, although 36 states, including most of the Western European states abstained, thus the support (104) came primarily from the Communist bloc, the Near Eastern states, and the "third world."

The General Assembly,

Having considered the item entitled "Question of Palestine",

Recalling its resolution 181 (II) of 29 November 1947, in which, inter alia, it called for the establishment of an Arab State and a Jewish State in Palestine,

Mindful of the special responsibility of the United Nations to achieve a just solution to the question of Palestine,

Aware of the proclamation of the State of Palestine by the Palestine National Council in line with General Assembly resolution 181 (II) and in exercise of the inalienable rights of the Palestinian people,

Affirming the urgent need to achieve a just and comprehensive settlement in the Middle East which, *inter alia*, provides for peaceful coexistence for all States in the region,

Recalling its resolution 3237 (XXIX) of 22 November 1974 on the observer status for the Palestine Liberation Organization and subsequent relevant resolutions,

1. *Acknowledges* the proclamation of the State of Palestine by the Palestine National Council on 15 November 1988;

2. *Affirms* the need to enable the Palestinian people to exercise their sovereignty over their territory occupied since 1967;

3. *Decides* that, effective as of 15 December 1988, the designation "Palestine" should be used in place of the designation "Palestine Liberation Organization" in the United Nations system, without prejudice to the observer status and functions of the Palestine Liberation Organization within the United Nations system, in conformity with relevant United Nations resolutions and practice;

4. *Requests* the Secretary-General to take the necessary action to implement the present resolution.

It is noteworthy that four of the member states that were original members of the United Nations Special Committee on Palestine in favor of the partitioning of Palestine into three states (Arab, Jewish, and internationalized Jerusalem) in 1947 abstained from voting on this resolution, acknowledging the willingness at this time for the Arabs to establish an independent state within the territories more or less originally allotted to them (Canada, Iran [not participating in the voting], Netherlands, and Sweden).

48

Security Council Commission, 1990

By 6 April 1989 437 Palestinians and 18 Israelis had been killed since the *Intifada* began in December 1987. Following a clash between Palestinian youths and the Israeli police outside of al-Aqsa Mosque in Jerusalem at the beginning of the holy month of Ramadan on Friday, 7 April 1989, the Israeli police minister issued orders on 10 April prohibiting the use of the mosque for prayer by some Muslims, regarded as direct interference in the religious affairs of those living in the occupied territories. Then, in the pre-dawn hours of 13 April the Israeli border police conducted a raid upon the village of Nahalin outside Bethlehem. According to an army investigation, the police were surprised by stone-throwing youths, and they opened fire with lead-tipped bullets, killing five and wounding at least twenty-five other inhabitants. This attack was considered one of the deadliest since the beginning of the uprising.

In response to the barring of one of the most important mosques of Islam during Ramadan, followed by the massacre at Nahalin, the General Assembly, during its annual in-

Source: S/21326. Courtesy of the U.S. Department of State and the Department of Public Information, United Nations.

vestigation into the "Question of Palestine," on
20 April 1989 passed a resolution deploring both
events and   requested the Security Council to
take up the matter with some urgency.

43/233   Question   of   Palestine

The General Assembly,

Having considered the item entitled "Question of
Palestine",
Guided by the principles of the Charter of the
United Nations and the provisions of the Universal
Declaration of Human Rights,
Gravely concerned at and alarmed by the deterio-
rating situation in the Palestinian territory occupied
by Israel since 1967, including Jerusalem,
Expressing its profound shock at the latest action
of members of the Israeli armed forces on 13 April
1989, which resulted in the killing and wounding of
Palestinian civilians in the town of Nahalin,
Having considered the statement of the Secretary-
General on 13 April 1989 relative to that raid,
Aware that Israel, the occupying Power, has imposed limitations on Palestinian Muslims that restrict
their participation in the life of their community and
in the observance of their religious rites and obligations,
Taking into account the need to consider means for
the impartial protection of the Palestinian civilian
population under Israeli occupation,
Considering that the current policies and practices of Israel, the occupying Power, in the occupied
Palestinian territory are bound to have grave consequences for the endeavours to achieve a comprehensive, just and lasting peace in the Middle East,
Reaffirming once again that the Geneva Convention
Relative to the Protection of Civilian Persons in Time
of War, of 12 August 1949, is applicable to the Palestinian and other Arab territories occupied by Israel,
including Jerusalem,
   1. *Condemns* those policies and practices of Israel, the occupying Power, which violate the human
rights of the Palestinian people in the occupied territory, including the right of freedom of worship, and,

in particular, the opening of fire by Israeli armed
forces, which has resulted in the killing and wounding
of defenceless Palestinian civilians, and specifically
the latest action of members of the Israeli armed
forces against the defenceless civilians in the Palestinian town of Nahalin;

2. *Demands* that Israel, the occupying Power,
abide scrupulously by the Geneva Convention Relative
to the Protection of Civilian Persons in Time of War, of
12 August 1949, and that it desist immediately from
those policies and practices which are in violation of
the provisions of the Convention;

3. *Requests* the Security Council to consider
with urgency the situation in the occupied Palestinian
territory with a view to considering measures needed
to provide international protection to the Palestinian
civilians in the Palestinian territory occupied by Israel since 1967, including Jerusalem;

4. *Stresses* the urgent need to expedite the convening of the International Peace Conference on the
Middle East, under the auspices of the United Nations
and in conformity with the provisions of General
Assembly resolution 43/176 of 15 December 1988;

5. *Requests* the Secretary-General to submit periodic reports on developments in the occupied Palestinian territory. [1]

During the succeeding year the conflict
continued to deteriorate, particularly with the
arrival of Soviet Jewish immigrants for whom
new settlements began to be constructed in the
occupied territories. The situation was further
exacerbated when, on Sunday, 20 May 1990, an
Israeli citizen, alleged later to have been men-
tally deranged, indiscriminately killed seven
Palestinian laborers and wounded eight others
near Tel Aviv. Despite an immediate curfew
ordered by the Israeli authorities to defuse the
situation, a large number of Palestinians

---

[1] United Nations. *Resolutions and Decisions adopted by the General
Assembly during its Forty-third Session. Vol. II: 22 December
1988-18 September 1989. General Assembly Official Records:
Forty-third Session, Supplement No. 49 A (A43/49/Addl)* (N e w
York: United Nations, 1989) 1.

demonstrated against the bloodshed, resulting in further loss of life when troops fired on the crowd with live ammunition. The following day the permanent representative of Bahrain sent a letter to the president of the Security Council requesting an emergency meeting to consider the situation in the occupied territories. At its meeting in New York on the 22nd, the Council decided to convene at the United Nations offices in Geneva on 25 May so that Yasir Arafat, over the objections of the United States, could address the Council. During 25-26 May, statements were made by the representatives of numerous European, Near Eastern, African, and Asian countries. On the 29th it recommenced its meeting at Headquarters in New York. On 31 May the representatives of Colombia, Côte d'Ivoire, Cuba, Ethiopia, Malaysia, Yemen, and Zaire submitted a draft resolution to the Security Council for debate and vote calling for a special Security Council commission be sent to the occupied territories. Prior to the vote the Israeli representative stated that "He rejected, in its totality, the idea of appointing a commission to examine the situation in the territories; and if such a commission was appointed, it would not be accepted by Israel, ..."[2]

The Security Council,
    Having considered the letter dated 21 May 1990 from the Permanent Representative of Bahrain to the United Nations, in his capacity as Chairman of the Arab Group for the month of May 1990,

    Having listened to the statement by His Excellency President Yasser Arafat,

    Reaffirming that the Geneva Convention Relative to the Protection of Civilian Persons in Time of War, of 12 August 1949, is applicable to the Palestinian and other Arab

---

2 United Nations Department of Public Information News Coverage Service, 31 May 1990, page 5 (paraphrasing his statements).

territories occupied by Israel since 1967, including Jerusalem,

Gravely concerned and alarmed by the deteriorating situation in the Palestinian territory occupied by Israel since 1967, including Jerusalem,

Bearing in mind that any deliberate planned act of violence in the region is a blow to peace,

1. *Establishes* a Commission consisting of three members of the Security Council, to be dispatched immediately to examine the situation relating to the policies and practices of Israel, the occupying power, in the Palestinian territory, including Jerusalem, occupied by Israel since 1967;

2. *Requests* the Commission to submit its report to the Security Council by 20 June 1990, containing recommendations on ways and means for ensuring the safety and protection of the Palestinian civilians under Israeli occupation;

3. *Requests* the Secretary-General to provide the Commission with the ncessary facilities to enable it to carry out its mission;

4. *Decides* to keep the situation in the occupied territories under constant and close scrutiny and to reconvene to review the situation in the light of the findings of the Commission.

Although supported by the other fourteen members of the Security Council, including the four other permanent members, the resolution was defeated by the veto of the United States. In his explanation for the veto, the U.S. ambassador stated, in part:

. . . The U.S. Government continues to support a special envoy of the Secretary-General to be dispatched on an urgent basis to look at the situation and report back to the Secretary-General. We continue to urge all parties to exhibit the necessary flexibility to permit such a mission.

The resolution before us today, however, seeks to advance a different vehicle which we cannot support. We cannot entertain any hopes for its rapid implementation. . . . it would become a vehicle which could be misused to generate needless controversy and dispute in the area, something clearly inappropriate, especially under present circumstances.[3]

According to a Department of State spokesman, the reason for the veto was classified as "highly secret."

---

[3] Department of State Incoming Telegram 31 May 1990. Courtesy of the U.S. Department of State.

Security Council Condemnation
of Israel, 1990

Beginning at 2 A.M. on 2 August Iraqi troops, without prior provocation or notice, invaded the neighboring state of Kuwait. That evening, the Security Council of the United Nations, meeting in an emergency session, passed the first of a series of resolutions condemning this act of aggression and calling for the immediate withdrawal of Iraq. On the following day thirteen members of the twenty-one member League of Arab States, meeting in Cairo, also denounced the invasion, but, at the same time, rejected any intervention or attempted intervention in "Arab affairs." The other eight representatives either remained neutral or declared themselves in favor of Iraq, including Yasir Arafat of the PLO. Concerned that Iraq might be contemplating an invasion of Saudi Arabia, President George Bush, following consultations with King Fahd, ordered the dispatch of U.S. troops and aircraft to the defense of the kingdom, and began to marshal an international, yet fragile, coalition of European and Arab states to put the Security Council resolution into effect. A few, including Egypt, and Syria, dispatched military forces to bolster those of Saudi Arabia and the United States.

Source: Courtesy of the Department of Public Information, United Nations.

The United Arab Emirates, without an army, permitted the stationing of U.S. forces on their territories.

At a time of continued international apprehension over the crisis in the Gulf, a Jewish fundamentalist group, calling itself the Faithful of the Temple Mount, announced plans to place on the Muslim holy site of the Dome of the Rock and al-Aqsa Mosque a cornerstone for the rebuilding of the Temple. Although prohibited from carrying out their plans by the Israeli Supreme Court, the zealots, on Monday, 8 October, began to march towards the mosque. Muslims, apparently having learned of their plans, and perhaps unaware of the Court's decision, gathered to stop the Faithful's action. The Palestinians began throwing rocks at the marchers, with some falling down upon Jewish worshippers gathered below at the western "Wailing" wall. Almost immediately the Israeli police began to fire upon the Palestinians with rubber, plastic, and live ammunition. The number of Arabs who died as a result was variously estimated at between 17 and 21, with over 150 wounded, considered to be the most bloody of all of the confrontations between the Palestinians and the Israeli forces since the beginning of the *intifada*.

Almost immediately the Palestine Liberation Organization, through Yemen, the one Arab nation on the Security Council, placed a draft resolution before the Council calling for the condemnation of Israel in the strongest terms, the immediate dispatch of an investigation team by the Council (rather than one by the Secretary-General), and the stationing of an U.N. observer team to protect the Palestinians. The United States, which invariably vetoes any resolution critical of Israel, was advised by her closest European allies not to automatically veto the resolution for fear of endangering the precarious Arab support for the international coalition against Iraq. After several days of intense diplomatic negotiations a U.S. resolution, which originally also was critical of the Palestinian demonstrators, was passed by the Council on a vote of 14-0, with Yemen abstaining. Membership of the Council, besides the five permanent members (China, France, Soviet Union, United Kingdom, and the United States), was composed of Canada, Colombia, Côte d'Ivoire, Cuba, Yemen, Ethiopia, Finland, Malaysia, Romania, and Zaire.

RESOLUTION 672 (1990)

Adopted by the Security Council at its 2948th meeting, on 12 October 1990

The Security Council,

Recalling its resolutions 476 (1980) and 472 (1980),

Reaffirming that a just and lasting solution to the Arab-Israeli conflict must be based on its resolutions 242 (1967) and 338 (1973) through an active negotiating process which takes into account the right to security for all States in the region, including Israel, as well as the legitimate political rights of the Palestinian people,

Taking into consideration the statement of the Secretary-General relative to the purpose of the mission he is sending to the region and conveyed to the Council by the President on 12 October 1990,

1. Expresses alarm at the violence which took place on 8 October at the Al Haram Al Shareef and other Holy Places of Jerusalem resulting in over twenty Palestinian deaths and to the injury of more than one hundred and fifty people, including Palestinian civilians and innocent worshippers;

2. Condemns especially the acts of violence committed by the Israeli security forces resulting in injuries and loss of human life;

3. Calls upon Israel, the occupying Power, to abide scrupulously by its legal obligations and responsibilities under the Fourth Geneva Convention, which is applicable to all the territories occupied by Israel since 1967;

4. <u>Requests</u>, in connection with the decision of the Secretary-General to send a mission to the region, which the Council welcomes, that he submit a report to it before the end of October 1990 containing his findings and conclusions and that he use as appropriate all of the resources of the United Nations in the region in carrying out the mission.

On 14 October the Israeli Cabinet adopted a statement in reply to the resolution and the speech by the president of the Security Council. In this statement the Israeli Government declared that both were ". . . totally unacceptable to us." It further proclaimed:

3. Jerusalem is not, in any part, 'occupied territory'; it is the sovereign capital of the State of Israel [a claim not acceptable by the United Nations or the United States]. Therefore, there is no room for any involvement on the part of the United Nations in any matter relating to Jerusalem, ...
4. Given the above, Israel will not receive the delegation of the Secretary-General of the United Nations.[1]

Despite pleas and pressures from Great Britain and the United States the Israeli prime minister, Yitzhak Shamir, remained adamant and announced the appointment of a governmental investigation headed by the former director of the Mossad, Israel's external intelligence agency. Without the cooperation of the Israeli Government the secretary-general of the United Nations, Javier Perez de Cuellar, determined that although he was prepared to send his mission to Jerusalem, he could not do so without assurances from the Israeli Government that it would not be barred from entry. Israel did not provide clarification on this point, so his own investigation committee was not sent. Angered by this direct affront to its earlier resolution, the members of the Security Council unanimously passed a second   on the

<hr>

[1] Quoted in: "Report submitted to the Security Council by the Secretary-General in accordance with Resolution 672 (1990). 31 October 1990." Pp. 2 and 3.

24th condemning this action of the Israeli Government:

RESOLUTION 673 (1990)

Adopted by the Security Council at its 2949th meeting, on 24 October 1990

The Security Council,
Reaffirming the obligations of Member States under the United Nations Charter,
Reaffirming also its resolution 672 (1990),
Having been briefed by the Secretary-General on 19 October 1990,
Expressing alarm at the rejection of Security Council resolution 672 (1990) by the Israeli Government, and its refusal to accept the mission of the Secretary-General,
Taking into consideration the statement of the Secretary-General relative to the purpose of the mission he is sending to the region and conveyed to the Council by the President on 12 October 1990,
Gravely concerned at the continued deterioration of the situation in the occupied territories,
1. Deplores the refusal of the Israeli Government to receive the mission of the Secretary-General to the region;
2. Urges the Israeli Government to reconsider its decision and insists that it comply fully with resolution 672 (1990) and to permit the mission of the Secretary-General to proceed in keeping with its purpose;
3. Requests the Secretary-General to submit to the Council the report requested in resolution 672 (1990);
4. Affirms its determination to give full and expeditious consideration to the report.[2]

In its statement issued on 14 October the government announced that it had also appointed an "independent commission of inquiry." This three man committee was headed by the former director of Mossad. Two days after the passage of the latest Security Council

---

[2] Courtesy of the Department of Public Information, United Nations.

resolution, the commission submitted its report, which came to the conclusion that the police had acted properly under the circumstances, although some senior officials were criticized for having failed to prepare adequately for the possibility of violence. The secretary-general refused to accept a copy of the report and on 31 October presented his own to the Security Council in which he stated that Israel had failed to protect the Palestinians under its authority by not adhering to the appropriate paragraphs of the Fourth Geneva Convention, which Israel has steadfastly maintained does not apply to the inhabitants under her control in the occupied territories. He concluded: "Clearly, the numerous appeals . . . to the Israeli authorities to abide by their obligations under the Fourth Geneva Convention have been ineffective. It is evident that for any measure of protection to be ensured, the co-operation of the Israeli authorities is, under the present circumstances, absolutely essential. Nevertheless, given the special responsibility of the high contracting parties for ensuring respect for the Convention, the Security Council might wish to call for a meeting of the high contracting parties to discuss possible measures that might be taken by them under the Convention."[3] As soon as the report was made public the Israeli Government attacked it, stating that it was "one sided" and "directed only toward Israel."

---

[3] "Report submitted to the Security Council by the Secretary-General in accordance with Resolution 672 (1990). 31 October 1990." Page 11.

Suggested Readings

The Arab-Israeli conflict is, without question, the most controversial subject of modern history, with the result that the literature upon it, both in book and article form, is immense. Furthermore, there are several journals which are almost entirely devoted to the subject. In order to maintain any kind of control over this literature numerous bibliographies have been compiled, so that, as early as 1973, I believed it useful to publish *The Arab-Israeli Dispute: an annotated bibliography of bibliographies* (Denver, American Institute of Islamic Studies. Bibliographic Series No. 7), which, of course, is now totally out of date. Therefore, because of its controversial nature and the amount of literature available it has been necessary for me to be extremely selective in bringing to the attention of the reader those books which I believe may be found useful, particularly upon specific subjects, hence the brief descriptions regarding each.

Reference Works

Legal Studies

Cattan, Henry. *Palestine and International Law: the legal aspects of the Arab-Israeli conflict.* Second edition. London, Longman, 1976.
> As the title states this is a detailed study of the legality, or illegality of the mandate, the U.N. partitioning of Palestine, the legitimacy of Israel, the settlements in the occupied territories

etc., under international law by a noted
specialist.   Will be regarded by some as having
a pro-Palestinian bias.

Quigley, John. *Palestine and Israel: a challenge to justice.*
Durham, North Carolina, Duke University Press, 1990.
An even more recent examination of the problem under international law by a professor of
law at Ohio State University.

Maps

Gilbert, Martin. *The Arab-Israeli Conflict: its history in
maps.* 4th ed.   London, Weidenfeld and Nicolson, 1984.
Contains over one hundred line maps with brief
accompanying descriptions, with pro-Israeli
bias.

United Nations Resolutions

Institute for Palestine Studies, The. *United Nations Resolutions and the Arab-Israeli Conflict.* 3 vols. Washington, D.C., The Institute for Palestine Studies, 1988.
Complete collection of the official texts of all of
the resolutions issued from 1947 through 1986
by the General Assembly, the Security Council,
and UN specialized agencies: I - 1947-1974; II -
1975-1981; III - 1982-1986.

Bibliographies

Khalidi, Walid and Jill Khadduri. *Palestine and the Arab-Israeli Conflict: an annotated bibliography.* Beirut,
Institute for Palestine Studies, 1974.
Listing, with very brief annotations, of 4,580
books and articles in both western and oriental
languages, arranged by historical period.
Although out of date the book remains valuable.

Readers

Laqueur, Walter and Barry Rubin. *The Israeli-Arab Reader:
a documentary history of the Middle East conflict.* 4th
edition.   New York, Pelican Books, 1984.
A very lengthy collection of documents
(frequently abbreviated), portions of articles,
speeches, etc., with occasional brief introduc-

tions. Decidedly pro-Israeli.

Rabinovich, Itamar and Jehuda Reinharz. *Israel in the Middle East: documents and readings on society, politics and foreign relations, 1948-present.* New York, Oxford University Press, 1984.

> Collection of laws, documents, resolutions, published articles, speeches, etc., illustrative of the history of modern Israel, arranged by period: I - 1948-56; II - 1956-67; III - 1967-73; IV - 1973-83. Intended to be pro-Israeli.

Introductory Works

Khouri, Fred. *The Arab-Israeli Dilemma.* 3rd ed. Syracuse, Syracuse University Press, 1985.

> One of the most widely used and objective college texts on the subject. Particularly strong on the period since partition. Includes documents and tables.

Smith, Charles D. *Palestine and the Arab-Israeli Conflict.* New York, St. Martin's Press, 1988.

> Although broader in historical scope than Khouri this is a more abbreviated version.

Hadawi, Sami. *Bitter Harvest: a modern history of Palestine.* Rev. ed. New York, Olive Branch Press, 1990.

> A Palestinian viewpoint by a noted historian. The book has been extremely popular and has gone through numerous reprintings.

Lucas, Noah. *The Modern History of Israel.* New York, Praeger Publishers, 1975.

> A good general history of the development of the state of Israel since World War I by a British historian. Now, of course, a little dated.

Sachar, Howard M. *A History of Israel: from the rise of Zionism to our time.* New York, Alfred A. Knopf, 1976.

> A lengthy, detailed history from the first World War to 1976 by a noted American historian with a decidedly pro-Israeli bias.

Sachar, Howard M. II: *A History of Israel: from the aftermath of the Yom Kippur war.* New York, Oxford University Press, 1987.

> A continuation of Professor Sachar's earlier history.

Works on Specific Topics

Aronson, Geoffrey. *Israel, Palestine and the Infitada: creat-
    ing facts on the West Bank.* 2nd ed. London, Kegan
Paul International Limited, 1990.
                Published in association with the Institute for
                Palestine Studies and therefore with a pro-
                Palestinian view.
Avineri, Shlomo. *The Making of Modern Zionism: the intel-
    lectual origins of the Jewish State.* New York, Basic
Books, 1986.
Brymen, Rex. *Sanctuary and Survival: the PLO in Lebanon.*
Boulder, Colorado, Westview Press, 1990.
                Covers the period 1970 to 1982.
Findley, Paul. *They Dare to Speak Out: people and institu-
    tions confront Israel's lobby.* 2nd ed. Westport, Con-
necticut, Lawrence Hill & Co., 1989.
                Because of America's deep involvement in the
                conflict from virtually the beginning it is nec-
                essary to obtain an understanding of the great
                influence of the Israeli lobby.
Gresh, Alain. *The PLO: the struggle within: towards an in-
    dependent Palestinian state.* London, Zed Books, 1987.
                Translated from the French.
Hart, Alan. *Arafat: a political biography.* Bloomington, In-
    diana, Indiana University Press, 1984.
                Based upon hundreds of interviews with Yasir
                Arafat and other PLO members, Hart provides
                an in-depth look at the leader and the history
                of the PLO.
Kamel, Mohamed Ibrahim. *The Camp David Accords.* Lon-
    don, KPI Ltd., 1986.
                The story behind the conference by the former
                Egyptian foreign minister and advisor to al-Sa-
                dat during the negotiations.
Kirisci, Kemal. *The PLO and World Politics: a study of the
    mobilization of support for the Palestinian cause.*
London, Frances Pinter (Pub.), 1986.
                A pro-Palestinian viewpoint.
Lall, Arthur. *The UN and the Middle East Crisis, 1967.* Revised
    edition. New York, Columbia University Press, 1970.
                A detailed study of the background to, and pas-
                sage of, Security Council Resolution 242, the
                basis of all attempted peace negotiations.
Lesch, Ann Mosely and Richard B. Parker. *Israel, Egypt and
    the Palestinians from Camp David to Infitada.*
Bloomington, Indiana, Indiana University Press, 1989.
McDowell, David. *Palestine and Israel: the uprising and be-*

yond. London, I. B. Tauris & Co. Ltd., 1989
Mallison, W.T., Jr. *The Balfour Declaration: an appraisal in international law.* North Dartmouth, Massachusetts, Association of Arab-American University Graduates, Inc., 1973.

> A reprint in booklet form of an article which appeared in a collection of articles published in 1971. Mallison, Professor of Law and Director of the International Law Program, George Washington University, presents a very lucid description of the intricate negotiations which led up to the letter by Balfour, together with its position under international law. Undoubtedly the best piece written on this very important document.

Marschall, Phil. *Intifada: Zionism, imperialism and Palestinian resistance.* London, Bookmarks, 1989.

> An examination of the conflict from a Socialist view.

Morris, Benny. *The Birth of the Palestinian Refugee Problem, 1947-1949.* Cambridge, Cambridge University Press, 1987.
Peretz, Don. *Intifada: the Palestinian uprising.* Boulder, Colorado, Westview Press, 1990.
Rubenberg, Cheryl A. *Israel and the American National Interest.* Urbana, University of Illinois Press, 1987.

> Comprehensive review of American-Israeli relations from 1947 through 1982, contending that this "special relationship" has damaged other U.S. relationships in the Near East.

Rubenberg, Cheryl. *The Palestine Liberation Organization: its institutional infrastructure.* Belmont, Massachusetts, Institute of Arab Studies, 1983.

> An attempt to present within a relatively brief format the diversity of opinions and subsidiary organizations found within the PLO.

Schiff, Ze'ev and Ya'ari Ehud. *Intifada: the Palestinian uprising. - - Israel's third front.* New York, Simon and Schuster, 1989.

> Translated from the Hebrew. An argument for an end to the occupation and the establishment of a Palestinian state for the survival of Israel.

Shemesh, Mosche. *The Palestinian Entity 1959-1974: Arab politics and the PLO.* London, Frank Cass, 1988.
Weizmann, Chaim. *Trial and Error: the autobiography of Chaim Weizmann.* New York, Harper, 1949.

The autobiography of, in many ways, the real founder and first president of the State of Israel.   Important for an understanding of Zionism after World War I.

Index

Because the words Arab(s), Jew(s) and Palestine occur, quite naturally, upon virtually every page of this book they are therefore not included within this index, except for special references to Palestine. Also, the names of individuals, places and publications, which are mentioned only peripherally, have been excluded.

About the Editor and Compiler

CHARLES L. GEDDES is Professor of History at the University of Denver. Since 1958 he has co-published and edited a number of volumes on Middle Eastern issues and written numerous articles on facets of Islam for both journals and encyclopedias. Among his books are *Islam in Paperback*, 1969; four separate guides to bibliographies; *Books in English on Islam, Muhammed, and the Qur'an: A Selected and Annotated Bibliography*; and a *Guide to Reference Books for Islamic Studies*.